Paradise Dreamed:

How Utopian Thinkers Have Changed
the Modern World

Paradise Dreamed

How Utopian Thinkers
Have Changed
the Modern World

Pamela Neville-Sington
and David Sington

BLOOMSBURY

First published in Great Britain 1993
Bloomsbury Publishing Ltd, 2 Soho Square, London W1V 5DE

PICTURE SOURCES

The Bridgeman Art Library: page 34

The British Library: pages x, xiv, 80, 130, 170;
plate pages 1, 2, 3, 4, 5, 6 *bottom*, 8

Oneida Community Mansion House: plate page 7

The Syndics of Cambridge University Library: page 190; plate page 6 *top*

A CIP catalogue record for this book
is available from the British Library

ISBN 0 7475 1293 0

Typeset by Hewer Text Composition Services, Edinburgh
Printed by Clays Limited, St Ives plc

This book is dedicated to
our parents
and to
Zuzanna Shonfield

A map of the world that does not include Utopia is not worth even glancing at, for it leaves out the one country at which Humanity is always landing. And when Humanity lands there, it looks out, and seeing a better country, sets sail. Progress is the realization of Utopias.

Oscar Wilde, 'The Soul of Man under Socialism'

Utopia? Oh, pardon me, I thought it was hell.

Max Beerbohm

Contents

Acknowledgements

We would especially like to thank the following people for their help and support, conversation and hospitality, newspaper clippings and the loan of their books: Julie Abraham, David Alexander, Libby Anderson, Francesca Bewer, Elizabeth and Bailey Bishop, Ellen and Franco Bianchini, Dr Elizabeth Cole, Dr Olga Dmitrieva, Rebecca Hardie, Jamila and Fran Hodgson, Sarah and Daniel Johnson, Jane Kilpatrick, Dr Peter Le Fevre, Susanne McDadd, Giles Mandelbrote, Dr Genevieve Miller, Dr Susan Morrison, Nadine and Brody Neuenschwander, Nancy Neville and Gareth Cadwallader, Jane Regan and Robert Duval, Laurie and Chris Simpson, Dr Barbara Sommerville, Swami Hansa and The Reverend Derek Watson. We would also like to thank Harv Neville for tapping into the NEXIS database, Dr David Starkey and Prof J. B. Trapp for their comments on Chapter 2, and Tom Freeman for reading the whole manuscript and giving us the benefit of his wit and wisdom. This book sprang from a series of radio progammes for the BBC World Service, and we would like to thank the original contributors: Prof Quentin Skinner, Prof Lisa Jardine, Dr Anthony Pagden, Dr Stephen Fender and Dr Krishan Kumar. *Paradise Dreamed* would never have seen the light of day had not Lady Zuzanna Shonfield lent us Poggio al Sole to finish the book. Finally, we are very grateful to our editor, David Reynolds, for his advice and patience.

Satirical view of Fourier's ideal society: J. J. Grandville, *Un Autre Monde*, 1844.

Prologue

During 1992 the *New York Times* used the words 'utopia' or 'utopian' on no less than 164 occasions. They occurred in connection with, among other things, Bill Clinton's presidential campaign, Russia's economic reforms, genetically engineered vegetables, the Seville Exposition, David Byrne's latest album, electronic banking, the courtship of dolphins, a public park in Zurich, a large greenhouse in the Arizona desert, basketball and the issuing of condoms in prep schools. The concept of utopia has indeed become ubiquitous, seeping into every corner of modern life. It is the purpose of this book to argue that this reflects more than the superficial use of a convenient term. The omnipresence of the word 'utopia', in fact, signals the profound influence which utopias, both literary and experimental, have had on the modern world.

However, the myriad different contexts in which the word 'utopia' appears also encapsulate the difficulty of establishing this influence. Given that everything from communism to *haute couture* is described as 'utopian', the problem is to write a book on the subject which is significantly shorter than the *Encyclopaedia Britannica*. The challenge is to distil the utopian essence from a general history of Western political and social thought since the Renaissance.

By what criteria, then, do we discern the utopian? Why do we include a discussion of the Shakers, but not the Amish? What makes Rousseau a utopian political philosopher, but not Hume? Samuel Butler once described the act of definition as 'the enclosing of a wilderness of ideas within a wall of words'. Utopia is a particularly fertile wilderness, and we have not attempted a precise definition, finding that any verbal walls we put up are quickly overgrown. Nevertheless, all our utopias share certain salient characteristics.

Perhaps the most striking of these is the rejection of history. The utopian is impelled, in Le Corbusier's words, to 'build on a clear site'. Again and again in this book we will come across utopians advocating a complete break with the past, protesting that they cannot achieve their aims if they are hampered by the ties of existing social institutions. More than anything else it is this desire to erase all traces of the world into which they were born that makes utopians the most radical of reformers.

A second attribute is one which, when combined with this predilection for annihilation, can make Utopia a dangerous place. Whereas most societies develop through a long period of historical change, a utopia is almost without exception the product of a single mind and expresses the values and world view of a lone individual. The insights and prejudices of that person are transformed into the mores of an entire community. For the members of such a utopia, non-comformity to these values is no longer simply a difference of personal outlook; it becomes a transgression of the norms of society, even treason to the great cause of the betterment of mankind.

If these tendencies are destructive, the creativity of Utopia lies in the comprehensiveness of its prescription for the ideal life. For literary utopians, especially, this means going into the minutiae of day-to-day living in their imaginary domains. Utopia, like God, is in the details.

Our approach is thematic rather than chronological, and we have concentrated on those utopias which have had the greatest impact on the modern world. This inevitably means that many well-known utopian experiments and works of fiction have not found their way into these pages. However, by bringing together and juxtaposing often contrasting utopian ideas on a single theme, we aim to show how, for the past five hundred years, developments in the fields of architecture and town planning, science and technology, sexuality and the role of women, even religion, have been anticipated and influenced by utopian thinkers. The final section of *Paradise Dreamed* traces the utopian pedigree of both American and Soviet Communist political institutions.

In its modern usage, the word 'utopia' has connotations of impracticality, even woolly-headedness. (Indeed, it has probably always had such connotations. A draft of Tyrone's peace proposals for Ireland has written across the top, in the hand of Elizabeth I's principal secretary, Robert Cecil, the one word 'Yewtopia'.) But, far from being idle dreamers, utopians have succeeded in changing the world in ways both trivial and profound. The prescience of utopian writers has been remarkable. While they have not always prophesied accurately the shape of things to come, they have often proved skilled social seismologists, perceiving with uncanny accuracy the fault lines, the areas of conflict, tension and instability running through contemporary society. Paradoxically, utopian writing may be the most realistic literary genre and utopian politics the most effective agent of social change.

Authors' Note

'Utopia' is the fictional island invented by Thomas More in his book *Utopia*. Besides referring to More's island, we also use 'Utopia' with a capital 'U' to describe the generic ideal state, the Platonic form of all 'utopias'. The inhabitants of More's island are, of course, 'Utopians'; 'utopians' with a small 'u' are those men and women who have followed in More's footsteps by drawing up plans for a perfect world or by actually attempting to create ideal communities. In all quotations, italics are original.

Map of the island of Utopia: Thomas More, *Utopia*, first edition, 1516.

PART ONE

ORIGINS

I' the commonwealth I would by contraries
Execute all things; for no kind of traffic
Would I admit; no name of magistrate;
Letters should not be known; riches, poverty,
And use of service, none; contract, succession,
Bourn, bound of land, tilth, vineyard, none;
No use of metal, corn, or wine, or oil;
No occupation; all men idle, all;
And women too, but innocent and pure;
No sovereignty. . . .

All things in common nature should produce
Without sweat or endeavour: treason, felony,
Sword, pike, knife, gun, or need of any engine,
Would I not have; but nature should bring forth,
Of its own kind, all foison, all abundance,
To feed my innocent people. . . .

I would with such perfection govern, sir,
To excel the golden age.
                    William Shakespeare, *The Tempest*

1. Cockaigne

Before Utopia, there was the Golden Age. As far as we can tell, it was the Greek poet Hesiod who first wrote about this idyllic time. Hesiod, who lived some time in the seventh or eighth century BC, was the son of a poor Boeotian farmer, who had fallen out with his brother over their inheritance. In his poem *Works and Days*, the disenchanted and melancholy Hesiod imagines the by-gone Golden Age when a golden race of mortal men lived like gods, 'with hearts free from sorrow and remote from toil and grief; . . . the fruitful earth spontaneously bore them abundant fruit without stint. And they lived in ease and peace upon their lands with many good things, rich in flocks and beloved of the blessed gods.' However, Hesiod relates that as time went on things deteriorated and the Golden Age gave way to the Silver Age, when men's foolishness caused them to live in discord and sorrow; the Silver Age was followed by the Bronze Age, when men delighted in war and violence. Finally, after a brief interlude featuring the Age of Heroes, we reach the Age of Iron. Hesiod laments: 'Would that I were not among the fifth race, but had either died before or were born afterwards. For now the race is iron. Neither by day does it have an end of toil and sorrow nor by night of wasting away.'

Hesiod's melancholy schema became a commonplace of the classical world. Some six hundred years later the Roman poet Ovid delivered the most famous rendition of the Golden Age in his *Metamorphoses*:

> Golden was that first age, which, with no one to compel, without a law, of its own will, kept faith and did the right. . . . The earth herself, without compulsion, untouched by hoe or ploughshare, of herself gave all things needful. . . . Then spring was everlasting, and gentle zephyrs with warm breath played with the flowers that sprang unplanted. Anon the earth, untilled, brought forth her store of grain, and the fields, though unfallowed, grew white with the heavy, bearded wheat. Streams of milk and streams of sweet nectar flowed, and yellow honey was distilled from the verdant oak.

Hesiod's and Ovid's pictures of primeval innocence are simply the most

3

famous of many literary versions of a myth that appears to be well-nigh universal. The Book of Genesis describes the Garden of Eden where 'made the LORD God to grow every tree that is pleasant to the sight, and good for food' (Genesis 2:9), and the Sumerian Epic of Gilgamesh, dating from the third millennium BC, tells of Dilmun, a place where

> ... the croak of the raven was not heard, the bird of death did not utter the cry of death, the lion did not devour, the wolf did not tear the lamb, the dove did not mourn, there was no widow, no sickness, no old age, no lamentation.

Modern anthropology may offer an explanation for the ubiquity of this myth. Comparison of the world's few remaining hunter-gatherer societies with those practising primitive agriculture shows that the hunter-gatherers, far from being deprived of nourishment, as one might assume, are in fact better fed than the agriculturists. They also enjoy far more leisure. Since a diet of meat, fruit, berries and nuts is so much more nutritious than the starch-dominated diet agriculture provides, the hunter-gatherer need work for only two or three hours each day. The only advantage of growing rather than gathering food is that crops can sustain a higher density of population. Thus, perhaps it was only the need to feed growing numbers that forced mankind to abandon a relatively easy way of life for the hard labour of the farm, leaving only a folk memory of those former lazy days.

Whatever one thinks of this theory, it is certainly true that fantasies about food have remained a constant feature of popular culture. Some of the most vivid were written by the Attic comic poets, whose aim was, in fact, to satirize the myth of the Golden Age. Athenaeus's *Deipnosophistae* ('Sophists at Dinner') is a collection, made in the second century AD, of 'windy discourses of the worthies' in which several gastronomic heavens are discussed. Athenaeus quotes from Crates's *Beluae* ('The Beasts'), dating from the fifth century BC, where no one need lift a finger at mealtime:

> Each object will automatically approach when ordered to. 'Table, set yourself. Get yourself ready. Mixing trough, start kneading. Wine cup, fill yourself! ... Fish, advance!' 'But I am not baked on the other side.' 'Then will you turn yourself over and salt yourself, stupid?'

4

COCKAIGNE

In the gourmand's paradise described by another fifth-century poet, Teleclides, the food does not even need to be told what to do:

> For every stream flowed with wine, and barley cakes fought with wheat cakes to enter the mouths of men, pleading to be gulped down. . . And fishes, coming to men's houses and baking themselves, would serve themselves upon the tables. . . . And pipes conducting sharp sauces ran beside those wishing them . . . and roasted thrushes with milk cakes flew down one's gullet. And there were pancakes elbowing each other aside at one's jaw and shouting their war cries. . . . Men were fat then.

These culinary daydreams were by no means confined to the ancient world. The fourteenth-century English poem entitled 'The Land of Cockaigne' (from the Germanic *kakan*, later *kuchen*, meaning 'cake') derides the gluttonous monks of the rich monasteries while describing a place for those at the bottom of the heap where

> There are rivers broad and fine
> Of oil, milk, honey and of wine;
> Water serveth there no thing
> But for sight and for washing. . . .
> There is a mighty fine Abbey,
> Thronged with monks both white and grey,
> Ah, those chambers and those halls!
> All of pasties stand the walls,
> Of fish and flesh and all rich meat,
> The tastiest that men can eat.
> Wheaten cakes the shingles all,
> Of church, of cloister, bower and hall.
> The pinnacles are fat puddings,
> Good food for princes or for kings.
> Every man takes what he will,
> As of right, to eat his fill.
> All is common to young and old,
> To stout and strong, to meek and bold. . . .
> Yet this wonder add to it –
> That geese fly roasted on the spit,
> As God's my witness, to that spot,

PARADISE DREAMED

Crying out, 'Geese, all hot, all hot!'
Every goose in garlic drest,
Of all food the seemliest.
And the larks that are so couth
Fly right down into man's mouth,
Smothered in stew, and thereupon
Piles of powdered cinnamon.
Every man may drink his fill
And needn't sweat to pay the bill.

Similar desires are echoed in American folk songs of the nineteenth and
twentieth centuries, such as 'The Big Rock Candy Mountains', where

The little streams of alcohol
Come a-trickling down the rocks. . . .
There's a lake of stew and of whiskey too.

In the 'Poor Man's Heaven'

There's strawberry pie
That's twenty feet high
And whipped cream they bring in a truck.

But, appealing as gastronomic delights are, the most important indul-
gence offered by these reveries is freedom from the necessity of labour.
Thus, in the Big Rock Candy Mountains

There ain't no short-handled shovels,
No axes, saws or picks,
I'm bound to stay where they sleep all day,
Where they hung the Turk that invented work.

These folk fantasies are all indirect expressions of dissatisfaction with
the status quo. This they have in common with utopias; and, in their
vivid depiction of what it would be like to live in an imaginary perfect
world, they established a tradition to which the architects of Utopia
are heirs. Yet these myths cannot themselves be counted part of the
utopian genre. The true utopia must also draw upon another tradition
originally rooted in antiquity, that of constitution building.

COCKAIGNE

The Greeks were natural politicians, indeed, they can be said to have invented politics and political philosophy. Living in small, independent city states, they had a need to draw up agreed systems by which they could be ruled. Thus, the most pressing issue in Greek life and philosophy became 'What is the best form of government?' Words such as *arete* (virtue) and *agathos* (good), which we now associate with moral philosophy, the Greeks used to describe political effectiveness. As early as the fifth century BC the historian Herodotus records a debate between three Persians on the pros and cons of democracy, oligarchy and monarchy.

The constitutions of the Greek states were often attributed to a single legislator, who sometimes acquired a semi-mythical status. One such was the great Athenian lawgiver and poet Solon. In early sixth-century Athens, according to Aristotle, 'the majority were enslaved to the minority and the commons were in opposition to the aristocracy. Civil strife became violent and for a long time they remained in a state of mutual antagonism, until both sides agreed to put Solon into political office as arbitrator.' Solon ended serfdom with his *seisachtheia* or 'shaking off of burdens', which secured the abolition of debts and the redistribution of land. But his most important and lasting reform was the law code, which touched upon almost every facet of civil society: murder, rape, treason, taxation, public morals, the family, land, commerce, religion. He introduced economic measures to encourage trade and industry and revised the archaic severity of the laws. He made property rather than high birth the basis of political power, and created a people's assembly of four hundred citizens to rule alongside the aristocratic council. By this subtle but effective restructuring of society, Solon endowed the lower classes with basic rights while allowing the rich to retain their wealth and privileges. As he himself wrote:

> For to the common people I gave so much power as is sufficient,
> Neither robbing them of dignity, nor giving them too much;
> And those who had power, and were marvellously rich,
> Even for these I contrived that they suffered no harm.
> I stood with a mighty shield in front of both classes,
> And suffered neither of them to prevail unjustly.

Solon's law code is perhaps the earliest well-documented example of pragmatic piecemeal reform. A more radical approach had been adopted by the Spartan lawgiver, Lycurgus. Almost nothing is known, certainly nothing is agreed upon, about Lycurgus: neither his origins, his dates (anywhere from the eighth to sixth centuries BC), nor his actual reforms and their purpose – even his historical authenticity is doubted by some. But, according to Plutarch, the Greek historian of the first century AD, Lycurgus remade the entire fabric of Spartan society. He redistributed the land equally among Sparta's citizens in order to 'banish insolence and envy and crime and luxury, and those yet more deep-seated and afflictive diseases of the state, poverty and wealth'. Other economic reforms included the abolition of gold and silver coinage, which put an end to financial corruption as well as to trade with other countries. Sparta isolated herself further by periodical deportations, and citizens were discouraged from travelling abroad.

Sparta was first and foremost a military state, and its institutions reflected this fact. The men did not eat at home with their families but in communal messes, or dining clubs. Members paid a subscription and contributed provisions. The fare was moderate and simple, consisting mainly of a thin black broth. Membership of these clubs was compulsory. There was no opting out in Spartan society: 'The system achieved equality through comformity'. This egalitarianism, however, did not extend to the ethnically distinct serfs, the Helots, who were ruthlessly suppressed.

The Spartan views on women and marriage were quite exceptional in the ancient world. Although girls lived at home, they did not learn the usual domestic arts of spinning and weaving, but were brought up as tomboys, playing outdoors, partaking in athletic training and bantering with the boys. These high-spirited girls grew up to be women renowned for beauty and toughness. One of Aristophanes's characters in *Lysistrata* greets a Spartan woman:

> Lampito, my sweet! Delighted to see you, darling,
> How pretty you look! How healthy you Spartans are!
> And my, what biceps! I believe you could throttle a bull.

Marriages were made on the basis of mutual consent, not by family arrangement. In order to banish jealousy, Lycurgan laws allowed for wife-sharing. However, Plutarch felt he had to defend Spartan 'free-love' against charges of immorality:

> The freedom which thus prevailed at that time in marriage relations was aimed at physical and political well-being, and was far

8

removed from the licentiousness which was afterwards attributed to their women, so much so that adultery was wholly unknown among them.

This sexual freedom encouraged the practice of eugenics among the Spartans, who came to believe that men and women should be selectively bred like domestic animals. Children were inspected at birth and unhealthy or deformed infants were left to die. Under Lycurgus's constitution, Sparta became a powerful state which rivalled Athens.

The most famous and influential example of the Greek predilection for constitutional experimentation was not a state, however, but a work of literature: Plato's *Republic*. It is perhaps surprising that Plato, a loyal Athenian born in 427 BC into an aristocratic family, drew more heavily upon the model of Lycurgus than that of Solon for his imaginary constitution. But, Plato had become disillusioned with his native city. The Peloponnesian War, waged between Athens and Sparta, had begun just before Plato's birth and ended in defeat and humiliation for Athens in 404 BC, when the philosopher was twenty-three. The turmoil of war and its aftermath provoked in Athens a series of democratic and oligarchic revolutions. It was under a restored democracy that, to the young Plato's horror and disgust, his teacher Socrates was sentenced to death on the trumped-up charge of impiety. Later in life Plato, looking back to this troubled time, wrote:

> I came to the conclusion that all existing states were badly governed, and that their constitutions were incapable of reform without drastic treatment and a great deal of good luck. I was forced, in fact, to the belief that the only hope of finding justice for society or for the individual lay in true philosophy, and that mankind will have no respite from trouble until either real philosophers gain political power or politicians become by some miracle true philosophers.

Thus it was that Plato founded the Academy in Athens in 386 BC as a school for statesmen, where would-be politicians might learn to be philosopher rulers. He composed the *Republic*, written in the form of a dialogue with Socrates as the narrator, in the first years of the Academy, and it can be viewed as a manifesto of the Academy's aims: a statement of its philosophical principles rather than a living and breathing paradigm of the ideal state. A large part of the *Republic* (whose title in Greek can mean indifferently 'constitution', 'state' or 'society') is not about politics or constitutions at all, but rather about education, ethics and philosophy: education because of its importance in creating the good citizen and statesman; ethics because the ancient Greeks equated the virtue of the individual with the virtue of the citizen; philosophy because it is the foundation of both. But, it is Plato's description of the constitution of his Republic which concerns us here.

Plato describes three classes in the *Republic*. The top two classes are the Rulers, who govern and make policy, and the Auxiliaries, a sort of combined civil service, military and police, who execute and implement government decisions. The Rulers and Auxiliaries together comprise the Guardians. Plato tells us next to nothing about the third class, made up of farmers, manufacturers and traders, except that the Guardians, in order to ensure that there is no excessive wealth or poverty among them, control all their activities.

Whereas this murky under-class are small-time capitalists, the Guardians are committed communists. They have no possessions, property, or family, and, like the Spartans, follow military-style discipline. They are entirely supported by the state, and their life is austere in the extreme: 'they shall eat together in messes and live together like soldiers in camp. They must be told that they have no need of mortal and material gold and silver', 'nor wear them as ornaments, nor drink from vessels made of them'. The reason for the enforced communism of the Guardians is to prevent corruption and disunity. Socrates states:

> If they acquire private property in land, houses, or money, they will become ... harsh tyrants instead of partners in their dealings with their fellow citizens, with whom they will live on terms of mutual hatred and suspicion; they will be more afraid of internal revolt than external attack, and be heading fast for destruction that will overwhelm themselves and the whole community.

To the charge that, under this regime, the Guardians cannot be very happy, Socrates responds:

> It would not in fact be in the least surprising if our Guardians were very happy indeed, [for] our purpose in founding our state was not to promote the particular happiness of a single class, but, so far as possible, of the whole community.

It is their education which teaches the Guardians to look to the interest of the community above their own or that of their class.

According to Socrates, 'the element in our constitution' to which this unanimity and devotion to a single common interest 'is especially due is the community of women and children in the Guardian class'. Plato believed that personal interests and affections, which were centred on the family, distracted a man from his duties to the state. Socrates therefore declares that the position of women, marriage and the production of children 'ought so far as possible to be dealt with on the proverbial basis of "all things in common between friends"' – as it was among the Spartans. Men and women Guardians are forbidden by law to set up house together, 'all the women should be common to all the men; similarly, children should be held in common, and no parent should know its child, or child its parent.'

With this community of women and children, Plato was thinking not only of the social cohesion of the Republic but also of the rights of women. In a later work, Plato wrote that 'almost every state, under present conditions, is only half a state' because women have no well-defined role in it. Thus, by abolishing the family, Plato was enabling women to pursue the same careers as men, for there is 'no administrative occupation which is peculiar to woman as woman or man as man; natural capacities are similarly distributed in each sex, and it is natural for women to take part in all occupations as well as men.' To this end, female Guardians receive the same intellectual and physical training as their male counterparts.

Nevertheless, begetting children is a vital part of the female Guardians' role in society. The state adheres to a strict eugenics policy to produce the best potential leaders. The Rulers hold festivals to match couples whom they wish to breed (the couples are supposedly unaware of this contrivance). Sex which has not been sanctioned by the Rulers is regarded as 'a sin and a crime'. Although the government provides an admirable child-care system, there is no question but that women's first duty is to 'bear children for the state'; for, although they work alongside men, 'in all women will be the weaker parties'.

One scholar has called Plato's Republic a 'Managerial Meritocracy', based on innate talent nurtured by a first-class education which is available to all (Plato stresses that there is mobility between the three classes). The focus of the *Republic* is on the philosopher rulers, those who 'have the capacity to grasp the eternal and immutable, while those who have no such capacity are not philosophers and are lost in multiplicity and change.' Plato uses the simile of a cave where men, prisoners since birth, see only shadows on the wall. The true philosopher is the man who breaks his chains and escapes the cave into the light to see the world as it really is. Once they have left the realm of shadows, these philosophers 'are unwilling to involve themselves in human affairs, and . . . their minds long to remain in the realm above'; they 'will take no practical action of their own accord, fancying themselves to be out of this world in some kind of earthly paradise.'

The philosopher ruler is the man who, however reluctantly, returns from the region of light and truth to the illusory world of the cave to liberate the prisoners and create an ideal state. However, to accomplish this, legislators, like an artist preparing a working surface, must first 'wipe the slate of human society and human habits clean', for they are 'unwilling to start work on an individual or a city, or draw out laws, until they are given, or have made themselves, a clean canvas'.

During his years at the Academy, Plato never lost his hope of turning a statesman into a philosopher ruler, although his confidence was occasionally shaken. In 367 BC he was invited to educate and train Dionysius II of Syracuse to become the ideal leader. Dionysius, twenty-eight years old at the time, was not an impressionable pupil and detested mathematics. The visit was not a success, and Plato left after a year. There were, however, partial successes. Hermias of Atarneus, in Asia Minor, took on two graduates of the Academy as advisors and turned his tyranny into a milder form of autocracy. In his last work, *The Laws*, the older and perhaps wiser Plato once again advocates the ideal society as described in the *Republic*, but then adds a second and third best constitution to provide lawgivers with a more practical choice. Plato's most important concession to reality in these alternative models is the absence of communism, which he admitted was too difficult to implement.

The *Republic* has always had as many detractors as admirers. One of its first and sternest critics was Plato's pupil, Aristotle (Plato nicknamed him 'the Brain'). Aristotle's mind was of a more practical nature than his teacher's, and his approach to the problem of the ideal society was to collect 158 constitutions of Greek states and to evaluate them on an historical and empirical basis. His findings, outlined in the second book of the *Politics*, made him a great sceptic of ideal states. He disapproves particularly of Plato's abolition of private property and the family. He points out that Plato has failed to account for human nature: 'Men pay most attention to what is their very own: they care less for what is common, and only when they feel themselves personally concerned.' It is not the possessions but the desires of mankind which need to be equalized. Family communism is impractical and, in any case, would not strengthen but water down affection among members of the community. As Aristotle remarks, Plato was unable 'to distinguish between unity and uniformity'.

Aristotle's overall conviction, that the best way forward is not, as Plato insists, to rebuild society from scratch but to draw upon examples of good government, past and present, prefigures the ideas of Sir Karl Popper, Plato's most bitter critic in the twentieth century. In the first volume of his work, *The Open Society*, entitled *The Spell of Plato* and originally published in 1945, Popper denounces Plato as a totalitarian and the worst sort of utopian who, believing that politics can be reduced to an exact science, draws up a blueprint of the ideal society and then ruthlessly puts it into effect. When Plato states that the Republic 'uses persuasion or compulsion to unite all citizens and make them share together the benefits which each individually can confer on the community', it would seem that such criticism is justified. In America the *Republic* was called the 'original philosophical charter of fascism'. Indeed, soon after the National Socialists came into power German academics began to point out the similarities between Plato's ideal state and the programme of the Third Reich.

However, the protests of Popper and others rest on the assumption that Plato intended the *Republic* as a model for an actual community. But, as we stated earlier, the *Republic* is a statement of philosophical principles rather than a blueprint for society. At one point, Plato describes his discourse on the Republic as a kind of daydream; elsewhere he speaks of it in terms of a state of mind:

> Whether it be in the infinity of past time, or in the future, or even at the present in some foreign country beyond our horizons, whenever men skilled in philosophy are somehow forced to take part in politics, then the society we have described either exists or existed or will exist, and the spirit of philosophy herself gain control.

The *Republic* is most concerned with the question of how to ensure that rulers are philosophers, and remain that way; Plato does not explore what life would be like for the ordinary citizen under such a constitution. A complete description of the ideal state required imaginative engagement with the texture of everyday reality, the synthesis of Plato's 'spirit of philosophy' with the plebeian perspective of Cockaigne. Utopia would have to wait two thousand years to be discovered.

2. A Little Book

A fruitful, pleasant and witty work, of the best state of a public weal, and of the new isle, called Utopia: written in Latin, by the right worthy and famous Sir Thomas More, Knight.

So reads the title page to the first English translation of a slim volume originally published in Louvain in 1516, whose influence on Western society has been incalculable. Thomas More was not the first to imagine a land of prosperity: from the Golden Age to Cockaigne, that mythical country had been a constant of human desire for two thousand years. Nor was he the first to describe the constitutional arrangements of an ideal society; that honour probably belongs to Plato. More's innovation was to conceive from the marriage of these two traditions something wholly new, a speaking picture of a just, prosperous and stable society, with its 'ground plan, elevation and bird's-eye view'. His genius was to give to his imaginary world 'a local habitation and a name'. To name something is, in a sense, to create it, and in naming his imaginary world More did not simply add a word to our language, he fashioned a new instrument of thought, a powerful weapon of social change: *utopia* – it has been on our lips, and in our minds, ever since.

The word itself is that favourite device of More, a pun, on the Greek *ou topos* (no place) and *eu topos* (good place). Its title thus embodies the enigma at the heart of *Utopia*: are we to take seriously this fantasy island, and, if so, is the book primarily a lament for the perfect society that can never be achieved, or is it meant as a blueprint for the construction of an ideal republic?

The author is as enigmatic as his book. Sir Thomas More loved good company and took 'such pleasure in jesting that he might seem born for it'. Yet Saint Thomas More wore a hair shirt and died a martyr to his faith. Born in 1478 in London, the son of a prominent lawyer, Sir John More, Thomas received a good education and went up to Oxford at fourteen, the normal age for that time. However, Sir John insisted that his son take up a career in the law, and More left Oxford after two years to enter the Inns of Court and follow in his father's footsteps. More experienced something of a spiritual crisis in his early twenties, and spent four years with the monks in the London Charterhouse while considering whether to take Holy Orders. During this time, he studied Greek with the humanist William Grocyn and lectured on one of the most important texts of the Middle Ages, St Augustine's *De Civitate Dei* ('On the City of God'). However, as his friend Erasmus later remarked, More, unable to shake off his desire for a wife, decided to become a good husband and father rather than a bad priest – although he continued to admire and at times long for the pious simplicity of monastic life. He married Jane Colt in 1504 or 1505 and had four children; after her death in 1511, he married a widow, Alice Middleton, whom he admitted to Erasmus 'was neither beautiful nor in her first youth'. More's household eventually grew to be quite large with the addition of Alice's child from her previous marriage, several wards and an adopted daughter.

His legal and diplomatic skills, as well as his acquaintance with London and its merchants, made More a valuable member of foreign trade embassies. Thus, he was eventually faced with another agonizing choice, this time between his London life as lawyer and family man (he was also an undersheriff of the city) and a political career at the court of Henry VIII. In February 1516 More wrote to Erasmus that he had refused a royal pension from the King: to accept would have meant being at court most of the time and away from his family in Chelsea. Nevertheless, in 1518 More took the plunge and became a Privy Councillor. His political career advanced: Under-Treasurer in 1521, Speaker of the House of Commons in 1523, Chancellor of the Duchy of Lancaster in 1525, Lord Chancellor in 1529. When the Catholic Church came under attack from Martin Luther in the 1520s, both More and Henry VIII became staunch and zealous defenders of the faith. However, Henry was soon seeking to annul his marriage to Catherine of Aragon, and to get his way he denounced the Pope's authority and established himself as supreme head of the Church in England. In 1534 More refused to take the oath demanded of each subject by the first Act of Succession, introduced that year. He was at once imprisoned as a traitor, condemned and beheaded in July 1535. His last words on the scaffold were reportedly that he was 'the king's good servant but God's first'. His execution shocked all Europe.

Before the religious and political world was turned upside down by Martin Luther, More and his fellow humanists had already been deeply concerned with the state of the Catholic Church and of society as a whole. They rejected the Aristotelian Scholasticism of the Middle Ages which had shrouded the Latin version of the Bible, the Vulgate, in what they considered obscure commentary and absurd logic for so long. The humanists sought to rediscover Scripture, pure and unadulterated, so that they and others might be moved to live by Christ's true teachings. The two things which were of the greatest help to them in this task were the revival of the Greek language and the invention of printing. In March 1516 Erasmus published for the first time the original Greek text of the New Testament, together with a revised version of the Vulgate.

This period, the height of the Renaissance, was a time of discoveries (or rediscoveries). Many classical texts, including Plato's *Republic*, which had been lost or forgotten during the Middle Ages, were brought to light and pored over by the humanists, eager to learn more about antiquity. Not only old worlds, but also new worlds were being explored: Christopher Columbus's voyages of discovery to the Americas began while More was at Oxford; those of Amerigo Vespucci followed while he was a young lawyer in London.

However, while the humanists welcomed these exciting revelations, they soon found both their faith and their reason severely tested. In examining the New Testament, scholars came to realize that it was not, as the contemporary Church contended, textually inviolate and inviolable. Much to the Church's horror, Erasmus was able to show that passages which were not in the original Greek had at some point made their way into the Latin Vulgate. And, as far as the New World was concerned, who could believe the extraordinary tales of strange monsters and stranger peoples which the explorers brought back with them?

It was this expanding world, where fact and fiction seemed to converge, and where old religious certainties were challenged, that gave birth to *Utopia*. The book began life as a humanist conspiracy in an Antwerp garden. In May 1515 More travelled to Bruges on Henry VIII's behalf to negotiate a commercial treaty with Flanders concerning the wool trade. By mid-July negotiations had come to a standstill, so More took the opportunity to visit Antwerp to meet a friend of Erasmus, Peter Gilles, about whom he had heard much. It was in Gilles's company that fact and fantasy began to intertwine in the garden of More's lodging, real and imaginary characters met and the stage was set for *Utopia*.

The book as published begins with an example of Utopian poetry in its original alphabet, together with a Latin translation. After this comes an introductory letter from the author to Peter Gilles, wherein he apologizes for taking so long to produce 'this little book about the

Utopian Republic'. After all, More admits, 'all I had to do was repeat what Raphael told us'. Raphael Hythloday (from the Greek meaning 'lover of nonsense') is the traveller whose tale More is supposed to be relating faithfully, and More is determined to get his facts straight. Did Raphael say that bridge across the river was five hundred or only three hundred yards long? And, 'another little problem' had cropped up: could Peter ask Raphael exactly where Utopia was in the New World? 'I'd gladly give what little money I possess to repair the omission. For one thing, it makes me feel rather a fool, after all I've written about the island, not to know what sea it's in. For another, there are one or two people in England who want to go there.'

Peter Gilles then joins in the joke with a letter of his own to another friend of More, the prominent humanist scholar Jerome Busleiden. Gilles recommends More's account – 'like Plato's *Republic*, only better' – but explains that just at the moment when Hythloday was describing Utopia's location, one of their company coughed so loudly that the information was lost. Gilles claims that he is determined to clear up the point, 'That is, if our friend Raphael is still safe and sound, for . . . Some people say that he has died somewhere on his travels'.

After this elaborate charade the book proper begins. Significantly, it is divided into two parts: More prefaces Hythloday's description of the island of Utopia, which comprises Book Two, with a preliminary dialogue in Book One, concerned mainly with the state of contemporary England. Erasmus tells us that whereas More composed Book Two 'when at leisure' that summer in Antwerp, he only decided to add Book One after he had returned to London in the autumn. This afterthought, however, transforms the whole work. It turns what might otherwise be read as simply another fantastic traveller's tale – albeit an unusually intelligent one – into a powerful social critique. The originality and importance of *Utopia* resides in its juxtaposition of a detailed examination of the workings of a just but imaginary society with a bitter denunciation of injustices that were all too real. Book One not only gives More's work its polemical bite but also alerts us to the author's central intention: to reveal, in Peter Gilles's words, 'the actual and potential causes . . . of every social evil'.

Book One opens with a brief but factual account of More's diplomatic mission to Flanders, and explains how he came to visit Peter Gilles in Antwerp. More then relates how one day, walking back to his hotel, he came across Gilles in the company of a sunburnt stranger, one Raphael Hythloday. Gilles describes Hythloday as a man of philosophical bent,

learned in Latin and especially Greek, who left his property in Portugal
to join the explorer Amerigo Vespucci: 'You know those *Four Voyages*
of his that everyone's reading about?' However, rather than return to
Europe with Vespucci on the last voyage in 1504, Hythloday chose
to remain behind in the New World along with twenty-three others.
(Here again fact meets fiction, for in his account Vespucci describes
such an incident.) Hythloday then begins to tell More and the others
gathered round him in the garden of his experiences, including

> ... the sensible arrangements that he noticed in various civilized
> communities. These were the points on which we questioned him
> most closely, and he enlarged most willingly. We did not ask him
> if he had seen any monsters, for monsters have ceased to be news.
> There is never any shortage of horrible creatures who prey on human
> beings, snatch away their food, or devour whole populations; but
> examples of wise social planning are not so easy to find.

But, before relating the main topic of the afternoon, the manners and
customs of the Utopians, More first gives an account of the conversation
leading up to it. The discussion between Hythloday, Gilles and More
begins with a dilemma familiar to the humanists, and one which they
felt keenly: should philosophers and scholars enter government service
and advise princes in an effort to better the commonwealth, or should
they remain aloof from the quagmire of politics and pursue their own
studies, like Erasmus, who begged and borrowed from friends and
patrons? Thus, after the intrepid explorer has described in general
terms the various peoples and places which he encountered on his
travels in the New World, Peter Gilles remarks, 'My dear Raphael,
I can't think why you don't enter the service of some king or other.
I'm sure any king would jump at the chance of employing you. With
your knowledge and experience, you'd be just the man to supply not
only entertainment, but also instructive precedents and useful advice.'
Hythloday answers Gilles in no uncertain terms: he does not wish
to find himself in servitude, nor even in service, to kings. In the first
place, monarchs are interested only in the pursuit of war, not peace;
in the second place, royal counsellors are too proud to profit from one
another's advice; they are bent only on winning the favour of their
superiors by flattery. Hythloday illustrates his point by describing
the 'curious mixture of conceit, stupidity and stubbornness' which he
came across on a brief visit to England in the time of Henry VII. He

recounts a conversation which he had at the table of the Chancellor, John Morton, a man whom 'one respected just as much for his wisdom and moral character as for his great eminence', and on whom both King and country depended. (The young Thomas More had once been a page in Morton's household.)

On that occasion Hythloday had challenged the Chancellor concerning the evils and injustices of contemporary English society, the result of the nobility and landed gentry seeking to enrich themselves at the expense of the poor. In Tudor England theft was a hanging offence; yet, asserted Hythloday, many were driven to it by sheer necessity since they had no other means of livelihood. Those affected included maimed war veterans who were offered no compensation from the government, the idle retainers of noblemen whose patrons died without making any provision for them, and those who were left to starve in the countryside after the rich had enclosed the common land, which once supported crops, to graze sheep whose wool was so valuable. On the subject of sheep, Hythloday remarked:

> These placid creatures, which used to require so little food, have now apparently developed a raging appetite, and turned into man-eaters. Fields, houses, towns, everything goes down their throats.

To make matters worse

> This wretched poverty is most incongruously linked with expensive tastes. Servants, tradesmen, even farm labourers, in fact all classes of society are recklessly extravagant about clothes and food. Then think how many brothels there are, including those that go under the names of wine-taverns or ale-houses. Think of the demoralizing games people play – dice, cards, backgammon, tennis, bowls, quoits – what are they but quick methods of wasting a man's money, and sending him straight off to become a thief?

Hythloday counselled Morton to 'get rid of these pernicious practices' and make laws that rectify these social injustices. (Legislation regulating apparel and fare – the so-called sumptuary laws – had, in fact, existed in England since the Middle Ages.) Upon hearing his proposed remedies Morton's other guests shook their heads and made wry faces. Yet, when Morton gave his cautious approval to Hythloday's ideas, these same hangers-on fell about praising the Chancellor for his great wisdom.

'So,' Hythloday remarks to More, 'you can guess how much notice people would take of me and my advice at Court!'

Hythloday subscribes to Plato's doctrine put forward in the *Republic*: although in an ideal world philosophers should become kings and kings philosophers, in a world full of foolishness the philosopher is better off abstaining from affairs of state – as Plato 'learned by experience with Dionysius' [of Syracuse]. The character of More, on the other hand, advocates the notion of 'civic humanism' as expressed by Cicero. In *De Officiis*, the Roman statesman declares that men should adhere to a more practical philosophy which is able to adapt itself to political vicissitudes. Cicero insists that we should place our talents at the service of the state and try our best 'to respect, defend and preserve concord and unity within the whole community of men'. More states his view plainly and simply: 'What you can't put right you must try to make as little wrong as possible.'

There is no doubt that the subject of royal service was on More's mind at the time he was writing Book One, for it was soon after his return from Flanders in the autumn of 1515 that he received the offer of a royal pension, to which he had to reply. (It may be this difficult decision to which Erasmus is referring when he states that More composed Book One 'in the heat of the moment'.) In October 1517, a few months after *Utopia* had come off the press, More wrote that Erasmus was wise to avoid being mixed up in 'the busy trifles of princes'. More had refused the pension, perhaps taking the advice of Hythloday, who stands by his principles and insists that social ills will never be remedied by half measures and compromises: kings and their counsellors must hear the truth.

If we're never to say anything that might be thought unconventional, for fear of its sounding ridiculous, we'll have to hush up, even in a Christian country, practically everything that Christ taught. . . . And most of His teaching is far more at variance with modern conventions than anything I suggested, except in so far as His doctrines have been modified by ingenious preachers – doubtless on your recommendation!

'We'll never get human behaviour in line with Christian ethics,' these gentlemen must have argued, 'so let's adapt Christian ethics to human behaviour. Then at least there'll be some connexion between them.'

Although he does not say so explicitly, one particular aspect of Christ's teachings in the Gospels leads Hythloday to his next point, the single most important principle put forward in *Utopia*: the benefit to be derived from the abolition of private property and the community of goods. Christ is constantly urging us to give up our worldly wealth. To the man who 'had great possessions' He said, 'Go thy way, sell whatsoever thou hast, and give to the poor, and thou shalt have treasure in heaven' (Mark 10: 21). Hythloday comments to More that 'to tell you the truth ... I don't see how you can ever get any real justice or prosperity, so long as there's private property, and everything's judged in terms of money.' He continues: 'When I consider all this, I feel much more sympathy with Plato, and much less surprise at his refusal to legislate for a city that rejected egalitarian principles [Megalopolis in Arcadia]. It was evidently quite obvious to a powerful intellect like his that the one essential condition for a healthy society was equal distribution of goods – which I suspect is impossible [under a system of private property].'

The fictitious More objects to this reasoning. He maintains that, without the motive of personal gain, people will become lazy and rely on others to do the work; riot and bloodshed will break out if individuals are not allowed their private possessions. In the Middle Ages this was the reasoning used by the Church Fathers, such as Thomas Aquinas, to justify private property, a necessary evil for mankind, weighed down as we are by original sin. Communism can only work among a community of saints; capitalism is for sinners. Thus, Paradise may have been set up on sound communist principles (though the Church Fathers were vague on this point), but God banished Adam and Eve to a dog-eat-dog world where 'men are at once punished and safeguarded' by the system of private property. Those who upheld this view once again cited Cicero, who remarked, 'What plague could ever be worse than to favour an equal distribution of goods?'

However, as we have seen, during this period humanists were stripping away the accretions of scholasticism from Church doctrine, and striving to get back to the original sources of Christianity. We have already remarked that while More was writing *Utopia*, his friend Erasmus was preparing the first edition of the Greek New Testament to be published, and it may well be that More was prompted to re-read the Gospels at this time. Perhaps, seeing them in the clear light of Erasmus's humanist scholarship, he was particularly struck by Christ's uncompromising attitude to private property. Indeed, the Acts of the

Apostles implies that the early Church had originally been organized along communistic principles: 'And all that believed were together, and had all things in common; And sold their possessions and goods, and parted them to all men, as every man had need' (Acts 2: 44–45).

Certainly, this was a period when Christian reformers were seeking to remake Catholicism in the image of the Early Church. In Florence in the 1490s the preacher Fra Girolamo Savonarola even managed briefly to establish such an austere Christian republic, claiming the Saviour as its head. The Florentines discarded their finery and donned plain, almost puritanical, attire; they burned many of their possessions, including books and paintings, on the 'Bonfire of the Vanities' in the Piazza della Signoria. Although Florence was not communist, it imposed a ten per cent tax on all property in an attempt to alleviate the gap between rich and poor. Savonarola was eventually burned at the stake as a heretic in 1498, but his reforming zeal made a great impression on the Christian humanists, especially Pico della Mirandola, whose biography More translated into English in about 1505.

It was probably for a complex variety of reasons, then, that by 1515–16 More was no longer willing to take on faith either the Church's verdict concerning private property and original sin or its condemnation of any attempt to create a true Christian state here on earth. He was also rejecting the very English view, as set out by the fifteenth-century lawyer, Sir John Fortescue, that the foundation of law is the protection of private property. More wanted to know whether a communistic society could work, and, if so, what it would be like. For his investigation, More could draw on other examples of communistic societies, both real and imaginary: the Guardian class in Plato's *Republic*, monastic communities and the Native American societies described by Vespucci where 'everything is shared in common'. The root of More's project is a rejection of the Church Fathers' view of human nature, and 'here we get to the heart of what is modern about *Utopia*': he sees private property not as a result of man's sins but as their primary cause, and sets out to describe a society whose institutions reflect this fact.

Hythloday replies to the 'orthodox' objections to communism made by the fictitious More:

> You're bound to take that view, for you simply can't imagine what it would be like – not accurately, at any rate. But if you'd been with me in Utopia, and seen it all for yourself, as I did – I lived there for more than five years, you know, and the only reason why

I ever left was that I wanted to tell people about the New World –
you'd be the first to admit that you'd never seen a country so well
organized.

And so, finally, at the invitation of More and his companions,
Hythloday sets out to give a description of Utopia.

Book Two, which comprises Hythloday's narration, begins with the
topography of the island. It measures two hundred miles across and is
in the shape of a new moon, with a large protected harbour. There are
fifty-four 'splendid big towns', models of urban planning, which are
similar not only in customs, laws and traditions, but also in layout
and general appearance. At the front of the first edition of *Utopia* is a
charming woodcut of the island, depicting the capital Amaurotum (from
the Greek word for 'obscure' or 'dark and dim') and the river Anydrus
(meaning 'waterless' in Greek), together with the following verse:

> NOPLACIA [*Utopia*] was once my name,
> That is, a place where no one goes.
> Plato's *Republic* now I claim
> To match, or beat at its own game;
> For that was just a myth in prose,
> But what he wrote of, I became,
> Of men, wealth, laws a solid frame,
> A place where every wise man goes:
> GOPLACIA [*Eutopia*] is now my name.

From the evidence of this poem, there is no doubt that More meant
the reader to have Plato in mind while reading *Utopia*. One might say
that More was picking up where the ancient philosopher had left off in
his *Republic*, which had been lost in the West for centuries until its
rediscovery in the early 1400s. Both More and Plato realized, as do all
utopians, the futility of trying to create an ideal society from existing
structures; it was necessary to abolish all historical traditions and social
conventions and start with a clean canvas – or an hitherto undiscovered
island. Both men to some extent believed in the importance of an ideal
ruler: the first leader of Utopia, Utopos, who transformed the islanders
from 'a pack of ignorant savages into . . . the most civilized nation in
the world', resembles one of Plato's philosopher kings. Both authors
advocated the abolition of private property. However, whereas Plato
established the communist system only among the Guardians, the élite of

his Republic, More showed himself to be a true egalitarian and extended communism to the whole of society.

More's Utopia differs from Plato's Republic in another vital respect: whereas Plato in effect destroyed the family by having not only possessions but also wives and children in common, More adheres to tradition and makes family life the most important institution among the Utopians (one eighteenth-century French translation calls them *bourgeois*). Within the family the Utopians are taught discipline and respect for their elders. Once a month 'wives kneel down at home before their husbands, and children before their parents, to confess all their sins of omission and commission, and ask to be forgiven. This gets rid of any little grudges that may have clouded the domestic atmosphere.'

Families live separately in individual state-owned houses, which are 'allocated by lot, and changed round every ten years'. (Vespucci reported a similar arrangement amongst certain inhabitants of the New World.) As for their government, the population is divided into groups of thirty households, each of which elects annually a local magistrate, called in their ancient language a *Syphograntus*. The *Syphogranti* elect the local Mayor (a post held for life) by secret ballot from among four candidates put forward by each quarter of the city. Other officials include the *Transibori*, elected annually, who act much like a Prime Minister's Cabinet. The Utopian system is basically a representative democracy. Every major issue is discussed in the Assembly of *Syphogranti*, who then explain it to all their households and report back to the Council of *Transibori*. There is no king; nor are there any lawyers: a fact which ensures that bureaucracy and red tape are kept to a minimum and disputes settled quickly. Official posts, such as ambassadorships, are always given to scholars.

The government of Utopia provides all the material as well as the social benefits of a welfare state: food, clothing, housing, education and medical treatment. The Utopians repay this debt to the state by working in the fields and at manual jobs in the cities for the required six-hour work day. Life, however, is rather regimented. As Hythloday explains, 'The chief business of the [*Syphogranti*] – in fact, practically their only business – is to see that nobody sits around doing nothing, but that everyone gets on with his job.' Utopians start the day at four o'clock in the morning: 'They have a six-hour working day – three hours in the morning, then lunch – then a two-hour break – then three more hours in the afternoon, followed by supper. They go to bed at 8 p.m., and sleep for eight hours.'

Even in their leisure time, Utopians' choices are restricted, for although 'they're free to do what they like', it is understood that they are 'not to waste their time in idleness or self-indulgence, but to make good use of it in some congenial activity. Most people spend these free periods on further education, for there are public lectures first thing every morning.' Too much privacy is considered a dangerous luxury in Utopia: meals are taken, when the bugle blows, in large communal dining halls; there are no locks on the doors; and people worship in public. Thus, the government is able to rely on peer pressure as well as the *Syphogranti* and the Utopians' own sense of civic duty, to keep people in line. Hythloday remarks that on the island 'everyone has his eye on you, so you're practically forced to get on with your job, and make some proper use of your spare time.' A twentieth-century reader cannot but be reminded of George Orwell's slogan 'Big Brother is Watching You'.

The Utopians not only do without money but also despise, like Plato's Guardians, the symbols of wealth to which Europeans were so attached, particularly gold and gems. (Again, Vespucci had told of strange tribes who disdained these precious commodities.) Thus, the Utopians relegate gold to the making of chamber-pots and shackles. The foreign dignitaries of Anemolia ('windy' or 'boastful'), parading through the streets of Utopia in a splendid array of gold and precious stones, prompt a child in the street to cry out:

'I say, Mother, just look at that great baby! Fancy wearing jewellery at his age!'
To which the mother would reply, very seriously:
'Sh, dear! I imagine he must be a clown attached to the embassy.'

Unlike the Europeans, the Utopians do not associate nobility with wealth and think anyone who does insane:

But what puzzles and disgusts the Utopians even more is the idiotic way some people have of practically worshipping a rich man, not because they owe him money or are otherwise in his power, but simply because he's rich.

According to the Utopians, virtue is its own reward, sometimes commemorated by a public statue, and virtue is the only true measure of nobility. One modern scholar believes that this is the main thrust of *Utopia*: 'Hythloday's description of Utopia in Book II should be read as an account of the social benefits that flow from espousing the true instead of the counterfeit view of nobility.'

Along with their concept of nobility, the Utopians' philosophy and religion are of key importance to the understanding of the work. Their philosophy of life is arrived at through reason, and 'their chief subject of dispute is the nature of human happiness – on what factor or factors does it depend?' Hythloday remarks disapprovingly that 'here they seem rather too much inclined to take a hedonistic view, for according to them human happiness consists largely or wholly in pleasure.' Pleasures can be physical, brought about 'by the discharge of some excess, as in excretion, sexual intercourse, or any relief of irritation by rubbing or scratching', or intellectual. The Utopians 'regard the enjoyment of life – that is, pleasure – as the natural object of all human efforts, and natural, as they define it, is synonymous with virtuous.' Furthermore, 'they say it's sensible to consult one's own interests, and a moral duty to consult those of the community as well.' With this very practical view of what is good, More comes very close to anticipating the nineteenth-century utilitarians, another example of his striking modernity.

However, 'in all their discussions of happiness they invoke certain religious principles to supplement the operations of reason, which they think otherwise ill-equipped to identify true happiness.' The Utopians are pagans: they knew nothing of Christ and his teachings until Hythloday's arrival on the island. Nonetheless, the founder, Utopos, recognized that religious strictures were the most effective way to maintain law and order within any society. Utopos demanded that his subjects take three things on faith: the immortality of the soul, reward and punishment after death, and the existence of Providence. According to Hythloday:

Anyone who thinks differently has, in their view, forfeited his right to be classed as a human being, by degrading his immortal soul to the level of an animal's body. Still less do they regard him as a Utopian citizen. They say a person like that doesn't really care a damn for the Utopian way of life – only he's too frightened to say so. For it stands to reason, if you're not afraid of anything but prosecution, and have no hopes of anything after you're dead, you'll always be trying to evade or break the laws of your country, in order to gain your own private ends.

Plato, too, at the end of the *Republic* reasons that the soul is immortal in order to evoke the notion of moral responsibility.

Although they have no knowledge of original sin as such, Utopians acknowledge that human nature is flawed. Crimes like adultery are not unknown, and their communistic system is intended precisely to overcome such basic human failings as idleness and greed. Thus, in *Utopia* More is not subscribing to the Pelagian heresy of the perfectibility of man. Nor is he contradicting St Augustine's view, set out in *De Civitate Dei*, that human nature, original sin or whatever one calls it must inevitably prevent man from attaining heaven on earth. And he certainly is not trying to describe an island of saints. Rather, More's central intention is to show that a purely rational approach to social organization would end up mimicking many aspects of Christ's teaching. In particular, the prosperity, stability and contentment of Utopian society are offered as evidence that the communism practised by the early Church, far from being an impractical ideal, is in fact the most sensible way to run society. The Utopians are portrayed above all as level-headed people who act always in their own enlightened self-interest. More even has his Utopians argue that acts of altruism ultimately stem from self-interest:

It's wrong to deprive someone of a pleasure so that you can enjoy one yourself, but to deprive yourself of a pleasure so that you can add to someone else's enjoyment is an act of humanity by which you always gain more than you lose. For one thing, such benefits are usually repaid in kind. For another, the mere sense of having done somebody a kindness, and so earned his affection and good will, produces a spiritual satisfaction which far outweighs the loss of a physical one. And lastly – a belief that comes easily to a religious mind – God will reward us for such small sacrifices of momentary pleasure, by giving us an eternity of perfect joy. Thus they argue that, in the final analysis, pleasure is the ultimate happiness which all human beings have in view, even when they're acting virtuously.

Hythloday remarks that 'whatever you may think of their doctrines, you won't find a more prosperous country . . . anywhere on earth.'

However, for a Christian, any code of conduct arrived at through reason alone, however admirable, must be flawed because of its ignorance of Christ's doctrines. Thus, some of the religious and moral principles which the Utopians hold to be sensible and rational, such as divorce

and married men in the priesthood, would have appeared misguided
to More's contemporary readers. Perhaps the clearest example is the
Utopian attitude towards death and dying. Utopian society condones
and even encourages euthanasia. If a disease is not only incurable,
but also painful, the priests and magistrates say to the unfortunate
invalid:

'Let's face it, you'll never be able to live a normal life. You're just
a nuisance to other people and a burden to yourself. . . . Since your
life's a misery to you, why hesitate to die? . . . Why don't you
break out and escape to a better world? Or say the word, and we'll
arrange for your release. It's only common sense to cut your losses.
It's also an act of piety to take the advice of a priest, because he
speaks for God.'

The Utopians' relentless and unblinking rationality extends to matters
of love, war and peace. When marriage is contemplated, the prospective
bride and groom are shown to each other naked. The Utopians think it
absurd that the Europeans take more precautions when buying a horse
than when choosing a wife. As for war, it is something, Hythloday
remarks, which the Utopians 'absolutely loathe. They say it's a quite
subhuman form of activity, although human beings are more addicted
to it than any of the lower animals.' Nevertheless, both men and
women undergo military training so that they will be able to protect
their country, to go to the aid of an ally or to deliver a people from
tyranny if called upon. However, the Utopians will go to great lengths
to avoid war, some of which sound slightly devious, such as offering
enemy troops a reward for the assassination of their leaders and hiring
mercenaries whenever possible. They seem to adhere to Machiavelli's
dictum that fraud is better than force.

Other practices among the Utopians which might seem somewhat
dubious to the modern reader include the institution of slavery and
an aggressive colonial policy. If the population of the Utopian cities
swells, they colonize any neighbouring land which is uncultivated.

If the natives won't do what they're told, they're expelled from the
area marked out for annexation. If they try to resist, the Utopians
declare war – for they consider war perfectly justifiable, when one
country denies another its natural right to derive nourishment from

any soil which the original owners are not using themselves, but are merely holding on to as a worthless piece of property.

The Utopians' rationalist justification of colonization was to be echoed many times as Europeans spread across the globe. It was the pretext used by American settlers in their westward expansion at the expense of the native peoples, and today similar claims are still made by Israelis who allege that they have 'made the desert bloom'.

Their wholly pragmatic approach is also responsible for the Utopians' enlightened policy of religious tolerance. Before Utopos's rule, the island's inhabitants had been caught up in dreadful religious wars. To stop the senseless fighting, Utopos decreed that 'everyone was free to practise what religion he liked, and to try and convert other people to his own faith, provided he did it quietly and politely, by rational argument.' The type of religious fanatic who cannot do enough good works is welcome in Utopia: these earthly saints 'cheerfully undertake all the rough, dirty and difficult jobs that the average person fights shy of.' However, anyone who is too fanatical in his attempts to win converts to his brand of religion, thus threatening to undermine the social order, is exiled or enslaved.

This tolerant attitude seems to be at odds with More's own vigorous persecution of Luther and other Protestant heretics in the 1520s. But, the stance taken by the Utopians on issues such as religious tolerance, divorce, married priests and euthanasia was never intended to represent More's own views. Rather, he is thinking out loud. What would life be like in a society whose members act in a wholly rational way? More brilliantly and dispassionately thinks through all the implications of this approach: the conclusions are the Utopians', not More's. However, we can guess that if Luther had been transported to the island of Utopia and continued his fiery preaching there, he would no doubt have been exiled for over-zealous and subversive behaviour.

In any case, one wonders how long it will be before Christianity becomes the dominant religion in Utopia since, according to Hythloday:

When we told them about Christ, His teaching, His character, His miracles, ... you've no idea how easy it was to convert them ... Perhaps they were unconsciously influenced by some divine inspiration, or perhaps it was because Christianity seemed so very like their own principal religion – though I should imagine they were also considerably affected by the information that Christ prescribed of His own disciples a communist way of life, which is still practised today in all the most truly Christian communities [referring to the monasteries which More had always admired].

The Utopians pray to God at the end of their church services:

> I thank Thee for all Thy blessings, but especially for letting me live in the happiest possible society, and practise what I hope is the truest religion. If I am wrong, and if some other religion or social system would be better and more acceptable to Thee, I pray Thee in Thy goodness to let me know it, for I am ready to follow wherever Thou shalt lead me.

More obviously did not intend that his readers regard the Utopian religion as in any way an improvement upon Christianity. Rather, More meant to shame Europeans into realizing just how far they had strayed from Christ's teachings in contrast to the heathen Utopians.

But was More going even further than this – was he, in fact, drawing up real guidelines intended to reorder Western European society? Erasmus was perhaps most familiar with More's purpose since he presided over the 'birth' of *Utopia*. More borrowed the name for his island before its conversion by Utopos, Abraxa, from Erasmus's *Moriae Encomium* ('The Praise of Folly'), published in 1511. According to Erasmus, More had encouraged him to write the *Moriae Encomium*, and its title was intended as a pun on the Englishman's name. More's *Utopia* might even be seen as a companion piece to Erasmus's earlier work: one takes folly as its theme, the other, reason. The two friends corresponded about More's fantasy, calling it *Nusquama nostra* (our Nowhere), and More entrusted its publication to Erasmus's care in Louvain (perhaps to avoid Henry VIII's censure).

There was no doubt in Erasmus's mind about the point behind *Utopia*. At the beginning of 1517 he wrote to a friend: 'As for More's *Utopia*, if you have not yet read it, be sure to ask for it when you want to be amused, or more truly, if you wish to see the very wellsprings of all troubles in the commonwealth.' In 1519 Erasmus stated: '*Utopia* he published with the purpose of showing the reasons for the shortcomings of a commonwealth; but he represented the English commonwealth in particular, because he had studied it and knew it best.' Both Erasmus and Peter Gilles aided More in his purpose by interjecting appropriate notes printed in the margin of the first edition, such as 'Would that the Same Procedure Were Followed Today in Our Councils', 'Yet Nowadays Blockheads and Loggerheads Devote Themselves to Scholarship, whereas the Best Endowed Talent Is Being Ruined by Pleasures' and, significantly, 'How Much Wiser the Utopians Are than the Common Run of Christians!'

Utopia was intended as a yardstick rather than a blueprint. With his fiction, More is challenging his fellow humanists to question society's long-held assumptions concerning the complex relationship between wealth, nobility, virtue and Christian doctrine. He is asking his readers to take seriously, though just for a moment, a society whose guiding principles are communism and social equality, then to consider whether contemporary European society stands up to comparison. At the end of the book the fictitious More comments that some of the customs and laws of the Utopians as recounted by Hythloday seem absurd:

> I cannot agree with everything that he said, for all his undoubted learning and experience. But I freely admit that there are many features of the Utopian Republic which I should like – though I hardly expect – to see adopted in Europe.

There is a letter to his co-conspirator Peter Gilles in which More remarks concerning one critic of *Utopia*:

> I do not see why he should appear to himself so open-eyed ... because he has detected that some little absurdities exist in the institutions of Utopia or that I have devised some things not expedient enough in the framing of a commonwealth. Why should he be so minded as if there were nothing absurd elsewhere in the world or as if any of all the philosophers had ever ordered the commonwealth, the ruler, or even the private home without instituting some feature that had better be changed? Why, if the memory of the greatest men, hallowed by time, were not sacred to me, I could in each of them quote points in the condemnation of which I should indubitably get a unanimous vote.

However, because *Utopia* draws such a vivid and compelling picture of its imaginary society, it broke the bounds of its author's original intentions. It was inevitable that many would read it as a call to action. Among the first to do so was the Spaniard Vasco de Quiroga who went to New Spain (Mexico) as a judge in 1531. When he saw the tragic situation brought about by the conquest of the indigenous peoples of Central America, he sought to create a 'humanistic program based upon More's *Utopia*, which, in his judgment, should serve as the Magna Charta of European civilization in the New World'. (Ironically, the day after Quiroga wrote his opinion addressed to the Spanish Court, Thomas More was beheaded.) Quiroga did not win over the Spanish government to his way of thinking. Nevertheless, he established hospital-villages in Santa Fe which were modelled after *Utopia* with all property in common, one magistrate for every thirty families, six-hour work days, distribution of goods according to need, and alternation of jobs in the fields and in the city.

The true importance of More's achievement is that in writing *Utopia* he fashioned a new form of discourse: *Utopia* is the first political thought experiment. The brilliance of More's insight is evidenced by the many ways in which Utopia prefigures modern society. Its communist system suffers from many of the drawbacks that are all too apparent in the twentieth-century history of state socialism. Utopia is a deeply conformist society: according to Hythloday, the Utopians all think along very similar lines. Among them, there is backsliding and even sin, but there is no dissent. It is a society that operates without any concept of individual rights, one which would no more tolerate the principled stand of the recalcitrant individual than did sixteenth-century Europe. Ironically, it is hard to imagine that More would have been any more at home in Utopia than he was in Henry VIII's England.

Utopia also has much in common with modern Western society. In Utopia, the Christian faith has yet to inform every aspect of political and social life; with us it has long ceased to do so. We, like the Utopians, consider our beliefs to be founded in rationality. Thus, we accept divorce and married priests, advocate religious tolerance, and are willing to contemplate euthanasia. Above all, the Utopians hold that no society can regard itself as truly just unless it has attained at least a degree of social and economic equality. And this belief, which is first fully articulated in *Utopia*, is a central tenet of modern liberal democracy.

In 1516 More drew a map of the future. The fact that our world resembles Utopia in so many ways stems from men's compulsion to measure themselves against this imaginary commonwealth and even to imitate it. The little book that first came off the press in Louvain nearly five hundred years ago is one of the founding documents of the modern world.

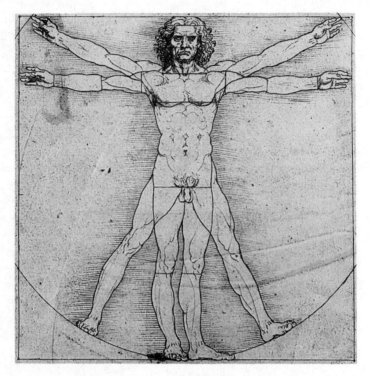

Leonardo da Vinci, Vitruvian man, *c.* 1492.

PART TWO

CITY

For we must Consider that we shall be as a City upon a Hill, the eyes of all people are upon us.

John Winthrop

But what distinguishes the worst architect from the best of bees is this, that the architect raises his structure in imagination before he erects it in reality.

Karl Marx, Das Kapital

> Forget six counties overhung with smoke,
> Forget the snorting steam and piston stroke,
> Forget the spreading of the hideous town;
> Think rather of the pack-horse on the down,
> And dream of London, small and white and clean,
> The clear Thames bordered by its gardens green.

William Morris, The Earthly Paradise

3. Cities on Hills

The first utopia was the city, according to the social philosopher Lewis Mumford. The ancient city in Mesopotamia and Egypt, ruled by divine kingship, guided by astrological symbols and dominated by a central temple, represented 'a glimpse of eternal order, a visible heaven on earth, a seat of the life abundant – in other words, utopia'. For most of man's history, life in the countryside was grim and brutish: as Aristotle remarked, outside the *polis* there were only beasts and heroes. In the Sermon on the Mount, Jesus used the image of the city to represent the Christian community: 'Ye are the light of the world. A city that is set on an hill cannot be hid' (Matthew 5:14): it was this urban image that the Puritan colonist John Winthrop echoed in the epigraph on the previous page when describing his utopian mission to the wilderness of the New World. The well-structured city was both a metaphor for the perfect society, and the only place where it could come into being. Inevitably, both Plato's *Republic* and Thomas More's *Utopia* have an essentially urban aspect. Indeed, all More's Utopians are city-dwellers; the land is cultivated by work details from the towns, so that the miseries of country life are shared out fairly:

> At regular intervals all over the countryside there are houses supplied with agricultural equipment, and town dwellers take it in turns to go and live in them. . . . Two years is the normal period of work on the land, so that no one's forced to rough it for too long.

However, neither Plato nor More devotes much space to the physical details of their cities. Utopia, like the Republic, is ideal by virtue of its social arrangements; its uniform, utilitarian architecture is simply a reflection of a rational, egalitarian polity. For More, the squalid state of contemporary London was a symptom of the sickness of society. But for other utopians, the arrow of causation pointed in the opposite direction: social problems were the result of ill-formed surroundings. Accordingly, the ideal city was not just the location of the perfect society, it was the means to bring it about. Though today neither our cities nor our society are ideal, the followers of this doctrine of

37

'salvation by bricks alone' have played a crucial role in shaping our environment.

The history of the ideal city begins with the Italian Renaissance. For most of Europe the collapse of the Roman Empire meant the eclipse of the city. In Italy, however, many of the towns established in classical times continued to be inhabited. But the medieval city was mainly a refuge from the wars in the countryside. It contained a jumble of conflicting social and economic interests. In Italian hill towns such as San Gimignano one can still see today remnants of the many fortified houses that were squeezed together inside the walls, testimony to the frequent clashes between factions and families that plagued city life.

Gradually, as Europe became politically more stable, the city's importance as a commercial and administrative centre grew, until on the Italian peninsula there arose a number of rich, powerful, sovereign city states. Their walls no longer enclosed fearful, feuding people, but inhabitants who exhibited civic pride, to be displayed in their architecture. It was in one such city, Florence, that two decisive steps were taken towards the creation of the ideal city.

In the early years of the fifteenth century the Florentine authorities were faced with a nagging problem. For over a century, since 1294, they had been erecting in the midst of the city a huge cathedral, designed to outdo those already put up by their rivals in Siena and Pisa. A series of master-builders, or *capomaestri*, had overseen the work, and with the decades the size of the edifice had grown. In particular, the east end had assumed the form of a large octagon. It had probably always been the plan to surmount this space with the ultimate civic status symbol, a dome (the Sienese and Pisan cathedrals already boasted them). The problem was that with a diameter of nearly 140 feet the octagon required a dome far bigger than anything attempted since Roman times, and nobody knew how it was to be built.

A dome is simply an arch rotated about its vertical axis, and the *capomaestri* of the Renaissance could conceive of only one way of constructing an arch: it had to be supported while it was being built upon a framework called 'centering'. A horizontal beam would be placed across the span to be covered and on this would be erected wooden scaffolding strong enough to carry the wedge-shaped stone blocks that would make up the arch. Only when the arch was closed by placing the keystone at its apex would the stonework be self-supporting, in effect held rigid by the force of gravity. But a span of 140 feet (and a height of 180 feet off the ground) was quite clearly too large to be crossed by wooden centering:

no tree was that tall, and any composite structure would be too weak. Well aware of these facts, successive *capomaestri* had busied themselves with any part of the cathedral rather than the dome.

Over the years a variety of schemes had been put forward, all impractical. The art historian Vasari tells us that at one point it was even suggested that the dome could be supported during construction by filling the entire cathedral with earth laced with pennies. When the dome was completed the children of Florence were supposed to carry away the earth to get at the money. But, in 1418, as a result of a public competition, the authorities finally appointed to oversee the work someone equal to the task.

That person was Filippo Brunelleschi. Born in 1377, he started his career as a goldsmith, but in 1401 he lost the commission for the reliefs on the new doors for the Florentine Baptistry to his arch rival Lorenzo Ghiberti. This disappointment prompted Brunelleschi to leave Florence for Rome. There he saw ruins on a scale far grander than anything he had come across before, including a huge building, the Pantheon, with a cast concrete dome 140 feet across. For a thousand years no one had understood how the Romans had put up such enormous structures, but Brunelleschi wandered among the ruins, gazing at them with the inquisitive eyes of the Renaissance, and began to puzzle out their secrets. It was his grasp of Roman engineering techniques that made him uniquely equipped to tackle Florence's cathedral dome.

Brunelleschi's idea was as simple as it was brilliant: in effect, he turned the arch on its side. By building the dome in inward-leaning horizontal courses of masonry and brick he was able to dispense with the centering altogether. While it was being laid each course, being relatively light, could be held in place by bonds to the one below it; but once the ring of masonry was closed it became self-supporting: in effect, it was a horizontal arch, and could no more collapse inwards than a vertical arch can collapse downwards. The completed course could then support the next one, which would be a little smaller and lean inwards a little further.

But Brunelleschi's crucial innovation was not in his design for the dome, it was in the manner in which he organized its construction. He sought at every stage to speed up the work; he used standardized structural components, which he had made in bulk ready for use; he supervised every aspect of the project himself, designing many special machines to expedite the building; he even arranged for a canteen high above ground level, so that the men working on the dome would not have to waste time climbing down to have their meals. Just what an organizational revolution this was can be appreciated from the fact that construction of the dome was begun in 1420, and was completed as far as the lantern by 1436. Whereas the cathedral walls had taken a century and a quarter and were still incomplete, Brunelleschi's masterpiece was all but finished in just sixteen years.

Never again would large-scale projects be left to a succession of *capomaestri*. The age of the master-builder was over; the age of the architect had begun. Utopias are, almost by necessity, the product of a single mind. Brunelleschi, by making it possible for one person to conceive of a large structure and actually see it raised within a lifetime, paved the way for the realization of utopias in stone. Florence's cathedral, *Il Duomo*, is the harbinger of the ideal city.

Nevertheless, Brunelleschi himself was more a practical engineer than a visionary. He studied Roman ruins in order to rediscover lost building techniques, but it seems he did not even know Latin. However, the next generation in Florence produced another genius who would exploit the new possibilities of architectural planning to lay the ideal city's intellectual foundations. Leon Battista Alberti was in fact born in Genoa in 1404, the illegitimate offspring of an important Florentine family temporarily in exile. The young Alberti received the very best education fifteenth-century Europe could offer, attending the Universities of Padua and Bologna. In about 1428 he was at last allowed to take up residence in Florence, where he met Brunelleschi. Like the older man, he began to make a study of the ruins of classical antiquity, but with a very different end in view. He was not interested in how the Romans built as they did, but why. He believed that their achievements were the result of adhering to eternal laws of form which underlay all the arts, and it was these laws he aimed to recover.

Alberti expressed his ideas in three theoretical treatises, on painting, sculpture and architecture, of which the last is by far the longest and the most important. *De Re Aedificatoria* was begun in Florence some time in the early 1440s, and a version was presented to Pope Nicholas V in 1452, although Alberti probably continued to work on it until his death in 1472. Just as the inspiration and source of Brunelleschi's dome lay in the physical remains of ancient Rome, Alberti's theoretical writing was inspired by and reflected the only technical treatise on any of the visual arts which survived from antiquity, Vitruvius's *De Architectura* (the text of which had been rediscovered a few decades earlier, in 1415, by the humanist Poggio).

In somewhat obscure and gnomic Latin, Vitruvius, a contemporary of Cicero, declared that the beauty of a building was not simply in the eye of the beholder but depended upon ensuring that its proportions obeyed certain basic mathematical relationships. This arithmetical principle ultimately derived from Pythagoras, who discovered that in a musical instrument a harmonious chord was the result of plucking strings whose lengths were related by simple numerical ratios. Thus, visual and musical beauty are different aspects of the same fundamental laws of harmony. Alberti believed that for any given architectural problem these laws of harmony would define an ideal solution; it was the architect's job to make his building conform to this ideal:

> I shall define Beauty to be a harmony of all the parts, in whatsoever subject it appears, fitted together with such proportion and connection, that nothing could be added, diminished or altered but for the worse.

This is a Platonic, indeed a utopian, conception of beauty.

Vitruvius had related architectural forms to the human frame: 'Without symmetry and proportion no temple can have a regular plan; that is, it must have an exact proportion worked out after the fashion of a well-shaped body. . . . In like fashion the members of temples ought to have dimensions of their several parts answering suitably to the general sum of their magnitude.' The human figure was linked in turn with the two most basic geometrical forms, the circle and the square.

> If a man lies on his back with hands and feet outspread, and the centre of a circle is located in his navel, then his hands and feet will touch the circumference: a square can also be produced in the same way . . . the height of a body from the sole of the foot to the crown of the head being equal to the span of the outstretched arms.

This association of the human form with the fundamental elements of geometry was reinforced in Alberti's mind by the Christian orthodoxy that Man was made in the image of God; it was therefore fitting that he should embody the harmonies of the universe. Thus, Alberti advocated that churches be centrally planned; that is to say, like a circle or a square, they should be symmetrical about a central point, such as the early Christian churches of the fourth century built on the pattern of a Greek cross.

In contrast, the churches of the Middle Ages were typically constructed in the shape of a Latin cross, symbolizing Christ's Crucifixion – and allowing for larger congregations. However, the concept of Christ fundamentally changed in the Renaissance, according to the art historian Rudolf Wittkower: 'Christ as the essence of perfection and harmony superseded Him who had suffered on the Cross for humanity; the Pantocrator replaced the Man of Sorrow.' Vitruvius's image of a man with limbs outstretched framed within a circle and a square became an icon of the Renaissance, illustrated in the printed editions of *De Architectura* and drawn time and time again by artists such as Leonardo da Vinci. Wittkower states:

> This simple picture seemed to reveal a deep and fundamental truth about man and the world, and its importance for Renaissance architects can hardly be overestimated. The image haunted their imagination.

Brunelleschi's technical advances had recreated the professional architect, a single intelligence able to oversee the transformation of an imaginary edifice into a real one. Alberti's theoretical manifesto gave that task a spiritual dimension and the architect a moral vision. With the publication of *De Re Aedificatoria*, architecture became a truly utopian calling. Indeed, Alberti included a technically detailed, though somewhat pedestrian, description of an ideal city, with particular emphasis on the necessity for good drainage and the circulation of fresh air, a preoccupation which he shared with Vitruvius. Alberti's treatise was imitated again and again; the drawing-up of architectural plans for the ideal city became a characteristically Italian form of utopian writing. None was more famous, nor had a more lasting impact on the world, than Filarete's *Trattato di Architettura*, which appeared in Milan in the 1460s.

In the second half of the fifteenth century, important architectural developments were taking place in the powerful Duchy of Lombardy. The Dukes of Milan, Francesco and his son Lodovico Sforza, were great patrons of the arts, and they attracted to the city such illustrious men as Donato Bramante from Urbino and, from Florence, Brunelleschi and Leonardo da Vinci. Another Florentine artist who lived and worked under the patronage of the Sforzas was Antonio Averlino (c.1400–c.1470), better known as Filarete ('lover of virtue' in Greek).

Filarete came to Milan from Rome, where he had been working, rather unsuccessfully, as a sculptor. He appears to have used the change of venue as an opportunity to change careers, for in 1456 we know that he began construction on a large hospital which was to bring together in one place the many charitable institutions then scattered about Milan (today it is part of the University of Milan, although much altered). The notion of centralization gave the hospital both its purpose and its architecture. Filarete designed this vast building as a cross within a square and placed the hospital church, itself centrally planned, at the central point, where the arms of the cross meet.

Filarete sought to apply Alberti's theories of harmonious proportion not only to individual buildings but also to the city as a whole, and this was to be his most valuable contribution. For Filarete, the Florentine architecture of Alberti and Brunelleschi embodied, according to one scholar, 'the true principle of order – political, social, and aesthetic – which could bring harmony and beauty to the whole society'. However, in the 1450s and '60s the predominant architectural style in Milan was still the 'Lombard' or late Gothic, which Filarete called the 'barbarous modern style'. Between 1461 and 1464 Filarete composed his *Trattato di Architettura* in which he pleads for the abandonment of the 'modern', putting forward a plan for an ideal city based on the 'antique', whose principles of aesthetic harmony will be reflected in the behaviour of its citizens.

Filarete's work was apparently intended as a meal-time entertainment for Francesco Sforza. The Duke, having suffered treachery at the hands of his brother and son, not to mention the murder of his beloved mistress by his jealous wife, was badly in need of political and social concord. To make his depiction of the ideal city more palatable, Filarete set it within a literary dialogue between the architect and his patron, brimming with digressions on such matters as hunting.

Filarete begins with a description of what had become the cornerstone of Renaissance architecture: the relationship between a building and the human body. The proportions and measurements of a building derive from those of the human frame; like the body, the building has 'entrances and exits', needs maintenance, but 'finally dies in its own time'. Filarete then admits the audacity of his desire to construct an ideal city:

> Perhaps to some it would seem better to begin with small buildings in order to show the mode and order of building and then to continue in order to the largest. I have had an idea about undertaking to construct a city in which we shall erect all the buildings that belong there, each with its own suitable orders and measures. But because I cannot build

it by myself, I want to talk first with the person who will bear the expense.

Sforzinda embodies the two perfect geometrical forms of the circle and the square throughout its design, which appears absolute, immutable and lucid. Situated in the Inda valley, on a gently sloping mountainside so as to be sheltered from the winds, its perimeter walls are in the shape of an octagonal star, formed by two overlapping squares within a circular moat (approximately $3^{1}/_{2}$ miles in diameter). Sixteen main arteries (alternately streets and canals for the easy passage of heavy goods) run from the outside wall to the central piazza, where the Ducal Palace and the cathedral are located. The other public buildings – the law courts, prison, mint, slaughterhouse, public baths, brothel and town hall – are situated in two smaller adjacent squares. The cathedral is a centrally planned building which reflects the symmetry of the city as a whole. As one scholar remarks, 'Centralised power is, of course, the counterpoint of the centralised plan: everything flows from the Duke as the creator and leader of Sforzinda.' The economy is also centralized: expenses and salaries are distributed by a central 'bank' and food distribution is tightly controlled by one man, who 'if possible . . . should not have relatives'.

Sforzinda has a population of 30,000, mainly tradesmen and skilled craftsmen, divided into neighbourhoods which are grouped around piazzas conveniently located halfway along each of the city's sixteen main transport arteries. Each square contains for the benefit of the locals the parish church, tavern, public baths, shops and a brothel. Filarete subscribed to Alberti's belief (derived from Vitruvius) that the various architectural orders mirror the social order. Thus, Filarete specifies the Doric order for the private houses of gentlemen, Corinthian for merchants, and Ionic for artisans.

One of the stranger institutions in Sforzinda is a 'House of Virtue and Vice', apparently a combination adult education centre and singles club, where citizens can not only pursue knowledge but also satisfy their more physical cravings. Passing through one doorway with the inscription 'Here enters the troop of pleasure-seekers who will later repent in grief', the lustful man enters a circular room where there are 'places for Venus and on the sides the rooms for Bacchus as well as bath, tap-rooms, and similar crafts pertaining to such places with games and other swindles, as is the custom, though an unfortunate custom'. Through the other doorway, with the inscription 'This is the path to acquire virtue with difficulty', are located rooms 'where all branches of knowledge are to be taught'. Statues of allegorical figures and inventors of every subject decorate each room; in the Astrology room carvings illustrate 'the means [the astrologers] use to measure the sky and the sun, to divide time and separate the planets'. Astrological calculations are called upon to determine the most propitious day to begin construction of the city and to guarantee social harmony for its citizens, among other matters.

In the middle of his treatise, Filarete describes how the workmen digging the foundations of Sforzinda discover a golden book, which tells of an ancient city once built on the same site by one King Zogalia. This gives Filarete a welcome opportunity to discuss the architecture of antiquity which he so admired. It also provides a poignant reminder that, as Filarete states, 'a city endures for the term conceded to it'. So that Sforzinda will not be entirely forgotten, marble and bronze plaques commemorating those who played a part in the construction of the city are embedded in the foundations of the first building. The architect explains to his patron:

> . . . as every man knows, things that have a beginning must have an end. When the time comes, they will find these things, and know our names and remember us because of them, just as we remember when we find something noble in a ruin or in an excavation. We are happy and pleased to find a thing that represents antiquity and [gives] the name of him who had it done.

However, soon after he completed the *Trattato di Architettura*, Filarete fell from grace in Milan. Undaunted, he returned to his native Florence and presented the same treatise to Piero de' Medici: a version dated 1465, richly illustrated with fanciful architectural drawings and dedicated to the Florentine ruler, survives today. Although never printed, Filarete's work was copied in manuscript and appeared in all the important Renaissance libraries, keeping alive the concept of the ideal city. The drawings contained in the 1465 manuscript may also have helped in the creation of a new form of architectural draftsmanship, representing buildings conceptually as well as technically.

Filarete's legacy had a marked influence on Leonardo da Vinci, who arrived in Milan from Florence in 1481. During his nearly twenty-year stay, Leonardo worked on his famous fresco, *The Last Supper*, studied the centrally planned building style advocated by Filarete and carried out research in anatomy, a science still very much in its infancy. Leonardo sought to revolutionize the field by depicting the human body and the functions of its parts in extremely detailed diagrams based on the various stages of dissection. Emboldened by Filarete's conceptual drawings, Leonardo thought to apply this approach to his own architectural drawings, making the link between the human body and architecture even more intimate. In a sketchbook which survives from this period, Leonardo drew imaginary, centrally planned churches from several different perspectives, including sections and bird's eye views. With these techniques he was able to provide a complete and complex picture of the three-dimensional form, whether it be a corpse or a cathedral.

A fellow Florentine, Donato Bramante, whose career was to epitomize High Renaissance architecture, arrived in Milan probably within a year of Leonardo da Vinci, and the two artists greatly influenced each other. Bramante, like Leonardo, was attracted to the harmonious proportions of the centrally planned building as depicted by Filarete. He made a study of the surviving early Christian churches in Milan which retained elements of this style and also worked on the reconstruction of several of these early structures.

Bramante's most important work, however, was done in Rome, where he fled after the invasion of Milan by the French in 1499. In Rome Bramante was confronted for the first time with the vast Pantheon, whose dome had so impressed Brunelleschi. When Pope Julius II, Michelangelo's patron, commissioned Bramante to rebuild the Old St Peter's (then a millennium old), the architect proposed a perfectly symmetrical cathedral revolving around a central point. However, his plan was altered at an early stage to a Latin cross to allow for long processions of the clergy and larger congregations. The structure which perhaps best represents Bramante's ideals is the Tempietto commemorating the spot where St Peter was crucified. As his model, Bramante looked to the *martyrium* of the early Christians, a religious monument (as opposed to a parish church) which was perfectly circular in shape.

Filarete's *Trattato di Architettura* had gone out of fashion by the middle of the sixteenth century: Vasari called it 'very ridiculous, and perhaps the most stupid book that was ever written'. However, Filarete's legacy cannot be so lightly dismissed. One modern scholar remarks:

There can be little doubt that Filarete's enthusiasm and, above all, his passionate advocacy of the centrally planned form, were of the greatest importance in the development of architectural theory in Milan. Since both Leonardo and Bramante were much occupied with the theory of centrally planned buildings in the 1480s and 1490s, the consequences for Europe as a whole can hardly be over-estimated.

What is more, Filarete's innovation of the star-shaped city was resurrected by military engineers all over Europe from the sixteenth century onwards as a design ideally suited to fortifications. The concept of centralized town planning, as we shall see in the next chapter, was extremely influential, especially in the nineteenth and twentieth centuries. But the only attempt made during the Renaissance to realize an ideal city in the spirit of Sforzinda took place at Sabbioneta outside Mantua.

Sabbioneta was the creation of one man, Vespasiano Gonzaga Colonna (1531–1591), who, in the best utopian tradition, saw his ideal city completed and in full operation during his lifetime. Vespasiano, born into a cadet branch of the Gonzaga family of Mantua, probably chose to develop the modest settlement around his castle at Sabbioneta because of its strategic position along an important route through the Po Valley. Vespasiano began his programme of expansion and rebuilding in 1556. Every available man was rounded up to work on the project, and in 1558 he had to apologize to the Duke of Mantua for not being able to contribute any manpower to the Duke's roadworks scheme. Vespasiano continued to coerce his citizens – another hallmark of Utopia. In 1562 he issued a proclamation ordering his subjects to reside within Sabbioneta's walls. At the time it must have seemed to these unwilling subjects that they were being forced to live in the middle of a permanent building site rather than an ideal city.

Vespasiano had learned military engineering while on campaign as a professional soldier, and his urban creation reflects his architectural expertise as well as his classical education. The 'state-of-the-art' defensive town walls form an irregular hexagon (a variation on Filarete's star-shaped design). The street plan is basically a grid pattern; but Vespasiano follows Alberti's advice in modifying the unrelenting rectilinearity of his scheme to enhance the town's visual interest. He also modifies the perspective by gradually decreasing the width of the streets as they converge on the centre of the town. As in Sforzinda, there are two main squares (though they are not adjacent) where the major public buildings are located, such as the Ducal Palace, church, castle, and Garden Palace. Other buildings commissioned by Vespasiano include a mint, a hospital, private housing and a *scuola di latina e greca lingua*.

The spirit of ancient Rome is ever present. In a speech delivered in 1562 at the inauguration of the humanist *Accademia* of Sabbioneta the scholar Mario Nizolio called the city 'a new Rome'. The statue of Vespasiano by Leone Leoni, which originally stood in front of the Ducal Palace, calls to mind the statue of the Roman emperor Marcus Aurelius on the Capitoline hill in Rome. It now decorates Vespasiano's tomb in the Church of the Blessed Virgin Mary Crowned (a centrally planned building in the style of Bramante). An ancient Roman statue of Pallas Athena – the goddess of war, symbol of wisdom and patron of the city – which rests on a fluted column, once held the central position in the architectural layout of Sabbioneta (it was moved this century, not far from its original place). The interior walls of the Ducal Palace and the Garden Palace (Vespasiano's private residence) are liberally decorated with frescoes (many now faded) depicting figures and themes from antiquity: the Caesars, Mars, Aeneas, Orpheus, *putti*, nymphs, satyrs and many more.

The *Sala dei Circhi*, one of the most beautifully decorated rooms in the Garden Palace, features frescoes of the Circus Flaminius and Circus Maximus. The detail and proportions of the latter, especially its double row of arches, are reflected in the architectural style of the *Corridor Grande*, the gallery adjacent to the palace, which forms part of the view from the windows of the *Sala dei Circhi*. The *Corridor Grande*, the third longest in Europe after those in the Vatican and the Uffizi, originally housed Vespasiano's collection of antique statuary, which at the time was second only to the Medicis'. Also in the *Sala dei Circhi* is a fresco depicting an ideal city. It has been strategically placed between the two windows looking out towards the central point of the town – where the statue of Athena originally stood – so that one takes in both the imaginary ideal city and the real one beyond it in a single glance. (The fresco includes a small circular temple reminiscent of Bramante's Tempietto.)

The image of the ideal city was also mirrored in the stage setting (now lost) for the theatre in Sabbioneta, designed by Vincenzo Scamozzi, Andrea Palladio's disciple. It was the first 'purpose-built' theatre of the Renaissance: previously, existing structures had been adapted for the task (such as Palladio's *Teatro Olimpico* in Vicenza, completed by Scamozzi four years earlier). Scamozzi's set depicted a 'city scene', probably similar to that in the *Teatro Olimpico*. The streets followed the gentle gradient of the stage upwards to a vanishing point, converging with the imitation-sky ceiling – creating an illusion that the entire theatre was open to the 'ideal city' of Sabbioneta outside.

The theatre shares Vespasiano's fascination with the classical world. Carved across the entrance of the building, in imitation of a Roman stone inscription, is the phrase 'ROMA QUANTA FUIT IPSA RUINA DOCET' ('How great was Rome its own ruin teaches'): it appears on the title page of *L'Idea dell'Architettura Universale* by Sebastiano Serlio. Two large wall frescoes on either side of the theatre's interior depict views of Rome, and along the gallery are statues of Greek and Roman gods and heroes. Lining the gallery walls are *trompe l'oeil* frescoes of Roman emperors as well as musicians, choir boys, knights, noble ladies, and even a clown's mask from the *Commedia dell'Arte* (Vespasiano founded a *Commedia dell'Arte* troupe in 1590).

Sabbioneta was a wholly planned city: Vespasiano regulated not only the layout and architecture, but also everything from education to the harvest. He treated the city like a giant theatre for his civic ceremonies and public entertainments, celebrating events such as his elevation to the Duchy. One scholar remarks:

> Just as the stage is built as a townscape, so the town itself is a stage: in 1586 Vespasiano had ordered marble sills to be installed on the houses along the main street, tightened building regulations and saw to the painted decoration of facades, . . . until the entire town – in the words of a contemporary – *sembrò . . . cangiata in un teatro* [seems transformed into a theatre].

Immediately after Vespasiano's death in 1591, all building and expansion ceased and Sabbioneta fell into decline. To visit the city today, with its fortified walls looming out of the mist on the flat, empty plain of the Po Valley, is a strangely haunting experience. Wandering the unpaved streets which suddenly peter out to nothing as they approach the outer walls, here and there the visitor comes across petrified fragments of Vespasiano's dream, a declamatory stone plaque, a statue. The city seems at once decayed and unfinished, but like Filarete's Sforzinda it does not lack memorials to its founder, and these lend the place a funerary air, as if the entire town were one huge mausoleum. Sabbioneta was the first and last ideal city of the Renaissance to have been built and lived in, but it died with its utopian creator.

However, the literary tradition of the ideal city had yet to produce its most famous creation. Eleven years after Vespasiano's death a very different sort of visionary painted a literary portrait of an urban utopia which was to become one of the most influential of the modern age.

Tommaso Campanella, the son of an illiterate shoemaker, was born in Calabria, southern Italy, in 1568. He entered the Dominican order at the age of fourteen, and soon began to show heretical proclivities. Rebelling against the orthodox Aristotelianism of his day, he believed that nature should be studied at first hand; he also showed a dangerous interest in magic and other occult sciences. Twice, in 1616 and 1632, he bravely defended Galileo and the new science.

For these heretical beliefs, Campanella was persecuted for most of his adult life by the Catholic Church and the Spanish monarchy, who ruled southern Italy at the time. He entered his first prison at the age of twenty-four and was only completely free at sixty-one. He suffered tortures, such as being suspended by rope above metal spikes for thirty-six hours, and inhumane confinement in windowless, damp dungeons with hands and feet bound. Extraordinarily, Campanella continued to write philosophical treatises throughout his imprisonment, often on scraps of paper smuggled in by gaolers whom he had bribed.

In 1599, Campanella became involved in a conspiracy to foment an uprising against both the Church and the Spanish authorities in Calabria, where poverty and destitution were rife. The provinces of southern Italy had been reduced to such a pitiful state by the depredations of the Spanish, often operating in league with the ubiquitous Inquisition, that many of the native population had been forced to take up banditry and organized brigandage as the only means of survival. Under these circumstances, it only needed the emergence of a leader who promised some chance of success to provoke a full-scale popular uprising.

It is unclear if Campanella himself was such a leader, but it does seem likely that he believed that old prophecies, recent natural disasters and astrological calculations all portended upheavals and great change for the year 1600, and that this belief was the inspiration of the planned revolt. What is certain is that the conspiracy was discovered and that Campanella and 150 others were arrested and removed to Naples. From the testimony produced at their trial it seems that the conspirators aimed at more than the simple overthrow of Spanish dominion: they wished to reorder Calabria as a theocratic, communistic state. Campanella only escaped execution by feigning madness. In 1601, from his dungeon, he wrote a sonnet which tells of a world made mad by a strange constellation. The few wise men who had escaped

... advised these madmen with well-chosen words to live the old way, with good food and dress. But everyone attacked them with

50

kicks and blows. So that the wise men were compelled to live as fools, in order to avoid death, because the greatest madman carried the royal burden. They lived with good sense only behind closed doors, in public applauding in deed and name the insane and wrong desires of others.

In the next year, less than three years into his imprisonment for the Calabrian plot, Campanella composed *La Città del Sole* ('The City of the Sun'). It describes an ideal society similar to that which he had so recently dreamed of establishing in his native land. Campanella's tale owes a great deal to More's *Utopia*. Like *Utopia*, it is in the form of a dialogue, in this case between a Knight Hospitaller and a Genoese sailor, a former shipmate of Columbus. (More's traveller, Raphael Hythloday, had sailed with another New World explorer, Amerigo Vespucci.) The Genoese explains that on a recent circumnavigation he was forced to put ashore in Taprobana, a name which was associated with both the modern islands of Sumatra and Ceylon. He emerged from a forest on to a great plain 'just below the equator' where 'I soon came upon a large company of armed men and women, and many of them understood my language. They led me to the City of the Sun.' Campanella proceeds to furnish the reader with a detailed description of this remarkable settlement:

Rising from a broad plain, there is a hill upon which the greater part of the city is situated, but its circling walls extend far beyond its base, so that the entire city is two miles or more in diameter and has a circumference of seven miles; . . . The city is divided into seven large circuits, named after the seven planets. Passage from one to the other is provided by four avenues and four gates facing the four points of the compass. . . . Entering by the northern gate, which is plated with iron and is raised and lowered by an ingenious device, you see a level area, some fifty paces wide, dividing the first circuit from the next. Girding the second wall there is a row of buildings which connect with it in such a way that you may say they are all one. Above them, there are ravelins raised on columns like friars' cloisters. These can only be entered on the concave side of the buildings. Then there are fine rooms separated from one another by thin walls and supplied with windows both on the convex and concave sides. . . . Beyond, you come to the second level area, two or three paces narrower than the first. From here you can see the second circuit with its ravelins and passageways. The inner side of this one has the columned cloister below and beautiful paintings on the surface above. . . . At the summit of the hill there is a spacious plain in the center of which rises an enormous temple of astonishing design.

This passage contrasts with the rather sketchy details More provides of the sensible but drab towns on his island: 'when you've seen one of them, you've seen them all,' Hythloday comments. While More says little about the Utopians' churches beyond the fact that they are 'impressive' but rather dark and 'contain no visual representations of God', Campanella gives us an elaborate depiction of a magnificent, centrally planned temple:

The temple is perfectly circular and has no enclosing walls. It rests on large, well-proportioned columns. The large dome has a cupola at its center with an aperture directly above the single altar in the middle of the temple. The columns are arranged in a circle having a circumference of three hundred paces or more. Eight paces beyond them are cloisters with walls scarcely rising above the benches which are arranged along the concave exterior wall. . . . Nothing rests on the altar but a huge celestial globe, upon which all the heavens are described, with a terrestrial globe beside it. On the vault of the dome overhead appear all the larger stars with their names. . . . The poles and circles are indicated, but not entirely since there is no wall below. Instead they are completed on the globes resting on the altar below. Seven lamps, each named for one of the seven planets, are always kept burning.

Despite their differences, Campanella shows his admiration for and indebtedness to More by borrowing many ideas and devices from *Utopia*. The Solarians (citizens of the City of the Sun) are not Christian but believe in the immortality of the soul; as with the Utopians, 'When the people learn the living truths of Christianity . . . they will submit to them.' The Solarians improve upon the Utopians' six-hour workday: they only work four hours. Both peoples despise gold, dress very simply (make-up is forbidden), prefer to avoid war 'by craft' but are well prepared to fight; in neither place is there much privacy.

However, since the publication of *Utopia* in 1516, men had started to look at the universe in a new way; accordingly, *La Città del Sole* reflects the strides that the fledgling experimental sciences had made since More's day and the importance they would have in any future world. Campanella declares that the sixteenth century 'has produced more history in a hundred years than the whole world did in the preceding four thousand', and describes the recent inventions of the compass, printing press and harquebus (portable fire-arm) as 'mighty signs of the imminent union of the world'. Campanella appreciated and acknowledged Galileo's contributions to science: thus, the Solarians 'have discovered the art of flying, the only art the world lacks, and they expect to discover a glass in which to see the hidden stars and a device by which to hear the music of the spheres.' (Campanella added this detail to his work in 1611, following Galileo's construction of his telescope in 1609.)

However, as we shall see in Chapter 5, science would only receive a central role in Utopia with the *New Atlantis* of the Englishman Francis Bacon, a contemporary of Campanella. It is the method of education preached in *La Città del Sole* which would fire the imagination of subsequent utopians, and which is Campanella's most memorable innovation.

As we have seen, Campanella despised the rigid and authoritarian scholasticism of his day. The Genoese sailor remarks that Europeans

> . . . term a man learned if he knows more than others do about Aristotle's grammar or logic or about some certain author – knowledge which requires only servile memory and which deprives the mind of vitality because it meditates upon books instead of things. Such inert stuff deadens the spirit which knows neither how God controls things nor how nature and nations operate.

Campanella was greatly influenced by the anti-Aristotelianism of his spiritual mentor and fellow Calabrian, Bernardino Telesio. Telesio urged that the route to true knowledge was through the senses rather than through reason: '*Non ratione*,' he declared, '*sed sensu.*'

Thus, the Solarians learn through observation, not so much of Nature herself, but of their own city, which has become a giant illustrated encyclopedia. The seven concentric walls of the City of the Sun are covered with pictorial representations, accompanied by commentary, of all human knowledge neatly categorized. As one scholar remarks, this is 'not unlike the cycles of frescoes in a Christian church – the facts of science have replaced the events of sacred history.' Each circuit is dedicated to a particular type of knowledge:

> On the exterior walls of the temple, on the curtains which are let down

when there is preaching so that it may be heard, all the stars are drawn in order, with three descriptive verses assigned to each one.

On the inner wall of the first circuit, all the mathematical figures – more than Euclid or Archimedes speaks of – are shown in their significant propositions. On the outer wall there is a map of the entire world with charts for each country setting forth their rites, customs, and laws; and the alphabet of each is inscribed above the native one.

On the inner wall of the second circuit there are both samples and pictures of all minerals, metals, and stones, both precious and nonprecious, with two descriptive verses for each one. On the outer wall all kinds of lakes, seas, rivers, wines, oils, and other liquids are shown with their sources of origin, their powers, and their qualities indicated. There are also carafes full of diverse liquids, a hundred and even three hundred years old, with which nearly all infirmities are cured.

On the inner wall of the third circuit every kind of herb and tree to be found in the world is represented. Moreover, specimens of each are grown in earthen vessels placed on the ravelins with explanations as to where they were first discovered, what their specific powers are, what their relation is to the stars, to metals, to parts of the body, and how they are used in medicine.

Other circuits are dedicated to such diverse topics as fish, birds, reptiles, serpents, insects and animals; diagrams of the mechanical arts displayed together with their inventors; and portraits of the founders of laws and of sciences as well as inventors of weapons.

I found Moses, Osiris, Jupiter, Mercury, Muhammad, and many others there. In a place of special honor I saw Jesus Christ and the twelve Apostles, whom they hold in great regard.

Campanella adds that the Solarians 'have teachers for these things, and, without effort, merely while playing, their children come to know all the sciences pictorially before they are ten years old' – and they continue to contemplate the world in like manner as adults.

Campanella realized that information absorbed in this effortless way from their surroundings would seem to the Solarians to be natural and inevitable, beyond all question. By making the visual environment into one great pedagogic exercise, he ensures that the citizens of his ideal commonwealth all share the same beliefs and expectations. Campanella had intuitively grasped the power and importance of propaganda in a centralized state, an insight which had a direct influence on the Bolshevik revolutionaries who seized power in Russia in 1917. Anatoli Lunacharsky, head of the People's Commissariat for Enlightenment, later explained that

> . . . according to Lenin himself, he got the idea of using art and poetry for propaganda from Campanella's *City of the Sun*, a seventeenth century description of a utopia in which the author mentioned the use of frescoes to serve, said Lenin, 'as vivid lessons to the young in natural sciences and history' and 'to awaken their civic consciousness' – to play, in short, 'a vital part in the education and upbringing of the new generation'.

Lenin was a pragmatist, and he did not fail to point out that 'our [Russian] climate is hardly suitable for the fresco[e]s dreamed about by Campanella. That is why I speak primarily of sculptors and poets.'

To celebrate the first anniversary of the Revolution in November 1918, Lenin decreed that artists should plaster the streets of Moscow and Leningrad with giant slogans, murals, banners and posters. The creed of the avant-garde artists who enthusiastically took up Lenin's call was 'Let us make the squares our palettes, the streets our brushes!' Campanella's City of the Sun had been realized, if only for a day.

Campanella's ideas inspired several generations of artists and policy makers in the years following the Russian Revolution. The Russian newspaper *Izvestia* hailed Campanella as one of the first communists; in the 1940s Campanella was among the philosophers studied in schools in the Soviet Union; his name appears on the obelisk in Red Square in Moscow along with other heroes of the Russian Revolution.

Every modern city is today covered with images and slogans, designed for the most part to sell us things rather than ideologies. But the fundamental idea behind communist propaganda and capitalist advertising is the same one that animated Campanella and the other utopian city planners of the Italian Renaissance: that thoughts which are embodied in our surroundings enter into our souls imperceptibly and irrevocably. To look around the twentieth-century metropolis is to see everywhere traces of the ideal cities of Alberti, Filarete and Campanella. The imposing bulk of a centrally planned St Paul's, the flashing neon exhortations of Times Square both echo, however faintly, the ambition of those early architects of Utopia to shape the citizen by setting him among forms in tune with universal harmonies, or to guide his thoughts by surrounding him with seductive images.

However, the utopian aesthetics of Alberti or Campanella have made little impression on the way the modern city functions. It was left to a later band of visionaries, who saw the city not as a backdrop but as an engine of production, to map the form and layout of the urban landscape we inhabit today. It is to these utopians of the machine age that we now turn.

4. Machines for Living

The eighteenth century saw the birth of the Industrial Revolution, and with it a new outlook on the world. Philosophers and scientists began to think of the universe as obeying simple laws, as an orderly and predictable mechanism, a celestial timepiece. The machine, the new emblem of harmony and order, became the industrial age's model for the ideal city, supplanting the Renaissance paradigm of the human body, which no longer seemed relevant to those striving to break away from the old order of religious and social authority. Thus, architects and town planners came to believe that 'the industrial process can provide the basic principle of order for a just, harmonious and beautiful society. The relations of co-operation and subordination which guide the factory are precisely those which must guide society as a whole.' Architecture developed from an aesthetic ideal into a force for change, 'a machine for living' in Le Corbusier's evocative phrase. This image of the machine and the reaction against it have shaped the debates about architecture and town planning over the last two centuries.

Claude-Nicolas Ledoux was the first architect to plan an ideal city around the industrial process. Born in Champagne in 1736, Ledoux trained as both engineer and architect before beginning his career with the Department of Waterways and Forests of Sens in eastern France, a region which was to become his principal architectural domain. One of his early patrons, Madame du Barry, the King's favourite, ensured him swift promotion. In 1771 the King gave him the important post of Inspector General of the Saltworks of Franche-Comté and, two years later, granted him, aged thirty-seven, the title *Architecte du Roi*. Ledoux's work covered a wide spectrum, from town houses, theatres, and royal stables to bridges, *barrières* or toll-houses, and factories, all of which were innovative and strikingly modern. But perhaps the greatest testimony to his extraordinary vision is the royal saltworks at Arc-et-Senans which Ledoux designed and built between 1774 and 1778 and which survives today as a museum.

Since the fourteenth century, the French monarchy had held a powerful monopoly of the salt trade. Salt was an immensely important and valuable commodity, since, before refrigeration, it was the only reliable means of preserving food. An organization known as the *Ferme Générale* was set up by the Crown in 1681 to levy the tax on this so-called 'white gold' and to control the saltworks around the country, where brine, piped in from local underground springs, was processed. Ledoux's task at Arc-et-Senans, an isolated spot near the Swiss border, was to design a factory where people both worked and lived, which would provide adequate supervision to safeguard the precious salt, and whose architecture would reflect its royal authority.

Ledoux designed his factory as ten separate buildings placed in a semicircle, surrounding a large open courtyard. For Ledoux, the semicircle was an aesthetic ideal, as 'pure as the arc described by the sun in its course', which also suggested an antique amphitheatre, a place where one could watch over the 'production' of salt. This design also allowed the free circulation of air, an important health factor for an industry in which lung diseases were prevalent.

A twelve-foot-high wall, crowned with thorns, and a dry moat originally enclosed the complex to prevent the theft of salt. There is only one entrance, for both people and goods: through the gatehouse, located at the apex of the semicircle and containing the guard rooms, two prison cells and other apartments, where all those coming and going could be closely scrutinized. This entrance is exactly in line with the main road, and its portico of eight heavy, baseless Doric columns immediately conveys to an approaching visitor an air of severe authority. The function of the factory is made clear along the walls on either side of the portico where the windows of the guard rooms are sculpted in the shape of overturned urns spilling forth petrified brine. This image is reinforced inside the portico by a low, rusticated arch framing a large grotto where sculpted springs of bubbling water symbolize the source of the salt.

Inside, the four rectangular stone buildings around the semicircular courtyard served as both workshops and workers' quarters. There were three types of workers: the *berniers* who boiled the brine to produce cakes of salt, the coopers who made the barrels to store and transport it, and the blacksmiths, whose job it was to maintain the boilers, machinery and other tools. Each workers' building comprises two low wings flanking a square section of rusticated stonework, with a large central archway. The floor plan of the building to the east of the gatehouse was divided between workshops and living space for the blacksmiths and their families; the building to the west was similarly laid out for the coopers and their families.

The *berniers* lived in the other two buildings around the courtyard, nearest to their much larger and separate workshops (*bernes*). The living quarters of the *berniers*, and also those of the blacksmiths and coopers, originally included separate bedrooms for each family, plus a communal kitchen and central hearth, which Ledoux imagined would heat the whole building while providing 'happy fireside evenings'. But Ledoux had underestimated the severity of the winters, and more fireplaces had to be added. Another instance in which he unwittingly sacrificed function to form was in the provision of natural light. As with the gatehouse, overturned urns spilling forth sculpted water constitute the windows in the workers' quarters, but these let in too little light.

The *bernes* comprise two long, low buildings along the diameter of the semicircle, adorned with neo-Palladian porches in rusticated stone. These *bernes* are situated next to the two small, elegant staff buildings ('Parisian *hôtels* in miniature') located at the corners. Between them is the director's house, from where production could be closely supervised.

The director's house, which also housed the chapel and administrative offices, stands opposite the gatehouse at the centre of the diameter, and is the focal point of Ledoux's grand design. The building's architecture conveys its royal, administrative and religious authority, and its floor plan reflects the hierarchy of those within, with the kitchens and accountants' offices below and the director's private apartments and chapel above. Below the steep pyramidal roof is a huge portico, comprising six massive Doric columns which are built of alternate round and square blocks of stone. These support a large triangular pediment pierced by an *oculus*, or 'eye', which surveys the factory grounds. Ledoux wrote: 'It is in this centre of knowledge that an indefatigable and vigilant eye follows the respective tasks of each hour and those that undertake them.' He even called the director's house the *temple de surveillance*. The central position of the house between the two *bernes* meant that it stood four-square across the flow of materials in the industrial process. Thus Ledoux provided a paved ramp which passed through the ground floor of the director's house to allow the easy passage of goods and workmen from one *berne* to the other, ensuring the smooth running of this living and working machine. (The passageway, however, proved too narrow for heavy ox-carts to negotiate and, moreover, created terrible draughts in the stone building.)

Everything about the saltworks at Arc-et-Senans conveys a spirit of surveillance and control – in the original plan Ledoux had even included two giant Doric columns in the open courtyard which were to act as beacons, watchtowers and belfries, 'the instruments of worker surveillance and time keeping'. However, Ledoux was genuinely, if sometimes misguidedly, interested in the workers' welfare. Behind the living quarters the architect laid out kitchen gardens to teach the workers the pleasures of cultivation, to enable them to feed their families and to ensure that they were always within sight of the authorities, even during their leisure hours. Ledoux imagines that the employees

> ... in these preferred places, augment and increase their existence under natural laws; each worker possesses the secret of the gods; surrounded by the sweetest illusions, he is with his wife and children during his hours of rest; he is sheltered from all costly distractions and from the bacchic delirium that could disturb his marriage, tempt or lead him to laziness. He finds, in this reunion with his dearest customs, his pleasures, the consolation for his hardships, the mustering of his needs.

However, Ledoux was not satisfied with this utopian factory community. Although no additions to the saltworks were made in reality, in the architect's mind the project kept growing. For the rest of his life, Ledoux continued to add to his design, completing the circle and creating plans for an 'industrial park', with tree-lined boulevards emanating from the centre and private and public buildings extending into the countryside. For Ledoux, 'everything is circular in nature; the stone that falls into the water propagates infinite circles; centripetal force is incessantly countered by a rotary motion; the air and the seas move in perpetual circles.' Ledoux believed, according to one scholar, that 'the discipline of the machine age must find its complement and fulfilment in the direct access to natural beauty'; therefore, the woodland setting for his 'ideal city' was also very important. The plans for the enlarged factory and city of Chaux are recorded in Ledoux's *L'Architecture Considerée Sous le Rapport de l'Art, des Moeurs et de la Législation* ('Architecture Considered in its Relationship to Art, Morals and Legislation'), published in 1804. The work is in the well-established utopian form of a conducted tour of Chaux, recounting to a visitor the lives of its imaginary inhabitants.

The central design principle of Chaux is that the form of each building represents its function. The public buildings include such utopian institutions as a 'House of Conciliation', 'a mighty cube rising on a sturdy podium' conveying unity, and a 'House of Ethics', with ascending forms suggesting man's ascent to justice. The 'House of Sexual Instruction', a public brothel where young people would exorcise their 'libertine pleasures' before enjoying the calmer and more ordered delights of marriage, has a floor plan resembling an erect phallus. Particularly rich in symbolism is the cemetery in the shape of a half-buried sphere: it at once suggests the city's circular plan, the eternal cycle of life, the realms of Heaven and Hades, and the earth itself. 'This round machine, is it not sublime?' Ledoux wrote.

Ledoux's housing for the workers, which consists of two-storey detached houses set in leafy suburbs, anticipates all subsequent town planning:

> The government, wishing to give models to the less fortunate of men, had constructed many houses that united every quality of utility and solidity and had not even neglected to give them a relative measure of architectural order.

Ledoux's communal dwellings for those who live and work in the forest, the charcoal burners, woodcutters, sawyers and coopers, are designed to echo what he thought was the pre-Classical architecture of primitive man, and yet to us they seem extraordinarily modern. Again, their form was meant to reflect their function. Thus Ledoux formalized the image of the primeval forest hut by creating new architectural innovations, such as a 'tree trunk' or 'log' order of columns. The coopers' house forms a double barrel; its facades recreate the hoops that bound the barrels. The charcoal burners' workshop is pyramidal in shape, representing the wooden pyres they used in their trade. Ledoux even imagines a wealthy stockbroker's house as a cylindrical form, suggesting the 'turning fortunes' of the markets. (One nineteenth-century observer remarked that Ledoux would have made 'the house of a drunkard in the shape of a bottle'.)

Despite its overtones of authority and surveillance, Ledoux meant his architecture to radiate equality: a circle, according to Ledoux, is not able to accommodate a hierarchical structure. Thus, the spherical cemetery assures the people of Chaux that in death all citizens return to the natural state of equality. The 'modernist' houses were an attempt to displace the thatched cottage and all that it stood for: 'To destroy the thatched cottages is to level the appearance of poverty with the comfort by which industriousness should be honored.' However, a circle has a centre, and at the focal point of Chaux was the ever-watchful director's house. Ledoux's architecture reveals the contradiction between the idealism and authoritarianism of modern town planning.

Charles Fourier, one of the major utopians of the nineteenth century, whom we will encounter several times in the course of this book, was greatly influenced by Ledoux's architecture. He was born in 1772, near the saltworks of Arc-et-Senans, in Besançon, the site of Ledoux's innovative municipal theatre. (It was the first modern theatre to banish the rabble, who had previously stood just in front of the stage, to the 'gods', and to put in their stead the orchestra pit and stalls for the more discerning and wealthier theatre-goers.) Fourier also admired Ledoux's architectural works in Paris, particularly the Hôtel de Thélusson, built for a Swiss banker's widow. Fourier described the *hôtel*, with its dramatic yet fanciful entrance, gardens and facades, as 'worthy of imitation in Harmony', Fourier's utopia. Like Le Corbusier a century later, Fourier carried a marked cane to measure an appealing facade as he walked the streets of Paris, and back in his tiny garret he worked out the 'mathematics of architectural harmony'. Fourier claimed that the sight of these impressive Parisian *hôtels*, set in beautiful gardens, 'suggested to me the idea of a unitary architecture whose rules I immediately determined'.

Fourier's utopia was based on communal living in one large building, which he called a 'phalanstery'. This was not, however, a cold, impersonal machine, like Ledoux's royal factory, but a vibrant one – always set on overdrive to accommodate, as one scholar puts it, 'every sex . . . talent, wealth, age and proclivity', providing 'spaces calculated for their every need, pleasure and whim'. The building itself, intended to house 1600 to 1800 people, was to be a massive structure adorned with ' "a multitude of colonnades, domes and peristyles" – a cross between a palace and a sumptuous resort hotel'. The central section, with a 1200-metre facade, is flanked by two long wings, and has a parade ground at the rear. The centre of the phalanstery is the place for quiet activities and contains the dining rooms, meeting rooms, library, studies, and so forth.

The wings are set aside for more boisterous activities. One wing is the place for 'noisy workshops', such as the forge and carpenter's shop, and also for the gatherings of children who, according to Fourier, 'are generally very noisy at work and even at music'. This arrangement, states Fourier, 'will avoid an annoying drawback of our civilized cities where every street has its own hammerer or iron merchant or beginning clarinet player to shatter the ear drums of fifty families in the vicinity.' The other wing contains the ballroom and reception halls for outside visitors and 'curiosity-seekers'.

Like Ledoux, Fourier conceived of his community of Harmony as a social machine set within a garden landscape of rolling hills with a good stream and forest nearby. The soil would, of course, be fertile, and crops would be grown according to their appeal, or 'quantity of attraction'. Thus, Arcs-et-Senans, Chaux and the phalanstery are very much prototypes of the garden city, and in the second half of the nineteenth century Fourier's concerns for community spirit and a 'green' environment were taken up in America by the great landscape architect, Frederick Law Olmsted.

Olmsted was a 'Fourierist sympathizer', with many friends in the Fourier-inspired Associationist movement in America. His best known work, Central Park in New York, was, according to one historian, 'an outdoor analogue to the phalanstery, the municipal park was a public meeting ground where social classes mingled and a communal spirit replaced selfish individualism.' In 1870 Olmsted described Central Park and nearby Prospect Park in Brooklyn as

> ... the only places in those ... cities where ... you will find ... all classes largely represented, with a common purpose, not at all intellectual, competitive with none, disposing to jealousy or spiritual or intellectual pride toward none, each individual adding by his mere presence to the pleasure of all others, all helping to the greater happiness of each.

The parks that Olmsted designed for New York and Boston were probably the immediate inspiration for the cityscape in the immensely popular American utopian work, *Looking Backward* (1888), by Edward Bellamy. In this, the well-to-do Bostonian Julian West goes to sleep in 1887 and wakes up in the year 2000 to a Boston wholly transformed, physically as well as spiritually. Bellamy knew Fourier's American disciple Albert Brisbane well, and the description of the future Boston also borrows many details from Fourier's writings.

Julian West's first impression of Boston in the year 2000 echoes Fourier's early impressions of Paris:

> At my feet lay a great city. Miles of broad streets, shaded by trees and lined with fine buildings, for the most part not in continuous blocks but set in larger or smaller enclosures, stretched in every direction. Every quarter contained large open squares filled with trees, along which statues glistened and fountains flashed in the late-afternoon sun. Public buildings of a colossal size and architectural grandeur unparalleled in my day raised their stately piles on every side.

Later in the book, West's words are an even stronger echo of Fourier's description of the phalanstery. West thinks of the 'glorious new Boston with its domes and pinnacles, its gardens and fountains, and its universal reign of comfort'. There is a communal restaurant straight out of Harmony. West is astonished by the 'magnificent architecture and richness of embellishment': 'It seemed that it was not merely a dining hall, but likewise a great pleasure house and social rendezvous of the quarter, and no appliance of entertainment or recreation seemed lacking.' Bellamy provides his Bostonians with covered walkways, a feature which he almost certainly borrowed from Fourier, who had made their benefits clear:

> To spend a winter's day in a Phalanstery, to visit all parts of it without exposure to the elements, to go to the theater and the opera in light clothes and colored shoes without worrying about the mud and cold, would be a charm so novel that it alone would suffice to make our cities and castles seem detestable. If the Phalanstery were put to civilized uses, the mere convenience of its sheltered, heated and ventilated passageways would make it enormously valuable.

An innovation which follows from covered walkways is the shopping mall, which Bellamy envisages with uncanny prescience. He describes a magnificent building whose facade was adorned with a 'majestic life-size group of statuary, the central figure of which was a female ideal of Plenty, with her cornucopia'. The interior was a 'vast hall full of light' flooding in from a glazed dome; at the centre was a magnificent fountain, 'cooling the atmosphere to a delicious freshness with its spray', around which were grouped chairs and sofas.

All in all, twentieth-century Boston is an architect's dream since, as West's host Dr Leete explains, 'Nowadays . . . there is no destination of the surplus wealth so popular as the adornment of the city.' Bellamy's future Boston is also environmentally sound: there are no chimneys nor any smoke. This is all in contrast to the Boston of 1887, where 'gusts of fetid air' came from 'the black doorways and windows' and the 'streets and alleys reeked with the effluvia of a slave ship's between-decks.' (Bellamy had once written, 'Cities are always pagan.') In the countryside are situated clubhouses, 'as well as country, mountain, and seaside houses for sport and rest in vacations'.

The most forceful image in *Looking Backward* is that of the future industrialized city as a machine humming with people and activity – a vision worthy of Ledoux. Distribution of goods in this welfare state is effected by a series of pneumatic tubes running through the city which are linked to warehouses; the system is likened to 'a gigantic mill'. The country functions with clockwork precision, and the administrators in Washington, DC need only carry out maintenance: 'The machine which they direct is indeed a vast one, but so logical in its principles and direct and simple in its workings, that it runs all by itself.' The 'industrial army', made up of all citizens, including women and disabled people, acts as a 'tremendous engine' and keeps this machine well oiled and ticking over.

The immediate impact of *Looking Backward* was such that for many people it proved Ledoux's assertion of a century earlier – that the industrial process can provide the model for the perfect society. This was a comforting thought to Americans of Bellamy's generation at a time when the large cities were plagued with labour strikes and violent riots. The essence of Bellamy's utopia, however, is its social organization, as we shall see in later chapters.

For those who looked to town planning for the answer to the unrest in America's cities, the Chicago World's Fair in 1893 was a seminal event. The fair, also known as the Columbian Exhibition, was held to celebrate the four-hundredth anniversary of Columbus's discovery of America, and it witnessed the first coherent expression of the City Beautiful Movement. Chicago had been the scene of some of the worst social unrest of the 1880s, thus the intention of the architect Daniel Burnham, director of the Exhibition, was in the words of one historian, 'to restore to the city a lost visual aesthetic harmony, thereby creating the physical prerequisite for the emergence of a harmonious social order'. Olmsted selected and laid out the site along the Chicago lakefront, placing the buildings in a naturalistic, park-like setting.

Although the famous Chicago School of Architecture had produced the first skyscraper (the Home Insurance Building of 1885) and was very much in the vanguard of the early modernist movement, the Exhibition committee deliberately chose classicism over modernism for the fair's pavilions. In a time of uncertainty in America, they wanted to emphasize their country's unique spirit of republicanism, and the architectural style best suited to that task was the classicism of the Greeks and Romans, and also of Thomas Jefferson, who helped the French architect Pierre Charles l'Enfant design Washington, DC.

The City Beautiful Movement became the dominant trend in American urban design from the 1890s to the 1920s. Its architecture and town planning reflect a policy of social containment: it was during this same period that fortress-like armories were erected in major cities all over America to house the newly formed strike-breaking force, the National Guard. Significantly, Burnham and the City Beautiful Movement took as their model for street planning Haussmann's Paris, laid out in the 1850s and '60s. Napoleon III's architect had, famously, made the boulevards wide so that the people could not raise barricades and riot.

But to some, architecture as a means of control and the city as machine were odious ideas. Both, of course, were central to Bellamy's utopian vision in *Looking Backward*, and William Morris, a leading member of the Arts and Crafts Movement in England, was horrified at the soullessness of Bellamy's future urban landscape. He remarked to a friend: 'I suppose you have seen ... "Looking Backward". ... Thank you, I wouldn't like to live in such a cockney paradise as he imagines.' In 1890, as a direct riposte to *Looking Backward*, Morris published his own utopian work, *News From Nowhere*, which offered a very different vision of the future of the city. Like Julian West before him, William Guest goes to bed in the nineteenth century and wakes up in the twentieth, but this time the venue is London.

Guest learns from one of his new acquaintances that the extraordinary transformation of both the social and physical landscape which he observes around him occurred only after a bloody revolution in 1955, not, as in *Looking Backward*, after a peaceful process of social evolution. More so for Morris than for Bellamy, society and the environment were powerful forces inextricably linked. The twentieth-century antiquarian, Hammond, tells Guest that after the revolution 'people flocked into the country villages.' The town, so to speak,

... invaded the country; but the invaders, like the warlike invaders of early days, yielded to the influence of their surroundings, and became country people; and in their turn, as they became more numerous than the townmen, influenced them also; so that the difference between town and country grew less and less.

Put in its historical perspective:

England was once a country of clearings amongst the woods and wastes, with a few towns interspersed, which were fortresses for the feudal army, markets for the folk, gathering places for the craftsmen. It then became a country of huge and foul workshops and fouler gambling-dens, surrounded by an ill-kept, poverty-stricken farm, pillaged by the masters of the workshops. It is now a garden, where nothing is wasted and nothing is spoilt, with the necessary dwellings, sheds, and workshops scattered up and down the country, all trim and neat and pretty.

England was a garden – but it was not a suburb. What suburbs there were had 'melted away into the general country' after the revolution. For Morris the terms 'suburban' and 'cocknified' seem to be almost synonymous, and it was this feature which he condemned in Bellamy's utopia, with its 'stately piles', garden squares, shopping malls and country clubhouses.

There are no shopping malls in Nowhere, and apart from London, no cities. Hammersmith, where both Morris and William Guest lived, has become a village outside London once again. Morris, who idealized the medieval aesthetic, made the landscape in *News from Nowhere* into a romanticized version of fourteenth-century England. Thus the bridge stretching across the Thames at Hammersmith resembles the Ponte Vecchio in Florence. The factories and chimneys along both shores of the river have been replaced by 'a line of very pretty houses, low and not large, standing back a little way from the river', built of red brick, roofed with tiles, and with a continuous garden in front of them, 'in which the flowers were now blooming luxuriantly, and sending delicious waves of summer scent over the eddying stream.' The guest house is decorated with a clay frieze on its facade; inside there are a marble mosaic floor, an open timber roof and a 'gaily painted' fresco on the wall. Here one felt 'that exhilarating sense of space and freedom which satisfactory architecture always gives to an unanxious man who is in the habit of using his eyes.'

In London some pre-revolutionary buildings still stand, such as the British Museum, National Gallery and the Houses of Parliament (now used to store manure). However, much of the architecture has been improved. Thus, along Piccadilly, 'on each side of the street ran an elegant arcade to protect foot-passengers, as in some of the old Italian cities.' Not even Morris, who had little sympathy for Fourier, could resist covered walkways – though he is careful not to credit Fourier with this by now standard feature of utopian cities.

Morris objected to Fourier for the same reason that he detested Bellamy: both advocated a central organizing principle for the city, an approach which is, indeed, at the heart of utopianism. In *News from*

Nowhere, the great change following the revolution had been an organic process, not the vision of one man or one principle. There is no central government in twentieth-century England as Morris envisages it, and town planning has become merely a matter of shared tastes. Hammond offers an example. In a local district

> ... some neighbours think that something ought to be done or undone: a new town-hall built; a clearance of inconvenient houses; or say a stone bridge substituted for some ugly iron one, – there you have undoing and doing in one.

There follows a number of public meetings to discuss and vote the proposed changes. If a vote is not unanimous, then the status quo is upheld unless the majority can persuade the minority to yield.

Morris also disparages communal living as a desperate measure for desperate times. The historian Hammond explains that 'the Fourierist phalansteries and all their kind, as was but natural at the time, implied nothing but a refuge from mere destitution.' Since the revolution and the virtual disappearance of poverty, 'separate households are the rule amongst us.' So deep-seated is his aversion to central planning or any sort of specialization of skills that Morris rejects the innovation which Brunelleschi had brought to architecture in the fifteenth century. In *News from Nowhere* the professional architect has been replaced by the master mason and craftsmen, who take pride in their workmanship and individuality.

However, back in the grim reality of the nineteenth-century English industrial landscape, philanthropists and town planners, motivated by an uneasy mix of paternalism and fear of social unrest, pursued their own visions of communities designed to pacify the working class and to ameliorate their living conditions. This had been a grave public concern in England since at least 1846, when the Report of Health of Towns Commission warned of the possible dangers resulting from the lack of public space in the city of Bradford: 'If the lower orders have not places where they can engage in sport and keep their minds engaged in matters of that kind, it is the very thing to drive them to Chartism.' The Great Exhibition of 1851, under the auspices of Prince Albert, addressed the issue with the display in Hyde Park of a 'Model House for the Working Classes'. The full-scale cottage, gothic in style, featured new developments in areas such as plumbing, insulation and the kitchen. The modular design allowed a number of these houses to be placed in rows or even piled into blocks (anticipating Le Corbusier's prefabricated modernist modules displayed at the Paris Exhibition of 1925).

The attention given to housing at the Great Exhibition encouraged philanthropic industrialists to build 'model' estates for their workers. For example, two years after the exhibition Titus Salt, Head Constable of Bradford in 1846 when the Report of Health of Towns was issued, began the construction of Saltaire, an unmistakably urban design of terraced houses on a grid plan located next to his mill near Bradford. There was always a strong tinge of morality and paternalism with regard to these housing estates. Salt did not allow pubs in the area. George Cadbury, who built Bournville for his factory workers near Birmingham, distributed a set of 'Rules of Health' to the residents which included such helpful hints as not to let tea brew for more than three minutes and not to sleep with their mouths open.

Perhaps the most visionary of these philanthropic industrialists, certainly the most flamboyant, was William Hesketh Lever, later first Viscount Leverhulme. Lever was at once 'tycoon and autocrat, patron and philanthropist'. He made his fortune in Sunlight Soap, and in 1888 tore down an old slum to make way for Port Sunlight, a housing estate for his workers located near his new factory near Liverpool. Whereas in 1853 Salt had simply aimed to provide his workers with decent but plain and utilitarian dwellings, Lever had a passion for architecture and, like Fourier, wanted to provide comfort and variety in a garden setting. However, once again, the well-meaning paternalism embraced the policy of containment:

A child that knows nothing of God's earth, of green fields, or sparkling brooks, of breezy hill and springy heather, and whose mind is stored with none of the beauties of nature, but knows only the drunkenness prevalent in the hideous slum it is forced to live in, and whose walks abroad have never extended beyond the corner public-house and the pawnshop, cannot be benefited by education. Such children grow up depraved, and become a danger and terror to the State; wealth-destroyers instead of wealth-producers.

Although the concept of Port Sunlight was in every way anathema to William Morris's utopian vision, the aesthetic influence of his Arts and Craft Movement can clearly be seen in Lever's design for his model village, both inside and out. One journalist of the period thought of Port Sunlight as a village from *News from Nowhere*:

It has all the picturesqueness of mediaeval England. It has all the convenience of the nineteenth century. Sanitary science of the Victorian era has married the picturesque of the days of Bluff King Hal, and the offspring is a village of health and loveliness.

Lever himself wrote:

The picture of a cottage crowned with a thatched roof, and with clinging ivy and climbing roses and a small garden foreground suggesting old-fashioned perfume of flowers and a home in which dwell content and happiness, appeals straight to the heart of each of us, and there are few who can resist its quiet, peaceful influence for the good.

Lever was as good as his word, and a modern architect has called Port Sunlight, which is still inhabited today by employees of the Unilever factory, 'the first and only good housing estate in England'. In accordance with Lever's specifications, there are not more that ten to twelve semi-detached (and some terraced) houses per acre. The architectural styles vary within the broad framework of the vernacular (one block is built in the Belgian style), and no house is built less than fifteen feet from the road. Allotment gardens and space for fowl runs and to hang washing are provided at the rear of each house (to keep the front tidy). Lever believed that 'a home requires a greensward and garden in front of it, just as much as a cup requires a saucer'; the maintenance of these front gardens, initially the responsibility of the tenants, was soon taken over by the company to ensure uniform neatness. Open spaces for recreation occur at 'frequent and convenient centres', and the public buildings, including a temperance hotel, gymnasium and open air swimming bath, are at the heart of the estate.

The industrialist also took great care with the house interiors, which were provided with fitted coat racks, gas, cupboards and hooks, boilers and ranges for cooking. Lever even ensured that there was a bathroom on the ground floor near the door so that the men returning from the factory could wash (with Sunlight Soap) before entering the main part of the house. Advice for tenants on interior decorating and furnishing was provided by the *Sunlight Yearbook* of 1898.

Lever's vision embodies many of the elements of Ledoux's 'industrial park' of Arc-et-Senans. In both, kitchen gardens keep the workers at home, out of trouble and within sight: a paternalistic concern close to a policy of surveillance. But there can be no doubt that Lever had the workers' interests at heart. His reforms were not restricted to design and architecture; he also improved the working conditions of his employees, introducing shorter hours, benefit and welfare schemes, all of which he called 'prosperity-sharing'. So as to allow the tenants to forget about work once they left the factory – and avoid marring the aesthetic effect of the landscaping – the soap factory was discreetly hidden from the view of the estate by a high red brick wall.

There is one building in Port Sunlight which is impressive yet looks out of place, the Lady Lever Art Gallery (1914–1922): it is classical in style, but built of reinforced concrete. The reason for this departure in design was Lever's introduction to the City Beautiful Movement on a visit in 1892 to the then unfinished Columbian Exhibition in Chicago. Its architecture and layout greatly impressed the industrialist at first:

> For picturesqueness of situation, beauty and extent of buildings, arrangement, conception and general execution it leaves nothing to be desired. . . . In addition to size which itself is always impressive, each building from a purely architectural point-of-view is well-conceived, duly proportioned and most admirably executed.

Lever soon had doubts concerning the appropriateness of the City Beautiful style for the art gallery at Port Sunlight, however, and he wrote to one of the architects:

> My suggestion of limestone and classical architecture [for the gallery] must not be taken as ruling out all other styles. This was my first impression, but Mr Simpson has expressed the view, and I think he is probably right, that it would be a little too hard for Port Sunlight Village, and that Renaissance, with red Runcorn stone would harmonise better with the Village. Please therefore feel at liberty to adopt whatever style you think best.

Nevertheless, the architect went ahead and built the Lady Lever Art Gallery in the classical style, set somewhat uncomfortably amid the English cottages of Port Sunlight.

The hugely influential Columbian Exhibition provided the immediate inspiration for another utopian venture in town planning, Ebenezer Howard's Garden City Movement in Britain. Howard, a stenographer by training, became disillusioned with his drab life in England and headed for America to become an homesteader in the state of Nebraska. Howard's attempt at pioneering ended in dismal failure and he returned home in 1893, paying a visit to the Exhibition in Chicago on the way. What he experienced there changed his life – and the English landscape – forever. Like Lever, Howard was greatly impressed with the City Beautiful Movement displayed at the Exhibition, as well as with the wealthy Chicago suburb of Riverside, which Olmsted had landscaped. While in America Howard fell under the spell of not only Burnham's and Olmsted's great visions, but also those of the spiritualist Cora Richmond. Cora Richmond had strong links with the American communitarian movement: she grew up in one of the Fourierist communities, Hopedale, and she was a friend of Robert Dale Owen, son of Robert Owen, the great English socialist and founder of the utopian community of New Harmony, Indiana (described in Chapter 10).

This heady concoction of urban design and spiritualism convinced Howard that there was a God-given order to the universe which made possible the creation of a harmonious society set within an ideal city. In this conception, Howard was going right back to the vision of Alberti in the Renaissance. For Howard, then, rebuilding the city was 'the Master Key' to all other social changes. Full of plans, he returned to England where there was much community-building in the air. One of the first things Howard did on his return was to organize the publication in Britain of Bellamy's *Looking Backward*, which had impressed him immensely, although he later rejected what he soon recognized as Bellamy's totalitarian blueprint for society.

Howard's alternative antidote to the horrors of the overcrowded city was a 'commonwealth' along the lines of Thomas More's Utopia: the population evenly distributed among a number of manageable towns, containing well-built houses and attractive gardens, and surrounded with a green belt of countryside. As with Ledoux's plans for Chaux, the towns – circular in shape – were to incorporate and harmonize the residential and the industrial. There was to be a strict limit on the size of the garden city – Howard suggested 32,000 people. As the first city reached its specified limit, another would be started a short distance away. Thus, over time, a vast planned network of garden cities would spread over the country, each connected to the others by an Inter-Municipal Railway. Howard called this vision 'Social City'.

In contrast to Ledoux, Morris and even Lever, Howard was more concerned with social fabric than with architectural style. Howard's cities were to be '*co-operative* commonwealths', superseding capitalism. The basic tenet was to eliminate the private landlord by transferring the ownership of land to the community; rents would finance roads, hospitals, libraries and schools, rather than lining the pockets of rich men. Howard also advocated 'gas and water socialism', that is, utilities provided by the town on a non-profit basis. He originally called his scheme 'New Jerusalem', and considered the names Rurisville and Unionville (all very American-sounding), but finally settled on Garden City since it was 'pictorially evocative while politically neutral'. Howard then set forth to preach the 'Gospel of the Garden City', under the title 'The Ideal City Made Practicable, A Lecture Illustrated with Lantern Slides'.

Not surprisingly, he came across opposition from several quarters. The English Socialists, or Fabians, disagreed as to what their fundamental goal for society should be: small co-operative communities or state socialism. In 1889 Sydney Webb, an advocate of the latter, complained that 'modern socialists are still reproached with the domestic details of an imaginary Phalanstery.' In that same year another Fabian stated that 'proposals for building new [cities] are about as useful as arrangements for protection against visits from Mr Wells' Martians.' *The Times* said in its review of Howard's book *To-morrow: A Peaceful Path to Real Reform* (1898; reissued in 1902 as *Garden Cities of Tomorrow*): 'If Mr Howard could be made town clerk of such a city he would carry it on to everybody's satisfaction. The only difficulty is to create it; but that is small matter to Utopians.'

Nevertheless, Howard still insisted that 'the essential idea is that a city can be founded, planned and governed *de novo* even in an ancient land like England.' As one scholar observes, *To-morrow* consists more of pages of calculations about finance than architectural elevations: 'Howard was writing not for utopian simple-lifers, but for hard-nosed Victorian businessmen who wanted to be sure they would get their money back. . . .' In 1899 Howard and eleven other men founded the Garden City Association to promote 'in its main features . . . the project suggested by Mr Ebenezer Howard in *To-morrow*'. Within a year, the Association had 325 members who had joined at a shilling per subscription, but this did not provide enough capital to begin building. In 1901, 'a change came over the Association [and] its affairs took a practical turn', in Howard's words.

A prominent barrister, Ralph Neville, took over the Garden City Association and within a few years had turned it into a respectable business proposition. He sold the idea to potential investors as a model industrial village along the lines of Bournville and Port Sunlight, intended to pacify and improve the conditions of workers rather than to transform society. Industrialists like Cadbury and Lever soon joined Howard and Neville on the board of the new Pioneer Garden City Ltd, then, once the site in Hertfordshire had been chosen, of the First Garden City Ltd. Under the influence of Cadbury, Lever and Neville, Howard's original collective venture became a private company, whose first responsibility was not to the residents but to its stockholders (although investors' dividends could not go above five per cent – 'philanthropy at five percent', as one commentator put it). The stenographer had proved 'no match for a cocoa millionaire or a soap magnate'.

Howard was to make compromises not only in the theory behind the Garden City but also in its design. He had envisioned a forward-looking city with a 'modern' geometric street plan and buildings. However, Unwin and Parker, the architects chosen by the First Garden City Ltd to design the new town of Letchworth in Hertfordshire, were strong advocates of the Arts and Crafts Movement. As a result, Letchworth bears more resemblance to William Morris's nostalgic look back to the medieval English village in *News From Nowhere* and to Lever's Port Sunlight than to Howard's optimistic endorsement of the future in *To-morrow*.

Although Letchworth and Port Sunlight look similar, their original inhabitants were very different types. The first residents of Letchworth were people of 'advanced' opinions, and the town was reputed to have more committees per capita than any other in England. The Company, concerned that Letchworth might gain a reputation as a 'colony of cranks', put out a press release stating that 'only one resident habitually wore a toga and sandals'. The newspapers were merciless. In 1907 the *Daily Mail* informed its readers that Letchworth offered a wealth of lectures on 'vegetarianism, social Christianity, [and] the raising of the moral tone of dustmen'. The papers also reported that the first factory to move to Letchworth, the Spinella factory, made 'corsets which Letchworth women obviously never wear, but which their husbands sell at great profit to the less enlightened women in other towns'.

Despite the scepticism of the press, Letchworth became a 'city on a hill' and Howard's ideas were hugely influential. In time his vision of a network of small towns, divided by green belts and linked by fast trains, thus easing the congestion of the large cities, was realized. One of the British Rail lines heading north out of Euston Station in London stops at Stevenage, Welwyn Garden City, Hatfield, Letchworth – all built on the Garden City principle. Some might lament that Howard's legacy gave us Milton Keynes; however, we must credit the Garden City Movement with the establishment of a green belt around London in the 1930s and '40s which, so far, has saved that corner of England from becoming a vast suburban nightmare.

In America the concept of the Garden City was embodied in commuter suburbs with names like Forest Hills Gardens, New York, and Greenbelt, Maryland. In 1913 the Garden City Society was founded in St Petersburg after a delegation of Russians had toured Letchworth and other garden city communities in Britain. In fact, despite the contempt of British Marxists, the Garden City Movement remained influential through the early years of the Soviet Revolution. Howard's concept seemed to answer Friedrich Engels's call for 'the abolition of the division between town and country', which he declared was no mere 'utopian ideal'. Lenin later formulated the goal of 'a resettlement of mankind (with the eradication of rural neglect, isolation from the world and barbarism, as well as of the unnatural accumulation of gigantic masses of people in large towns)'. Many workers' settlements were designed as garden cities around the new industrial factories, such as electric power stations and oilfields, and the Great Moscow Plan of 1921–25 envisioned that city's historical nucleus surrounded by three belts of industry and parks, garden cities and woodland.

By 1928, however, official Soviet policy deemed the Garden City Society of Leningrad a 'bourgeois relic'. In the *Great Soviet Encyclopaedia* of 1932, under 'Garden Cities', Ebenezer Howard was called a 'petit-bourgeois intellectual'. Soviet socialism, in respect of industry, agriculture and domestic housing, became collective: individual dwellings with gardens at the back were out. According to one official at the time, Stalin's first Five Year Plan (1928–1932) called for the 'putting into practice all that, until recently, was [considered] fantasy and utopia'. With such encouragement and inspired by the avant-garde movement, many fantastical architectural designs were floated in the 1920s – some literally, such as Malevich's cosmic city, 'a sort of urban earth satellite', Krutikov's 'Flying City' and Iozefovich's floating House of Congresses, which could be moored at various cities to conduct business. The main battle was between the urbanists, who wanted to house everyone in tower blocks, and the de-urbanists, who advocated linear communities connected by road ('automobile socialism' – resembling something like Southern California today). However, by 1931 the avant garde was dead and to suggest the abandonment of the city was considered state treason. The urbanists, for a time, won, and 'Le Corbusier was their god'.

75

Not since Ledoux had an architect had the conviction that his 'total architecture' or 'machine for living' could alone change society. From Fourier to Howard the physical environment as reflected in town planning had been just one, though a key, element in the general transformation of society. But, to Le Corbusier, his unique vision of architecture and town planning were the only means to bring about change. Le Corbusier stated in uncompromising terms in his work, *Vers une Architecture* ('Towards a New Architecture'):

> Architecture or Revolution.
> Revolution can be avoided.

That is to say, his new architecture, once established, would revolutionize social attitudes without the need for outright political revolution.

Born Charles-Edouard Jeanneret in the Swiss watchmaking town of La Chaux-de-Fonds, 'Le Corbusier' reinvented himself in 1920, taking his pseudonym from his maternal grandfather. In *Das Kapital* Karl Marx had described La Chaux-de-Fonds as 'one huge manufactory', and this peculiar environment helped to shape Le Corbusier's conception of society as thousands of minute components tightly fitted together into a planned harmony. In his early days, Le Corbusier was an adherent of the Arts and Crafts Movement; he travelled in England and made sketches of Hampstead Garden Suburb in his notebooks. However, he soon rejected both the artisan aesthetic and the small town ideal as obsolete and eagerly entered into the Machine Age. Le Corbusier was heir to that belief, held first by Ledoux and later by Bellamy, that the industrial process should provide the basis for the social order. For Le Corbusier, the factory machine and its products were both a model and an inspiration to the worker:

> The machines that cover the floor of the factory are examples to him of power and clarity, and make him part of a work of perfection to which his simple spirit never dared to aspire.

Le Corbusier stated, in a phrase which could have come from Bellamy's pen, that contemporary society was 'profoundly *out of gear*'.

Le Corbusier had the true utopian credentials: in putting forward his solution to society's problems he rejected all that had come before:

The existing centres must come down. To save itself, every great city

must rebuild its centre. . . . WE MUST BUILD ON A CLEAR SITE!
The city of today is dying because it is not constructed geometrically.

In complete contrast to Howard and Morris, Le Corbusier wished to
glorify the power of the big city. Existing cities were not dense enough;
they gave too much expression to 'anarchic individualism'. The city should
be a centre for great bureaucracies whose administration of society would
bring the order and harmony Le Corbusier sought. In 1922 he proposed
his 'Contemporary City for Three Million People', which would represent
'an act of faith in favour of the present'. The decision by some enlightened
city council to build it would mean that the 'radiant hour of harmony,
construction and enthusiasm' had finally arrived.

Le Corbusier 'placed his ideal city on a perfectly flat plain, a *tabula
rasa*, unmarked by man or nature'. Its geometric grid plan served the city's
modern communication and transportation systems: 'A modern city,'
according to Le Corbusier, 'lives by the straight line in a practical sense.'
Sixty-storey office and administrative skyscrapers are placed at its centre;
these are surrounded by luxurious high-rise residential superblocks for
the élite (captains of industry, scientists, intellectuals, artists, etc). All the
buildings are constructed of steel, reinforced concrete and glass and are
set amidst park space. Subordinate office and industrial workers live in
garden suburbs on the outskirts of the green belt which surrounds the
central area of the city. At the very heart of the Contemporary City
is a central piazza, a transportation hub with an airport set above the
main intersection of north-south, east-west superhighways. The 'fearful
symmetry' of this city is reminiscent of the Italian Renaissance. As one
scholar remarks, it

> . . . symbolized the victory of reason over chance, of planning over
> anarchic individualism, of social order over discord. . . . The sky-
> scraper, this tool given by the engineer to the architect, permitted Le
> Corbusier to reconcile the seeming opposites of urban design: density
> and open space.

The Contemporary City is a twentieth-century version of Chaux,
designed to encourage speed and efficiency. Both Le Corbusier and
Ledoux place their administrators at the centre to enable them to keep
their fingers on the pulse of the industrial society and oversee the flow
of important materials, whether they be salt or people and transport.
In both the Contemporary City and Chaux the residential buildings

surround the administrative heart, within close reach, and both complexes have a garden setting. The many communal comforts provided by Le Corbusier's apartment blocks are perhaps closer to Fourier's phalanstery. As in Howard's original Garden City scheme, the apartment blocks were to be jointly owned by residents and run as non-profit co-operatives – there would be no private houses or land.

His efforts to see his architectural ideals realized in Paris led Le Corbusier to declare, 'France needs a Father. It doesn't matter who' – just someone who would back his *plan voisin*, which entailed razing the historic Marais quarter of Paris to make way for identical X-shaped towers. But he found French bureaucrats incapable of initiative (he called them 'Messieurs les Non'), and the capitalists – including the Voisin aircraft and automobile company from which the plan took its name – too conservative. Le Corbusier decided that society needed not only a plan, but a strong authority from above. His work *La Ville Radieuse* (1935), a revised version of the Contemporary City, is therefore dedicated to 'Authority'. Just as Fourier and his contemporary utopians, Saint-Simon and Robert Owen, had looked to the authoritarian Napoleon to realize their utopias, so Le Corbusier courted first Stalin's Russia, then Mussolini's Italy, and finally Pétain's Vichy government to begin work on his city.

Le Corbusier's ideas appealed to the Soviet government, and in 1928 the architect was invited to enter a competition for the design of the Palace of the Soviets. The Palace was to be a monumental structure, a 'symbolical expression of the magnificent results of the proletarian dictatorship', celebrating the first Five Year Plan. However, Le Corbusier's design was turned down in favour of a standard-issue monument in 'the Italian Renaissance style' by a Russian architect. Le Corbusier left the USSR feeling 'insulted'. Stalin had decided that stark modernist architecture did not suit his Monumental Propaganda Plan. Nevertheless, modernism, also known as the International Style, thrived in Europe and America, and Le Corbusier contributed pavilions to the Paris Expositions of 1925 and 1937. The contribution of his utopian city to the twentieth century can be seen in the tower-block housing estates which went up on the outskirts of all the major Western cities.

High-rise living has not been hailed as a great success, owing mainly to the growing perception that these estates had answered Le Corbusier's prescription only too well: they were machines for living, soul-destroying machines which annihilated not only the anarchy of individualism but individualism itself – and which also had a tendency to come to bits.

MACHINE FOR LIVING

In England as early as 1955, Le Corbusier's legacy was deemed by the *Architectural Review* 'subtopia'. Some date the symbolic end of modernism to 3.32 p.m. on 15 July 1972, when the Pruitt-Igoe housing project in St Louis – a prize-winning example of Le Corbusier's vision – was condemned as uninhabitable for its low-income residents and dynamited.

Morris's objections to Bellamy have been echoed in modern criticisms of Le Corbusier. The Post-modernists, like Morris more than a century before them, reject the notions of absolute truth, rational planning and the standardization of people's lives, and advocate instead a conception of the urban fabric as necessarily fragmented, a 'palimpsest of past forms'. Post-modernists are essentially anti-utopian.

Nevertheless, the utopian impulse to create a rational order out of the jumble of an unplanned city has played a vital part in the construction of the modern world. Utopians like Filarete and Ledoux pioneered the idea that the city should be conceived as a whole, as a living organism or a working machine. That original utopian inspiration is the foundation of the discipline of urban planning without which late twentieth-century city life is virtually impossible, as the teeming, unplanned cities of the South demonstrate.

But, if that is Utopia's success, its failure lies in its attachment to inappropriate models of human society. Neither the universal laws of harmony posited by Renaissance utopians, nor the industrial machinery worshipped by Ledoux and Le Corbusier, have much to do with the way real flesh-and-blood people live and act. Utopian architects and planners sought to build the precincts of human happiness without much bothering to inquire into the nature of the men and women who would inhabit them. The result was, all too often, an environment which alienated rather than succoured.

The ideal city remains perhaps a somewhat frightening prospect, for behind the promise of a totally planned environment there lurks the threat of total social control. Indeed, the ideal city, were it ever to be created, could only be maintained by a strong central authority, since real cities tend to spread or decay – they do not remain static as the ideal city must to retain its special status. If for no other reason, therefore, the schemes of men like Ledoux, Howard and Le Corbusier can never be fully realized; yet their partial implementation has had a tremendous impact on our landscape. We live surrounded by the fragments of their utopian dreams.

Title page to Francis Bacon, *Instauratio Magna*, at the front of the *Novum Organum*, 1620.

Part Three

MACHINE

We live not in Plato his Commonwealth, but in times wherein abuses have got the upper hand.
Francis Bacon, 'Speech Upon the Case of Sir Thomas Parry'

The imagination of the poets has placed the golden age in the infancy of the human race. . . . The golden age of the human race is not behind us; it lies before us, in the perfection of the social order.

Henri de Saint-Simon,
De la Réorganisation de la Société Européenne

The European talks of progress because by the aid of a few scientific discoveries he has established a society which has mistaken comfort for civilization.

Benjamin Disraeli

5. The College of the Six Days' Works

The myths always had it that in Paradise, be it the Garden of Eden, Arcadia or the Golden Age, man did not work. The Land of Cockaigne, with its flying roasts and rivers of potable fluids, was the quintessential dreamscape of the working man, 'conceived in defiance of the biblical idea – reinforced by their own experience – that work is man's curse'. However, utopians have always been more realistic, accepting that men must labour for their daily bread. Utopias have generally offered not a world freed from work, but a world where its fruits, and the burden of producing them, are apportioned fairly. Thomas More allowed the incentive of shorter working hours; others, like Tommaso Campanella, believed that, properly managed, work could actually be fulfilling. However, utopians up to and including Campanella were unanimous in the belief that the pie which was to be distributed was of a fixed size: everyone had to make do as best he could with the limited goods on offer, and luxury was to be considered a sin.

Utopia itself set the puritanical tone. The Utopians are guaranteed a mere six-hour workday:

> They don't wear people out ... by keeping them hard at work from early morning till late at night, like cart-horses. That's just slavery – and yet that's what life is like for the working classes nearly everywhere else in the world.

In fact, the Utopians

> ... never force people to work unnecessarily, for the main purpose of their whole economy is to give each person as much time free from physical drudgery as the needs of the community will allow, so that he can cultivate his mind – which they regard as the secret of a happy life.

However, the price to be paid for this 'Social Chapter' is that consumer goods are limited to the bare essentials needed for a 'comfortable life'. With some occupations such as dressmakers and tailors thus made obsolete (everyone wears the same drab clothing in Utopia and fashions never change), more people are free to take on the really essential work. Farming, a task which More obviously deemed to be particularly unpleasant, is done by rotation: everyone must spend at least two years in the countryside. But the restricted working day is possible above all because, quite unlike the practice in contemporary Europe, the entire population, including women, must work – there can be no slackers or the system breaks down. Hythloday explains that

> . . . if you took all those engaged in non-essential trades, and all who are too lazy to work – each of whom consumes twice as much of the products of other people's labour as any of the producers themselves – if you put the whole lot of them on to something useful, you'd soon see how few hours' work a day would be amply sufficient to supply all the necessities and comforts of life – to which you might add all real and natural forms of pleasure.

However, as we saw in Chapter 2, the promise of leisure is not sufficient on its own to motivate the Utopians to work. The *Syphogranti*, or local magistrates, make sure 'that nobody sits around doing nothing', and, if that is not enough, 'everyone has his eye on you, so you're practically forced to get on with your job.' There are slaves to perform those tasks that no one wants to do, such as slaughtering animals in the abattoirs located outside the city.

In Tommaso Campanella's *La Città del Sole*, the Solarians, all of whom contribute to the labour force, also subscribe to the belief that work is not an end in itself, but simply the means of producing the necessary goods and services. Presumably super-fit as a result of their programme of eugenics, the Solarians are able to cut the working day to four hours. The extra leisure time is taken up in games, debating, reading, teaching or walking. Nevertheless, Campanella was the first utopian to suggest that job satisfaction and self-fulfilment were also important factors in people's working lives. Career counselling is performed by astrological forecast:

> The particular inclination of each person is seen in his birth, and in the division of labor no one is assigned to things that are destructive to his individuality but rather to things that preserve it.

Job flexibility is encouraged as well; thus, 'the one who learns the greatest number of skills and practices them best is judged to have the greatest nobility.' Campanella dispels all the unpleasant connotations of work which linger in More's *Utopia*. Work is not a dirty word in the City of the Sun: 'Anyone who is assigned any particular task performs it as though it were a high honor. They keep no slaves, since they are sufficient unto themselves and more.'

Although the Solarians, whose city is one huge classroom, are extremely well educated, their learning essentially consists of the passive absorption of facts rather than the active exploration of the world. Their most important accomplishment is their mastery of the ancient wisdom of astrology; however, in his emphasis on this arcane art Campanella was already behind the times. For he lived at the threshold of the Age of Science, a period in which the belief began to take hold that technology could be used to increase man's knowledge, skills and the fruits of his labour. The first thorough treatment of the potential benefits of modern science, especially in 'the relief of man's estate', is to be found in Francis Bacon's *New Atlantis*, which became one of the most influential works in the utopian genre.

Bacon, an exact contemporary of Campanella, was born in 1561, the son of Sir Nicholas Bacon, Lord Keeper, and nephew of Sir William Cecil, later Lord Treasurer Burghley. At the age of twelve Bacon entered Trinity College, Cambridge, and left at the end of two years to study law at the Inns of Court, like Thomas More before him. In 1584, during the reign of Elizabeth I, Bacon was elected to Parliament and was to continue as a member for the next thirty-six years. In 1591 he met and began to act as advisor to the young Earl of Essex, an impulsive and passionate nobleman who became greatly attached to the older Bacon. Through his friendship with Essex, Bacon hoped to forward his political reforms and gain promotion in the government. (Essex also helped Bacon out when he was short of money.) However, Bacon's ambitions were frustrated on all fronts. He was passed over for two government posts, Attorney-General and Solicitor-General, after incurring the Queen's anger for refusing to support her request for money from Parliament. Bacon commented on the matter, 'There is a variety allowed in counsel, as a discord in music to make it more perfect.'

Although he was the Queen's favourite, the dashing Essex was becoming a dangerous friend. After a series of military successes abroad, the admiration which he drew from his troops posed a threat to the Queen, who had no standing army to protect her position at home. The relationship between Elizabeth and her favourite worsened in 1599–1600, after Essex returned from a disastrous campaign to quell the rebellion in Ireland. Bacon, an advisor to the Queen as well as to Essex, tried to steer a middle course, but only managed to offend both parties. Essex, whose restlessness and frustration soon took the form of wild schemes, rode into London on 8 February 1601 with two hundred men, calling on the citizens to rally round him against the Queen's ministers. Bacon, Essex's friend, took the role of prosecutor in the subsequent trial. Essex was found guilty of treason and executed.

Elizabeth I died two years later, in 1603. Bacon's political fortunes improved somewhat under the new monarch, James I. He was appointed Attorney-General in 1613, Lord Keeper, like his father, in 1617, and Lord Chancellor the next year. Also in 1618, he was raised to the peerage as Baron Verulam, and in January 1621 took a step higher, to become Viscount St Albans. However, Bacon had made enemies along the way, and in the spring of 1621 his political career came to an abrupt end when he was found guilty of taking bribes in court (ironically, Bacon had decided against the persons who had given him money). The Great Seal of office was taken from him, he was imprisoned in the Tower, fined £40,000 and banned from both Parliament and the Court.

Bacon spent only a few days in the Tower, and the fine was assigned by the King to trustees for Bacon's own use. But Bacon never returned to politics, and he died a few years later, in 1626, a victim of his own scientific curiosity. Driving through the snow near Highgate he was suddenly seized by the intuition that freezing might preserve meat. He immediately alighted from his coach, purchased a chicken and proceeded to stuff it with snow. This impulse was to prove unwise, for in doing so he caught a fatal chill and died of bronchitis. His last letter, to the Earl of Arundel, reveals his enthusiasm to the last:

> My very good Lord, I was likely to have had the fortune of Caius Plinius the elder, who lost his life by trying an experiment about the burning of the mountain Vesuvius. For I was desirous to try an experiment or two, touching the conservation and induration of bodies. And for the experiment itself, it succeeded excellently well. But in the journey between London and Highgate . . .

For Bacon's predecessor in both the Lord Chancellorship and Utopia, Thomas More, political duties were an unwelcome distraction from intellectual pursuits. In Bacon's case, however, politics were a means to promote his philosophical and scientific ideas. His purpose was to harness the wealth and power of the state in the cause of advancing man's knowledge of the natural world, both because such knowledge was valuable in itself, and, more importantly, because he realized that it was the key to improving the material conditions of human life. Bacon's aims were sketched out in the *Instauratio Magna* ('The Great Instauration'), the title of which denotes both a great restoration and a great founding. He published this work, in Latin, in 1620, as an introduction to his treatise on scientific method, the *Novum Organum* ('The New Instrument'). In the *Instauratio Magna* Bacon states that his goal is 'to lay the foundation, not of any sect or doctrine, but of human utility and power' in order to 'command nature in action'. Probably some time around 1614 Bacon decided to put the *Great Instauration* aside and instead try to draw attention to his scheme by means of a more popular tale, a fable in the manner of More's *Utopia*. The work, *New Atlantis*, written in English, was published posthumously by Bacon's secretary, William Rawley, in 1627. Rawley begins his preface:

> This fable my Lord devised, to the end that he might exhibit therein a model or description of a college instituted for the interpreting of nature and the producing of great and marvellous works for the benefit of men, under the name of Salomon's House, or the College of the Six Days' Works. . . . Certainly the model is more vast and high than can possibly be imitated in all things; notwithstanding most things therein are within men's power to effect.

New Atlantis was a work of propaganda for a revolutionary view of the role of science in society, and as such it has proved immensely influential.

It begins with the account of how a European ship, lost somewhere in the South Seas, stumbles upon an unknown island. The first-person narrator, an unspecified member of the ship's company (though there are faint indications that he might be the first officer), describes how the sailors drop anchor in 'a good haven, being the port of a fair city; not great indeed, but well built'. However, it soon becomes apparent that a landing is out of the question, for 'straightways we saw divers of the people, with bastons [truncheons] in their hands, as it were forbidding us to land; yet without any cries or fierceness, but only as warning us off by signs that they made.' Soon, an official comes aboard and hands the captain a scroll in 'ancient Hebrew, and in ancient Greek, and in good Latin of the School, and in Spanish' which informs the Europeans that they are indeed forbidden to land, and must leave the coast within sixteen days, although fresh supplies and medical attention for the sick will be provided. The curiosity of the sailors – and reader – is stirred:

> We were much perplexed. The denial of landing and hasty warning us away troubled us much; on the other side, to find that the people had languages and were so full of humanity, did comfort us not a little. And above all, the sign of the cross to that instrument [the scroll delivered by the islanders] was to us a great rejoicing, and as it were a certain presage of good.

The European visitors are eventually permitted to land, although security on the island, called Bensalem, remains tight. They are quarantined in the Strangers' House for several days before being allowed into the city, and even then they cannot wander too far beyond the city walls. Nevertheless, the sailors are greatly overwhelmed by the hospitality they find, and believe 'that we were come into a land of angels, which did appear to us daily and prevent us [anticipate our needs] with comforts, which we thought not of, much less expected.' (None of the islanders accept 'tips', 'for they call an officer that taketh rewards, "*twice paid*" – ironic in the light of Bacon's fall from grace.)

The Europeans learn from the governor of the Strangers' House, a Christian priest, that the Bensalemites received the Gospel about twenty years after the ascension of Christ, when an ark carrying the Old and New Testaments miraculously appeared in a pillar of light. The priest also explains the history of the island. Three thousand years ago, Bensalem was known and visited by ships and people of all nations, Phoenicia, Carthage, Egypt, Palestine, Persia, Arabia, China and 'the great Atlantis (that you call America), which have now but junks and canoes, abounded then in tall ships.' A number of these foreigners chose to remain and settle in Bensalem at that time, and their descendants still flourish. Within a hundred years, Atlantis was 'utterly lost and destroyed' by a deluge. However, 'the poor remnant of human seed which remained in their mountains peopled the country again slowly' with 'simple and savage people'.

The priest goes on to explain how Bensalem's policy of isolation came about. A king, named Solamona,

> . . . recalling into his memory the happy and flourishing estate wherein this land then was, so as it might be a thousand ways altered to the worse, but scarce any one way to the better; thought nothing wanted

to his noble and heroical intentions, but only (as far as human foresight might reach) to give perpetuity to that which was in his time so happily established.

Therefore, he ordained that strangers should not be permitted to visit the island for fear they would disrupt the status quo. As for the few foreigners (numbering thirteen only) who have seen Bensalem and returned to their homeland, 'whatsoever they have said could be taken where they came but for a dream.'

On a walk about town, the Europeans discover something about the islanders and their customs, while continually meeting 'with many things right worthy of observation and relation; as indeed, if there be a mirror in the world worthy to hold men's eyes, it is that country.' The family as an institution is honoured annually in an elaborate ceremony, the 'Feast of the Family', held for any man who lives to see thirty of his descendants, all above three years of age, gather about him. (This would have seemed an enviable achievement to the average seventeenth-century man, whose life expectancy was about forty years.) During the feast, family discords are settled; help, advice and sometimes reprimands are handed out. A Jewish merchant named Joabin, living proof of the society's religious tolerance, explains to the strangers that the 'chaste' people of Bensalem regard marriage as 'the faithful nuptial union of man and wife, that was first instituted', unlike the Europeans who regard it as 'a remedy for unlawful concupiscence'. Therefore, there is no need for 'stews [brothels], no dissolute houses, no courtesans, nor any thing of that kind'; nor is polygamy practised. As for 'masculine love', 'they have no touch of it.'

By this point in the narrative the reader is bursting with impatience: just what is the secret of Bensalem which allows its citizens to live such felicitous lives? Fortunately, Bacon is at last ready to reveal all. The conversation between the Jew and the strangers is interrupted by news of the imminent arrival of one of the 'Fathers of Salomon's House'. Salomon's House, sometimes called the College of the Six Days' Works, was founded (confusingly) by King Solamona. It is the institution which sets Bensalem apart from all other countries, the key to its success. The Father is the subject of quasi-religious awe – none of his kind has been seen for twelve years – and he enters the city in a stately procession:

He held up his bare hand as he went, as blessing the people, but in silence. The street was wonderfully well kept: so that there was never any army had their men stand in better battle-array, than the people stood. The windows likewise were not crowded, but every one stood in them as if they had been placed.

Soon the narrator is summoned to the presence of this priest-like figure, who explains the 'manifesto' of Salomon's House, which turns out to be a succinct summary of the aims of modern science. First and foremost:

> The End of our Foundation is the knowledge of Causes, and secret motions of things; and the enlarging of the bounds of Human Empire, to the effecting of all things possible.

The heart of Bacon's utopia is revealed to be the single-minded, even ruthless, pursuit of scientific knowledge, co-ordinated from the College of the Six Days' Works, the centre of discovery and innovation. The experiments and inventions of this institution, which are mostly of a practical nature, are lovingly described: caves house experiments in refrigeration as well as hermits 'by whom also we learn many things'; towers provide views of meteors and other atmospheric phenomena; salt lakes test desalination plants; among the wells and fountains is found the Water of Paradise which prolongs life; spacious houses enclose ecological mini-environments (forerunners of Kew Gardens); orchards and gardens provide herbal medicines; wildlife parks preserve rare species (more common animals are dissected); furnaces allow the study of heat, perspective-houses optics, sound-houses acoustics and engine-houses motions of all sorts; there are also perfume-houses, a mathematical house and houses of deceits of the senses. In effect, Bacon invents the specialist research laboratory, perhaps the single most important innovation of all time. The products of these laboratories include telescopes, microscopes, piped music (a common feature of nineteenth-century utopias), submarines and flying machines. Information on 'the sciences, arts, manufactures and inventions of all the world' is collected by three of the Fellows of Salomon's House, who travel incognito every twelve years and remain abroad until a new mission sets out.

Some critics see a sinister side to Bacon's *New Atlantis*, not only in certain of the customs of the Bensalemites, such as their initially hostile attitude towards strangers, but in the absence of any discussion of the body politic or society as a whole on the island. However, this is to misunderstand Bacon's real interest in writing *New Atlantis*. As Rawley suggested in his preface, he was mainly concerned with describing the organization of the House of Salomon. Bacon realized that his scientific utopia surpassed all others in scope and imagination; therefore, the first part of the work, where he describes the history of the island and its customs, is really just a subtle parody of his two most famous predecessors in Utopia, Plato and Thomas More.

It is evident that Bacon found More's Utopia a very dull place indeed. Therefore, he ensures that, unlike the Utopians, the Bensalemites are not deprived of high fashion: on almost every festive occasion people get out their colourful Persian-style finery. Their dignitaries, as they process through the streets decked out in satin and gold, are not laughed at, as are the foreign ambassadors in *Utopia*, but admired. (The Bensalemites, however, do not trade in gold and silver, only in light.) Joabin remarks to the Europeans that he has 'read in a book of one of your men [More], of a Feigned Commonwealth, where the married couple are permitted, before they contract, to see one another naked.' He goes on to explain that the inhabitants disliked this, 'for they think it a scorn to give a refusal after so familiar knowledge.' The Bensalemites' remedy: friends observe the prospective bride and groom swimming in what they call 'Adam and Eve's pools' on their behalf. It is telling that the names in *New Atlantis* conjure up not the improbability of such a society, as in Utopia, but its goals: Utopia means 'nowhere' in Greek, Bensalem 'the son of peace' in Hebrew.

Bacon is only gently mocking More; he has a much more serious point to make in his criticisms of Plato. In Bacon's eyes, the philosopher's preference, as stated in the *Republic*, for the life of contemplation over action in an imperfect world suffocated any notion of experimental science and technology for centuries. For Bacon, Plato's Atlantis myth perfectly symbolized this halt to progress. As the title of his book suggests, Bacon sought to rewrite the myth in *New Atlantis*.

According to Plato in the *Critias*, Atlantis is an island located just beyond the Pillars of Hercules (that is, the Straits of Gibraltar) which possessed luxuries and 'all those sweet-scented stuffs . . . in marvellous beauty and endless abundance'. Among other things, the inhabitants constructed hot and cold springs and a complex irrigation system – projects which Bacon would have lauded. But, the 'portion of divinity within them was now becoming faint and weak through being ofttimes blended with a large measure of mortality.' Therefore Zeus caused the island to be completely swallowed up by a large earthquake which 'has created a barrier of impassable mud which prevents those who are sailing out from here [the Straits of Gibraltar] to the ocean beyond [the Atlantic] from proceeding further.'

To Bacon, the impasse created by the sunken Atlantis also represented an impasse in men's minds which prevented them from breaking free of the ancient philosophy and 'sailing uncharted waters'. Navigation, which had greatly advanced since Thomas More's day, was an important metaphor for discovery and progress in Bacon's writings. Magellan's ships had circumnavigated the globe, and 'a globe encompassed became a globe reduced'. In 1566 a youth wrote a thank-you note for a sphere which he had received: 'Before seeing it, I had not realized how small the world is.' In comparing himself and his new scientific method to Columbus's voyage to the New World, Bacon stated:

Lastly, even if the breath of hope which blows on us from that New Continent were fainter and less distinct, yet (if we do not wish a completely abject spirit) we must by all means make the test. For there is no comparison between the danger of not trying and the danger of not succeeding: since by not trying we throw away the chance of an immense good; by not succeeding we only incur the loss of a little human labor. From the things said and also from those unsaid, it seems to me, there is hope in reserve not only to make a bold man try, but also make a prudent and sober man hope.

Thus, Bacon explicitly states in *New Atlantis* that the great Atlantis was not destroyed by an earthquake, 'as your man [Plato] saith', but by a flood. The implication is that Atlantis, that is America, was not an obstruction to navigation, but rather an opportunity for exploration. (The Fellows of the House of Salomon provide a prediction and advisory service for earthquakes, floods and other natural disasters.) Significantly, the original title page of the *Instauratio Magna*, at the front of the *Novum Organum*, has an engraving of a ship sailing confidently through the Pillars of Hercules with the caption 'Multi pertransibunt & augebitur scientia' ('Many will pass through and knowledge will be multiplied'). Before Columbus's voyage, the coat of arms of the Spanish royal family had featured the Pillars of Hercules with the motto *Ne Plus Ultra* ('No More Beyond'). After Columbus's discoveries, the negative was erased from the arms, leaving the motto *Plus Ultra* ('More Beyond'). Bacon had written in 1608:

Distant voyages and travels have brought to light many things in nature, which may throw fresh light on human philosophy and science and correct by experience the opinions and conjectures of the ancients. Not only reason but prophecy connects the two. What else can the prophet mean who, in speaking about the last times, says: Many will pass through and knowledge will be multiplied [Daniel 12:4]. Does he not imply that the passing through or perambulation of the round earth and the increase or multiplication of science were destined to the same age and century?

If some critics have found *New Atlantis* sinister, others have complained that it is incomplete. It ends abruptly after the Father has finished his description of Salomon's House. Bacon's secretary, Rawley, suggests why this is so. He states that Bacon

... thought also in this present fable to have composed a frame of Laws, or of the best state or mould of a commonwealth; but ... his desire of collecting the Natural History diverted him, which he preferred many degrees before it.

Bacon typically left his writings unfinished, perhaps because in the field of science he inevitably preferred experiment to theory. However, it is likely that *New Atlantis* ends as Bacon always intended.

Bacon's campaign for the advancement of science and reorganization of knowledge was carefully designed, and 'his major writings were assigned exact positions in the over-all plan for [the] *Instauratio Magna*'. Thus, he stipulated that *New Atlantis* be published in the same volume as the *Sylva Sylvarum* ('A Forest of Materials') 'in regard it hath so near an affinity (in one part of it) with the preceding Natural History'. Bacon almost certainly had no intention of providing *New Atlantis* with a description of good government. Elsewhere he identifies government as a separate science which is 'secret and retired': secret in the sense that some things are 'hard to know, and some because they are not fit to utter'. Some critics take this to mean that not even the Fellows of Salomon's House attempt to delve into the murky waters of politics: a dangerous situation since these scientists effectively rule Bensalem through their science.

But could not Bacon simply be saying that government is too complicated and impenetrable and, in any case, there is no point talking about it because the study of politics is not the way forward: it has been tried and has failed? Rather, technology and the new science, as exemplified by the House of Salomon, are the only hope. More's Utopians endeavour to overcome the great stumbling block of mankind, original sin, through their well-ordered institutions. However, for Bacon, 'the true ends of knowledge' are 'a restitution and reinvesting (in great part) of man to the sovereignty and power . . . which he had in his first state of creation.' In other words, learning has the potential to undo the consequences of the Fall. In leaving *New Atlantis* apparently unfinished, Bacon may also be deliberately echoing the structure of the *Critias*, the only extant uncompleted dialogue by Plato: it stops abruptly before Zeus makes his speech on the destruction of Atlantis.

We have mentioned the Fellows' experimental apparatus and some inventions. But what is the philosophical basis of their science, and how exactly does the House of Salomon run its operation? At the beginning of the seventeenth century thinkers such as Campanella and Bacon believed that man could only understand the world through his senses and that all knowledge must be based on the direct study of nature. Bacon, indeed, heralded Campanella's mentor, Telesio, as 'a lover of truth' and 'the first of the new men'. Campanella's Solarians were open-minded concerning scientific matters. They praised Ptolemy and admired Copernicus, but did not venture to declare who was right on the question of the earth's relation to the sun, since not all the evidence had been gathered.

Campanella had taken the first step towards the concept of progress by recognizing the increasingly fast pace of invention and innovation: 'Our present century . . . has produced more history in a hundred years than the whole world did in the preceding four thousand!' Bacon, too, realized that the same inventions which Campanella had admired – printing, gunpowder and the compass – had 'changed the appearance and state of the whole world . . . so that no empire, sect, or star, appears to have exercised a greater power and influence on human affairs than these mechanical discoveries.'

Nevertheless, Campanella remained fascinated by astrology and, as we shall see, his eugenics programme in *La Città del Sole* was based on the alignment of the planets. Bacon, however, was well ahead of his time even among scientists in condemning all vestiges of the old science:

> The sciences themselves which have had better intelligence and confederacy with the imagination of man than with his reason, are three in number: Astrology, Natural Magic, and Alchemy.

But the far more serious offence in Bacon's eyes was the fact that both Telesio and Campanella had constructed a philosophical system before all the necessary data had been collected. In this, they were as bad as Plato:

All these [Plato, Aristotle, *et al*] invented systems of the universe, each according to his own fancy, like so many arguments of plays; ... Nor in our age ... has the practice entirely ceased; ... Telesius ... and Campanella have come upon the stage with fresh stories, neither honoured by approbation nor elegant in argument. .... Each has his favourite fancy; pure and open light there is none; every one philosophises out of the cells of his own imagination, as out of Plato's cave.

For Bacon, a system should spring not from the imagination but from the observation of nature. In the inductive method which Bacon preached, general principles arose from the study of a large number of particular experiments. However, Bacon realized that this alone was not enough: the scientist must then proceed back again from generals to particulars to carry out further experiments and gain fresh insights: 'For our road does not lie on a level, but ascends and descends; first ascending to axioms, then descending to works.' This method would achieve 'a true and perfect marriage between the empirical and rational faculty ... building in the human understanding a true model of the world' and leading to valuable inventions.

The House of Salomon is the very embodiment of Bacon's scientific method. The division of labour among the thirty-six Fellows (according to Judaic belief, thirty-six just men sustain the world) creates a highly centralized scientific organization. Each post to which the Fellows are assigned contributes a single step to the whole inductive process, in effect institutionalizing it. Thus, the Merchants of Light, as we have seen, voyage around the world to gather books and other information; Depredators and Mystery-men collect all the experiments outlined in the books and elsewhere; Pioneers or Miners carry out selected experiments, while Compilers classify and list these 'to give the better light for the drawing of observations and axioms out of them'. Dowry-men or Benefactors observe the experiments and study the results in order to determine how these might benefit men's lives and contribute to knowledge. At this stage all the Fellows meet in order to discuss the findings so far, after which the Lamps direct new experiments 'more penetrating into nature than the former' which are performed by Inoculators. Finally, Interpreters of Nature use the results of these experiments to derive greater observations and scientific axioms.

Bacon's description of the College of the Six Days' Works is perhaps the most important passage in all utopian writing. Bacon was the first person to delineate the fundamental methodology of modern science. The late twentieth-century research laboratory may not compartmentalize its activities so rigidly as Salomon's House (nor assign its scientists such catchy titles), but it follows basically the same procedure: the literature search to check that no one else has answered the question already; the design of the experiment; the analysis of the data to draw a tentative conclusion; the hurried fax to the patent lawyer; the assembly of the distinguished luminaries on the funding council; the authorization of further more penetrating (and expensive) investigations; and, finally, perhaps, the acceptance of a new generalizing theory. Bacon's genius was to perceive the power of this interplay between experiment and theory, and to realize that knowledge based upon, and verified against, not 'the cells of [the] imagination', but the observation of Nature, could be collective. He grasped that his scientific method could harness the individual mind of the scientist to a greater, shared quest, and that the power of the communal enterprise of science would transform the world.

To put it simply, the scientist in *New Atlantis* has replaced the philosopher ruler of Plato's *Republic*. As early as 1603 Bacon had compared the value of the inventor's work with that of the hero and lawgiver, whose contribution lasted only a short while, whereas 'the work of the Inventor . . . is felt everywhere and lasts forever'. Thus, in the two long galleries in Salomon's House, statues of the principal inventors and explorers have pride of place, along with cases displaying their inventions and discoveries – no statesmen or lawgivers are so honoured.

As we have noted, *New Atlantis* was intended primarily as a work of propaganda, to 'draw men's minds' to Bacon's scheme. And for the Lord Chancellor, the establishment of something like the College of the Six Days' Works was a central concern of his political career. In a private memorandum of 1608, Bacon considered the possibility of setting up a research institute, at Westminster, Eton, Winchester or, preferably, Trinity College, Cambridge, where he could command both 'wits and pens'. But Bacon, writing before Galileo had published his most important work and two generations before the brilliant successes of Newtonian physics demonstrated the power of experimental science, was ahead of his time.

> It deserveth not to be read in Schooles
> But to be freighted in the ship of Fooles

was the comment scribbled by Sir Edward Coke in the copy of the

Novum Organum which Bacon presented to him, above the engraving of the ship passing through the Pillars of Hercules. King James I was overheard to remark that Bacon's book, like the peace of God, 'passeth all understanding'.

It was only after the tumults of the English Civil War and Cromwell's Protectorate that Bacon's vision became a reality. Although, as Samuel Pepys noted in his diary, the newly restored Charles II 'mightily laughed at [the scientists of] Gresham College for spending time only in weighing of ayre, and doing nothing els since they sat', he had a keen interest in science, weighing himself before and after a game of tennis. The King also wanted to create an English learned society to rival the renowned French Academy. Thus in 1662 he chartered the Royal Society, whose object was, according to the Society's first historian, Thomas Sprat, 'to overcome the mysteries of all the Works of Nature', and to apply this knowledge 'for the Benefit of humane life'. Its Fellows 'have contriv'd in their thoughts, and courageously begun an *Attempt*, which all *Ages* had despair'd of' with the same spirit of tolerance as portrayed in *New Atlantis*, 'freely admitt[ing] Men of different Religions, Countries, and Professions of Life'.

All scholars agree that Francis Bacon was the source of inspiration for the Royal Society; they only argue about the degree of his influence. In 1665 Joseph Glanvill remarked: 'Solomons House in the *New Atlantis* was a Prophetick Scheam of the Royal Society.' Thomas Sprat states that the Royal Society owed its inspiration to Bacon, to the 'one great Man, who had the true Imagination of the whole extent of this Enterprize, as it is now set on foot'. Abraham Cowley, a botanist, contributed an ode to Sprat's *History of the Royal Society* which rhapsodizes:

> Bacon, like Moses, led us forth at last,
> The barren Wilderness he past,
> Did on the very Border stand
> Of the blest promis'd Land,
> And from the Mountains Top of his Exalted Wit,
> Saw it himself and shew'd us it.

The engraved title page shows Bacon sitting beside the bust of Charles II.

The Royal Society had its critics – and its problems, some of which were inherent in Bacon's model of the House of Salomon. People were eager for results, but Bacon's methodical gathering of information had the same disadvantages as entering masses of data into a computer today: the process can be tedious and slow going; real progress has to await that flash of insight which is the true stuff of science. Christopher Wren, a member of the Royal Society, explained that 'in many Things we must be content to plant Crab stocks for Posterity to graft on [crab-apple trees often served as the original stock for more desirable strains of apples].'

The founders of the Royal Society had hoped that it would follow *New Atlantis* in having monetary rewards for useful inventions as well as the financial support from the government which the Fellows of the House of Salomon obviously enjoyed. Although Bacon had believed, with King Solamona, that 'it is the glory of God to conceal a thing, but the glory of a king to search it out', Charles II would not fund the Royal Society. But the new breed of gentleman scientist, imbued with the English amateur spirit, persevered in the belief

> ... that the most *profitable* Tryals are not always the most *costly*: that the best Inventions have not been found out by the *richest*, but by the most *prudent*, and *Industrious* Observers: that the right Art of *Experimenting*, when it is once set forward, will go near to sustain it self. This I speak, not to stop mens future Bounty, by a Philosophical Boast, that the *Royal Society* has enough already: But rather to encourage them to cast in more help; by shewing them, what return may be made from a little, by a wise administration.

In spreading the idea of the value of experimental science throughout society, Bacon had founded the English empirical tradition without which the first – British – Industrial Revolution could never have happened. Throughout the eighteenth and nineteenth centuries gentlemen of independent means, even aristocratic landowners, contributed to the rapid development of science, engineering and agriculture. Bacon, Lord Chancellor and Viscount St Albans, had made experimentation respectable.

Bacon was a typical utopian in his belief that to bring about real change men must start again from scratch:

> It is idle to expect any great advancement in science from the superinducing and engrafting of new things upon old. We must begin anew from the very foundations, unless we would revolve for ever in a circle with mean and contemptible progress.

But, in contrast with all previous attempts at ideal worlds, Bacon's *New Atlantis* is not a static society, certainly not in its scientific community. Bacon made philosophy, for the first time, not just the love of truth but also the ally of progress for the benefit of man. Whereas the question which had dogged Plato and Thomas More was whether the highest life was to be found in contemplation or public service, Bacon makes the two not only compatible but inseparable. In *New Atlantis* the things that are of greatest service to mankind are the inventions and axioms which are arrived at through contemplation. Science, therefore, constitutes the highest good.

Bacon had a very high reputation among the French *philosophes* of the eighteenth century. In his introduction to the *Encyclopédie*, Jean le Rond d'Alembert praises Bacon's bold claim that philosophy 'did not yet exist'. Rousseau called him 'perhaps the greatest of philosophers'. He even captured the imagination of the English Romantics: Shelley wrote that Bacon's 'eagle spirit soared'. H. G. Wells called *New Atlantis* the first of the truly modern utopias, remarking 'that Utopia of Bacon's has produced more in the way of real consequences than any other Utopia that was ever written.'

But not everyone has admired *New Atlantis*, finding its exaltation of a scientific élite sinister. The Fellows of the House of Salomon distrust government so much that they

> . . . have consultations, which of the inventions and experiences which we have discovered shall be published, and which not: and take all an oath of secrecy, for the concealing of those which we think fit to keep secret: though some of those we do reveal sometimes to the state, and some not.

This is the most controversial passage in *New Atlantis*. To some, Bacon was simply being prescient, anticipating the moral dilemmas which would haunt scientists. (Would the option to keep their discoveries secret from the state have allowed the scientists on the Manhattan project to master atomic fission without destroying Hiroshima?) To others, Bacon raises the spectre of a scientific establishment pursuing clandestine experiments without any thought of the consequences or morality of their actions, a state of affairs that could eventually lead to atrocities like the Nazi scientists' experiments in the death camps. Robert Oppenheimer, the American physicist who led the project which developed the atomic bomb, had no illusions about the motivation of real scientists:

When you see something that is technically sweet, you go ahead and do it and then argue about what to do about it only after you have had your technological success. That is the way it was with atomic power.

Bacon admits that the Fellows of the House of Salomon are not infallible. They are susceptible to the temptation to fake their results, and the society, which hates 'all impostures and lies', has 'severely forbidden it to all our fellows, under pain of ignominy and fines, that they do not shew any natural work or thing, adorned or swelling'. For Bacon, the only source of intellectual and moral integrity can be religion. He clearly states the limitations of scientific aspiration:

The first, that we do not so place our felicity in knowledge, as we forget our mortality; the second, that we make application of our knowledge to give ourselves repose and contentment, and not distaste or repining; the third, that we do not presume by the contemplation of nature to attain to the mysteries of God.

Today, we inhabit a world created by science, where the products of technology have, as Bacon thought they would, ameliorated many of the social problems that afflicted the society of his day. But lately, many people have begun to grow wary of the gifts that science offers us, perceiving a hidden price that may not be worth paying. The biologist Sir Peter Medawar likened such people to bad workmen blaming their tools. He never ceased to believe in Bacon's view that scientific learning would make the world a better place: 'To deride the hope of progress is the ultimate fatuity, the last word in poverty of spirit and meanness of mind.' Progress, Medawar argues, quoting Thomas Hobbes's *Leviathan*, is part of our very nature:

There is no such thing as perpetual tranquillity of mind while we live here because life itself is but motion, and can never be without desire, or without fear, no more than without sense . . . there can be no contentment but in proceeding.

This, above all, was Bacon's message too.

6. The Religion of Newton

If Bacon was the first philosopher of the Age of Science, Isaac Newton was its greatest hero. His discoveries in physics and mathematics seemed to bring order out of chaos. Alexander Pope expressed a sense of Newton's cosmic significance when he wrote his famous couplet:

> Nature and Nature's laws lay hid in night:
> God said, *Let Newton be!* and all was light.

Newtonian mechanics revealed a harmonious universe operating according to simple and intelligible laws, eternal and benign, the ultimate expression of a beneficent Creator imbued with justice and rationality. As described by Newton, the handiwork of God pre-ordained the values of the Enlightenment.

But the order of the cosmos contrasted sadly with the ruinous disorder and injustice of terrestrial affairs. To many utopians, the remedy seemed obvious: seek to understand, and thereby solve, the problems of society by applying the methods of scientific inquiry advocated by Bacon and so triumphantly implemented by Newton (who quite explicitly claimed to have followed Baconian practice). Thus Utopia became scientific and the social sciences were born.

The first utopian to envision such a social science was Henri de Saint-Simon. Born in 1760 into one of France's most blue-blooded aristocratic families, which claimed direct descent from Charlemagne, Saint-Simon was a child of the Enlightenment: he met Rousseau and was tutored by d'Alembert, Denis Diderot's 'co-conspirator' in the great project of the French *philosophes*, the *Encyclopédie*. He later remarked of his generation that their education had made 'revolutionaries' of them.

Saint-Simon's rebellion began early: at thirteen he refused to take his first communion because he thought it a meaningless act. In 1777, at the age of sixteen, he entered the army as a second lieutenant, and in 1781, having risen to the rank of captain, he fought under General Washington against the British at Yorktown. His participation in the American War of Independence was an inspiration, as he later recorded:

I occupied myself much more with political science than with military tactics. . . . To study the advance of the human mind in order subsequently to work for the improvement of civilisation: that was the aim I set myself.

In America he had seen the basis of 'a regime infinitely more liberal and more democratic than the one under which the peoples of Europe lived'.

Before he returned to France, Saint-Simon travelled to Mexico and conceived of an extraordinarily ambitious plan to build a canal across the Isthmus of Panama, linking the Atlantic and Pacific Oceans. The Viceroy of Mexico, to whom Saint-Simon offered the idea, turned it down, but such schemes for the modernization of transport and communications would remain dear to the Frenchman's heart. On his return to Europe, he eagerly took up the Spanish government's challenge to construct a canal between Madrid and the Atlantic Ocean. However, events at home in France made the project impossible, and Saint-Simon returned to a nation in the grip of revolution.

At the beginning of the French Revolution, Saint-Simon was made president of the municipal assembly of his home district Falvy, where his goal in office was 'to organise a great industrial establishment, to found a scientific school of improvement'. His efforts to raise finances for this project were threatened by the growing political turmoil, and he realized that, as an aristocrat, he was a prime candidate for Robespierre's guillotine. He renounced his aristocratic title in a ceremony of 'republican baptism' but, despite this precaution, was imprisoned by the secret police as a 'counter-revolutionary'.

Saint-Simon managed to survive the Revolution and set out on a number of different careers – as a wine merchant, a trader on the Paris corn-exchange and a manufacturer of republican playing cards, in which the King, Queen and Knave were replaced by representations of Genius, Liberty and Equality. However, by 1798, all these ventures had ended in failure, and with what little money he had salvaged, he devoted himself to his great passion, science.

Saint-Simon enrolled in courses in physics and mathematics at the École Polytechnique, but perhaps the most important part of his studies was in physiology at the École de Médecine, for this was to lead him to his theory of social organization, or 'social physiology'. Saint-Simon came to view man's history as falling into three distinct stages: the polytheism of Greece and Rome, the Christian monotheism of the Middle Ages and the positivism of the Enlightenment, that is the reliance on positive fact, observable phenomena and the laws which govern them. Saint-Simon believed that the great upheavals of the French Revolution had marked the changeover from a theological-feudal society, dominated by the priestly and military ruling classes, to the new (and by implication better) social order.

This theory of historical change anticipates Karl Marx, for whom each phase of history was defined by the economic relations between classes; for Saint-Simon the characteristics of each period were primarily ideological and doctrinal. In Marxist theory the engine of historical change is economics; for Saint-Simon it was the advancement of scientific knowledge, which forced in turn a renewal of the moral foundations of society. Common to both men, however, was the idea that history should be understood as an orderly and essentially predictable progression of distinct epochs which were moving inevitably towards the creation of Utopia.

Unlike Marx, Saint-Simon hoped that the times of revolution were in the past; where the example of the American Revolution had inspired him with hope, the French one filled him with dread. 'The philosophy of the last century was revolutionary; that of the nineteenth century must be organisational,' he declared. He saw contemporary Europe seized by a new and potentially dangerous class conflict between property holders, non-property holders and a floating intellectual class. (The 'bourgeois' class of idle landowners, soldiers and lawyers would, according to Saint-Simon, eventually dissolve away.) His mission in life was to issue warnings and guidelines to the property holders in order to prevent revolution among the masses. 'Obey history or be crushed by it,' Saint-Simon declared in 1803 in *Lettres d'un Habitant de Genève à ses Contemporains* ('Letters of an Inhabitant of Geneva to his Contemporaries').

Saint-Simon wanted to enlist the aid of all the sciences, and to this end he petitioned Napoleon to implement Bacon's scheme for the total systemization of knowledge under the control of the 'Council of Newton' – a tribute to the great scientist. In *Lettres d'un Habitant de Genève* he calls upon his contemporaries to subscribe money at Newton's tomb to the most distinguished scientists and artists of the day, the fund to be administered by the President of the Royal Society of London. Saint-Simon's immediate aim was to endow the savants, the scientists and artists, with the sort of financial resources hitherto enjoyed by the Church. Indeed, the ultimate goal was nothing less than the establishment of a totally new religion, one in accord with the level of enlightenment achieved by mankind.

Saint-Simon therefore advocates the transformation of his association of savants into the 'Religion of Newton', organized like the Catholic faith on an international basis, and administered by the world's most eminent scientists and artists. Though this proposal may strike us as rather fanciful, we should remember that the French Revolution saw various attempts to establish new cults to replace Catholicism – Robespierre's 'Cult of the Supreme Being', for example. However, Napoleon's Concordat with the Vatican soon made it clear that the authorities were no longer interested in supplanting the Church. Saint-Simon, therefore, quietly dropped the anti-Christian aspects of the Religion of Newton and recast it as a programme for increasing the spiritual influence of science rather than a formal institution to rival the Church.

Saint-Simon's social science, as an empirical science, was founded on Baconian principles: he believed that the study of man and society must be based entirely on experiment and observation. In his investigations, he strove to follow the 'golden rule' of science: 'Man should believe only those things avowed by reason and confirmed by experience.' Only by this approach, Saint-Simon argued, could mankind develop a general theory of history which would reveal the fundamental causes of historical change, a theory with the power to predict the future as well as explain the past; for the causes of future events must exist in the present time, and these should be observable and analysable on a scientific basis.

The agents of change that would cause society to move towards the new order were to be science and industry. As we have seen, Saint-Simon thought to invest the spiritual power of his new society in a 'priesthood of scientists'; the temporal power would be in the hands of the economic administrators or 'industrials'. Although initially the 'priesthood of scientists' was to be the central authority, as in Bacon's *New Atlantis*, over the years Saint-Simon came to bestow greater power upon the industrialists, for it was their economic activity which fed and clothed all other members of society, including the scientists. These 'captains of industry' would have a 'hands off' policy: 'Governments will no longer command men; their functions will be limited to ensuring that useful work is not hindered.' One historian remarks that 'the idea of a transition from arbitrary government to scientific administration was almost certainly derived, at least in part, by Saint-Simon from Bacon's argument that a truly scientific society can dispense with power politics.' The Marxist slogan 'From the government of men to the administration of things' and the concept of the 'abolition of the state', are drawn from Saint-Simon's ideas.

However, Saint-Simon did not advocate a communistic society, nor was he a free-marketeer. He wanted to put the national budget in the hands of the experts, believing that this would ensure a low-maintenance, low-tax economy. The law on property should be reformed 'to render it most favourable to production'. Thus, farmers would be given entrepreneurial rights over landed property. Public revenue would not be wasted on the army, police or courts, but invested in science and industry to promote social welfare, transport and communications schemes, and useful employment; for the main tenet of Saint-Simon's new social order was 'All men will work. They will all regard themselves as workers attached to a workshop.' More and Campanella had looked upon work as a necessity; Saint-Simon considered it a basic human right:

> The most direct way to bring about an improvement in the moral and physical well-being of the majority of the population is to give priority in State expenditure to the provision of work for all fit men, so as to assure their physical existence; to disseminate as quickly as possible among the proletarian class the positive knowledge which has been acquired; and finally to ensure that the individuals composing this class have forms of leisure and interests which will develop their intelligence.

Work created social cohesion; thus, in Saint-Simon's industrial society, an atmosphere of harmony and co-operation would exist between industrialists and workers, and class war could be avoided. Unlike Marx, Saint-Simon believed that class differences were a necessary part of society.

Saint-Simon outlined a number of specific proposals for the reorganization of existing political institutions to create his utopia. One, set out in the journal *L'Organisateur* in 1819, called for the transformation of the Chamber of Deputies (the French equivalent of the House of Commons) into an industrial chamber, to be called the 'Chamber of Execution', composed of the heads of industry and elected by industrials. There was also to be a 'Chamber of Invention', consisting of artists and engineers, whose chief tasks were to be 'drainage, land clearance, road building, [and] the opening up of canals [which] will be considered the most important part of this project'. It would also be responsible for organizing the 'festival of hope', to encourage the people to co-operate with the plans for public works, and the 'festival of remembrance', to 'show the people how their present position is better than that of their ancestors'. The third and last chamber, the 'Chamber of Examination', made up of scientists, was to examine all the projects proposed by the Chamber of Invention, organize festivals for specialist groups (such as children, mothers and workers), and oversee education. The education system was to be divided into three grades, for citizens of three different levels of wealth. 'Its aim will be to ensure that young people are as capable as possible of conceiving, directing and carrying out useful work.'

Saint-Simon saw his general system being adopted throughout industrialized Europe. The interdependency between nations which would inevitably result, together with vast improvements in the transport and communications network, would make co-operation necessary if peace were to be maintained and nationalist rivalries suppressed. In a booklet entitled *De la Réorganisation de la Société Européenne* ('On the Reorganization of European Society'), Saint-Simon envisioned a formal European federation:

> Europe would have the best possible organisation if all its constituent nations were governed by parliaments, and if they recognised the supremacy of a common parliament set above all national governments and invested with the powers of settling their disputes.

The first step towards that goal was to be an *entente cordiale* between England and France. Saint-Simon had declared confidently:

> There will undoubtedly come a time when all the peoples of Europe will feel that questions of common interest must be dealt with before coming down to national interests. Then evils will begin to lessen, troubles abate, wars die out. That is the goal towards which we are ceaselessly moving, towards which the advance of the human mind is carrying us! But which is more worthy of man's prudence: to be dragged there or to hasten towards it?

Saint-Simon published *De la Réorganisation* in 1814 to coincide with the Congress of Vienna, whose delegates were determining the shape of Europe after the Napoleonic Wars. Nothing came of Saint-Simon's ideas in the nineteenth century. However, his utopian scheme was never entirely forgotten, and he can claim to be the intellectual father of the European Community.

From about 1820, Saint-Simon returned to his original idea of scientists taking on a priestly role in society, though this time he envisioned his religion not as an alternative to Christianity, as before, but as the *true* Christianity. He wrote in 1821:

> I believe that the new spiritual power will be composed at first of all the existing Academies of Science in Europe, and of all persons who deserve to be admitted to these scientific corporations. . . . I believe that the direction of education, as well as of public teaching, will be entrusted to this new spiritual power. I believe that the pure morality of the Gospel will serve as the basis of the new public education, and that, for the rest, it will be pushed as far as possible in conformity with positive knowledge. . . . Finally, I believe that the new spiritual power will settle a fairly large number of its members throughout all the communes, and that the principal mission of these detached scholars will be to inspire their spiritual charges with a passion for the public good.

It was this new Christianity which Saint-Simon's disciples took hold of and refined after the master's death in May 1825. The charismatic leader of the Saint-Simonians, Barthélemy Prosper Enfantin, formed the movement into a Church, with himself and one other as 'Supreme Fathers'. The sect was much more critical of the institution of private property than Saint-Simon ever was, and, in effect, advocated a collectivist society. The Saint-Simonians also added a psychological dimension to Saint-Simon's labour theories. They asserted that human personalities are of three basic types, those naturally given to scientific, artistic or manual work, and emphasized that allocating the right job to the right man was a simple matter which would ensure individual happiness and industrial efficiency. Their views struck a chord, and by mid-1831 the Saint-Simonians numbered 40,000. Among their admirers and supporters were John Stuart Mill, Thomas Carlyle, George Sand, Hector Berlioz and Franz Liszt.

The Saint-Simonians established a utopian community at Ménilmontant, outside Paris. Here they practised their religion, wore red, white and blue uniforms, and followed Saint-Simon's dictum 'All men will work'. The days were punctuated by parades, recitations, songs and symbolic events. The community became something of a tourist attraction: up to 10,000 Parisians gathered behind a ribbon to watch the sons of respected families work the land like peasants. However, Enfantin began to advocate free love as a replacement for the institution of monogamous marriage. He also began a quixotic search for the female Messiah, 'the emancipator of her sex', but in vain.

These views on sexual liberation were too extreme for many Saint-Simonians and for the French authorities. In 1832 the Saint-Simonians of Ménilmontant were charged with outrages against public morals and brought to trial. They conducted their own defence, often using crude and graphic imagery. At one point the judge declared: 'The defense is degenerating into a scandal.' Enfantin was sentenced to a year in gaol.

After his release Enfantin, along with many other ex-Saint-Simonians, began to work towards Saint-Simon's original aspirations, taking up careers in industry to promote the large-scale projects of which Saint-Simon had only dreamed. As one historian puts it, these 'visionaries soon became the architects of French capitalism, the planners and entrepreneurs'. Enfantin led the way with the construction of a railway network in France and in many other countries of Europe. Other former Saint-Simonians founded the Crédit Mobilier bank in order to aid economic expansion and industrialization in France. Finally, the technical scheme dearest to Saint-Simon's heart, the building of a large waterway, was realized in the Suez Canal (opened 1869), the brainchild of the one-time Saint-Simonian, Ferdinand de Lesseps. (De Lesseps later set about constructing a Panama Canal, Saint-Simon's original idea, but the project ended in failure owing to unfamiliarity with the terrain, corruption and yellow fever.)

It has often been observed that modern French society has two salient characteristics that set it apart from other European countries: its centralized state planning and a certain love affair with technology. The *dirigisme* is usually identified as a product of the French absolutist tradition as refined by Napoleon, and the technophilia ascribed to the pen of Jules Verne. But surely Saint-Simon is also an important influence. His dream of a technologically orientated state, decisively planned by scientists and industrialists, boldly undertaking ambitious public works, but also concerned with the careful education of the succeeding élite, seems to prefigure many of the distinguishing features of modern France. Saint-Simon would surely have applauded the French government's decision, apparently taken at one cabinet meeting, to respond to the oil crisis of the early 1970s by replacing virtually all the country's power stations with nuclear reactors; he would certainly have admired the single-mindedness with which that goal has been pursued. It is perhaps not too far-fetched to see the Minitel computer screens attached to many French telephones and the TGV slicing orthogonally across the French countryside as late-blooming flowers of Saint-Simon's utopian vision.

As we have noted, Saint-Simon's hero was Newton: the English scientist also inspired Saint-Simon's contemporary, Charles Fourier, whom we met briefly in Chapter 4. Fourier claimed that four apples had been famous – or infamous – in history: 'Two were famous by the disasters which they caused, that of Adam and that of Paris, and two by services rendered to mankind, Newton's and my own.' Fourier's apple cost him fourteen sous in a Paris restaurant, when he knew that elsewhere the same amount bought a hundred apples. He concluded that something was wrong with the world:

> From that moment were born the investigations which, at the end of four years, made me discover the theory of industrial series and groups and subsequently the laws of universal movement missed by Newton.

Fourier believed that his law of 'passionate attraction', that is, the tendency of every passion naturally to seek its own gratification, was analogous to gravitational attraction in the physical world. Just as Newton's discovery of gravity had enabled him to perceive the orderly structure of the cosmos, so Fourier believed that his discovery of this fundamental psychological law would reveal an equally harmonious social order.

Fourier, born in Besançon in 1772, was the son of a prosperous cloth merchant and a prudish, stingy and extremely pious mother. At the age of seven Fourier was so terrified by the idea of Hell that he confessed to fornication and simony just as an insurance policy. At this same age he swore an 'Hannibalic oath' against commerce, vowing never to enter his father's business. As a child he preferred music, drawing, arithmetic and flowers. Nevertheless, after several attempts to escape his fate, Fourier was forced to follow in his father's footsteps. In 1791, in the midst of the French Revolution, he was apprenticed to a cloth merchant in Lyon, a career which he continued to loathe but which paid the bills. His experience as a travelling salesman gave him a valuable insight not only into the economic situation in France, but into that of Europe as a whole.

During these years of revolution, Fourier saw a country afflicted with unemployment, poverty and class conflict. Following Lyon's unsuccessful rebellion against the revolutionary government, Fourier lost most of his inheritance and nearly forfeited his life. Like Saint-Simon, his experiences of the French Revolution gave him a lasting horror of social upheaval. Fourier, who lived alone in boarding houses, kept cats and cultivated flowers, spent all his spare time setting down the theories which, he passionately believed, would relieve man's misery. He wrote:

It is a *shop sergeant* who is going to confound all the weighty tomes of political and moral wisdom. . . . Eh! This is not the first time that God has made use of a humble agent to bring low the mighty.

In his efforts to find a patron, Fourier sent copies of his works, including *Le Nouveau Monde Industriel* ('The New Industrial World'), to princes, bankers, academicians, scientists, Madame de Staël and Lady Byron. He returned to his boarding house each day at noon to greet the hoped-for benefactor – who never came.

The cantankerous Fourier had no time for either Saint-Simon or his disciples: he claimed that, whereas the Saint-Simonians were trying to change human nature, he was 'the only reformer who has rallied round human nature by accepting it as it is'. He despised as hypocrites those, including Saint-Simon, who tried to fool people into loving their work as a social duty. Civilization had played a dirty trick on mankind by making work a 'veritable industrial hell'. Men and women suffered long hours 'crouched in an unhealthy workshop' – yet, at the same time, there never seemed to be enough work to go around, as was evident from the problem of chronic unemployment. Fourier considered 'the first of the natural rights [to be] the RIGHT TO WORK', not because it created social cohesion, as Saint-Simon claimed, but because it fulfilled a natural passion. Fourier set out '*To find a new Social Order* that insures the poorest members of the working class sufficient well-being to make them constantly and passionately prefer their work to idleness and brigandage to which they now aspire.' As one scholar states: 'Fourier offered to do no less than to free man from the biblical curse, to liberate him from work that was painful, enslaving, and destructive of his integrity.'

Fourier's utopia, which he dubbed Harmony, rested on the notion of 'industrial attraction' or 'attractive labour'. As we saw in Chapter 4, he conceived of establishing small co-operative communities or associations, which he called phalanxes. Labour wages were to be abolished; instead, all members of the phalanx were to receive dividends proportional to their contributions in work, capital and talent, something like a joint-stock company. Labour would be made attractive by allowing men to work at as many tasks as they liked, in a group with friends and lovers who were attracted to each other, the work itself and its product. The system promised a 'social minimum', that is a guaranteed annual income, to provide both economic and psychological security. Fourier believed that a child's education should allow the unrestricted development of an individual's natural passions, and to this end encouraged a progressive curriculum which included 'FERRETING, or the penchant for handling things, exploring, running around, and constantly changing activities . . . Industrial *din*, the taste for noisy jobs . . . [and] *Aping*, or the imitative mania'.

The basic mechanism behind Fourier's system was the 'passionate series', which he defined as a 'league of various groups, graduated in ascending and descending order, passionately joined together because they share a common liking for some task, such as the cultivation of a fruit'. Workers had to be 'passionately engaged' in their job, not forced into it by motives of 'need, morality, reason, duty and constraint'. Inequality and competitiveness within a series were a good thing, as they stimulated creativity. In fact, every sort of character was accommodated, including the 'Butterfly' type who had a short attention span and liked to 'flutter about from pleasure to pleasure'. Thus, in *Le Nouveau Monde Industriel* Fourier describes how a typical 'Butterfly', the rich Mondor, enjoys a busy, fun-filled schedule, beginning at 3.30 a.m. and ending at 10.30 p.m., which comprises five meals, mass, two public functions, a concert or some such entertainment, an hour and a half at the library, plus his eight tasks for the day: hunting, fishing, gardening and tending pheasants, fish-tanks, sheep and two different greenhouses. Fourier adds: 'It is obvious from this description that only a few moments are left for sleep. Harmonians sleep very little.'

Once the system in Harmony was running like clockwork, Fourier foresaw the creation of 'armies', not military but industrial. Women would work alongside men in corps, which would be organized, naturally, according to each member's capacities and inclinations. Fourier was an early environmentalist, and, like President Franklin Roosevelt's Civilian Conservation Corps a century later, the major tasks undertaken by Fourier's 'troops' were reforestation, bridge-building, and land reclamation. Fourier reckoned that civilization had so ravaged the earth that it would 'take at least a hundred years' to reforest the Alps and Pyrenees. In addition, he preferred horticultural work to manufacturing. To reduce the need for it, he determined that goods produced at Harmony would be durable and well made. Those factories which were necessary should be made elegant and luxurious by features such as marble veneers. As for the nasty jobs which no one wants to do – those 'foul functions' such as cleaning sewers and slaughterhouses – Fourier made them the responsibility of a special corps of the industrial army, the 'Little Hordes', also known as 'God's Militia'. The Little Hordes were made up of boys from the ages of nine to fifteen, who were 'unruly, peevish, scurrilous and overbearing' and loved to 'wallow in the mire and play with dirty things'.

In their different ways, both Fourier and Saint-Simon were inspired by the intellectual triumphs of Newtonian physics. But as the nineteenth century wore on the products of the Industrial, rather than the Scientific, Revolution were coming to dominate civilization. It was natural that utopians should take industry as a model for society: the mechanization of labour had increased its output by prodigious amounts; could not the same organizational principles be applied to social relations in order to improve the workings of the state to the benefit of all its citizens? However to some eyes this utopian vision was fatally flawed. With the growth of factory and office-based wage labour, the worker acquired a double aspect, as producer and consumer. The danger was that the very productivity of the industrial society would smother the human spirit under a comfortable blanket of material abundance, reducing the citizen to a passive recipient of largesse: not Utopia, but Cockaigne. This argument underlies much of the contemporary debate about the 'consumer society', and its origins can be traced to William Morris's reaction to Edward Bellamy's utopian romance *Looking Backward*.

Bellamy's book, as we noted in Chapter 4, was published in Boston in 1888; and it soon became, after *Uncle Tom's Cabin*, the bestselling novel of the century in America, and only the second novel in American literature to sell a million copies. Bellamy's hero, Julian West, is an independently wealthy and well-educated member of late nineteenth-century Boston society. He admits, 'Living in luxury, and occupied only with the pursuit of the pleasures and refinements of life, I derived the means of my support from the labor of others, rendering no sort of service in return.'

In 1887, at the age of thirty, West is engaged to the beautiful and equally upper-crust Edith Bartlett. But the date of the marriage keeps having to be put back owing to delays in completing a new house for the couple. 'The cause of a delay,' West states, 'calculated to be particularly exasperating to an ardent lover was a series of strikes, that is to say, concerted refusals to work on the part of the bricklayers, masons, carpenters, painters, plumbers, and other trades concerned in house-building.' However, something rather more extreme is about to part the lovers for ever. One evening, West, a chronic insomniac, descends into his subterranean chamber, a cellar well insulated against outside noise and damp, and calls for Dr Pillsbury, a 'Professor of Animal Magnetism', to hypnotize him into a deep sleep, as Pillsbury often does. On this occasion the doctor evidently overdoes things, for the next thing West knows, he has woken up in the year 2000.

His twentieth-century host, Dr Leete, explains that he came upon the subterranean vault – and West, still in a trance, his body perfectly preserved – while digging foundations for an underground laboratory in his back yard. The rest of the novel is largely a dialogue between Leete and West on the workings of the future society and its improvements upon West's own time, interrupted periodically by a blossoming romance between West and Leete's charming daughter, Edith (coincidentally the great-granddaughter of West's nineteenth-century fiancée). As its title implies, *Looking Backward* is supposedly written from the standpoint of the dawn of the twenty-first century, where West has become, appropriately, a professor of history.

From the perspective of his times, at the height of the Industrial Revolution, Bellamy was able to envision a bigger 'pie in the sky' than any of his predecessors in Utopia. Bacon had foreseen that the central concern of society would become not the redistribution of the same modest pie, but how technology could guarantee a bigger pie – plenty for everyone. Yet for Bellamy, technology on its own was not enough; society itself must mirror the efficiency of the machine. Dr Leete remarks to West that the nineteenth-century corporations had 'the military efficiency of a mob, or a horde of barbarians'; for 'Competition, which is the instinct of selfishness, is another word for the dissipation of energy, while combination is the secret of efficient production.' According to Bellamy, the capitalist system is far from efficient; in fact, it is incredibly wasteful owing to mistaken undertakings, competition and mutual hostility in industry, periodic crises in the economy and the permanent problem of idle capital and labour.

Both efficiency and production had been increased, explains Dr Leete, when the nation, in a peaceful transition process, became the 'one capitalist', the 'sole employer', in the monopoly to end all monopolies: 'The epoch of trusts had ended in The Great Trust.' This had come about, according to Leete, 'as the result of a process of industrial evolution which could not have terminated otherwise. All that society had to do was to recognize and cooperate with that evolution, when its tendency had become unmistakable.' The people of the United States are 'organizing now for industrial purposes on precisely the same grounds that they had then organized for political purposes'.

In *Looking Backward*, Bellamy describes a society which has followed the prescription: 'From the governing of men to the administration of things.' Dr Leete explains to West that 'almost the sole function of the administration now is that of directing the industries of the country.' This 'machine . . . is indeed a vast one, but so logical in its principles and direct and simple in its workings, that it all but runs itself': its only source of fuel is statistics. Thus Boston in the year 2000 has achieved Saint-Simon's goal of the 'abolition of the state': there are no parties or politicians, no legislation (which means no lawyers), and no Internal Revenue Service.

By the year 2000, with this 'prodigious increase of efficiency', industry is able to provide goods in abundance and 'the wealth of the world had increased at a rate before undreamed of . . . the organization of the industry of the nation under a single control, so that all its processes interlock, has multiplied the total product over the utmost that could be done under the former system.' People no longer have to be abstemious in their day-to-day living, as in More's Utopia where fashions never change and clothes are strictly sensible and hard-wearing. In answer to West's comment that Leete's society does not seem to encourage thrift, his host replies: 'The nation is rich, and does not wish the people to deprive themselves of any good thing.'

The year 2000 is duly cluttered with innovations and gadgets – though many are patently unscientific. Awnings automatically cover the sidewalks in bad weather. Charge cards (made of pasteboard) replace money – Bellamy even foresaw American Express: 'An American credit card . . . is just as good in Europe as American gold used to be.' Goods are selected at local 'shopping malls', the orders are sent to a central warehouse, from where the shipments, no matter what size, are prepared and delivered – all through a system of pneumatic tubes (the implication is that the ground below Boston is a rabbit warren of these tubes, large and small). Bellamy anticipated electricity and even Radio Three, with a small selection of good music piped into every room: a great improvement over the musical evenings in one's parlour with Aunt Bess and Cousin Harriet playing a duet. This 'radio' can even be rigged to give wake-up calls. Thus the society which greets Julian West at the start of the twenty-first century resembles nothing more closely than a gigantic machine, linked by pneumatic arteries.

The cornerstone of Bellamy's utopia is the industrial army, an idea borrowed directly from Fourier. Bellamy compares this huge, quasi-military body, to which every member of society belongs, to 'a disciplined army under one general – such a fighting machine, for example, as the German army in the time of Von Moltke [the Franco-Prussian War of 1870–71]'. Everyone serves in this army between the ages of twenty-one and forty-five years old. Vocational training and apprenticeships are provided: 'A man's natural endowments, mental and physical, determine what he can work at most profitably to the nation and most satisfactorily to himself.' The number of hours to be spent at work are determined by the job's appeal, evident from the level of demand for that particular kind of work – the less popular the job, the fewer hours required. The existence of the industrial army also stimulates technical innovation. Everyone has a vested interest in devices for 'lightening the burden': 'This fact,' says Dr Leete, 'has given a prodigious impulse to labor-saving inventions in all sorts of industry.'

As with the military, a hierarchy of rank exists in Bellamy's industrial army, but one rewarded by status and honour only, since every worker receives equal pay (that is, credits). All workers are judged on merit and divided into three categories of excellence; the best in their occupation wear badges of distinction. If the incentive of working for Uncle Sam is not enough, the officers of the nation, much like Thomas More's *Syphogranti*, 'hold their followers up to their highest standard of performance and permit no lagging'. The claims and justifications are not so very different from those of More and of Campanella:

> There is far less interference of any sort with personal liberty nowadays than you were accustomed to. We require, indeed, by law that every man shall serve the nation for a fixed period, instead of leaving him his choice, as you did, between working, stealing, or starving. With the exception of this fundamental law, which is, indeed, merely a codification of the law of nature – the edict of Eden – by which it is made equal in its pressure on men, our system depends in no particular upon legislation, but is entirely voluntary, the logical outcome of the operation of human nature under rational conditions.

Bellamy rejected Fourier's idea of complete self-fulfilment through work and returned to the sense of duty and the utilitarian principles of More's Utopians: Bellamy's American Utopia of the year 2000 reflects 'the true self-interest of a rational unselfishness, and [appeals] to the social and generous instincts of men'. In return, the system guarantees that the basis of every man's claim to his particular share of the national product 'is the fact that he is a man': his title to such a claim 'is his humanity'. When West remarks that 'human nature itself must have changed very much', Dr Leete's reply echoes Marx: 'The conditions of human life have changed, and with them the motives of human action.'

William Morris found the motives ascribed to human action in *Looking*

Backward deplorable: as we noted earlier, he wrote his own utopia, *News From Nowhere* (1890), as a riposte to Bellamy's consumer paradise. Born in 1834 to wealthy middle-class parents, Morris read medieval history at Oxford, where he befriended the artist Edward Burne-Jones. On leaving university, Morris became a designer and producer of stained glass, wallpapers, textiles, furniture and ceramics as well as a poet. He came late to politics: in 1883 he joined the Liberal Party, but soon proclaimed himself a socialist and founded first the Socialist League, dedicated to revolutionary socialism, and later, in 1890, the Hammersmith Socialist Society. Appropriately, *News from Nowhere* begins with the protagonist, William Guest, leaving the Socialist League after a heated debate on 'what would happen on the Morrow of the Revolution'. Guest returns home to Hammersmith via 'that vapour-bath of hurried and discontented humanity, a carriage of the underground railway', and falls into bed. The next morning he awakes to the twenty-first century.

Morris's criticism of *Looking Backward*, that 'cockney paradise', extended not only to the aesthetics of the physical environment (discussed in Chapter 4) but also to the attitude to work – indeed, Morris believed the two were related. As far as Morris was concerned, Bellamy had 'his mind fixed firmly on the mere *machinery* of life' – not its quality. Thus, in *Looking Backward*

> ... though [Bellamy] *tells* us that every man is free to choose his occupation and that work is no burden to anyone, the impression that he produces is that of a huge standing army, tightly drilled, compelled by some mysterious fate to unceasing anxiety for the production of wares to satisfy every caprice, however wasteful and absurd, that may be cast up amongst them.

Morris accused Bellamy of regarding work as a necessary (and worse, a *mechanized*) evil: work, 'instead of being pleasurable, is a regimented obligation'. Yet, at the same time, Morris claimed, Bellamy neglected to give a convincing and reassuring picture of people at leisure. For Morris, work and leisure are one and the same.

Like Fourier, Morris believed that manufacturing and mechanization were not among civilization's benefits. In *News from Nowhere*, one of Guest's twenty-first-century hosts, Hammond, explains the ethos of the manufacturers in the nineteenth century who were caught up in something called the World-Market which demanded the production of more and more goods, irrespective of their usefulness or quality. Under this system, work became nothing more than 'the ceaseless endeavour to expend the least possible amount of labour on any article made, and yet at the same time to make as many articles as possible. To this "cheapening of production", as it was called, everything was sacrificed', including the happiness and comfort of the workman at home and at work. Morris was scathing of the spineless remedies proposed by Bellamy, who envisioned a peaceful transformation of society and whose 'only idea of making labour tolerable is to decrease the amount of it by means of fresh and ever fresh developments of machinery'.

Hammond relates to Guest the events of the great revolution of 1955. After years of social unrest under a capitalist system which had made only partial and wholly inadequate concessions to State Socialism, the workers' leaders put forward a 'Resolution' which, as Hammond remarks, was in fact a declaration of war, demanding that the government hand over 'the management of the whole natural resources of the country, together with the machinery for using them into the power of the Combined Workers'. The workers' leaders called meetings in Trafalgar Square and other places around England, and terrible, bloody riots broke out between the protesters and government, eventually turning into full-scale civil war. Destruction of wealth and goods took place on a vast scale, and by the time the conflict had ended the class system had been annihilated and England had to be rebuilt almost from scratch: 'The world was being brought to its second birth; how could that take place without a tragedy?' remarks Hammond. Morris, as a Marxist, could only envision the truly co-operative society arising from the complete destruction of the old order in a violent socialist revolution.

Hammond goes on to confide to Guest that

> . . . when men began to settle down after the war, and their labour had pretty much filled up the gap in wealth caused by the destruction of that war, a kind of disappointment seemed coming over us, and the prophecies of some of the reactionists of past times seemed as if they would come true, and a dull level of utilitarian comfort be the end for a while of our aspirations and success. The loss of the competitive spur to exertion had not, indeed, done anything to interfere with the necessary production of the community, but how if it should make men dull by giving them too much time for thought or idle musing?

The remedy to this state of affairs was the production of art – 'or work-pleasure, as one ought to call it', which

. . . sprung up almost spontaneously, it seems, from a kind of instinct amongst people, no longer driven desperately to painful and terrible over-work, to do the best they could with the work in hand – to make it excellent of its kind; and when that had gone on for a little, a craving for beauty seemed to awaken in men's minds, and they began rudely and awkwardly to ornament the wares which they made; and when they had once set to work at that, it soon began to grow.

Like Fourier, Morris believed that the secret of man's happiness was to release that hidden instinct, the passion to work and the 'craving for beauty'. However, Morris recognized in Fourier's utopia a paradox: the Harmonians' liberated passions are confined within a highly regulated and centralized system. As we remarked in Chapter 4, Morris's rejection of any form of centralization is not at all typical of the utopians. There is no national government in his utopia: affairs are managed democratically at the local level and the chapter on politics in *News From Nowhere* takes up less than half a page. Nor is there any sort of indoctrination programme for the young – no schools at all, in fact. The children learn to read, write and speak several languages in the same way they learn the more practical arts such as cooking, carpentry and thatching – by imitating the adults and other children. Book-learning is considered altogether dull, though some are naturally inclined to it.

As to the fate of machines after the revolution, Hammond explains: 'Work that was pleasure began to push out the mechanical toil, which they had once hoped at the best to reduce to narrow limits indeed, but never to get rid of.' So, 'machine after machine was quietly dropped under the excuse that the machines could not produce works of art.' As in Harmony, there is no real division of labour, and idleness no longer exists. One man whom Guest meets in the twenty-first century, a weaver, also dabbles competently in history, mathematics and machine printing (which, however, is beginning to die out in favour of hand printing). The 'golden dustman', Boffin, also writes reactionary novels. Everything in Nowhere, from silver belt-buckles to goblets, is exquisitely wrought and durable. There is no difficulty in finding work which suits everybody's talents and inclinations (Guest notes that a road crew he meets resembles an Oxford boating party). But, if the work is too unpleasant, people do without the product altogether. The only problem is that these happy craftsmen may run short of work one day.

Morris was not, however, advocating a return to the Middle Ages. Technology still exists, but it is very much the slave of society, not its saviour: 'All work which would be irksome to do by hand is done by immensely improved machinery.' Though, admittedly, 'this is not an age of inventions. The last epoch did all that for us, and we are now content to use such of its inventions as we find handy, and leaving those alone which we don't want.' Thus many of the folk gather together in 'Banded-workshops' to share large equipment, such as kilns, but mainly to enjoy companionship. No smoke emanates from the workshop furnaces: Morris implies that Nowhere is supplied with electricity generated by wind and water. Science is still pursued, 'though it is no longer the only innocent occupation which is thought worth an intelligent man spending his time upon, as it once was.'

Both Morris and Fourier had a new attitude to work: the point of labour was not simply to produce goods for consumption, but to achieve self-fulfilment. With this outlook, the citizens of Nowhere and Harmony have no desire to maximize production, and so can conserve energy and material resources, lessening their impact on the natural environment. These utopias boast clean air, clean energy, unspoilt countryside, decent housing, pleasant workshops, a minimum of manufacturing and an evenly distributed population. In short, they are an environmentalist's heaven. Fourier and Morris thus pioneered the 'appropriate technology' advocated by E. F. Schumacher in *Small Is Beautiful* (1973). This 'utopian technology', remarks one of its proponents, is 'a technology which is satisfying to work with, can be controlled by both the producers and the community by whom the products are used, conserves natural resources, and does negligible damage to the environment.' However, as we have noted, Morris despised the authoritarian elements in Fourier's system, a tendency with which he might also find fault in much of the green movement today.

Notwithstanding Morris's protests, technological progress accelerated in the twentieth century, creating the 'cockney paradise' he dreaded, based on consumerism and the mechanization of work. Nevertheless, Morris was far from being its only critic. One of the most powerful denunciations of the industrial consumer society appeared in 1932 in the form of Aldous Huxley's anti-utopian novel, *Brave New World*. The anti-utopia, or dystopia, though different in tone and outlook, shares with the classical utopia the aim of mirroring the evils of contemporary society in order to bring about change. In fact, the chief distinction between utopia and dystopia may lie only in the attitude of the reader: it is reported that some American college students of the late 1950s took *Brave New World* for a straightforward utopia.

Aldous Huxley was born into a family of scientists: both his grand-father, Thomas Henry Huxley, and his older brother, Sir Julian Huxley, were eminent biologists. As a boy Aldous had wanted to follow in their footsteps, but a condition of near-blindness which developed when he was sixteen put a halt to a career in science. He turned to writing instead. He scorned the faith which men had put in reason, progress and science since the eighteenth century: it had all been a cruel illusion. Huxley's future society does not create the institutions or material conditions to serve the citizen; rather, through behavioural conditioning, it moulds the citizens to serve the institutions.

Brave New World opens in the Department of Hatcheries and Condi-tioning, where the Director is giving a tour to a group of new students. He explains Bokanovsky's Process:

> One egg, one embryo, one adult – normality. But a bokanovskified egg will bud, will proliferate, will divide. From eight to ninety-six buds, and every bud will grow into a perfectly formed embryo, and every embryo into a full-sized adult. Making ninety-six human beings grow where only one grew before. Progress.

As the Director declares, this is 'the principle of mass production at last applied to biology'. Biological birth, 'mother', 'father' no longer exist. A human being has become a product whose role in society is decided in the 'Social Predestination Room', based on the most up-to-date statistics to achieve the greatest efficiency.

The industrial principles applied to nearly every aspect of life in *Brave New World* are those of Henry T. Ford, whose theory of mass production produced in 1909 the first popular motor car, the Model T. His creed was: 'Machinery is accomplishing in the world what man has failed to do by preaching, propaganda or the written word.' He also held the same view on administration as Saint-Simon: 'Substituting the engineer for the politician is a very natural step forward.' Thus, in *Brave New World*, the ten World Controllers, scientists loyal to the system, simply maintain the status quo. In Huxley's work Henry Ford is revered as 'Our Ford' and the year zero is dated to the first appearance of the Model T.

Bokanovsky's Process has become 'one of the major instruments of social stability' in *Brave New World*, creating 'standard men and women; in uniform batches', decanted 'as socialized human beings, as Alphas or Epsilons, as future sewage workers or future . . . Directors of Hatcheries' or World Controllers. Various techniques are applied to the test-tube babies: 'Nothing like oxygen-shortage for keeping an [Epsilon's] embryo below par.' Future chemical workers are exposed at the embryo stage to lead, caustic soda and chlorine to build up a tolerance; the tubes containing future rocket-plane engineers are constantly rotated to improve their sense of balance.

'And that,' put in the Director sententiously, 'that is the secret of happiness and virtue – liking what you've *got* to do. All conditioning aims at that: making people like their unescapable social destiny.'

From these more 'crude' methods, babies graduate to various forms of psychological conditioning, including the Pavlovian technique and hypnopaedia or sleep-teaching. In the 'Neo-Pavlovian Conditioning Rooms' toddlers are exposed to beautiful roses together with colourful illustrated books. When they draw near to these objects, a siren goes off and an electric shock is administered to the toddlers. The result: 'Books and loud noises, flowers and electric shocks . . . They'll be safe from books and botany all their lives.' Huxley mocks Thomas Jefferson's claim that 'all men are created equal'. In *Brave New World*, 'All men are physico-chemically equal', but beyond this scientific fact the gulf between the classes is unbreachable.

Hypnopaedia was the 'greatest moralizing and socializing force of all time'. Slogans are repeated over and over again as children sleep so that, if any doubt or uncertainty should enter their minds as adults, an appropriate phrase will quickly fill the void and peace will be restored: 'Cleanliness is next to fordliness', 'Never put off till tomorrow the fun you can have today', 'Everybody's happy now', 'Progress is lovely'. Sleep lessons are also given in 'Elementary Class Consciousness'. Here, Huxley satirizes the Marxist view that the proletariat must become aware of its own miserable position in society before it can become truly revolutionary. In *Brave New World* class consciousness serves to cement the status quo:

Alpha children wear grey. They work much harder than we do, because they're so frightfully clever. I'm really awfully glad I'm a Beta, because I don't work so hard. And then we are much better than the Gammas and Deltas. Gammas are Stupid. They all wear green, and Delta children wear khaki. Oh no, I *don't* want to play with Delta children. And Epsilons are still worse. They're too stupid to be able. . . .

There is a whole range of synthetic drugs to quell potentially dangerous emotions: Violent Passion Surrogate, Pregnancy Substitute for women, and *soma*, for as they say in *Brave New World*, 'when the individual feels, the community reels' and 'a gramme [of *soma*] is better than a damn'. Like most utopians the Brave New Worlders reject history and live only in the present: 'Was and will make me ill, I take a gramme and only am.' Ford's dictum, 'History is bunk', has been taken to heart. *Soma* and sex are society's safety valves: 'The *soma* habit was not a private vice; it was a political institution, it was the very essence of the Life, Liberty and Pursuit of Happiness guaranteed by the Bill of Rights,' as Huxley later remarked in *Brave New World Revisited*. Sex, made safe by Malthusian drills and contraceptive belts, is encouraged on the premise that it uses up that excess energy and emotion which could otherwise lead to dissatisfaction.

In this Brave New World, the hours of labour vary, not according to the nature of the task, as in Bellamy, but in relation to the worker's social standing. As for the lower orders, the Deltas and Epsilons, the Controllers feel 'it would be sheer cruelty to afflict them with excessive leisure. . . . Seven and a half hours of mild, unexhausting labour, and then the *soma* ration and games and unrestricted copulation and the feelies. What more can they ask for?' A shorter working day was tried once, but the experiment only created 'unrest and a large increase in the consumption of *soma*; that was all. Those three and a half hours of extra leisure were so far from being a source of happiness, that people felt constrained to take a holiday from them.' The many plans for labour-saving devices are left to attract dust in the Inventions Office.

Like Bellamy's Boston in the year 2000, the Brave New World of the year A.F. (After Ford) 632 encourages consumption: 'Self-indulgence up to the very limits imposed by hygiene and economics. Otherwise the wheels stop turning.' Once again, Huxley is taking his cue from Henry Ford, who saw consumerism as a social duty. 'To consume – to consume more and more progressively – to be able to say in the evening "I have consumed more to-day than I consumed yesterday", this now is the duty the individual owes to industrial society', as one of Ford's critics put it in 1925. Thus, in *Brave New World*, many of the slogans of hypnopaedia encourage consumer spending: 'We always throw away old clothes', 'Ending is better than mending', 'The more stitches, the less riches'. This is a long way from Morris's well-made and durable products.

Huxley paints a dire picture of the future. He implies that the faith humanity has put in science and technology since Bacon's *New Atlantis* will ultimately prove misplaced. Sir Isaiah Berlin comments that *Brave New World* is 'certainly the most influential expression of disillusionment with purely technological progress'. Huxley's charge is that the material abundance provided by technology tempts us to trade our freedom for mere comfort, reducing us to passive consumers, willingly manipulated by advertising and propaganda. What is most shocking about *Brave New World* is its pessimism. In the end, the only alternative on offer is the 'right to be unhappy'.

But if technology poses a threat to human freedom in *Brave New World*, this is as nothing compared to the challenge offered by the psychologist B. F. Skinner in his utopian novel *Walden Two* (1948). Skinner, as a strict behavioural determinist, denied that freedom really exists at all. There is simply cause and effect; what we believe to be free will is wholly an illusion. The key to the perfection of society is simply to acknowledge this fact and act upon it:

> The Good Life is waiting for us – here and now! . . . It doesn't depend on a change in government or on the machinations of world politics. It doesn't wait upon an improvement in human nature. At this very moment we have the necessary techniques, both material and psychological, to create a full and satisfying life for everyone.

Born into a middle-class Protestant family in Susquehanna, Pennsylvania (a place with good utopian credentials, as we shall see in Chapter 10), Skinner became one of the foremost psychologists of the twentieth century. He began to develop his concept of 'behavioural engineering' in the late 1930s, and ten years later published *Walden Two* – to near-universal execration. The university professor had decided to set out his behavioural theory in fictional form in order to avoid producing 'just another scientific paper marred "by foot and note disease" '. However, *Walden Two* appeared in the same year as George Orwell's great anti-utopia *Nineteen Eighty-Four*, which describes a totalitarian regime relying on 'Thought Police', 'reality control' and 'Newspeak' to coerce its citizens – the world was just not ready for Skinner's ideas on controlling men's behaviour. 'Not even the effective satire of Huxley is adequate preparation for the shocking horror of the idea when positively presented,' remarked two critics in 1952. However, the next generation rallied round Skinner's call for 'the Good Life' here and now, and in the 1960s and '70s a number of communities were established which took *Walden Two* as their 'bible' – one such, Los Horcones in Mexico, is still going today. (Skinner did not always approve of his progeny, and complained that his ideas were often distorted by 'the Maharishi and whatnot'.)

Walden Two begins with two young soldiers, Rogers and Jamnik, recently returned from World War II, disillusioned with civilian life. They persuade a former college teacher, Professor Burris, to join them and their respective girlfriends on a visit to an experimental community, Walden Two, founded by a former colleague of Burris in psychology, T. E. Frazier. On the first day of their tour, the visitors, including a sceptical colleague of Burris, Professor Castle, come across an 'organic' lawn mower: a flock of sheep which is moved around the lawn by means of a portable electric fence. Frazier remarks: 'the curious thing is that most of these sheep have never been shocked by the fence'; the lambs have learned to avoid it from the behaviour of their elders. There is also, adds Frazier, a sheep dog to keep them in line.

During the course of their stay, Burris and his party learn from Frazier that a similar but much more sophisticated method of 'behavioural engineering' is applied to community members. Skinner despairs of creating first-rate 'citizens' out of first-generation converts. Only the second generation, born in the community, with no memory of a life without an 'electric fence', can truly benefit. Thus, in Walden Two, the first two years of a baby's life are spent in an isolated environment, with climate controls and glass walls (safety glass, of course) to protect the child from all early aggravations. A child grows up knowing 'nothing of frustration, anxiety or fear. It never cries except when sick.' Skinner raised one of his own daughters in such an 'air crib' (dubbed the 'baby-in-the-box' by *Ladies Home Journal* at the time), and suggested volume controls to ease the parents' irritation and frustration.

When the child graduates from the 'air crib' in Walden Two, he or she is subjected to a series of what can only be described as 'teases' to condition his or her reaction to emotions. To stave off the feeling of discouragement, the child is taught to pull a ring once to hear a nice tune; then he is made to pull the same ring twice to hear the tune, then three, four, five times. Ideally, he is learning 'perseverative behaviour' without showing any frustration or rage. This is adding a new twist to Darwinian theory: 'The traditional use of adversity is to select the strong. We control adversity to build strength.' Frazier adds: 'It may not surprise you to learn that some of our experiments miscarried; the resistance to discouragement became almost stupid or pathological. One takes some risks in work of this sort, of course. Fortunately, we were able to reverse the process and restore the children to a satisfactory level.'

Although the tortures meted out to toddlers in Walden Two may not seem so very different from the roses and electric shocks of Huxley's

Pavlovian conditioning, they are, in fact, based on different premises. Whereas the Pavlovian technique conditioned only emotions and feelings in relation to specific events or objects, what one may call knee-jerk reactions, Frazier's aim is to teach an individual how to react properly to a whole array of experiences, many unexpected. Frazier explains:

> You can't foresee all future circumstances, and you can't specify adequate future conduct. You don't know what will be required. Instead you have to set up certain behavioral processes which will lead the individual to design his own 'good' conduct when the time comes. We call that sort of thing 'self-control'. But don't be misled, the control always rests in the last analysis in the hands of society.

There are two kinds of control which a society can exert on its citizens, negative and positive. According to Skinner, nineteenth-century liberalism did not understand the concept of 'positive reinforcement'. Rather, it presumed that individuals should be left free to act as they wish; negative control, that is punishment, was only used when an individual's behaviour interfered with another's freedom. However, as Skinner states elsewhere, there is no such thing as this liberal concept of 'natural' freedom: 'To refuse to control is to leave control not to the person himself, but to other parts of the social and non-social environments.' Frazier declares at one point: 'I deny that freedom exists at all. I must deny it – or my program would be absurd.' Castle, the archetypal liberal philosopher, proposes to 'dump the science of behavior in the ocean' and give people back their freedom. Frazier asks him:

> 'How could you give them freedom?'
> 'By refusing to control them!'
> 'But you would only be leaving the control in other hands.'
> 'Whose?'
> 'The charlatan, the demagogue, the salesman, the ward heeler, the bully, the cheat, the educator, the priest – all who are now in possession of the techniques of behavioral engineering.'

Following in the by now firmly established tradition of Saint-Simon, Skinner thought that the way to achieve a 'government based upon a science of human behavior' was to replace the politicians with planners and managers, the only people competent to run a community properly. In Walden Two these administrators are appointed, not elected, for, as

Frazier explains, 'The people are in no position to evaluate experts. And elected experts are never able to act as they think best.' The key to the success of Walden Two is its willingness to embrace Bacon's optimism concerning the power of science and technology: 'A constantly experimental attitude toward everything – that's all we need. Solutions to problems of every sort follow almost miraculously.' History, as in all utopias, is deemed useless: 'History tells us nothing,' Frazier remarks.

Day-to-day life in Walden Two has been aptly described as 'a kind of dull, mid-western small town with a well-endowed arts centre'. There are no competitive sports. Personal contacts are arranged through a Social Manager, as in Fourier (see Chapter 8). Walden Two also comes complete with all the conveniences of Utopia: covered walkways and piped music. (Although Skinner is writing in the age of radio, he encourages the simple pleasures of amateur music-making which Bellamy found so painful.) The community dining hall (in a feature reminiscent of Disneyworld) offers its guests a choice of surroundings decorated in a number of different styles, such as quaint Early American, the traditional 'English inn', or modern Swedish decor. There are few possessions and no money, thus ensuring complete economic equality. No prematurely aged, occupationally disabled people, no criminals, and far fewer sick people are to be found in the small community (perhaps owing to the required medical examinations before joining the experiment). No member ever dresses badly, for sloppy dress is a sign of indolence or carelessness, 'both of which are born of weariness'. Several weeks at Walden Two, apparently, and you are even ready to give up smoking and drinking.

'Puppy love' is taken seriously in the community, and girls as young as sixteen are encouraged to have children. Marriage, sanctioned by the Manager of Marriages, is the normal practice, but not mandatory. In any case, husband and wife usually choose to live apart, and the care of the children, as we have seen, is given over to the experts. 'Walden Two replaces the family, not only as an economic unit, but to some extent as a social and psychological unit as well.' 'The significant history of our times . . . is the story of the growing weakness of the family,' Frazier remarks. 'Home is not the place to raise children.' Skinner himself commented in an interview, 'I prefer to turn child-raising over to a specialist. I just can't believe that an ordinary parent can do a good job.'

Skinner's solution to the labour problem is not very original; in fact, as Frazier acknowledges, in many ways it very closely resembles Bellamy's system, but on a small scale. Everyone has on average a four-hour work day and is paid in credit. The Managers assign different credit values to different kinds of work, and adjust them on the basis of demand. Skinner's New England upbringing, like Bellamy's, ensured that work was regarded as a necessary evil in Walden Two, and leisure a serious occupation. To allow the members to choose whatever job they please is an extravagance, a waste of resources, since this would inevitably result in misplaced talents. But, says Frazier, 'our educational system will see to that', steering children towards what they do best, not what they aspire to be. As in Fourier's utopia, children are part of the work force too: 'It's no hardship; it's accepted as readily as sport or play.'

As for motivation, extra incentive 'comes when a man is working for himself'. In any event, the Managers can count on the middle-class Puritan work ethic which permeates Walden Two: 'The really intelligent man doesn't want to feel that his work is being done by anyone else.' Like Bellamy's Bostonians of the future, the members feel they have a vested interest in creating labour-saving devices. To 'avoid the goat and loom', technology flourishes. Walden Two is striving to eliminate all 'uncreative and uninteresting work', for 'What we ask is that a man's work shall not tax his strength or threaten his happiness. Our energies can then be turned toward art, science, play, the exercise of skills, the satisfaction of curiosities, the conquest of nature, the conquest of man.'

The conquest of nature and man focuses, of course, on the science of behaviour. The possible fields of research to be carried out at Walden Two are the design of personalities, control of temperament and of motivation, capacities of the group (communal science) and the 'Superorganism', that is groups of artists and scientists who work together as smoothly and efficiently as an NFL football team. The community's doctors also have 'extraordinary powers' to ask for 'intelligent co-operation' in experiments. Frazier comments, with much the same enthusiasm as Bacon:

> We must never be free of that feverish urge to push forward which is the saving grace of mankind. . . . It's no solution to put the brakes on science until man's wisdom and responsibility catch up. As frightening as it may seem – as mad as it may seem to the contemplative soul – science must go on. We can't put our rockets and our atomic piles in museums . . . But wait until we've developed a science of behavior as powerful as the science of the atom, and you will see a difference.

Problems undoubtedly lay ahead for Walden Two in relation to its neighbours, however. Although Skinner rejects politics as a forum for action, he is ready to take over local politics. Frazier explains that the

Planners decide how to vote, and the Political Manager draws up the 'Walden Ticket', which everyone must endorse. By being able to throw six or seven hundred votes around in this way, Frazier explains, they have 'cleaned up the township and are in a fair way to cleaning up the county'. But the Planners are prepared to go even further. By buying up half the farms that do business in a particular town, they can virtually control it by applying pressure to local businesses and manipulating real estate. 'We can make the area very uncomfortable for noncooperative landowners' and, Frazier adds, as for the person who refuses to co-operate, 'all we can do is make his personal demise as painless as possible, unless he's intelligent enough to adjust to the new order.' It comes as no surprise to learn that Walden Two has a host of lawyers working for it.

What is most disturbing about *Walden Two* is its open contempt for the notion of human freedom. However, this is what gives the book its value. We have already noted Frazier's remark 'I deny that freedom exists at all. I must deny it – or my program would be absurd.' This may be shocking, but Skinner would claim that Frazier is merely being honest in acknowledging the hidden assumption behind all the social sciences. As Skinner put it elsewhere: 'The hypothesis that man is not free is essential to the application of scientific method to the study of behaviour.' Skinner's point is surely just. The desire that had motivated utopian reformers since the time of Newton, a desire still shared by the social sciences – to uncover the laws that determine human behaviour and human history – rests upon the conviction that human behaviour is an effect caused by external agencies. To admit the autonomous, uncaused free will of the individual into the equation would be to render the entire calculation meaningless. Walden Two brings us right up against a truth that most shy away from, that to the social sciences human beings are marionettes.

This 'cause and effect' view of humanity is a product of a Newtonian conception of the cosmos. To Newton and his followers, the universe consisted of particles, 'hard, massy and impenetrable', in constant motion according to simple laws. The French mathematician Pierre Simon de Laplace (1749–1827), called 'the Newton of France', saw that the logical corollary of this view was the proposition that if one could somehow become appraised of the exact position and momentum of every single one of these particles, one would in principle be able to calculate not just the entire future history of the universe, but its past too. Laplace's postulate exposes both the pretension and the ultimate implausibility of the Newtonian world view: it posed philosophical problems which could not be solved until the discovery of quantum mechanics.

Quantum physics answers Laplace by maintaining that *in principle* the exact position and momentum of even one particle, let alone a universe of them, is unknowable. There is an irreducible uncertainty about any particle's behaviour which can never be overcome. At a certain level, the cosmos is inherently unpredictable. Today, the same sense of uncertainty is seeping through the human sciences. Our growing understanding of the importance of biological factors in shaping human behaviour has undermined the view that environmental conditioning can exercise unlimited control over our actions. Once one accepts that genes, as well as purely random effects in our biological development, distinguish us as individuals and cause us each to respond to the same phenomenon in a different way, the prediction of human behaviour becomes an impossible task, and Frazier's boasts sound less like threats, more like foolishness:

> We can achieve a sort of control under which the controlled, though they are following a code much more scrupulously than was ever the case under the old system, nevertheless *feel free*. They are doing what they want to do, not what they are forced to do. That's the source of the tremendous power of positive reinforcement – there's no restraint and no revolt. By a careful cultural design, we control not the final behavior, but the *inclination* to behave – the motives, the desires, the wishes. . . . [Men] never strike against forces which make them want to act the way they do.

Somewhere between the uncertainty of the quantum and the unpredictability of the individual human organism, modern science has created a tiny space for the concept of free will to worm its way back into the cosmos. As it does so, it is undermining not only Skinner's behaviourist utopia, but also the whole utopian project of the social sciences. *Walden Two*, like Laplace's determinism, exposes both the pretension and the ultimate implausibility of scientific utopianism. Utopia helped to create science, but science cannot create Utopia.

Woman and boy of Tahiti: Sydney Parkinson, *Journal of a Voyage to the South Seas*, 1784.

PART FOUR

SEX

Therefore God's universal law
Gave to the man despotic power
Over his female in due awe.
John Milton, 'Samson Agonistes'

Where women walk in public processions in the streets the same
  as men,
Where they enter the public assembly and take places the same as
  the men;
Where the city of the faithfullest friends stands,
Where the city of the cleanliness of the sexes stands,
Where the city of the healthiest fathers stands,
Where the city of the best-bodied mothers stands,
There the great city stands.
Walt Whitman, 'Song of the Broad Axe'

Pleasure's a sin, and sometimes sin's a pleasure.
Lord Byron, 'Don Juan'

7. Sex and the Savants

Modern life is lived surrounded by sexual imagery; where once sex was not considered a fit topic for conversation, it now sometimes appears to be the only topic of conversation. This sexual liberation seems such a recent phenomenon that it is tempting to agree with Philip Larkin that

> Sexual intercourse began
> In nineteen sixty-three . . .
> Between the end of the *Chatterley* ban
> And the Beatles' first LP.

But the reader will perhaps not be surprised to learn that present-day sexual attitudes spring from a long tradition of utopian thinking about the uses of desire. Today, those attitudes are under attack from an unlikely alliance between radical feminists and religious and political conservatives, unfettered sexuality being perceived by the one group as a threat to women, by the other as a threat to family life. The argument all too easily becomes bogged down in a confusing melange of issues: sexual equality, abortion, pornography, divorce, homosexuality. But, from More onwards, utopians have sought to accommodate the sex urge within an ideal community, and in their imaginary worlds one can see with startling clarity the connection between sexual mores and the shape of society. The insights gained force us to re-examine the terms of the debate about the 'permissive society'.

Sex entered the utopian sphere with the ceremony which Thomas More's traveller Hythloday describes as preceding every marriage in Utopia: 'The prospective bride, no matter whether she's a spinster or a widow, is exhibited stark naked to the prospective bridegroom by a respectable married woman, and a suitable male chaperon shows the bridegroom naked to the bride.' The Utopians think choosing a wife is every bit as important and tricky as buying a horse and, therefore, 'take every possible precaution'. In their eyes, the European practice of betrothal is 'unbelievably careless':

You judge a whole woman from a few square inches of face, which is all you can see of her, and then proceed to marry her – at the risk of finding her most disagreeable, when you see what she's really like. No doubt you needn't worry, if moral character is the only thing that interests you – but we're not all as wise as that, and even those who are sometimes find, when they get married, that a beautiful body can be quite a useful addition to a beautiful soul.

Could the ascetic More, who according to a contemporary biographer did not marry his second wife for 'bodily pleasure' and may not even have had sexual relations with her, really have approved of such a liberal attitude? Unlikely as it seems, his son-in-law William Roper relates that More went some way towards putting Utopian theory into practice by allowing the younger man to catch a glimpse of his two daughters naked in order to choose between them.

Even more surprisingly, More's Utopians appear to be advocates of the 'pleasure principle'. They believe that 'pleasure is the ultimate happiness which all human beings have in view'. The Utopians are 'impelled by reason as well as instinct to enjoy [themselves] in any natural way which doesn't hurt other people, interfere with greater pleasures, or cause unpleasant after-effects'. This almost sounds like a manifesto of the swinging Sixties, but on closer examination it is clear that the Utopians, while they have dispensed with what they regard as irrational and unnecessary prudishness about the human body, have anything but a permissive attitude to sexual matters. The 'greater pleasures' that Hythloday refers to are primarily intellectual – 'the satisfaction that one gets from understanding something, or from contemplating truth' – or spring from a general sense of physical well-being – 'the calm and regular functioning of the body'. Sexual intercourse is relegated to the 'lower' physical pleasures, along with the relief from irritation achieved by rubbing or scratching – and 'they don't think much of pleasures like that, except in so far as they're necessary.'

In fact, sex in Utopia is rigidly controlled; its function is not merely to give pleasure, but to strengthen the mainstay of society, the family. Thus the only sexual relations which can be tolerated are between man and wife; adultery is punishable by slavery, and a second offence by death. Also:

Any boy or girl convicted of pre-marital intercourse is severely punished, and permanently disqualified from marrying . . . The Utopians are particularly strict about that kind of thing, because they think very few people would want to get married – which means spending one's whole life with the same person, and putting up with all the inconveniences that this involves – if they weren't carefully prevented from having any sexual intercourse otherwise.

The point of mutual inspection before marriage is to ensure that the partners find each other sufficiently attractive to allow sex to fulfil its proper function, as a compensation for the rigours of married life. The importance they attach to marriage is underlined by the Utopians' attitude towards divorce – they tolerate it only when it creates two happy marriages out of one miserable one: 'Divorce by mutual consent is allowed on grounds of incompatibility, when both husband and wife have found alternative partners that seem likely to make them happier.'

The Utopians' view of the relationship between sex and marriage may seem rather crude, even demeaning, but the experience of the last few decades surely endorses their position. As the rising number of children born out of wedlock illustrates, for many people the lack of strong social sanctions against extra-marital sex has robbed marriage of much of its point. The imaginary example of Utopia suggests that it is this, rather than the availability of divorce, which is in the long run the greater threat to the institution of marriage.

For many feminists, of course, what marriage institutionalizes above all is the subjugation of women, and again this aspect of married life is made strikingly explicit in Utopia. Although Utopian women are slightly more liberated than European women of More's time in that they learn trades alongside men and are even able to become priests (a suggestion which both Luther and Tyndale proposed and More strenuously rejected a decade later), they are nevertheless ultimately subservient to men. Once a month, as we noted in Chapter 2, wives must kneel down before their husbands to 'confess all their sins of omission and commission, and ask to be forgiven.' The husband makes no such confession to his wife.

The Utopian emphasis on the family could find no greater contrast than in Campanella's *La Città del Sole*. Here, the family has been abolished and there are no permanent sexual relationships. But sex is in many respects even more rigidly controlled than in Utopia, for the Solarians are the product of a comprehensive programme of eugenics, and all conception is under state control. One of the three cabinet ministers who assist the supreme ruler is called Love, and it is his task to ensure that men and women are properly matched for breeding. There are regular wrestling matches 'in the manner of the ancient Greeks' (i.e. in the nude) to allow Love and his delegates to pair couples for the best results:

Tall handsome girls are not matched with any but tall brave men, while fat girls are matched with thin men and thin girls with fat ones, so to avoid extremes in their offspring.

As we have seen, the Solarians' guiding star is the science (as Campanella would have seen it) of astrology, and so not only does the state decide who will mate with whom, it also dictates when they will do it. The most propitious hour is determined by the official Astrologer to ensure the best possible outcome:

On the appointed evening, the boys and girls prepare their beds and go to bed where the matron and senior direct them. Nor may they have intercourse until they have completely digested their food and have said their prayers. . . . At the proper time, the matron goes around and opens the cell doors.

Romantic love is tolerated, but only if it remains unconsummated:

If a man becomes enamored of a woman, he may speak and jest with her, send her verses, and make emblems out of flowers and branches for her. But if his having intercourse with her is deemed undesirable by reason of the offspring that might result, it will by no means be permitted.

Thus sex has been placed firmly at the service of the state: the very opposite of free love. However, Campanella seems well aware that unregulated sexual desire perpetually threatens to bring his elaborate procreative edifice tumbling down, and so he is careful to buttress it with some safeguards. Men may mate freely with women who are pregnant or barren, and counselling is provided for those who are 'troubled by Venus'. However, no such accommodation is made for women, and Campanella is entirely typical of his age in assuming that a strong sexual urge is a uniquely male characteristic, although he does admit that occasionally a woman may be tempted to make herself sterile 'in order to become a wanton', and so the Solarians have taken steps to discourage this.

Campanella, like Plato, believed that the institution of the family only encouraged self-love. Children stay with their natural mothers only until they are weaned, then the state takes over child-care. These provisions allow women to enjoy a greater degree of equality than in the European society of Campanella's time. Plato, who also advocated eugenics in his

Republic, had come to the same conclusion in the fifth century BC. Discussing the duties of the female Guardians, Plato states:

> If the only difference apparent between [men and women] is that the female bears and the male begets, we shall not admit that this is a difference relevant for our purpose, but shall still maintain that our male and female Guardians ought to follow the same occupations. . . . [However,] women will be the weaker parties.

In the City of the Sun, therefore, men and women receive the same education and are trained in the mechanical, speculative and military arts. Women have an equal voice in the state council and may do any job for which they are qualified. However, Campanella assumes that it will be the men who really run things, and there is no doubt that in the City of the Sun the role of women, like the role of sex, is first and foremost procreative.

The Solarians, like More's Utopians, are pagans (although their Genoese visitor, like Hythloday, is sure that they will soon convert to Christianity). Thus neither society subscribes to the Church's doctrine that sex is inherently sinful. However, in both places sexual desire is clearly regarded as a potentially subversive force that must be carefully channelled if the commonwealth is to prosper. Hanging over both the Utopians and Solarians is the shadow of original sin which decrees that human nature is irredeemably flawed. It was not until the eighteenth century that the view gained ground that man's nature – and his desires – were basically good. The *philosophes*, that group of fashionable and influential savants of the French Enlightenment who tended towards atheism, stood original sin on its head: man's corruption comes, not from the Fall, but from the failings of society. The search was on to 'find a society in which it would be almost impossible for a man to be depraved or evil', as Morelly states in the *Code de la Nature* (1755).

In the same year that these words were published, Jean-Jacques Rousseau took a decisive step in this search by elaborating the myth of the 'noble savage' in his *Discours sur l'Origine et les Fondements de l'Inégalité Parmi les Hommes* ('Discourse on the Origin and Foundations of Inequality Among Men'). Rousseau, born in 1712, was the son of a Swiss watchmaker. He was apprenticed to a boorish and cruel engraver, and ran away after three miserable years. Rousseau lived among the noble and wealthy society of Piedmont and Savoy for some time, then finally made his way to Paris at the age of thirty. Although he moved in the same circles as the *philosophes*, he always felt something of an outsider and had many quarrels with them. Some of his writings, especially *Du Contrat Social* ('On the Social Contract'), which became Robespierre's bible during the French Revolution, brought official disfavour, and Rousseau spent the rest of his life travelling to escape persecution, both real and imagined.

The *Discours sur l'Origine de l'Inégalité* was Rousseau's entry in a competition, sponsored by the Academy of Dijon, for the best essay on the question 'What is the origin of inequality among men, and is it authorized by natural law?' His approach to this problem was to trace the history of man back to its origins in order to uncover man's true nature. Rousseau imagines earliest man as a rather unreflective, simple being, 'eating his fill under an oak tree, quenching his thirst at the first stream, making his bed at the foot of the same tree which furnished his meal, with all his needs satisfied'.

In this early stage, man is a solitary creature with no responsibilities, not even family. Men and women unite 'fortuitously, according to chance encounters, opportunity and desire'. Mothers take sole charge of raising their children until they are old enough to survive alone. According to Rousseau, these savages

> . . . lacking among themselves any kind of moral relationship or any known duties, can be neither good nor evil and had neither vices nor virtues. . . . it could be said that savages are not wicked precisely because they do not know what it is to be good.

At one point Rousseau states point blank, 'Man is naturally good.' He likewise concludes that these simple men enjoyed a kind of primitive equality: the few inequalities that existed, for example in physical strength, were either rooted out by nature or of no real consequence.

Of course, Rousseau's depiction of the first humans as asocial creatures is historically incorrect. Modern anthropologists believe our ancestors were social even before they were human, vindicating Aristotle's famous dictum that 'Man is a political animal', more accurately translated as 'Man is a city-dweller'. However, the historical veracity of the noble savage is not the point, as Rousseau is at pains to explain:

> The research which can be conducted on this subject need not be taken as historical truth, but only as hypothetical and conditional arguments, better suited to explain the nature of things than to reveal their true origin.

In other words the noble savage is a thought experiment, a truly utopian creation.

However, man, 'blessed' with the faculty of self-improvement, would not allow his kind to remain in this simple, happy state forever. Rousseau remarks: 'The first man who, having fenced off a plot of land, thought of saying "This is mine" and found people simple enough to believe him was the real founder of civil society.' Public esteem as well as private property came to have value among men, and both contributed to the foundation of inequality and the birth of the hitherto unknown passions of greed, pride and envy. Society soon created laws and a moral code intended to protect property and men, but which merely institutionalized inequality and vice. Villages, towns and eventually cities, 'the abyss of the human species', were the result. These advances, Rousseau asserts, which 'have apparently been so many steps towards the perfection of the individual', have been 'in fact, towards the decrepitude of the species'. (Shortly after writing the *Discours*, Rousseau got into a bitter dispute with a neighbour over some butter which had been delivered to the wrong address – proof indeed that private property was the source of conflict and injustice!)

Rousseau argues that the violent passions which so disrupt society are in fact a product of the frustrations and inequalities created by social life. In his natural state man is easy-going, since everything to satisfy his simple wants is readily to hand: 'Nothing is so gentle as man in his primitive state.' He singles out one newly created passion as perhaps the most dangerous of all:

> Among the passions that stir the heart of man, there is an ardent, impetuous one which makes one sex necessary to the other, a terrible passion which braves all dangers, overcomes all obstacles, and which, in its fury, seems calculated to destroy the human race, which it is destined to preserve. What will become of men, prey to this unbridled and brutal rage, without modesty, without restraint, and fighting every day over the objects of their love at the price of their lives?

The problem, as Rousseau sees it, is not the physical urge of sex but the moral sentiment of love, which 'fixes it exclusively upon a single object'. He continues:

> The moral aspect of love is an artificial sentiment, born of social custom and celebrated by women with much care and cleverness to establish their ascendancy and to make dominant the sex that should obey.

In the state of nature this artifice did not yet exist, and so the sexual urge had yet to acquire its destructive power:

> Limited to what is physical in love, and fortunate enough to be ignorant of those preferences that inflame this sentiment and increase its difficulties, men must feel the ardors of their temperament less frequently and less sharply, and must, consequently, have fewer and less cruel disputes among themselves.

Rousseau illustrates his argument with the example of the Caribs, who 'among all existing people . . . have, up to now, deviated least from the state of nature', and who consequently 'are in fact the most peaceful in their loves and the least subject to jealousy, although they live in a scorching climate, which always seems to cause these passions to grow more active.' He concludes: 'It is, therefore, incontestable that love itself, like all the other passions, has acquired only in society that impetuous ardor which often makes it fatal to men', and which makes necessary laws to contain it.

The immediate reception of the *Discours* was mixed. Voltaire, for one, was not impressed. He wrote to Rousseau:

> I have received your new book against the human race. I thank you for it. . . . The desire to walk on all fours seizes one when one reads your work. However, as I lost that habit more than sixty years ago, I unfortunately sense the impossibility of going back to it.

Nor did it please the Academicians of Dijon, who did not even read the work to the end. However, the *Discours* soon established itself as one of the most read and discussed works of political philosophy. Its impact was truly revolutionary. Not only did it mark a radical change in the perception of human nature, but also, by condemning the entire history of society as a descent towards perdition, it legitimized the dissolution of all traditional social forms – a dissolution put into practice a few decades later by the French revolutionaries.

As we have seen, the noble savage is a utopian conception, and indeed the *Discours* shares with the whole utopian genre elements of the Golden Age myth. Nevertheless, a solitary acorn-eater is hardly a satisfactory foundation for an ideal society, and it may seem that by ascribing all man's ills to his social interactions, Rousseau is denying the very possibility of ever achieving Utopia. However, he suggests that man was at his happiest, not in the asocial state of nature, but at a second stage of development, when he had formed small family groups. Rousseau clearly has in mind the native societies which Europeans had encountered in the New World:

> As long as men remained content with their rustic huts, as long as they confined themselves to sewing their clothing of skins with thorns or fish bones, to adorning themselves with feathers and shells, to painting their bodies with different colors, to improving or embellishing their bows and arrows, to carving a few fishing boats or a few crude musical instruments with sharp stones, in a word, as long as they applied themselves only to tasks that a single man could accomplish and only to arts that did not need the cooperation of several hands, they lived free, healthy, good, and happy lives.

He goes on to observe that 'this period of the development of human faculties, maintaining a happy medium between the indolence of the primitive state and the petulant activity of our self-love, must have been the happiest and most enduring epoch.' Although Rousseau fails to draw a detailed picture of this ideal state, it exerted a powerful attraction upon the *philosophes*, one of whom, Denis Diderot, developed it into a full-blown utopia, his *Supplément au Voyage de Bougainville* ('Supplement to the Voyage of Bougainville').

Diderot, born in 1713 in the provincial town of Langres, was sent to Paris to study with the Jesuits. His father's ambition for his gifted son was that he should join the Church. But Diderot was a rebel and, after completing his studies, preferred to take up lodgings in Paris's Latin Quarter to pursue his own literary, scientific – and amorous – interests. In 1747 he became involved in a project which would dominate his life for the next twenty years, the *Encyclopédie*. Its aim was to set forth all man's accumulated knowledge in the arts and sciences, and the multi-volume work came to be the *philosophes'* manifesto. The French authorities, particularly the Jesuits, thought many of its articles, submitted by such free-thinkers as Rousseau, Voltaire and d'Alembert, were heretical, and they strove either to censor or to ban the project altogether. Although he was repeatedly thrown into gaol, Diderot, through his energy and tenacity, saw the *Encyclopédie* completed. Towards the end of his life, his renown was such that in 1773, the ruler of Russia, Catherine II, invited him to her court for an extended visit. (In their private discussions on reform, Diderot in his excitement, it was said, slapped Catherine's thighs until they were black and blue, and Catherine had to put a table between them to protect her limbs.)

Diderot was probably the least inhibited and most eloquent of the *philosophes* on the subject of sexuality. He frequently spoke of sexual pleasure as 'the greatest pleasure that can be imagined' and he gave his daughter a graphic talk on the birds, bees and human anatomy. His views on sexuality and marriage were, inevitably, coloured by his personal experience in these matters. Although he eloped with the woman he loved in opposition to their parents, the marriage soon proved to be a disaster and a curse. He and his wife were incompatible, and Diderot's numerous love-affairs did not sweeten his wife's temperament. Diderot once said of marriage that it was as crazy as any other vow except that, instead of promising to keep your body locked up in the large cell of a monastery, you promised 'to keep a small part of it locked up in a small cell.'

Diderot struck at a pillar of the Catholic Church, the monastic orders, when he condemned celibacy as both unnatural and cruel in his novel *La Réligieuse* ('The Nun') and elsewhere (for example, in the article on 'Celibacy' in the *Encyclopédie*). He based the story of *La Réligieuse* on an actual case of a woman who petitioned the government to be released from her monastic vows. (Vows could be made binding when a girl was sixteen, and only the state could grant a release from them.) Diderot sympathetically describes the extremes to which celibate men and women are sometimes driven when their natural desires are denied them: homosexuality or sexual hysteria, leading to madness. He also believed that the denial of normal sexual appetites led to acts considered by society to be 'unnatural', such as homosexuality and sodomy.

But Diderot saved his most impassioned attacks for the institution of marriage, the very bedrock of society. He did not believe in the constancy of love and called Nature as his witness. Everything in Nature is in a perpetual state of transition and flux; the sky is never for one moment the same. How, then, can we expect the human heart to remain constant? Diderot believed that the real victims of marriage were women. In early 1772 he wrote a short treatise entitled simply *Sur les Femmes* ('On Women'), prompted by a brief love affair he had had in 1770 and also by the forthcoming marriage of his beloved daughter Angelique. According to one of Diderot's biographers, 'Mme Diderot cried all the time before [the wedding] and Diderot cried, or felt like crying, all the time after it. . . . His daughter's impending change of roles probably made especially vivid to his imagination the status of a woman, biologically and socially.'

In this small treatise, Diderot is sometimes poetic: 'When you write of women you should dip your pen in the rainbow and scatter the dust of butterfly wings on your words'; sometimes bitter: 'More civilized than us on the outside, they have remained true savages within, all of them more or less machiavellian'; and even downright condescending: 'Oh women! what extraordinary children you are!' But, despite the occasional patronizing remark, *Sur les Femmes* contains open and frank discussions on sexual hysteria and the effect on women of menstruation, pregnancy and menopause. Diderot is equally revealing about the male psyche. He states that when a man says '*Je t'aime*' to an attractive woman 'It really means: "If you would like to sacrifice your innocence and your morals; lose your respect . . .; kill your parents with grief and allow me one moment of pleasure, I would be most obliged."' Perhaps the most chilling moment in *Sur les Femmes* is Diderot's description of the private hell of a woman trapped in an unhappy marriage:

I have seen an honest woman shudder with horror at the approach of her husband; I have seen her plunge into the bath, thinking that she could never scrub hard enough to remove the stain of her [wifely] duty. . . . Many women die without having experienced the extreme of desire.

Diderot, following Rousseau, saw the origin of all this misery in the morality and laws imposed by civilized society:

In almost all countries the cruelty of the civil law has combined with the cruelty of nature, against women. They have been treated like imbecile children. There is no kind of vexation which among civilized nations may not be exercised with impunity by a man against a woman.

It is this insight which led Diderot to explore the possibility of an ideal society among Rousseau's noble savages.

Like Thomas More's, Diderot's venture into utopian waters was prompted by a contemporary voyage, that of Louis-Antoine de Bougainville. The accounts of Bougainville's travels to the South Sea island of Tahiti seemed to confirm Rousseau's depiction of that second and most perfect stage of man's development. The descriptions of free love, in particular, captured the public's imagination. In November 1769, about six months after Bougainville had returned, the *Mercure de France* published an article by the expedition's naturalist, Commerson, describing

Tahiti as a 'Utopia . . . the only corner of the earth where men live without vices, without prejudices, without needs, without strife.'

In 1771 Bougainville published his own account of the voyage, in which he sought to correct some of these initial reports. Although he had at first been attracted – and even overwhelmed – by the sight of Tahiti, its balmy shores and beautiful women, he soon saw that this paradise and its inhabitants had not escaped the scourges of humanity: disease, superstition, avarice, tribal warfare and inequality. Diderot wrote a review of Bougainville's book, and, inspired by its description of an albeit flawed island paradise, sat down to write the *Supplement to the Voyage of Bougainville: A Dialogue Between A and B on the Disadvantage of Attaching Moral Ideas to Certain Physical Acts Which Have Nothing to Do with Them*. It circulated in manuscript in instalments in 1773–74, and, like most of Diderot's writings, was not published until after his death.

The *Supplément* is divided into three parts. In the first part, two anonymous interlocutors, known only as A and B, discuss Bougainville's recently published *Voyage Autour du Monde* ('Voyage Around the World'). B also describes how Aotourou, the native Tahitian whom Bougainville introduced into Parisian society, 'threw himself on the first European woman he met, and very seriously intended to show her the courtesy of Tahiti', and comments that he won't learn much from civilized man. B then produces two fragments of Bougainville's journal, supposedly left out of the published account, picking up where Bougainville had left off. These fragments together comprise the second part of Diderot's *Supplément*.

The first fragment begins with an islander's farewell to Bougainville and his ship. The speaker is an old man, the father of a large family and, therefore, like patriarchs in *New Atlantis*, greatly honoured among his people. The old man begins with an impassioned attack upon European colonialism. Most utopias are very robust and capable of dealing with any incursions – indestructible, in fact. But Diderot depicts a fragile society at the point when it is about to collapse under the impact of the European sailors. The old man declares:

We are innocent; we are happy: and thou canst not but spoil our happiness. We follow the pure instinct of nature: thou hast sought to efface its character from our souls. Here all things belong to all men. Thou hast preached some strange distinction between 'thine' and 'mine'. . . . We are free: and see thou hast planted in our earth the title of our future slavery.

Diderot is here in agreement with Rousseau that private property corrupts society. However, he parts company with his fellow savant on the question of whether civil society, its laws and notions of morality are the inevitable result of man's inherent drive to improve his lot. Rather, as Diderot has the old Tahitian explain, civil societies are created out of particular needs: the need to supply food and other goods which people crave and demand. Civil society creates laws because people, whose needs conflict, have to be restrained. These laws can only be enforced effectively by imposing moral constraints on people. However, in Tahiti there are no material needs: food is plentiful and riches are not coveted. Thus, since there are no needs, there are no laws; since there are no laws, there are no morals or 'virtues'.

The second fragment of Bougainville's journal produced by B is devoted to the subject of free love Tahitian style. It takes the form of a conversation between the chaplain who accompanies Bougainville on his voyage and his Tahitian host, Orou, who speaks the King's French. On the first night, when it is time for bed, Orou offers the chaplain some native hospitality:

'Thou hast had supper, thou art young and in good health. Sleep alone, and thou wilt sleep badly. Man needs a companion by his side at night. Here is my wife, here are my daughters. Take your choice. But you would oblige me by fixing for preference on my youngest daughter who has not yet had a child. . . .'

The chaplain replied that his religion, his calling, good morals and honourability forbade him to accept these offers.

Orou replied: 'I do not know what thou meanest by religion, but I cannot think well of it, if it forbids thee to enjoy an innocent pleasure, to which nature, the sovereign mistress, invites us all – to give existence to one like thee: to make a fitting return to a host who has welcomed thee warmly and to enrich a nation, by increase, with one subject the more. . . . See the care thou hast spread on all these faces. They fear thou has remarked in them some faults which have made thee disdain them. . . . Be generous.'

THE CHAPLAIN: It is not that: they are all four equally beautiful: but my religion! but my calling!

. . . Here, the candid chaplain admits that never had Providence

145

enforced him to so formidable a temptation. He was young: he was excited: he was tormented. . . . The frank chaplain adds that [Thia, the youngest] clasped his hands and gazed on him with the most touching and expressive looks: that she wept: that her father, mother, and sisters withdrew: that he remained alone with her and after repeating 'But my religion, but my calling' he found himself next day lying beside this girl. . . .

The worthy chaplain tells us he spent the rest of the day touring the island and visiting the cabins. In the evening after supper father and mother besought him to sleep with their second daughter, and Palli presented herself in the same undress as Thia. Several times during the night he cried out 'But my religion, but my calling' and the third night he was stirred by the same remorse with the eldest, Asto. The fourth night, as in honour bound, he consecrated to the wife of his host.

Thus, through humour, Diderot attacks what he regards as the cruel and unnatural practices of marriage and celibacy. Because the Tahitians do not make such vows which go against human nature, the crimes so abhorred in European society, fornication, adultery and incest, simply have no meaning in Tahiti.

However, as Orou hinted to the chaplain, the point of love-making among the savages is not to satisfy sexual desire but to bear children and so increase the wealth of the island. It is not so much free love which reigns in Tahiti as a kind of natural economics. To the Tahitians, the birth of a child 'means an increase of fortune for the cabin and of strength for the nation, arms and hands the more in Tahiti'. Diderot, like most of his compatriots in the eighteenth century, firmly believed that France's population was declining and that an increase in population led to prosperity. (Thomas Malthus's revolutionary theory of overpopulation first appeared in 1798, fourteen years after Diderot's death.) In fact, the subject comes up several times in the *Encyclopédie*, under 'Population', 'Celibacy', and '*Jouissance*', where it is stated that 'the propagation of beings is the greatest object of nature'.

Thus, according to Orou, sexual morality depends entirely upon whether a country has more or fewer children than it can feed: if more, then European morality is practical; if fewer, then Tahitian promiscuity is the answer:

Are the morals of Tahiti better or worse than yours? It is a question that can be easily settled. Has the country of thy birth more children

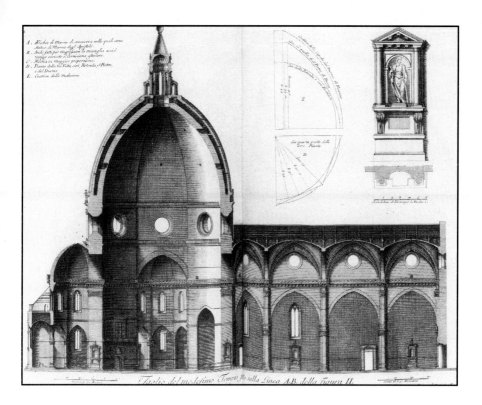

Section and elevation of Bramante's dome, S. Maria del Fiore, Florence.

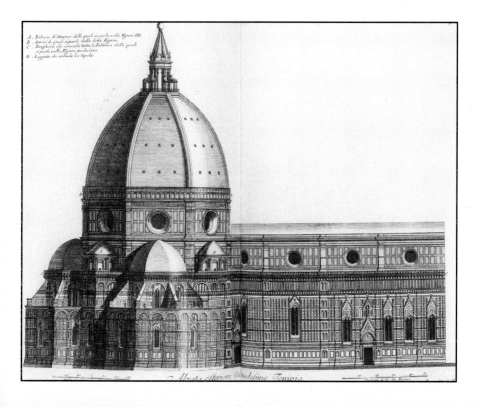

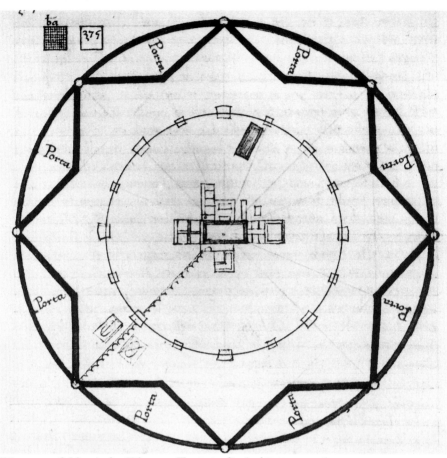

Diagram of Sforzinda: Filarete, *Trattato di Architettura*, 1465.

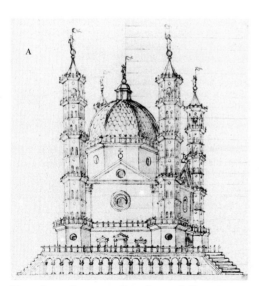

Drawing of a centrally planned church:
Filarete, *Trattato di Architettura*, 1465.

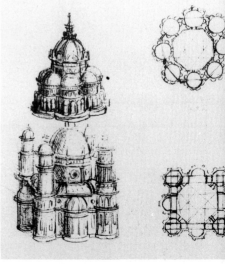

Leonardo da Vinci, drawing of centrally
planned churches, *c.* 1489.

ew of the ideal city of Chaux: Ledoux, *L'Architecture*, 1804.

View and plan of the spherical cemetery at Chaux: Ledoux, *L'Architecture*,
1804.

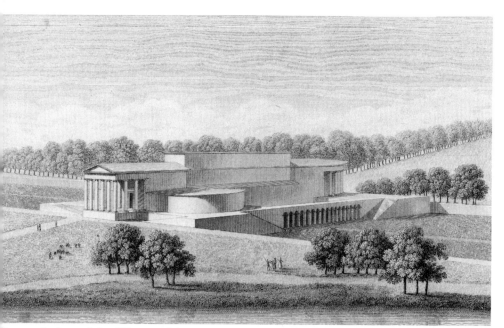

iew and plan of the 'House of Sexual Instruction' at Chaux: Ledoux, *L'Architecture*,
804.

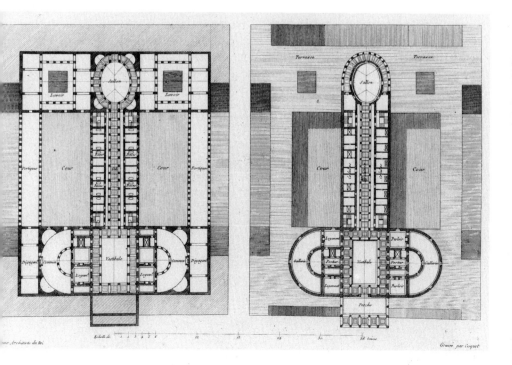

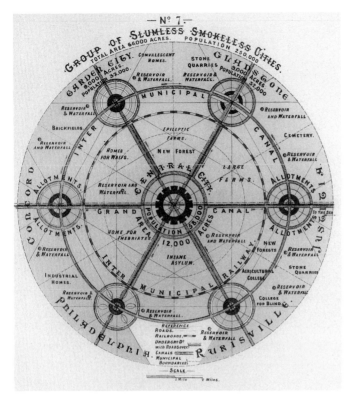

'Group of Slumless Smokeless Cities': Ebenezer Howard,
To-morrow: A Peaceful Path to Reform, 1898.

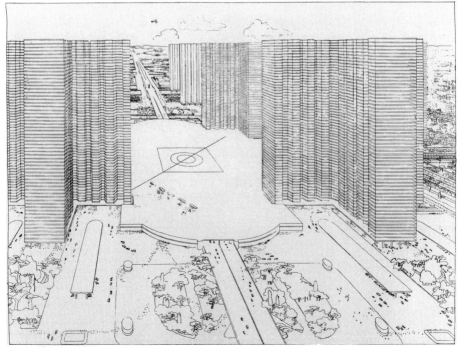

Le Corbusier, Contemporary City for Three Million People, 1922.

neida Community, New York, *c.* 1875.

e Oneida 'stirpicults', *c.* 1875.

'New Harmony – All Owin' – No Payin'', by George Cruikshank, 1843.

than it can feed? In that case thy morals are neither better nor worse than ours. Can it feed more than it has? Then our morals are better than thine.

Orou eventually reveals the true nature of Tahitian hospitality:

> We are more robust and healthy than you; but we perceived you surpassed us in intelligence and immediately we decided that some of our fairest wives and daughters should gather in the seed of a race which is better than our own. It is an experiment we have made which may well be profitable. We have extracted from thee and thine the only advantage possible. And, believe me, savages as we are, we also know how to calculate.

'Free love', it turns out, is not so free after all in Tahiti. It amounts to a form of landing tax for visitors. For the Tahitians themselves, procreation is governed by complex rules and there are harsh penalties if these are transgressed. On the island, when a man and woman decide to live together, they must share the same hut for at least one month so it is known who has fathered any children conceived. At the end of this period either party can choose to move out, whether it be to return to his or her parents or to seek another mate. When they are born, children remain under their mother's care and are to her a dowry which she brings to any new partner. Motherly love has been replaced by the sentiment of self-interest: children are cherished for the wealth they bring. The sexual desires of sterile women are ignored and they are even punished with banishment or slavery if found with a man. According to one scholar, 'Tahiti has less a moral code of conduct than a science of community planning.'

Diderot's *Supplément* was the first utopian work to expound the belief that perhaps the greatest flaws in European society stem, as one scholar puts it, from a 'misadaptation of sexuality. As sexuality links man's physical, mental, and social functioning, the greatest ills are produced when its mechanisms are distorted.' But, despite Diderot's evident sympathy for women, his Tahiti is no paradise of female emancipation. For Diderot the primary function of sexuality remained conception, a belief that carried with it the implication that the principal role of women was child-bearing. This view of the female sex as an instrument for the perpetuation of mankind inevitably allotted women a subordinate position in society. The utopia of true sexual equality could only be achieved by breaking the link between sex and procreation, a link forged by two thousand years of Christian thinking.

But sex as pure pleasure was perhaps too radical an idea even for Diderot. The third and final part of the *Supplément* returns to the discussion between A and B:

A: . . . What is to be done then? Shall we return to nature? Shall we submit to laws?

B: We will preach against insensate laws until they are reformed. And meanwhile we will submit to them. He who of his own authority infringes a bad law authorizes everyone else to infringe a good one. It is less inconvenient to be mad among madmen than to be wise all alone. Let us cry out continually that shame, punishment, and disgrace have been attached to things innocent in themselves. But let us not do those things: for shame, punishment, and disgrace are the greatest of all evils. Imitate the worthy chaplain. Be a monk in France, a savage in Tahiti.

While working on the *Supplément*, Diderot urged his daughter Angelique, newly married, to conform diligently to society's moral conventions. He recognized that what was most important, for a woman at least, was the appearance of virtue. Diderot writes: 'One revolts against this injustice, but that person is wrong. People have the right to judge women on appearances.'

The Marquis de Sade, born a generation after Diderot, would never have given this piece of advice to his daughter. Sade took human sexuality to its extremes. Like the *philosophes*, he believed that Nature, not God, ruled the world. However, his Nature was not the generally hospitable, pastoral paradise of Rousseau, nor the benign, creative force of Diderot. Rather, the uncompromising Sade saw Nature as cruel and amoral, and regarded destruction as a force as potent as creation. According to Sade, society is a conspiracy by the weak, whose idea of pleasure is virtue, against the strong, whose idea of pleasure is vice. Sade thus discards all conventional morality, and 'insists, more blatantly than Freud ever dared, that sex rules the world and that there is no sex without cruelty.' Sade does not believe that sexual perversion is a result of repression, as Diderot claims. In Sade's dark world, all forms of sex are natural and sexuality equals domination. Sexual pleasure must be had for its own sake, regardless of whether it causes pain to oneself or anyone else.

Born into an aristocratic family, Sade married, at the age of twenty-three, a woman from the upper middle class aspiring to a title. Because of his continual refusal to conform to society, he spent a third of his life in gaols and insane asylums, where he staged plays for his fellow inmates. His crimes, which included beating women, attempted poisoning (apparently an unforeseen effect of giving aphrodisiacs to prostitutes) and sodomy, began soon after his marriage. Perhaps not surprisingly, his mother-in-law was instrumental in keeping Sade locked away for so long. He fared best during the Revolution, when he held various government posts, but was back in gaol by 1793. It was in prison that most of his works were written. One of Sade's modern translators comments that, if Sade had not spent so much time locked away, 'he would not then have fantasized so luridly and chronicled dreams which chart the darkest corner of human sexuality or, as some prefer to say, drawn new maps of hell.'

In one of Sade's fantasies, entitled *Philosophie dans le Boudoir* ('Philosophy in the Bedroom'), three men and two women, drawn from various social classes, attempt to co-ordinate simultaneous orgasms by contorting their bodies and using every available erogenous zone. Their host, the greatest libertine of the age, entertains his exhausted guests by reading aloud from a pamphlet he picked up on the street, entitled 'Yet Another Effort, Frenchmen, if you would Become Republican'. The basic principle set forth in this utopian constitution, which extends to all members of society and both sexes, is that no one may deny a citizen the satisfaction of any of his or her erotic desires. Adultery, incest, sodomy and even rape are no longer deemed crimes: 'We wonder that savagery could ever reach the point where you condemn to death an unhappy person all of whose crime amounts to not sharing your tastes.' Free love reigns, and children do not know their parents but are truly *les enfants de la patrie*, as the line in *La Marseillaise* goes. During the 1848 revolution which swept across Europe, Sade's constitution was lifted from its pornographic context and reprinted by the followers of Saint-Simon.

By far the most important aspect of Sade's sexual paradise (or hell) is his insistence that women have erotic desires as well as men, and that they should have every opportunity to satisfy them:

I say then that women, having been endowed with considerably more violent penchants for carnal pleasure than we, will be able to give themselves over to it wholeheartedly, absolutely free of all encumbering hymeneal ties, of all false notions of modesty, absolutely restored to a state of Nature; I want laws permitting them to give themselves to as many men as they see fit; I would have them accorded the enjoyment of all sexes and, as in the case of men, the enjoyment of all parts of the body; and under the special clause prescribing their surrender to all who desire them, there must be subjoined another guaranteeing them a similar freedom to enjoy all they deem worthy to satisfy them.

Diderot had never gone anything like so far in his claims for female sexuality.

What's more, unlike Diderot, Sade loathed the mothering instinct and had no interest in the size of the population nor even in the continuation of the human race:

> Let us make no mistake about it, this propagation was never one of her laws, nothing she ever demanded of us, but at the very most something she tolerated. . . . Why! what difference would it make to her were the race of men entirely to be extinguished upon earth, annihilated! she laughs at our pride when we persuade ourselves all would be over and done with were this misfortune to occur!

One of the more experienced members of the orgy, Madame de Saint-Ange, gives a young female initiate some practical advice on birth control, which includes alternative forms of love-making, sponges and condoms. She also discusses female hygiene and recommends abortion if necessary: 'We are always the mistress of what we carry in our womb.' (Abortion and infanticide were, of course, capital crimes in France at this time.)

> O charming sex, you will be free: as do men, you will enjoy all the pleasures of which Nature makes a duty, from not one will you be withheld. Must the diviner half of humankind be laden with irons by the other? Ah, break those irons; Nature wills it.

Here at last was the separation of sexuality from procreation necessary for the emancipation of women. Freed from the duty to conceive and bear children, the women of Sade's utopia were finally able to join men on a truly equal footing, albeit in what most would consider a nightmare of sexual cruelty.

Sade's most gruesome imaginings are contained in *Les 120 Journées de Sodome* ('The 120 Days of Sodom'), a blow-by-blow account of a four-month orgy in a gothic castle, featuring every species of sexual anomaly, as well as horrid tortures and murders. Yet here again men and women enjoy complete equality: anal intercourse is almost always preferred by Sade's characters for its denial of sexual difference. Angela Carter remarks, 'Sade remains a monstrous and daunting cultural edifice; yet I would like to think that he put pornography in the service of women.' As Simone de Beauvoir observes, 'The supreme value of his testimony lies in its ability to disturb us. It forces us to re-examine thoroughly the basic problem which haunts our age in different forms: the true relation between man and man' and every possible combination thereof.

Sade's writings are, even by today's standards, the most extreme pornography. He argued that pornography gives 'free flight and rein to those tyrannical desires which, despite himself, torment man ceaselessly.' Without it, men will 'seek outlets for it, it will be vented upon nearby objects; it will trouble the government.' Whether one accepts this justification or not, it is striking that this pornographer *extraordinaire* is also a radical feminist. Sade's utopia of sexual licence suggests that it is only when sexual desires have been freed that women can escape a purely procreative role, to be regarded as equal partners, in bed and in the world at large.

8. Promiscuity and Prudery

In the opening decade of the nineteenth century Charles Fourier wrote the following 'general proposition':

Social progress and changes of period are brought about by virtue of the progress of women towards liberty, and social retrogression occurs as a result of a dimunition in the liberty of women. Other events influence these political changes; but there is no cause which produces social progress or decline as rapidly as a change in the condition of women. . . . In summary, the extension of the privileges of women is the fundamental cause of all social progress.

By their legitimation of sexual desire and the attacks they mounted against conventional Christian morality, especially the institution of marriage, the French *philosophes* and utopians of the eighteenth century had succeeded in making the relationship between men and women a central issue of social reform. Women's rights and sexuality had played no part in the earlier utopias of More, Campanella and Bacon, whereas utopian thinkers who came after Diderot and Sade could not escape the 'Woman Question'. Thus the nineteenth century looked set to make even greater strides towards a liberalization of sexual attitudes and the achievement of female emancipation. However, as it turned out, in both the realms of Utopia and the real world the nineteenth century saw more of the social retrogression that Fourier had warned against than of the progress of women towards liberty that he undoubtedly hoped for.

Fourier was the spiritual successor to both Diderot and the Marquis de Sade. He shared with Sade 'a sense of the power of the sexual drive and an appreciation of the diversity of individual erotic needs'. But he did not revel in sexual abuse, nor did he think that the desire to dominate was the driving force behind sex. He condemned as unnatural sexual acts in which a person was abused, injured or used against his or her will (although flagellation among consenting adults was acceptable). Nor was Fourier an anarchist like Sade. For Fourier, 'sexual liberation would not lead to the collapse of social bonds but to the reinforcement of social harmony.'

Like Diderot, Fourier believed that the passions were 'hungers' and great harm was done to a person's constitution when these were ignored or frustrated. A moral code was only needed to hold these passions in check because a misguided society had perverted them. In such conditions, 'free love' was an empty statement, an act of rebellion which could not succeed in satisfying the passions. Fourier's great mission was to create a society that went with the grain of human desires, rather than one which attempted to smother and manipulate them. He remarked:

It is easy to compress the passions by violence. Philosophy suppresses them with a stroke of the pen. Locks and the sword come to the aid of sweet morality. But nature appeals from these judgements; she regains her rights in secret. Passion stifled at one point reappears at another like water held back by a dike; it is driven inward like the humor of an ulcer closed too soon.

Elsewhere, Fourier commented, 'Nature driven out through the door comes back through the window.'

Fourier preached the 'flowering of the passions': 'Happiness consists in having many passions and many means to satisfy them.' In Harmony, Fourier's utopia, 'the man who devotes himself most ardently to pleasure becomes eminently useful for the happiness of all!' The perfect hedonist would be the perfect Harmonian. This new breed of men would emerge only after Harmony had guaranteed to every man and woman the right to a 'sexual minimum', a kind of minimum wage in human relations. In Harmony, the threat of sexual deprivation, along with that of hunger, would be permanently banished so that every man and woman could truly be free to fulfil his or her potential: 'No one capable of love [will ever] be frustrated in his or her desire.' Even the sexual minorities – lesbians, homosexuals, sodomites, fetishists and flagellants – would be catered for. Fourier admitted to his own personal mania: 'I discovered that I loved lesbians and was eager to do anything to please them.'

In the phalanx, the heart of Fourier's new world order, amorous affairs are run by an elaborate hierarchy of officials: a pontiff (always an elderly woman who is well versed in matters of the heart), high priests, matrons, confessors, fairies, fakirs and genies. Each of these dignitaries has a part to play in the Court of Love, which holds nightly sessions after the children and the Vestals (chaste young men and women under twenty) have gone to bed. The Court of Love is a kind of singles club, which sponsors fetes, entertainments and orgies. Fourier, like the best Club Med or 'Love Boat' organizer, plans for every minute of the day. Certain institutions specialize in sexual philanthropy, caring for the poor, the elderly and 'perverts' – all those, in fact, whose sexual needs are normally denied in the civilized world.

Fourier is particularly concerned for the comfort and enjoyment of travellers. After assessing their sexual needs and proclivities, the phalanx arranges introductory orgies:

> When the Head Fairy waves her wand a semi-bacchanalia gets underway. The members of both groups [of men and women] rush into each other's arms, and in the ensuing scramble caresses are liberally given and received. Everyone strokes and investigates whatever comes to hand and surrenders himself or herself to the unfettered impulses of simple nature. Each participant flits from one person to another, bestowing kisses everywhere with as much eagerness as rapidity. Everyone also makes a special point of encountering those individuals who caught his or her eye earlier. . . . The opening caresses and exploratory activities should last no more than a few minutes, barely a quarter of an hour.

To break up the skirmish in order to get on to the next round of entertainment, diversionary tactics are employed: homosexuals and lesbians are 'thrown into the fray to attack people of their own kind' to 'create a general distraction'. The senior confessors can then easily call a halt to the proceedings. One scholar aptly describes this as 'the fantasy of the traveling salesman who spent restless lonely nights in grubby provincial hotels'.

The Court of Love also upholds the amorous code, which is not coercive, but simply ensures that everyone finds their right place in society according to their sexual needs and desires. The Court gives out 'amorous tithes', 'indulgences' and 'penances' in parody of the Catholic Church. Court officials keep a card file of the personality and sexual proclivities of each member of the phalanx (ideally numbering 1600 to accommodate all possible combinations), and the files are frequently updated.

Not surprisingly, marriage has no place in Harmony. Man's erotic desires are far too complex to be thus strait-jacketed. (Fourier drew up a pseudoscientific list of the drawbacks to marriage, such as monotony and 'disappointing in-laws'.) It was obvious to Fourier that 'both the law and [the Christian] religion admit only one goal in love and that goal is procreation . . . they forbid purely sentimental relationships, for those unions would produce neither Christians nor citizens.' Christianity sanctioned and even encouraged brutality and tyranny within marriage. Fourier cites the familiar example of a girl married against her will: 'Her deflowering, a veritable debauch, an obvious case of rape, is no less sacred in the eyes of the law and of religion.' Marriage was not in the interest of either sex, but Fourier identified women as its principal victims.

Like the Marquis de Sade, Fourier argued that men and women were subject to the same emotional and sexual needs; therefore, they should enjoy the same rights and privileges. In his phalanx Fourier eliminates all the tedium and drudgery from women's lives by providing communal housekeeping and child-care, which begins immediately after the baby is born. (Babies were not to be swaddled and strapped into cradles, but placed in specially constructed hammocks which enabled them to move freely and see what was going on – the forerunner of B.F. Skinner's 'baby-in-the-box'.) Boys and girls receive exactly the same education to eliminate preconceived notions of sexual roles.

Fourier acknowledged that certain conditions had to be met before any society, even Harmony, could accept total sexual liberation. He remarks that until venereal disease has been completely eradicated 'Harmony will be more circumspect about love than civilization now is.' Fourier would not have expected to see his new amorous world implemented today, in the AIDS era. In any case, he was well aware of a sea change in attitudes following the seizing of the French throne by Louis Philippe in 1830. The new regime insisted upon a strict moral code. Realizing that these radical ideas might endanger the success of his larger utopian vision, Fourier suppressed the work whose central theme was love and sex in the phalanx, *Le Nouveau Monde Amoureux* ('The New Amorous World'). It remained in manuscript until, appropriately, the 1960s.

Fourier's self-censorship was just one example of a backlash against any realignment of sexual roles. In the predominantly rural, pre-industrial societies of Europe, husbands and wives had worked side by side. With the industrialization and urbanization of the nineteenth century, men's occupations increasingly took them out of the home, and the women were left behind to raise the children and manage domestic affairs. The gap between men and women, especially in the middle classes, widened. This setback for women's social freedom was accompanied by a new, puritanical view of sexuality. The 'cult of true womanhood' arose, while at the same time the fledgling women's movement was subsumed in Marx's class war. As a feminist wrote in 1917: 'The woman movement has been almost synchronous with socialism (like Jill, tumbling after).'

In *Der Ursprung der Familie, des Privateigentums und des Staats* ('The

Origin of the Family, Private Property and the State') of 1884, Friedrich Engels offers a Marxist analysis of women's oppression. In yet another version of the 'noble savage' myth, Engels claims that women were free and, indeed, enjoyed matriarchal authority in the primitive communistic society:

> In the old communistic household, which comprised many couples and their children, the task entrusted to the women of managing the household was as much a public and socially necessary industry as procuring of food by the men.

But, with the rise of civilization and private ownership,

> . . . the overthrow of mother-right was the *world historical defeat* of the female sex. The man took command in the house also; the woman was degraded and reduced to servitude, she became the slave of his lust and a mere instrument for the production of his children. . . . The first class oppression coincides with that of the female sex by the male.

Engels, therefore, declares that 'the first condition for the liberation of the wife is to bring the whole female sex back into public industry, and that in turn demands the abolition of the monogamous family as the economic unit of society.' However, his idea of freedom for women is limited to 'matriarchal authority' and 'mother-right' – there is no mention of their sexual needs and desires. Sade's message had been lost.

What is more, in the puritanical climate of Victorian Britain, this attack on the institution of marriage was something of an embarrassment to Marxist social reformers. They preferred to concentrate on the class struggle, which in any case took precedence over the battle of the sexes in Marxist theory. The issue of whether marriage would be abolished in a communist state plagued the Socialist League. William Morris wrote to Bernard Shaw in 1885 that 'we of the S. L. must before long state our views on wedlock quite plainly and take the consequences, which I admit are likely to be serious.'

Morris's *News from Nowhere* reveals the author's feelings on the 'Woman Question' – perhaps more clearly than he intended. Soon after he wakes up in the future, William Guest encounters three young women 'flitting to and fro' and finds them pleasant to look at, 'shapely and well-knit of body':

As to their dress, which of course I took note of, I should say that they were decently veiled with drapery, and not bundled up with millinery; that they were clothed like women, not upholstered like armchairs, as most women of our time are.

These same young girls arrange the flowers for the table and cheerfully serve Guest and his male companion, Robert, breakfast. They are not shy, but one of them blushes when Guest takes her for a much younger woman.

To his credit, Guest is puzzled by this image of the woman of the future. He asks the old antiquarian, Hammond, who claims to 'understand "the Emancipation of Women movement" of the nineteenth century': 'But about this woman question? I saw at the Guest House that the women were waiting on the men: that seems a little like reaction, doesn't it?' Hammond responds: 'Does it? . . . perhaps you think housekeeping an unimportant occupation, not deserving of respect. I believe that was the opinion of the "advanced" women of the nineteenth century, and their male backers'. He continues:

Come, now, my friend, . . . don't you know that it is a great pleasure to a clever woman to manage a house skilfully, and to do it so that all the house-mates about her look pleased, and are grateful to her? And then, you know, everybody likes to be ordered about by a pretty woman: why, it is one of the pleasantest forms of flirtation.

Guest pursues the matter: 'Don't you remember that some of the "superior" women wanted to emancipate the more intelligent part of their sex from the bearing of children?' Hammond replies, taking a position close to Engels, 'I *do* remember about that strange piece of baseless folly, the result, like all other follies of the period, of the hideous class tyranny which then obtained.' He assures Guest that maternity is highly honoured in his society:

So that, you see, the ordinarily healthy woman (and almost all our women are both healthy and at least comely), respected as a child-bearer and rearer of children, desired as a woman, loved as a companion, unanxious for the future of her children, has far more instinct for maternity than the poor drudge and mother of drudges of past days could ever have had; or than her sister of the upper classes, brought up in affected ignorance of natural facts, reared in an atmosphere of mingled prudery and prurience.

Morris's society of the future is strictly monogamous, although partners may be changed by mutual consent. Human nature has improved, but not that much: Hammond admits that love is still the cause of what sadness and conflict there is in society.

Edward Bellamy's view of the woman of the future in *Looking Backward* is not much more enlightened. Bellamy, like Morris, was sympathetic to the plight of contemporary women: the poor who died from overwork and the well-off but intellectually frustrated who 'languished under house arrest'. With collective housekeeping, time-saving gadgets and centralized kitchens, Bellamy's future does offer women freedom from drudgery. However, Edith, the daughter of Julian West's host in the future, does not strike one as a convincing prototype of the 'new woman'. Her father describes her as an 'indefatigable shopper', and, like Morris's young nubiles, she is particularly adept at arranging flowers, with a charming tendency to blush.

All women work (though we never discover the vocation of either Edith or her mother). Women belong to a separate branch of the labour army, 'under exclusively feminine regime', which requires lighter duties and shorter hours (female judges and a place in the President's cabinet for the lady general safeguard female interests). But Dr Leete makes it clear that this is a state of affairs which men tolerate to make the little women happy:

> The men of this day so well appreciate that they owe to the beauty and grace of women the chief zest of their lives and their main incentive to effort, that they permit them to work at all only because it is fully understood that a certain regular requirement of labor, of a sort adapted to their powers, is well for body and mind, during the period of maximum physical vigor.

Like Hammond, Dr Leete has the advantage of hindsight and claims that he understands the limitations of the women's movement of the nineteenth century:

> It is in giving full play to the differences of sex rather than in seeking to obliterate them, as was apparently the effort of some reformers of

your day, that the enjoyment of each by itself and the piquancy which each has for the other, are alike enhanced. In your day there was no career for women except in an unnatural rivalry with men. We have given them a world of their own, with its emulations, ambitions and careers, and I assure you they are very happy in it.

The primary role of women in *Looking Backward* is still procreative. Women leave the industrial army when they have children and may return to the workforce at any time, though there seems to be no provision for child-care (Dr Leete states that mothers normally work for five to fifteen years rather than the full twenty-five). Motherhood is honoured mainly because it serves society's interests: 'Can you think of any service constituting a stronger claim on the nation's gratitude than bearing and nursing the nation's children?' asks Dr Leete. Conventional marriage persists, but because matches are based on love rather than money, the forces of natural selection are given full play, producing a spontaneous eugenics programme.

Julian West deduces from all that he has learned about the future that 'until the nation was ripe for the present system of organized production and distribution, no radical improvement in the position of woman was possible.' One scholar remarks that 'in the year 2000 Bellamy's women are still frozen to the pedestal' and this goes for Morris's future world, too.

However, there were attempts to escape the straitjacket of Victorian morality and experiment with different forms of relationship between the sexes. One such, by the Oneida Perfectionists of upstate New York, demonstrates just what it was possible to get away with, even in the middle of the Victorian century – if you were prepared to confine yourself to the middle of nowhere. The founder, John Humphrey Noyes, was born into a prosperous upper-middle-class family in Putney, Vermont, in 1811. His father successfully went from teaching to business and finally into politics as a US Representative in Congress. His mother, who was deeply religious, was the second cousin of President Rutherford B. Hayes. Noyes fulfilled the expectations of his family by going to Yale Theological Seminary in New Haven, Connecticut. However, he became discouraged with his studies there and sought guidance from his Bible, whereupon it fell open at the passage: 'Fear not ye: for I know that ye seek Jesus, which was crucified. He is not here' (Matthew 28: 5, 6). Noyes immediately abandoned both the seminary and orthodox religion. He joined America's homeless, wandering the streets of New York for three weeks, eating nothing, craving only 'the strongest stimulants, such

as cayenne pepper'. Finally, his brother Horatio rescued him and arranged
for his return to New Haven. During this exploit Noyes formulated his
own theology, which he called Perfectionism, and which he proceeded
to preach throughout the North-East.

Noyes rejected the notion, then prevalent among many social reformers, that to better mankind one must first enhance his environment. He
criticized previous attempts at reform by both religious and social groups:
'Revivalists failed for want of regeneration of society, and the Socialists
failed for want of regeneration of the heart.' 'The idea prevails generally
in the world,' he told his followers, 'that character cannot be radically
changed . . . the whole theory of Christianity is based on the assumption
that character can be improved, yea, radically changed.' Noyes's message
was a comforting and appealing one:

> The truth is, the way of salvation is a pleasurable process. Pleasure is
> more valuable than pain in its results; and the way that Christ proposes
> to save us, on the whole, is not by suffering, but by making us happy.
> The happiest man is the best man, and does the most good.

Allied to this emphasis on happiness was a courageously frank attitude
to sexual matters that is strikingly modern:

> Sexual shame is factitious and irrational. The moral reform that arises
> from the sentiment of shame attempts a hopeless war with nature.

The central tenet of Noyes's Perfectionism was 'complex marriage'.
Noyes considered monogamous marriage 'a tyrannical institution that
did not exist in heaven and eventually would be abolished on earth.'
'The law of marriage "worketh wrath",' he wrote. However, after an
early romantic disappointment, he returned home to Putney and in 1838
married a woman he hardly knew, who nevertheless proved to be devoted
to him and his cause. Asserting control over his family (his father was by
this time an alcoholic), he proceeded to arrange his siblings' marriages to
create a 'community'. Before his own wedding, he wrote to his fiancée,
outlining his ideas on complex marriage:

> We can enter into no engagements with each other, which shall limit the
> range of our affections, as they are limited in matrimonial engagements
> by the fashion of this world . . . the object of my connexion with her
> [my yoke-fellow] will be, not to monopolize and enslave her heart or

my own, but to enlarge and establish both, in the free fellowship of God's universal family.

Noyes's matrimonial experiment began in secret in this tiny enclave in Vermont amongst his few followers and resembled nothing so much as wife-swapping. The secret soon got out and Noyes, charged with adultery, escaped to New York State. In the revolutionary year 1848 Noyes set up a new community in Oneida, isolated from the outside world. To avoid the mistakes of Vermont, members were carefully screened. Thus secured, Noyes set about 'perfecting' his doctrine of complex marriage. He believed that 'the restoration of true relations between the sexes is a matter second in importance only to the reconciliation of man to God.' And, he wrote elsewhere, 'The great problems of our relation to God and of the relation of the sexes, which the Fourierists postpone as of no pressing importance, we consider the first to be solved.' This is, of course, an unfair criticism of Fourier – Noyes would not have known *Le Nouveau Monde Amoureux*.

It is all the more extraordinary, then, that the Oneida Community seems in many of its details to have been the incarnation of Fourier's Harmony. Noyes's work *Bible Communism* reads like a more sober version of one of Fourier's writings. He states, for example, that 'in vital society labor will become attractive. Loving companionship in labor, and especially the mingling of the sexes, makes labor attractive.' According to Noyes, for believers to love each other in close communal Association (a favourite Fourierist word), they must love each other fervently and physically, 'not by pairs, as in the world, but *en masse*'.

Noyes was not advocating orgies, however. In Oneida, arrangements for sexual intercourse between two people were made through a third party, much like Fourier's 'aunts'. To avoid intimacy and 'special love' developing – and so endangering the smooth operation of complex marriage – couples were forbidden to spend the night together. Young people were the most prone to love's affliction; Noyes therefore established a system of hierarchy whereby older members were paired with younger members. It was considered very much against the 'public spirit' for a woman to refuse the advances of any man within the community, particularly as her action might suggest that she had grown too fond of one person.

If 'special love' persisted between members, then sexual privileges were taken away. 'Special love' was even condemned among families who joined Oneida, that is between husband and wife, parent and child (community child-care was provided). Peer pressure was invoked by evenings of mutual criticism instituted and often presided over by Noyes, who always had the last word.

The Oneida Community was, not surprisingly, accused of immorality by outsiders. A contemporary journalist described complex marriage as an unprecedented 'combination of polygamy and polyandry, with certain religious and social restraints'. Noyes retorted to such criticisms:

> The thing we have done for which we are called 'Free Lovers,' is simply this: We have left the simple form of marriage and advanced to the complex stage of it. . . . The honor and faithfulness that constitutes an ideal marriage, may exist between two hundred as well as two; while the guarantees for women and children are much greater in the Community than they can be in any private family.

Noyes's views on procreation were influenced by personal experience. His wife had five difficult childbirths: all but one were premature or stillborn. Noyes came to conclude that there were two kinds of sexual intercourse, 'amative' and 'propagative', and tailored his theology accordingly. God originally created Eve as a companion and 'helpmeet' for Adam. The subject of children didn't come up until after the Fall. However, Noyes disapproved of conventional contraception: 'A woman is less convenient than the ordinary means of masturbation [of which he didn't approve in any case].' Nor could he put his blessing on *coitus interruptus*, for 'after marriage it is as foolish and cruel to expend one's seed on a wife merely for the sake of getting rid of it, as it would be to fire a gun at one's best friend merely for the sake of unloading it.' And, besides, this method was 'a drain on the life of man, and when habitual, produces disease.'

Noyes's eventual solution was *coitus reservatus*, also known as male continence, a kind of 'celibate intercourse' based on the principle 'It is the glory of man to control himself, and the Kingdom of Heaven summons him to self-control in ALL THINGS.' Noyes likened male continence to rowing near a waterfall. The nearer one gets to the falls, the harder it is to return: 'If he is willing to learn, experience will teach him the wisdom of confining his excursions to the region of easy rowing, unless he has an object in view [propagation] that is worth the cost of going over the falls.'

Male continence not only proved to be a very effective method of birth control, it also produced unexpected benefits. To avoid accident during the learning stages, women past menopause inducted young men in the mysteries of *coitus reservatus*, while the older, more experienced men did the same for the young women. This arrangement was even more ingenious than Fourier's sexual philanthropy in guaranteeing that older members were not left out. Also, it appears from a revealing comment made by Noyes that the women were more likely to achieve orgasm through male continence: 'My wife's experience was very satisfactory, as it had never been before.'

So, complex marriage, which at first sight seems to institutionalize sexual freedom, was in fact underpinned by the most rigorous sexual self-denial. This ambiguity was reflected in the status of women in the Oneida Community: freed from the encumbrance of raising children, they were able to work alongside the men in the community's light industry (primarily the manufacture of animal traps). Photographs show them in front of the communal Mansion House, sporting short hair and mid-length skirts over trousers. But the appearance of sexual equality is misleading. Noyes believed that 'man is naturally the superior' of the two sexes. 'Woman,' he wrote, 'is comparatively passive, and man is active; and the active party should be responsible for the passive.' According to the Oneida *Handbook* of 1875, their women had 'not ceased to love and honor the truth that "the man is the head of the woman" and that woman's highest God-given right is to be "the glory of man".'

Just how subservient the women were is evident in the 'scientific' breeding programme which Noyes decided to implement at Oneida in 1868–69. As early as 1848 he had written:

The time will come when involuntary and random procreation will cease, and when scientific combination will be applied to human generation as freely and successfully as it is to . . . animals.

Noyes called his system 'stirpiculture', from the Latin *stirps*, meaning stock or stem – the word 'eugenics' had not yet been coined.

The Oneida men willingly offered themselves, as Noyes's 'true soldiers', 'to be used in forming any combinations that might seem to you desirable.' The women, for their part, signed a document which stated:

1. That we do not belong to *ourselves* in any respect, but that we *do* belong first to *God*, and second to Mr *Noyes* as God's true representative.
2. That we have no rights or personal feelings in regard to child-bearing

which shall in the least degree oppose or embarrass him in his choice of
scientific combinations.
3. That we will put aside all envy, childishness and self-seeking,
and rejoice with those who are chosen candidates; that we will, if
necessary, become martyrs to science, and cheerfully resign all desire
to become mothers, if for any reason Mr Noyes deem us unfit material
for propagation. Above all, we offer ourselves 'living sacrifices' to God
and true Communism.

Noyes himself, believing in the superiority of his family line, sired ten of
the fifty-eight 'stirpicults' while his eldest son was responsible for three.

This eugenics programme was, in fact, the undoing of the Oneida
Community. Although 'special love' between parent and child was still
discouraged, it was unavoidable when the stirpicults began to arrive and,
together with the jealousy felt by those martyrs not chosen for the cause,
proved divisive. While contention within the community raged, outside
disapproval, which had never entirely abated, was renewed with even
greater vigour. The most serious charge concerned the induction of under-
age girls into the joys of complex marriage. Sexual relations for women
at Oneida began soon after menstruation, which normally occurred at
about thirteen, but sometimes as early as ten. Noyes realized that he
could face charges of statutory rape, and so in 1879 he fled to Canada.
The community voted, in the face of outside pressure, to give up complex
marriage. However, the collapse of the Oneida Community posed a real
dilemma: how could the unmarried women become reintegrated into a
prudish society which had already condemned them as promiscuous? As
some members remarked at the time: 'By jolly, they've got to take care
of the women and children.'

The solution was to turn Oneida into a joint-stock company, allowing
members to continue living in the Mansion House, and working in and
drawing dividends from the Oneida industries. Oneida Ltd survives to
this day, and you can still buy the cutlery it produces. At its dissolution,
the leaders of the Community said of their fellow utopian pioneers:

> . . . the truth is, as all the world will one day see and acknowledge, they
> have not been pleasure-seekers and sensualists but social architects,
> with high religious and moral aims, whose experiments and discoveries
> they have sincerely believed would prove of value to mankind.

Despite its rather ignominious end, the Oneida Community was a remarkable phenomenon. For over thirty years Noyes was able to create sexual relationships radically different from anything in the outside world. But this was only possible because the community was literally hidden away in the backwoods of America. The new breed of feminists, whose aim was the reformation of society at large, faced much greater difficulties. Society's prudishness made any open discussion of sexuality, especially by women, out of the question. With sexual liberation off the agenda, the feminists were left with only two choices: either to reject sex altogether, becoming the sort of 'new woman' satirized as a cigar-smoking spinster who marches on Parliament; or to take the same tack as Morris and Bellamy, idealizing the 'true woman' of the domestic sphere.

As we shall see in the next chapter, one solution to this dilemma was already to be found in the Shaker religion: Shakers rejected both sex and motherhood, choosing instead to live together as brothers and sisters, separate but equal. The American feminist and utopian, Charlotte Perkins Gilman, on the other hand, imagined motherhood without sex or men.

Gilman, the great-niece of the author of *Uncle Tom's Cabin*, Harriet Beecher Stowe, held motherhood to be 'the foundation stone of a society'. She was drawn to Bellamy's *Looking Backward* and even lectured to the Nationalist Clubs which his vision had inspired. In various books and articles, she advocates women in the workforce, collective housekeeping and centralized kitchens, all components of Bellamy's utopia. By thus alleviating the drudgery and isolation which the traditional home imposed on women, it could become what it had always claimed to be, a caring atmosphere to return to at the end of the day.

But Gilman rejected Bellamy's Marxist, male-dominated view of the Great Change. She sought to return women to centre stage. She wanted feminists and socialists to work together, but believed that women alone were in the best position to lead the way towards a genuinely co-operative society. She argued, like Fourier before her, that it was the social constraints on women which were holding back human potential. The liberation of women would inevitably lead to the liberation of men, who suffered from the equally stifling role of sole provider and authority.

Gilman's life poignantly reveals the struggle to reconcile the two principal feminist ideals of the late nineteenth century, motherhood and freedom. After the birth of her only child, she suffered from severe post-natal depression. She then became the victim of the neurologist S. Weir Mitchell's famous 'rest cure', which decreed that she must never leave her baby and never take up pen and paper again. Mitchell, along with Sigmund Freud, believed that women's increased intellectual activity and the spread of nervous disorders were directly related. Gilman soon rejected Mitchell's treatment and went on to write a fictional account of her experience, 'The Yellow Wallpaper'. She divorced, creating a scandal when she not only blessed her ex-husband's marriage to her own best friend, but also chose to 'abandon' her daughter to their care. Nevertheless, for Gilman, motherhood was a sacred trust and source of fulfilment.

Like other feminists of her generation, Gilman opposed contraceptive devices and abortion. She felt they encouraged female sexuality outside the bonds of wedlock, threatening to undermine the primacy of the mother within the family, women's trump card. However, she believed in 'voluntary motherhood', advocating that it was the woman, not her husband, who had the right to decide when to have a child and to abstain from sexual intercourse accordingly. Gilman distrusted the idea of sexual liberation because she thought it would only serve to replace one form of subordination with another. Sex for women, whether inside or outside marriage, often meant venereal disease and difficult, possibly life-threatening pregnancies; it was rarely carefree pleasure.

In her utopian fantasy, *Herland*, serialized in 1915, sex has been abolished. The novel begins when three male explorers in Africa, hearing of a land of female warriors, set out to find this kingdom of Amazons. The three men represent different 'types'. Jeff is a Southern gentleman, chivalrous and sentimental about women. According to Terry, 'there were two kinds of women – those he wanted and those he didn't; Desirable and Undesirable.' As for the narrator, Van, he is the sort whom women like but never love. The three explorers enjoy fantasizing about what they will find. Terry 'had visions of a sort of sublimated summer resort – just Girls and Girls and Girls.' He boasts, 'I'll get myself elected king in no time – whew! Solomon will have to take a back seat!'

The reality, of course, is very different. The men are taken prisoner by a group of middle-aged but athletic women with short hair. Van remarks, 'We found ourselves much in the position of the suffragette trying to get to the Parliament buildings through a triple cordon of London police.' They try manfully to escape (Terry wants to 'get to where the real women are – the mothers, and the girls'), but without success.

The explorers find it very difficult to accept that there really are no men. Finally, one of the women explains that, several thousand years earlier, their entire male population had been wiped out by war and disease. The women thought they were doomed until one among them bore children by parthenogenesis. From this one Mother, there descended a line of 'New Women' who, when they felt the 'Supreme Desire' for children, discovered that they could conceive spontaneously, without men and without sex. However, to prevent overpopulation, each woman is limited to one child, and only then if she is healthy – a kind of asexual eugenics. When the urge of motherhood comes upon her at an inopportune time, she must distract her thoughts (presumably rather like a man having to take a cold shower).

The children – all female, of course – are cherished by the whole community. Child-care is a communal service, provided by the most skilled women. One of the female characters in the sequel to *Herland*, *With Her in Ourland*, sums up their attitude to motherhood: 'Motherhood is venerated in your world, as it is in Herland, but with you it is used to confine women and children, not help them grow.'

In Herland, a mother is no longer 'completely wrapped up in her own pink bundle of fascinating babyhood, and taking but the faintest theoretic interest in anybody else's bundle, to say nothing of the common needs of all the bundles.' Herlanders are not familiar with the concepts of home and family. Van comments: 'All the surrounding devotion our women have put into their private families, these women put into their country and race. All the loyalty and service men expect of wives, they gave, not singly to men, but collectively to one another.'

The Victorian male explorers had expected a land of women to be full of 'feminine vanity', 'frills and furbelows', dull submissive monotony, pettiness, jealousy and hysteria. Instead, they found daring social inventiveness, social consciousness, sisterly affection, health, vigour and calm temper. 'These women, quite unassisted by any masculine spirit of enterprise, had ignored their past and built daringly for the future.' To Van, Herland was 'like – coming home to mother', but not 'the under-flannels-and-doughnuts mother, the fussy person that waits on you and spoils you'. Terry calls it 'Ma-land' and complains, 'Oh, well, of course, if you like a perpetual Sunday school, it's all very well. But I like Something Doing. Here it's all done.'

The women of Herland, too, feel that their single sex society lacks something. They envision a bi-sexual world 'full of continuous lovers, ardent, happy, mutually devoted', all of which makes for greater creativity. The visitors eventually marry three young, attractive and very independent Herlanders (the men insist on a ceremony to make it all look 'proper'). Jeff and Van find true companionship and happiness with their wives. Terry, however, cannot dispel his belief that 'there never was a woman yet that did not enjoy being *mastered*.' He is convicted of marital rape, and exiled.

The social conventions of her day meant that Gilman could not, and probably did not even want to, imagine a world where sexual liberation reigned. Instead, *Herland* is an attempt to reconcile the restricted choices left to educated Victorian women, sanctified motherhood or sexless intellectual pursuits. By depicting a society which functions smoothly without men, Gilman implies that the 'Woman Question' is really the 'Man Question'. However, the reader cannot help wondering if the re-introduction of the opposite sex into Herland does not spell the beginning of the end for this utopia, and the novel finishes on a note of uncertainty.

Ultimately, Gilman's utopian vision is crippled by this inability to embrace sexual freedom. A survey of sex in Utopia reveals the close association between sexual liberation and sexual equality. It is no coincidence that the Marquis de Sade and Charles Fourier, who both dreamt of a sexually indulgent society, are among the most truly egalitarian in their attitudes towards men and women. This connection is borne out by recent history. It was the widespread availability of the contraceptive pill in the 1960s, breaking once and for all the link between sex and procreation, which ushered in both the 'permissive society' and the modern women's movement. The last few decades have seen not only a growing tolerance for sexual relations outside marriage and forms of desire long considered 'deviant', but also the entry of women into all levels of the workforce and legislation to safeguard their rights.

But this change is not without its critics. Religious conservatives reject both sex as pleasure and the modern emancipated woman. This double backlash was evident during the 1992 American Presidential campaign. When Dan Quayle, then Vice-President, complained about the sympathetic television portrayal of a single, working woman who decides to have a baby on her own, he was attacking both the sexual permissiveness that allowed her to become pregnant in the first place, and the idea that a woman can choose motherhood outside the traditional family. This self-styled 'moral majority' continues to strive for political influence.

The feminist writer Margaret Atwood has imagined a future where the most extreme elements within this religious fundamentalism have gained power. In her dystopia *The Handmaid's Tale* (1985), growing immorality and a declining birthrate (caused in part by a series of chemical and nuclear accidents) provoke a fundamentalist coup in the United States. The first act of the new regime is to take away women's charge cards and their jobs, two things which Bellamy had bestowed upon them in *Looking Backward*.

In Atwood's nightmare of the future, a repressive puritanism has replaced the promiscuity of the late twentieth century, and women have returned to their 'natural' role in society: to be 'sacred vessels' and bear children. The biblical story of the childless Rachel, who says to her husband Jacob, 'Behold my maid Bilhah, go in unto her; and she shall bear upon my knees, that I may also have children by her' (Genesis 30:3), is re-enacted on a national scale. Thus, if a Wife is infertile, her husband takes a Handmaiden. Infertile women who are not married become either domestic servants (Marthas), controllers of other women (Aunts) or outcasts (Unwomen). On the rare occasion of a birth all the women gather together and go through a kind of sympathetic ritual – a moment of great female solidarity, except that the Handmaidens, who have lost their personal names and identities, are not allowed to speak to one another.

Lately, conservative critics of sexual permissiveness have been joined by radical feminists who see its manifestation in pornography as degrading to women. For example, under pressure from feminists lawyers, Indianapolis recently enacted a law banning all pornography (though the law was later struck down as incompatible with the First Amendment of the US Constitution). There is a certain irony in this. Conservatives wish to outlaw pornography because they believe to do so would bolster precisely those 'family values' which feminists have long attacked as a cloak for patriarchy. Certainly, the evidence from Utopia is that those societies which are most reticent about sexual matters are also those in which the role of women is most clearly circumscribed. Women who would restrict the expression of sexuality perhaps risk undermining the foundations of their own liberty. The Utopia of human freedom is also the Utopia of human desire.

'Shakers at Meeting. The Final Procession': Arthur Boyd Houghton,
The Graphic, 14 May 1870.

PART FIVE

RELIGION

'Tis the gift to be simple,
'Tis the gift to be free,
'Tis the gift to come down
Where we ought to be,
And when we find ourselves
In the place just right,
'Twill be in the valley of love and delight.

When true simplicity is gain'd,
To bow and to bend
We shan't be ashamed,
To turn, turn will be our delight
'Till by turning, turning
We come round right.

'Simple Gifts' – Shaker Hymn

9. Third Class Ticket to Heaven

The religious and the utopian are clearly kin. The desire to live in harmony with God usually implies a desire to live in harmony with one's fellow man, and perfect harmony is found only in Utopia. Nevertheless, orthodox Catholicism has always been inimical to utopian thought. (Thomas More was canonized despite, rather than because of, his role as the creator of the genre.) As we noted in Chapter 2, Saint Augustine declared the belief that perfection could be achieved on earth a heresy, and the doctrine of original sin did not offer much hope for the reformation of man's character. In the Catholic tradition, the only utopia is the Kingdom of Heaven, which may be achieved within us or in the after-life, but which man cannot create in this sublunary sphere.

However, one strain within the Protestant tradition has proved fertile ground for utopian ideas – in fact, it could be said to be the religious version of Utopia – and that is millenarianism. Its origin is to be found in the last book of the New Testament, the Revelation of St John the Divine, also called the Apocalypse. All Christians believe in the Second Coming of Christ, but the Book of Revelation suggests that His coming is imminent: 'Blessed is he that readeth, and they that hear the words of this prophecy, and keep those things which are written therein: for the time is at hand' (Revelation 1:3). The book is full of signs, portents, strange beasts and even stranger apparitions. In it, St John recounts a vision which revealed to him the rather complicated sequence of events which will precede the end of the world. The passage in St John's prophecy from which the millenarians take their doctrine describes an angel come down from heaven who:

> . . . laid hold on the dragon, that old serpent, which is the Devil, and Satan, and bound him a thousand years, And cast him into the bottomless pit, and shut him up, and set a seal upon him, that he should deceive the nations no more, till the thousand years should be fulfilled.

During this thousand-year period, or millennium, with Satan safely put away, a small elect 'lived and reigned with Christ' while their tormentors were damned, not to live again 'until the thousand years were finished.

This is the first resurrection.' The final battle between God and Satan would occur 'when the thousand years are expired, [and] Satan shall be loosed out of his prison, And shall go out to deceive the nations which are in the four quarters of the earth.' God would triumph, the Last Judgement would take place and there would be 'a new heaven and a new earth': the holy city, new Jerusalem, would come down out of heaven, and God dwell with men (Revelation 20–21:3).

However, St John's prophecy, like all prophecies, is obscure, and Christians have inevitably differed as to the nature and timing of the millennium and its exact relation to Christ's Second Coming. The conventional belief (sometimes called post-millenarianism) is that Christ's Coming will follow the millennium: it is therefore postponed to the far distant future. On the other hand, a minority opinion (pre-millenarianism) holds that Christ's second advent precedes the millennium: it is therefore either close at hand or, in fact, has already taken place. (John Humphrey Noyes, for example, thanks to a feat of biblical exegesis, discovered that the Second Coming had occurred in AD 70.)

It is around this latter belief that radical utopian sects have gathered. Freed by Christ's return from the shackles of original sin, they no longer see any obstacle to attaining the perfect life in the here and now.

Throughout the history of Christianity, millenarianism has been a prime ingredient of revolutions, as was evident in the turmoil of the English Civil War when, according to one contemporary, 'the spirit of the whole Creation is about the Reformation of the World' and, thus, 'all sorts of people dreamed of an *Utopia*.' A potent brew of revolution and millenarianism prompted utopian sects to spring up all over England: the Ranters, libertines with dreams of free love; the Diggers, whose principle of common property led them 'to digge, and to take possession of the commons for the poor on George-Hill in Surrey'; the Levellers, with a programme of universal male suffrage and other civil rights; and the Fifth Monarchy men, who believed that Oliver Cromwell was the forerunner of the Messiah.

The discovery of the New World had fuelled the fires of millenarianism, for the virgin American continent was regarded as the lost Paradise, the wilderness which God had promised to transform into Eden (Isaiah 51:3). Indeed, Christopher Columbus thought that he had discovered the Garden of Eden at the mouth of the Orinoco in Venezuela where four rivers meet, matching the biblical description (Genesis 2:10). At the time he fled in terror, but he remained convinced that 'God made me the messenger of the new heaven and the new earth, of which He spoke in the Apocalypse by Saint John, after having spoken of it by the mouth of Isaiah; and He showed me the spot where to find it.'

It was in the mid-seventeenth century, following the tumults of the Thirty Years War in Europe and the Civil War in England, that Europeans began in earnest to view the American continent as the stage upon which would be enacted the events described by St John. Men such as John Milton's Oxford tutor, Joseph Mede, believed that recent catastrophic events in Europe signalled the approach of the millennium and that the final battle between God and Satan would be fought in America. Millenarians, seeking the new Eden as well as refuge from persecution in the Old World, led the way in establishing the American colonies. William Penn, for example, looked upon Pennsylvania as a 'holy experiment' intended as 'an example ... to the nations' and named the capital Philadelphia, 'the city of brotherly love', after one of the seven Asian churches commended by God in the Book of Revelation (Revelation 1:11; 3:7). From the Pilgrim Fathers onwards, dozens of sects travelled steerage to find in those virgin lands their version of heaven on earth.

Once established in the fertile ground of America, utopian millenarianism took root and reached its fullest flowering. The utopianism of these sects was so radical that it created what can reasonably be regarded as entirely new religions. Most of these proved short-lived, but two in particular continue to exert a powerful influence over America.

The Shakers, or the 'Believers in Christ's Second Appearing', were one of many sects which made the perilous journey from England to America to escape oppression and to live out the millennium on its shores. The founder of the Shakers, Ann Lee, was born in Manchester in 1736. She was the second in a family of eight children, whose poverty was typical of the English Midlands at the beginning of the Industrial Revolution. Her father was a blacksmith; her mother died early, possibly in childbirth. Ann too married a blacksmith and bore four children after painful deliveries; all four died in infancy or early childhood. Seeking consolation, Ann joined a breakaway sect of the Quakers, known as the 'Shaking Quakers'. Often accused of witchcraft, Ann was gaoled several times for disturbing the peace, and it was in a Manchester prison that Christ first appeared to her. Her fellow 'Shakers', on hearing Ann's testimony, also 'experienced' Christ and accepted her leadership.

A few years later, in 1774, having been called by the Spirit to the Promised Land, nine 'Believers in Christ's Second Appearing' landed in New York. Ann's husband accompanied the small group to America and, according to Ann, 'would have been willing to pass through a flaming fire

175

for my sake, if I would but live in the flesh with him.' However, she had early on decided that celibacy was to be a central tenet of her faith, and her husband left her for another woman. Ann returned to her maiden name, Lee, and worked as a laundress in New York City until the group was able to buy some land in Watervliet, New York, where they gathered in 1776, the year of the American Revolution.

'Mother' Ann Lee, as her followers call her, continued to be persecuted for her beliefs even in the Promised Land. The idea that a woman could be leader of a religious movement defied the tradition of the Protestant Church; celibacy was a threat to that sacred American institution, the family. She was accused of being a British spy as well as a witch, and on one occasion was 'worked over by a bunch of toughs who ostensibly wished to find out if she were really a woman.' Incidents such as these probably hastened her death in 1784.

It was only in 1787, the year in which the Constitution of the United States was signed, that the Shakers took the decision to live apart from their neighbours in isolated communities, the first being at New Lebanon, New York. These small communities, based on celibacy and, when it was found to be practical, the common ownership of goods, constituted a kind of 'lay monasticism'. Each village was divided into 'families' of thirty to a hundred people which functioned as independent economic units. In part thanks to the waves of religious revivalism sweeping America, Shaker missionaries gathered many converts, some from the professional classes, though most from the poor and working classes. The Shakers also took in orphans and other unwanted children, but as a social service rather than a recruitment policy since only one child out of ten normally chose to remain within the sect as an adult. At the time of Mother Ann Lee's death there were about a thousand Believers in New England; by the 1840s there were between 5500 and 6000 in eight communities, a high proportion of them women.

Shaker theology has always been the subject of controversy. Their view of the Second Coming is rather sophisticated and has often been misunderstood. According to the few remaining modern-day Shakers, Mother Ann Lee did not consider herself, as has sometimes been claimed, the second Christ in female form. Rather, she was simply the first 'among many to be drawn into the unifying experience of Christ alive and fully present in-through-with us all'. In other words, Christ's Second Coming is not fixed in time but is an on-going event among Believers: 'The Shaker Way begins where other Christians expect the pilgrimage of Faith will one day end: the Second Coming of Christ for Glory.'

Crucial to Shaker belief is Mother Ann's interpretation of original sin: the original sin with which the serpent tempted Adam and Eve was sex and the forbidden fruit was lust. Thus marriage is actually institutionalized lust, or, as Mother Ann is supposed to have expressed it, 'Marriage of the flesh is a covenant with death and an agreement with Hell.' (Compare Archbishop Cranmer's view of marriage in the *Book of Common Prayer*: 'It was ordained for a remedy against sin, and to avoid fornication; that such persons as have not the gift of continency might marry, and keep themselves undefiled members of Christ's body.')

After Mother Ann Lee's experiences of marriage and especially childbirth, one can understand her attitude. She was expressing the deep-seated fears of many women in an era of unreliable contraception and medical ignorance. The Bible had a grim message for women, the cursed descendants of Eve: 'I will greatly multiply thy sorrow and thy conception; in sorrow shall thou bring forth children; and thy desire shall be to thy husband, and he shall rule over thee' (Genesis 3:16). The Shakers believed that:

> ... this same curse has been more or less felt by the fallen daughter of Eve to this day. ... Thus the woman is not only subjected to the pains and sorrows of childbirth, but even in her conception, she becomes subject to the libidinous passions of her husband.... This slavish subjection is often carried to such a shocking extent, that many females have suffered an unnatural and premature death, in consequence of the unseasonable and excessive indulgence of this passion in the man. Thousands there are, no doubt, who are able to bear sorrowful testimony to the truth of this remark.

This passage was written by two Shaker men in 1823. In an age when all other authorities, both religious and lay, urged couples to 'be fruitful and multiply', only the Shakers took these anxieties seriously and offered women and men relief from large families.

The rejection of sex and all its consequences raised women to a position of complete equality with men in the Shaker doctrine: this was truly the only Western religion based on the equality of the sexes. Although there was no getting around the fact that Eve was primarily responsible for the Fall, Mother Ann Lee's life and beliefs had redeemed women and shown them to be free from inherited sin. Those women who chose to live a celibate life among the Shakers thereby escaped 'the fallen and cursed state of their sisters in the World'. The Shakers were committed to 'the equal dignity of women and men together as making up the Body of Christ in a complete humanity, male and female'.

Shaker women were always men's equals, not only in theological doctrine, but also in community administration. Celibacy and communal child-care, for those who already had children when they joined, allowed Shaker women in the nineteenth century a degree of equality in leadership greater than that argued for or achieved by even the most militant secular advocates of female emancipation. Each community was ruled by two elders, one woman and one man, who were subject to a central ministry and chief elder, either male or female, at New Lebanon.

It may seem curious that the Shakers tended to stick to the traditional division of labour between men and women. But in an agrarian community men's work hardly seems more exciting or interesting that women's work: mucking out a stall and cleaning a privy are equally unpleasant tasks. The Shakers could divide jobs between men and women without compromising their belief in equality because the real power at the top of the hierarchical structure was shared equally between the sexes. As one modern writer puts it, 'For the Shakers, equality for women did not mean "doing what men do".' In modern society, the division of labour is an issue precisely because women do not have equal status.

The Shaker doctrine of celibacy was reflected in their architecture, which was designed to keep the sexes apart as much as possible. Although men and women lived under one roof, the buildings were large enough to accommodate separate entrances for men and women and either separate or very wide staircases to minimize contact between the sexes. One elder described this living arrangement as 'monks and nuns, without the bolts and bars'. The sexes were separated even in death. At the original Shaker cemetery in Harvard, Massachusetts, the graves of men and women are segregated into neat rows, marked by simple cast-iron medallions on posts with only the deceased's name, resembling 'chaste parking meters'.

Shaker life offered a real refuge from the outside world, but it also demanded extraordinary commitment. Although there were varying degrees of membership – novitiates, for example, retained their property and family life – those who sought full admittance to the community had to give up all personal ties. Hervey Elkins, who in 1853 left the Shakers after fifteen years, criticized 'the regime which mildly separates man and wife, parent and child . . . and directs them all to seek a less local, and more general bond of union.' He added that 'no pity, in their acts or measures, was ever shown to social or earthly ties.'

Applicants were asked practical questions, such as 'Can you liquidize your debts?', 'Do you drink?' and, if so, 'How much?' New members had to make confession of their sins to the elders, and the 'Millennial Laws' dictated every facet of Shaker life, from slicing bread and carving meat to walking on the stairs in a certain way to save the carpets. (Just to be on the safe side, these same laws stipulated that men and women could not milk cows together nor 'look at beasts when they copulate'.) Shaker government was not democratic but authoritarian: 'Order meant uniformity, obedience to strict rules and regulations, and subordination of self,' according to one scholar.

The songs and dances that were an important part of Shaker worship have now entered into American folk art – the songs are perhaps best known through Aaron Copland's arrangements. The puzzling spectacle of these otherwise austere people dancing received a mixed press from outside observers, who were often invited to attend meetings. Ralph Waldo Emerson called it 'senseless jumping, this shaking of their hands, like paws of dogs'. An English lady described it as a 'swinging step somewhat between a walk and a dance', while the Shakers flopped their hands with 'a penguin kind of motion'.

In the late 1830s and '40s, in response to the spiritualism which had become fashionable across America, Shaker meetings became even more energetic. Some Shakers, especially young girls who were said to have 'received Mother Ann's gift', would break into whirling dances and experience visions. One poster at Harvard announced that one 'Miss Chase, the Teetotum' would demonstrate at a 'Shaker entertainment' her ability 'to perform 1500 to 2000 whirls'.

The visions, or 'gifts', grew increasingly imaginative, and an extraordinary range of historical figures, from Christopher Columbus to Napoleon, Queen Isabella to Elizabeth I, began to make their presence known to the Shakers. One eye-witness described a certain spiritual visitation made by a tribe of Indians. There

> . . . ensued a regular pow-wow, with whooping and yelling and strange antics. . . . The sisters and brothers squatted down on the floor together, Indian fashion, and the Elders and Eldresses endeavored to keep them asunder, telling the men they must be separated from the squaws, and otherwise instructing them in the rules of Shakerism.

This same spectator thought that 'some of the old folks who eyed me, bit their lips and smiled' during these performances. 'It appeared to me,' he concludes, 'that whenever any of the brethren or sisters wanted to have some fun, they got possessed of spirits, and would go to cutting up capers.'

Eventually, the bouts of spiritualism were discouraged by the elders, who believed, quite rightly, that these eccentric performances did not enhance the Shakers' reputation. In the nineteenth century public opinion was divided on the Shakers. Nathaniel Hawthorne found everything so neat at Hancock, Massachusetts that it was 'a pain and constraint to look at it'. In his description of the community at New Lebanon in *American Notes*, Charles Dickens applies the adjective 'grim' to almost every object he sees, both animate and inanimate. He was particularly scathing about Shaker women. In a Shaker store which he visited, 'the stock was presided over by something alive in a russet case, which the elder said was a woman; and which I suppose *was* a woman, though I should not have suspected it.'

Although literary men may have thought the Shaker Way too austere, to the new breed of social scientists the Shakers were a living testimony to the feasibility and virtues of communism. For Friedrich Engels the Shakers were an inspiration to the working class and, more importantly, a justification for a socialist state. He wrote in 1845: 'In America and, generally speaking, in the world the first to found a society organized according to the principle of common ownership of goods were the people called the Shakers.' Engels knew the Shakers only from travel literature and chose to ignore their theological doctrines 'as of no importance to us here'. Knowing almost nothing about them, however, did not prevent him from painting a very rosy picture of Shaker life as a Marxist Cockaigne:

The Shakers labor only to pass the time; otherwise they would have nothing to do. Among them no one is forced to work against his will and no one fusses uselessly in his job. They have no poorhouses, no homes for the aged, because they have no poor, no needy, no widows, no abandoned orphans. They know no poverty and have nothing to fear. In their ten villages there is not a single policeman; there are no judges, no lawyers, no soldiers, no prisons, and yet everything functions normally.

Engels concludes that

. . . people living communally live better and work less, that they have more leisure time in which to develop their minds, and that they become better and more moral men than their neighbors who stayed in the system of private property. . . . This is important news for all men, but it is especially important for the poor workers.

Whatever their contribution to the revolutionary cause, the Shaker legacy to American life and culture is a rich one. Perhaps best known today for their simple, well-crafted furniture and buildings, which have a place in the history of American design, the Shakers took as their motto Mother Ann Lee's exhortation: 'Put your hands to work, and your hearts to God, and a blessing will attend you.' Another member restated the sentiment more prosaically: 'A man can show his religion as much in measuring onions as he can in singing glory hallelujah.' Their furniture design was above all practical. Heavy pieces were on castors, and chairs could be hung up on pegs to help sweeping. Although the Millennial Laws forbade Shakers to lean their chairs against the walls, the habit persisted, prompting them to devise wooden ball-and-sockets which keep the back legs flat on the floor when the sitter leans back.

Contrary to popular myth, the 'classic' Shaker furniture which now sells for astronomical sums at auction was only made during a fairly brief period of their history, from about 1790 to 1830, and it clearly reflects the American Federalist style of the time. The Shakers were not caught in a time capsule, and, as keen business people, they were always aware of the marketplace: their designs reflected the fashions and trends of the day. Thus, after about 1830, the Shakers began to manufacture and market more solid, heavy pieces of furniture, wholly in line with Victorian tastes. The Shakers' practicality and modernity can also be seen in their invention of appliances which are now standard in American homes: the revolving oven (an idea now applied to microwaves) and the washing machine.

The Oneida Perfectionist John Humphrey Noyes, who turned his attention from religious to socialist doctrines in the 1860s and wrote the monumental *History of American Socialisms* (1870), disapproved of the Shakers' celibacy. Nevertheless, he recognizes the Shakers' importance: 'We are indebted to the Shakers more than to any or all other Social Architects of modern times.' Noyes observes that the Shakers' success served as an inspiration to the many communitarian experiments, both religious and secular, which sprang up in the first half of the nineteenth century. The Shakers saw themselves as part of this American communitarian tradition and proclaimed in 1848: 'We view all labors of this kind as providential and beneficial to mankind, and preparatory to the order of the true work.'

After the American Civil War the communitarian movement waned and Shaker membership declined. The establishment of state orphanages made the Shakers' larger social role less significant and also dried up a small but important source of young converts. Their numbers had dropped to a thousand by 1910. Today, at the last 'living' Shaker village, Sabbathday Lake, Maine, there are eight Shakers and at Canterbury, New Hampshire, there is one: nine in all, the same number which originally emigrated to America in 1774.

The sad dwindling of the Shakers is not, however, the inevitable fate of utopian religious endeavours. Another new religion planted in American soil has today a worldwide membership approaching nine million, and the Mormons continue to gather converts at a rate of several thousand a week. The founder of Mormonism, Joseph Smith, was born in Vermont, but his parents, plagued by bad luck, moved from place to place, attempting to flee poverty. They eventually settled in New York State in the heart of the Burnt Over Region (so-called because of the blazing fires of revivalism which swept across it). The Smiths were God-fearing, Bible-carrying people, but they did not belong to any church in particular: none seemed to offer the answers which they were seeking.

It was in Manchester, New York, at the age of fourteen that Smith began having visions. After a false start with a 'seer-stone' which was supposed to lead to hidden treasure, he hit the jackpot. On 21 September 1823 Smith beheld the angel Moroni, who stated that

> . . . the preparatory work for the second coming of the Messiah was speedily to commence; that the time was at hand, for the Gospel in all its fulness [sic] to be preached in power, unto all nations, that a people might be prepared for the millennial reign.

Moroni went on to explain that God had chosen Smith to reveal to the world the Book of Mormon, which was engraved in hieroglyphics on golden tablets and lay buried in a nearby hillside. It took Smith four years to uncover the tablets. As soon as he had finished translating the holy scripture with the help of a magic breastplate, the angel Moroni took back the originals, leaving the English version, now the authoritative one, behind.

The story as told in the Book of Mormon begins in about 600 BC, when a Hebrew prophet called Lehi flees from the Israelites' captivity in Babylon and voyages to America with his two sons. The sons and their descendants divide into irreconcilable factions: the devout Nephites who are hard-working and disdainful of luxury, though prone to backslide into ungodliness every so often; and the evil Lamanites who become idle, savage and dark-skinned. Christ made an appearance on the American continent after his crucifixion and resurrection in Jerusalem and reunited the Nephites and Lamanites for a time. However, one thousand years after Lehi first arrived in America, both sides had again fallen by the wayside. A great battle ensued in which the Lamanites finally destroyed the Nephites, but not before their prophet Mormon had engraved their history upon golden plates. He entrusted these to his son Moroni, who buried them for safekeeping. This Moroni was the angel who appeared to Joseph Smith in 1823. The Lamanites continued to inhabit the continent, and their descendants are the Indians whom Columbus first encountered in 1492. Up until that moment God had kept America hidden from the world, reserving it for His people, and it was He who inspired Columbus's voyage.

Not only had God steered Columbus in the direction of the American continent, He also took care of the last big obstacle to His grand design. According to one historian,

> . . . when the Book of Mormon first appeared on March 26, 1830, it verified what most Americans already knew. It was God who had delivered the United States from British monarchy and endowed it with republican liberties. Speaking in the Lord's name, the pre-Columbian Mormon prophet Jacob proclaimed that America would 'be a land of liberty unto the Gentiles' and promised that there would 'be no kings upon the land'.

Smith claimed that 'Zion will be built upon this continent.' In doing so, he was consciously echoing the millenarian language not only of the early Puritan settlers of North America but also of the Founding Fathers of the American Revolution. Thomas Paine, whose religious convictions fell somewhere between atheism and deism, had come up with the same line as Smith in 1776. He proclaims in *Common Sense*:

> Even the distance at which the Almighty hath placed England and America is strong and natural proof that the authority of the one over the other, was never the design of heaven. The time likewise at which the continent was discovered, adds weight to the argument, and the manner in which it was peopled, increases the force of it. The Reformation was preceded by the discovery of America: As if the Almighty graciously meant to open a sanctuary to the persecuted in future years, when home should afford neither friendship nor safety.

However, according to Joseph Smith, Christ's Second Coming, to be followed by the millennium, would not occur until the Saints, as the Mormons called themselves, had completed God's plan by creating in America a state worthy of a divine ruler.

The Book of Mormon – which Mark Twain called 'chloroform in print' – gave people like Joseph Smith's parents all the answers they were seeking and more. The Reverend Alexander Campbell of Kirtland, Ohio, Smith's contemporary and leader of the rival millenarian sect, the Disciples of Christ (Ronald Reagan's church), remarked:

> This prophet Smith, through his stone spectacles, wrote on the plates of Nephi, in his book of Mormon, every error and almost every truth discussed in New York for the last ten years. He decides all the great controversies – infant baptism, ordination, the trinity, regeneration, repentance, justification, the fall of man, the atonement, transubstantiation, fasting, penance, church government, religious experience, the call to the ministry, the general resurrection, eternal punishment, who may baptize, and even the question of free masonry, republican government and the rights of man.

Smith's genius was to do more than simply offer yet another interpretation of the Bible, making his followers just one of many Protestant sects; instead, he had discovered (or invented) his own version of scripture and so fashioned an entirely new religion.

The Book of Mormon was also Joseph Smith's 'clarion call against the world he grew up in'. According to Smith, the American republic, which had started out with such high hopes, was crumbling like the Nephite nation before it, and the fall of the United States would herald the millennium. Smith invoked the same republican virtues which the Founding Fathers had held up in 1776. Thus, at one point, the Nephites are described in the battle against the Lamanites as

> ... inspired by a better cause; for they were not fighting for monarchy nor power; but they were fighting for their homes, and their liberties, their wives, their children, and their all; yea for their rights of worship and their church; and they were doing that which they felt it was the duty which they owed to their God.

God was a republican.

Smith's earliest converts were family, friends and neighbours. The group made their first base in Kirtland, Ohio, in 1831 when a large number of Campbell's followers converted to Mormonism. From Ohio, missionaries were sent to the wayward Israelites, the Indians, in Missouri, which was soon proclaimed 'the land of promise'; in that same year 1200 Mormons began to build the new Zion at Independence, Missouri. However, the local inhabitants felt threatened by the Mormons: their sense of separateness and superiority, their strict theocracy (anathema to the United States Constitution) and the special place for the Indians in Mormon doctrine, were all cause for suspicion. The Saints were driven out of Independence.

In 1839, after a number of similar setbacks elsewhere, the Saints (numbering 5000 by now) arrived in Illinois and started once again to plan for Zion – this time at Nauvoo on the Mississippi River. They were initially made to feel at home: the two political parties, the Whigs and Democrats, each hoped for the Mormons' vote. Thus the state legislature granted an unusually favourable charter to the new settlement of Nauvoo, making it an almost independent body with its own militia, the Nauvoo Legion. With such encouragement, the Mormons duly laid out streets and began constructing a large temple, all under the central authority of the Mormon Church. By 1842 the population had grown to between 14,000 and 15,000.

However, once again the Mormons' neighbours grew alarmed, especially about the Saints' refusal to celebrate the Fourth of July and rumours of polygamy amongst Smith and his Apostles. Polygamy had been a Mormon doctrine since 1843, but was kept secret until 1852. Joseph Smith held up the polygamy practised by the Hebrew Patriarchs in the Old Testament as justification and maintained that a woman cannot enter the heavenly kingdom without a husband to introduce her. According to one nineteenth-century observer, Sir Richard Burton:

Politically considered, the Mormons deem it [polygamy] necessary to their existence as a people. . . . they hold population, not wealth, learning, civilization, nor virtue, to be the strength of a nation.

Burton offers another reason for the practice: 'Servants are rare and costly; it is cheaper and more comfortable to marry them.' Mormon girls rarely remained single past the age of sixteen. The Mormons themselves were divided on the issue of polygamy: Joseph Smith's wife, for example, never accepted it. One early convert, who later denounced the Mormons, remarked that he didn't need Smith's line to seduce women.

The citizens of Illinois inevitably began flinging the serious accusation of being un-American at the Mormons: it was said by their enemies that Mormonism was an American Islam and Joseph Smith the new Mahomet. As if to irritate his enemies further, in 1844 Smith began a 'quixotic' campaign for President of the United States and sent out more than three hundred followers to canvass for votes. One local protester explained:

Five years have passed, and the helpless band of exiles that sought our hospitality in the inclement season of winter, have become the most powerful people that ever organized a distinct community under our republican institutions.

Another protester invoked 'the noble spirit which led to the American Revolution of '76' to fight against the Mormon tyrants.

In June 1844 Joseph Smith and his brother Hyrum were assassinated. The Mormons continued to be persecuted, and by the end of 1845 they had finally had enough of the United States and decided to look for a Zion well outside the nation's borders. Smith's successor, Brigham Young, declared that 'I never intend to winter in the United States [again]'; this nation is 'as corrupt as Hell from the president down clean through the priests and the people'. On 5 February 1846, Young led his 'captive people', the 'nation of Israel', out of bondage, westward towards the land of milk and honey. They stopped in Utah on 24 July 1847 on the shores of the Great Salt Lake and founded a new city.

We have already referred to the account of the Mormons written by the British explorer, Sir Richard Burton, published in 1861. This was the third of his 'Holy Cities' trilogy, describing his journeys to Mecca, Harar in East Africa, and Salt Lake City. Burton, who was sympathetic to the Mormons, found in Utah, then a US Territory, an America in miniature, determined to outdo the original. The city, laid out on a grid with houses 'almost all of one pattern' gave 'a suburban look to the settlement'. The street plan was in compliance with the description of the Heavenly Jerusalem found in the Revelation of St John: 'And the city lieth foursquare, and the length is as large as the breadth' (Revelation 21:16). Burton, who arrived at Salt Lake City together with a group of new converts from Britain, testifies that these newcomers were taken into the fold and cared for by the Mormons in a way which sadly contrasted with the welcome given to poor immigrants disembarking in New York. During Burton's visit the Mormons celebrated their Independence Day (24 July) with a picnic, three-gun salute, flags waving, the band playing

'The Star-Spangled Banner' (retitled 'The Standard of Zion'), and dancing in the evening, ending with a rendition of 'Home Sweet Home'. All American as apple pie.

The Mormon government was a theocratic version of the United States Constitution. The Prophet, as head of the Mormon Church, was also President for life. Their Legislative Assembly consisted of an Upper House and a House of Representatives, or Lower House. The Mormons had, however, improved on the original design: elected representatives had limited terms of office (an issue in the United States today), candidates had to be *bona fide* residents of the districts they represented, and no member of the Legislative Assembly could hold any appointment created while he was in office.

Fourteen years after their exodus from Nauvoo, Burton saw a nation still very much at war with America. The Utah Mormons had reputedly murdered a US Army captain and massacred a group of pioneers, the latter atrocity in revenge for the stabbing of one of their own. The Mormons themselves boasted of attacking and burning a US Army supply train. Burton notes that 'Mormon' had become a word of fear. The Americans believed that the Mormons, also known as 'White Indians', were in league with their 'Israelite brothers', the Red Indians, against the pioneers. Burton reports that the Mormon militia were indeed counting on the help of the Yuta Indians in case of an attack by the US Army.

For the Mormons' part, Burton observes, 'they make scant pretension of patriotism. They regard the States pretty much as the States regarded England after the War of Independence. . . . Theirs is a deep and abiding resentment.' They 'despise a political system' in which 'every vital interest of the state is merged in the all-absorbing question of "who shall be the next president".' Brigham Young 'mourned to see the corruption, and he sometimes felt a blush for being an American.' Burton writes:

> They held that the laws of the United States are better adapted to secure the happiness of a small community than to consolidate the provinces of a continent into one huge empire. . . . They declared themselves to be the salt of the Union, and that in the fullness of time they shall break the republic in pieces like a potter's vessel.

However, the Mormons considered Washington, Jefferson and 'other sages of the Revolution' 'as Latter-Day Saints in will if not in deed'. Burton was writing his account just at the outbreak of the American Civil War, which the Mormons regarded as 'at once retribution for their injuries, and the fulfillment [sic] of the denunciations of Joseph the Seer against the "Gentile land of strife and wickedness".'

Despite Burton's prediction in 1861 that 'time [would] strengthen, not efface' the Mormons' resentment against the United States, Utah achieved statehood in 1896 and Mormonism has become an extremely successful religious force in America. Like many religions, it has split into a number of rival denominations. Nevertheless, the Mormon Church is on a per capita basis probably the richest in the world, with extensive property holdings in many countries. In the United States Mormons now outnumber Episcopalians; in 1990 they claimed 331,000 new converts. Nevertheless, among Americans, the Mormons remain a separate people, with their own security division supposedly run by former FBI agents. The general opinion in Utah, where Mormons make up three-quarters of the population, is that 'you don't rise in this state embarrassing the Mormon Church or making them look bad.' Although the US government outlawed polygamy in 1890, there are reputedly more than 30,000 Mormons still practising it today, mainly in Utah and Arizona.

Mormonism has had as great an influence on the American fabric as the Shakers. The Mormons made a vital contribution to the westward expansion of America in the nineteenth century: between 1840 and 1890 some 55,000 converts emigrated from Britain to Utah and the West. Edward Bellamy visited the Mormons at Salt Lake City in 1883 to observe their co-operative economy wherein the head of each family 'consecrated' all possessions to the Church, receiving in turn an 'inheritance' to sustain his family. Bellamy was impressed, and this curious hybrid of state ownership and private property may have inspired his picture in *Looking Backward* of a nationalized industry whose work force is motivated by the Religion of Solidarity. Bellamy's Nationalist Clubs are said to have 'respected Mormon economic doctrines as representative of advanced social planning'. (The Mormons eventually abandoned this co-operative system for the simpler one of ten per cent tithes.)

The appeal of Joseph Smith was that 'in the guise of a prophet of the coming millennium, [he] in effect posed as the conservative defender of an older America' which was beginning to crumble under the pressures of rapid industrialization. In this cause Smith and his successors threw back in America's face much of the pseudo-religious millenarian rhetoric of the early republic that had equated the Kingdom of God with the United States. It is a remarkable fact that such millenarian rhetoric is still a feature of American politics. When President Ronald Reagan, a product of Campbell's Disciples of Christ, described Soviet communism as the 'Evil

Empire' and 'the focus of all evil in the world', for many Americans he was making a cryptic reference to the Book of Revelation. One American historian reports that many of his fellow countrymen recognized the birthmark on Mikhail Gorbachev's forehead as 'the mark of the Beast' from the Apocalypse (Revelation 13:17).

The observations made by the Frenchman Alexis de Tocqueville during his visit to America in the early 1830s still ring true today. He notes that 'from the beginning, politics and religion contracted an alliance which has never been dissolved'. 'There is no country in the world in which the Christian religion retains a greater influence over the souls of men than in America.' In 1992 one of out every sixteen people in the United States was reported to be a religious fundamentalist, often a member of a pre-millenarian sect. Tocqueville further remarks that in America one is surprised to 'meet a politician where you expected to find a priest'. Certainly, this was true in the Presidential election campaigns of the 1980s, when 'preachers and politicians were stumbling over each other' – figures such as the Reverends Jesse Jackson, Jim Bakker, Jimmy Swaggart, Jerry Falwell and Pat Robertson, all of whom were either running for office or courting George Bush and Ronald Reagan. President Clinton, born and raised a Southern Baptist, gave his manifesto a biblical ring by dubbing it 'The New Covenant'.

Why does religion, and in particular its utopian manifestation, millenarianism, wield such influence over a nation where separation of Church and State is guaranteed by the Constitution? Part of the answer is that the Founding Fathers never intended to lessen religion's impact on the country. Rather, as one modern commentator observes, they argued that churches, once freed from the constraints which bind an established institution, 'would have greater moral force . . . and in this they proved prophets.' Equally, millenarianism, with its imperative to strive for perfection here on earth, is in tune with the American cast of mind which, as we shall see in the next section, has always been utopian. Shakers and Mormons both encouraged and drew strength from this powerful millennial force, and in doing so created new worlds on the American continent. As the year 2000 approaches, and churches everywhere, from America to Korea, are proclaiming the coming of Christ's millennium, we would do well to remember the power which St John's prophecy continues to hold.

Boris Kustodiev, cover of *The Communist International*, 1919.

PART SIX

STATE

With mental eye exulting now explore,
And soon with kindred minds shall haste to enjoy
(Free from the ills which here our peace destroy)
Content and Bliss on Transatlantic shore.
> Samuel Taylor Coleridge, 'On the Prospect
> of Establishing a Pantisocracy in America'

We Americans have the power to begin the world
over again.
> Ronald Reagan

Utopias have turned out to be much more realizable than seemed possible
before. Now we are faced with another tormenting question: how to
avoid their being realized in full.
> Nikolas Berdyaev

I must Create a System, or be enslav'd by another Mans.
> William Blake, 'Jerusalem'

10. The Pursuit of Happiness

For nearly half a century of Cold War two great powers struggled to dominate the planet. This was a conflict of military might, economic vigour and machiavellian diplomacy. It was also a clash between rival utopian visions of the future of humanity. In the West we are used to thinking of the Soviet Union as an attempt to create a utopia, and we attribute its failure to the impossibility of that goal. But America too has endeavoured to enact Utopia on a national scale – albeit in a different way.

Ever since Thomas More, the New World has been haunted by the vision of Utopia. Columbus's discoveries, and later the settling of North America by Protestant sects, were hailed as signs of a religious utopia, the millennium. The rhetoric of millenarianism was, as we have seen, employed again in the eighteenth century by the propagandists of the American War of Independence. However, even without this millenarian veneer, the American Revolution qualifies as a utopian project. The Founding Fathers were not content simply to shake off the shackles of British rule. They were about the task of creating an ideal republic to be a model for all nations. As Thomas Paine declared in 1792:

> The independence of America, considered merely as a separation from England, would have been a matter but of little importance, had it not been accompanied by a revolution in the principles and practise of governments. She made a stand, not for herself only, but for the world.

The patriarchs of the young American republic had the confidence of all utopians that their actions would be imitated around the globe, and subsequent revolutions at first seemed to confirm their expectations. The first nation to follow their shining example was France. In 1789, with the cry of *Liberté, Égalité, Fraternité*, Frenchmen rose against tyranny and oppression. In the beginning, Americans looked upon the French Revolution as a fulfilment of the principles of 1776, and the French seemed to return the compliment. The revolutionaries in Paris symbolically presented George Washington, the first President of the United States, with the key to the fallen Bastille, the 'early trophy', remarked Thomas Paine, 'of the Spoils of Despotism and the first ripe fruits of American principles transplanted into Europe'. The first draft of the manifesto of the French Revolution, the Declaration of the Rights of Man and of the Citizen, was drawn up by Lafayette, the hero of the American War of Independence, with the advice of Thomas Jefferson, then US ambassador in Paris.

However, Americans soon discovered that supporting revolutions abroad was a tricky business, and successive United States administrations found that they had to check their initial enthusiasm. Thus, once the full extent of the Terror in France became known, many Americans began to think of the French Revolution as merely an aborted attempt to imitate their own success. In their eyes, the American Revolution, not the French, remained the true prototype of international revolution (although it is interesting to note that America's War of Independence was not styled the 'American Revolution' until the French Revolution had made the term popular).

Undaunted, the United States continued to back foreign revolutions. However, the government soon found itself in another awkward position when the slaves on the Caribbean island of Saint Dominique rebelled against their French masters. The American President at the time, John Adams (1797–1801), in keeping with the nation's policy of supporting revolutions, willingly aided the rebels with arms and provisions. However, the American South, terrified of slave rebellions at home, prevented the United States officially recognizing the new Haitian Republic (established in 1806) until the Civil War.

American leaders such as Adams and Jefferson also welcomed the colonial rebellions against the Spanish in Latin America, but were nonetheless sceptical. Jefferson wrote in 1821:

> I feared from the beginning that these people [South Americans] were not yet sufficiently enlightened for self-government; and that after wading through blood and slaughter, they would end in military tyrannies, more or less numerous. Yet as they wished to try the experiment [in republicanism], I wished them success in it.

The United States continued to support revolutions around the world, from the Greek revolt in 1821 to the overthrow of the Second French Empire in 1870. One Virginian declared in 1830, echoing the utopian sentiments of Thomas Paine:

THE PURSUIT OF HAPPINESS

We stand under a fearful responsibility to our Creator and our fellow citizens. . . . It has been his divine pleasure that we should be sent forth as the harbingers of free government on the earth, and in this attitude we are now before the world. The eyes of the world are upon us; and our example will probably be decisive of the cause of human liberty.

As late as 1992, George Bush was still describing America as 'the last, best hope of mankind'. Such a statement from a European politician would sound distinctly odd, but Americans imbibe utopianism with their mothers' milk. The assumption that it is America's duty to show the rest of the world how to run its affairs has often guided the nation's foreign policy and lent to it a certain moralizing tone (Woodrow Wilson's administration, 1913–21, was a notable example). Indeed, it is impossible to understand United States foreign policy without taking into account this utopian legacy.

What, then, were the principles which animated the enterprise and which the Founding Fathers believed it their task to proclaim to the world? The ideas upon which the new republic was founded were set out by Thomas Jefferson in 1776 in the Declaration of Independence:

> We hold these truths to be self-evident, that all men are created equal, that they are endowed by their Creator with certain unalienable Rights, that among these are Life, Liberty and the pursuit of Happiness.

In stressing the equality of men, Jefferson was drawing upon a utopian tradition instituted by Thomas More and followed by many of his imitators, notably Campanella. Yet in both *Utopia* and *La Città del Sole* the basis of equality is community of goods; Campanella's utopia is quite hierarchical in other respects. In contrast, the egalitarianism of the Founding Fathers was based not on a levelling of material circumstances, but on a levelling of status – America was to be a society without distinctions of rank. For Alexis de Tocqueville, writing in 1832–33, this was the key to understanding American life:

> The more I advanced in the study of American society, the more I perceived that this equality of condition is the fundamental fact from which all others seem to be derived and the central point at which all my observations constantly terminated.

As one historian observes, the revolution in America was 'from hierarchy to equality, from a world where people knew their place to a world where they made their place'.

It is here that the utopian creed of equality divides into two irreconcilable attitudes which have defined the shape of ideological and political conflict ever since. The European utopian tradition, from More through Rousseau to, as we shall see, Marx, understood equality to mean above all an equal distribution of economic resources. In America, the new republic was based on a more limited egalitarianism, created by extending the Anglo-Saxon tradition of equal status before the law into the 'equality of condition' that so struck Tocqueville. Jefferson, in the Declaration of Independence, laid the foundation for the doctrine of 'equality of opportunity', which is America's distinctive contribution to political theory.

Jefferson's original draft of the Declaration, which read 'all men are created equal and independent', hints at another fundamental American trait, rugged individualism. The words 'Life, Liberty and the pursuit of Happiness' conjure up an image of a nation of restlessly independent individuals, carving out of the raw timber of an unpeopled continent their own version of the good life. This is certainly close to what Jefferson had in mind for his republic: a country without as aristocracy or a peasantry, a utopia of small landholders, hard-working and educated to civic virtue. As America developed, of course, individualism found its expression less in tilling virgin soil than in that brand of entrepreneurial capitalism which is America's great strength, success in which constitutes the American Dream. For most Americans, this is what is meant by the 'pursuit of Happiness'.

But Jefferson's words have also provoked a different response from those who have found it impossible to pursue happiness within America's acquisitive and competitive society. With the same confidence with which the Founding Fathers created a new nation, some of these nonconformists have attempted to remake society in small, to carve out of the same raw timber of America mini-utopias – pursuing happiness not as individuals but in small isolated communities. It is to this alternative version of the American utopia, the communitarian movement, that we now turn.

In the first few decades of the new republic, America's unique combination of radical credentials, political stability and cheap real estate attracted utopian enthusiasts from all over Europe. One such, looking back on his experiences, wrote:

I was a sharer in the general vortex, though my little World described the path of Revolution in an orbit of its own. What I dared not expect from constitutions of Government and whole Nations, I hoped from Religion and a small Company of chosen Individuals, and formed a plan, as harmless as it was extravagant, of trying the experiment of human Perfectibility on the banks of the Susquahannah [sic]; . . . Strange fancies! and as vain as strange! yet to the intense interest and impassioned zeal, which called forth and strained every faculty of my intellect for the organization and defence of this Scheme, I owe much of whatever I at present possess, my clearest insight into the nature of individual Man, and my most comprehensive views of his social relations.

These words were penned by the Romantic poet Samuel Taylor Coleridge who, together with Robert Southey, planned to set up a utopian idyll, a 'Pantisocracy', in Pennsylvania. Although Coleridge and Southey never made the journey across the Atlantic, 'Pantisocracy' became a byword in nineteenth-century America for a radical and wildly idealistic utopian experiment.

Coleridge and Southey met as undergraduates in 1794. They shared a passionate enthusiasm for poetry, progress and the French Revolution – as well as the perennial student dilemmas of debts and family disapproval. Coleridge, it was rumoured, plotted to etch the words 'Liberty' and 'Equality' on the lawns of St John's and Trinity Colleges, Cambridge. Southey, beset by troubles at home, had been wavering between suicide, joining the French Revolutionary Army and emigrating to America to build a farm 'on ground uncultivated since the creation' and live in seclusion until 'cooked for a Cherokee, or oysterised by a tiger'. The thought of emigrating to America to establish an ideal society seemed to the two poets to solve all their problems. Coleridge, with his love of vibrant words, baptised their utopia 'Pantisocracy' ('all-governing society') and the precepts by which they were to live 'Aspheterism' ('nothing of one's own').

The philosophy behind Pantisocracy was inspired chiefly by the works of two people: the political theorist William Godwin and the scientist and philosopher Joseph Priestley. Both these men, though firmly rooted in the English traditions of rationalism and utilitarianism, were influenced greatly by the French Revolution. Godwin, the husband of Mary Wollstonecraft and father of Mary Shelley, advocated the abolition of property and believed that 'Man is perfectible, or in other words susceptible of perpetual improvement'. Priestley was, according to Coleridge, 'the author of modern Unitarianism', a religious sect which Coleridge joined while an undergraduate. Unitarians combined dissenting Christianity and the ideas of the Enlightenment, and conceived of spiritual and secular progress as one. In essence they rejected the notion of inherited original sin and believed that humans had a natural capacity for good. After he was attacked by a 'Church and King' mob for his unconventional views, Priestley chose to emigrate, not to France, but to the calmer shores of America in 1794 – to the banks of the Susquehanna, in fact (later recommended to Coleridge by a land agent as a spot secure from 'hostile Indians' where 'literary Characters make *money*').

Southey and Coleridge abandoned their university courses and repaired to Bristol to work out the details of their pantisocratic community. Two others, George Burnett and Robert Lovell, joined them, and at one point all four pantisocrats were engaged to the daughters of their Bristol landlady, Mrs Fricker. Once established in Pennsylvania, the group (to include the Fricker sisters but not their mother, at Coleridge's insistence) was to practise absolute equality, with no servants, community of goods and free speech. Southey mused:

> When Coleridge and I are sawing down a tree we shall discuss metaphysics: criticise poetry when hunting a buffalo, and write sonnets whilst following the plough.

The issue of whether or not to dispense with marriage vows in the wilderness remained unsettled.

However, by August 1795, the plans for the great Pantisocracy had fizzled out. The course of true love did not run smoothly for Coleridge. Money was always a problem, and Coleridge and Southey each became suspicious that the other did not have his heart in the project. As the years passed, the Romantics grew more conservative because, they said, the world had changed. Coleridge looked back nostalgically on the venture. Southey, however, held a grim view of his youthful enthusiasms. In his work, *Sir Thomas More*: Or, *Colloquies on the Progress and Prospects of Society* (1829), the spirit of Thomas More appears to one Montesinos and states:

> We have both speculated in the joy and freedom of our youth upon the possible improvement of society; and both in like manner have lived to

dread with reason the effects of that restless spirit, which . . . insults Heaven and disturbs the earth.

At the time when Coleridge's head was full of Pantisocracy, another utopian who would make the journey across the Atlantic was working hard to make a profit in the spinning mills of Manchester. Like Coleridge, Robert Owen was a friend of Godwin and was influenced by his radical ideas on communism and the perfectibility of man. By 1800, long after Coleridge's pantisocratic dream had turned sour, Owen became manager and co-owner of the New Lanark Mill in Scotland, from where he would become one of the most important utopian thinkers of the nineteenth century. Whereas the first warm glow of the French Revolution had been Coleridge's immediate inspiration, it was the economic, social and intellectual upheavals following the Napoleonic wars which moved Owen to create a 'new moral world'.

What Owen found at New Lanark, a remote mill town with a population of 1700 to 1800 people, was typical of the newly industrialized world. The mechanization of spinning had resulted in the increased employment of women and very young children in the factories. It was common practice for mill-owners virtually to buy workhouse children from public authorities glad to be rid of them. When Owen arrived at New Lanark, these pauper children, from five to ten years old, made up a third of its inhabitants. According to Owen, the workers were 'intemperate and immoral' and 'theft was very general'.

Owen resolved to set right, in his own back yard at least, the social ills of the Industrial Revolution. By 1815, he had managed to reduce working hours from fourteen or more a day to ten and three-quarters and to ensure that the factory employed no child under ten years of age. At the same time, he enlarged the workers' cottages, which were owned by the company, and improved sanitation. Owen also made better goods at cheaper prices available in the village shops. Once these reforms were in place, New Lanark actually achieved better results in production and trade than its unenlightened rivals. Because of his success at New Lanark, Owen became known as 'Mr Owen, the Philanthropist' or 'the benevolent Mr Owen', and phrenologists pronounced the bump of benevolence on his skull unusually large: 'His name was everywhere linked with successful, paternalistic schemes for improving the lot of the poor.' In 1815, for example, Owen campaigned for a Bill to regulate the employment of children in the textile industry. After much fierce opposition, the Factory Act, so compromised as to be almost useless, was passed through Parliament in 1819. It did, however, establish an important precedent for government interference with industry.

Owen was not just a philanthropist and social reformer. He was deeply influenced by the philosopher John Locke's notion of the *tabula rasa*, which held that man's mind was, at birth, a 'clean slate'. Owen declared that

> ... Man becomes a wild ferocious savage, a cannibal, or a highly civilised and benevolent being, according to the circumstances in which he may be placed from his birth.

Thus, at New Lanark, Owen had reasoned the workers out of drunkenness and irregular habits, with reprimand the only form of punishment. (He devised a 'silent monitor', a sort of barometer of conduct conspicuously hung by each person's workplace.) Owen's principle was 'diminished responsibility': the motto on his journal, *The Crisis*, reads, 'The character of man is formed FOR – not BY himself.'

Education was a key word in Owen's vocabulary. He insisted that children be 'trained and educated without punishment or any fear of it'. Teachers with special training should 'speak to them with a pleasant countenance, and in a kind manner and tone of voice'. Proper schooling was essential to the reformation of society since

> ... children are, without exception, passive and wonderfully contrived compounds; which, by an accurate previous and subsequent attention, founded on a correct knowledge of the subject, may be formed collectively to have any human character. And although these compounds, like all the other works of nature, possess endless varieties, yet they partake of that plastic quality which, by perseverance under judicious management, may be ultimately moulded into the very image of rational wishes and desires.

Owen also pioneered adult education since he believed that 'education should extend from the cradle to the grave'. Perhaps his finest achievement in New Lanark was the building of an Institute for the Formation of Character where people of all ages were taught.

By 1813 his successful reforms at New Lanark had convinced Owen that

> ... any character from the worst to the best, from the most ignorant

to the most enlightened, may be given to any community, even to the world at large, by applying certain means, which are to a large extent at the command, and under the control, or easily made so, of those who possess the government of nations.

The philanthropist had become a utopian. Following the Battle of Waterloo (1815) when the farmers' and manufacturers' 'most extravagant customer', war, disappeared, leaving recession and unemployment in its wake, Owen proposed to create self-supporting communities of about 1200 people in order to relieve the poor. These towns were to be miniature welfare states, with provisions for education and social needs, and the inhabitants were to be housed in 'parallelograms', something like Fourier's phalansteries.

By 1817 Owen's ambitions had grown still further: he planned to relocate not just the poor and homeless, but everyone, from every class and walk of life, to these Owenite communities, set up all over Britain. He rejected class divisions, believing that 'the rich and the poor, the governors and the governed, have really but one interest.' Future generations, raised and educated in these 'Villages of Unity and Mutual Co-operation', would be free of those social ills which plagued early nineteenth-century Britain:

As the easy, regular, healthy, rational employment of the individuals forming these societies will create a very large surplus of their own products, beyond what they will have any desire to consume, each may be freely permitted to receive from the general store of the community whatever they may require.

This line of thought led to the logical conclusion that 'individual accumulation of wealth will appear as irrational as to bottle up or store water in situations where there is more of this invaluable liquid than all can consume.' 'It may be safely predicted,' Owen wrote, 'that one of the new associations cannot be formed without creating a general desire throughout society to establish others, and that they will rapidly multiply.' However, not everyone was impressed. A contemporary, one Mr Peacock, caricatured Owen as 'Mr Toogood', the 'co-operationist . . . who wants to parcel out the world into squares like a chess-board, with a community on each.'

Owen sent his earlier proposals, laid out in his book *A New View of Society* (1813–14), to prime ministers, presidents, kings, professors and even to Napoleon in exile on the island of Elba. Owen never hesitated to propose his radical ideas to all and sundry, and he never learned to recognize the polite brush-off, let alone ironic remarks. In 1818 Owen travelled on his own initiative to the Congress of Sovereigns held at Aix-la-Chapelle. There he personally shoved copies of a pamphlet he had had specially printed into the hands of all the rulers present, except the Tsar, whose 'dress fitted so tightly to his person, that, having no pockets' he snapped: 'I have not place to put it in. Who are you?' William Hazlitt remarked at the time that 'Mr Owen is the first philosopher we ever heard of, who recommended himself to the great by telling them disagreeable truths.'

As Owen's ambitions grew more utopian, he naturally turned to the one place where he was sure of a sympathetic hearing: the United States. In 1824 he travelled there, to be wined and dined in Philadelphia, Washington, DC and elsewhere, and to meet with a veritable host of American Presidents, past, present and future: John Adams, Thomas Jefferson, James Madison, James Monroe, John Quincy Adams, Andrew Jackson and Martin Van Buren. In Washington, Owen delivered not one but two addresses to the House of Representatives, conferred with President Monroe and even sat down with a group of Choctaw and Chickasaw chiefs – all in an effort to advance his ideal society. Owen, delighted at this regal reception from the Americans, prophesied that

> . . . the whole of the district north of the Ohio River comprising all the free States will be ripe for the change before the . . . year 1827. . . . Our operations will soon extend to the blacks & the Indians who by singular circumstances have been prepared in a peculiar manner for the change which I propose.

Lecturing and meeting statesmen were not Owen's only reasons for travelling across the Atlantic. He proposed to set up a model society on the American frontier which would 'spread from Community to Community, from State to State, from Continent to Continent, until this system and these *truths* shall overshadow the whole earth, shedding fragrance and abundance, intelligence and happiness, upon all the sons of men!'

Owen's communitarian system fitted into an American tradition which had already been well established by the Shakers (whom Owen admired) and other religious sects. Ideal communities were 'hot property' in the early nineteenth century: the minute one utopian community put its land up for sale, another grabbed the ready-made paradise. Thus the French socialist Etienne Cabet bought the Mormons' settlement at Nauvoo, Illinois and Robert Owen purchased the property of the Rappites (a religious sect) at Harmony, Indiana.

The papers were signed at New Harmony (newly dubbed) on the morning of 3 January 1825. Owen departed for the East that afternoon, putting his son William in charge. According to John Humphrey Noyes, Owen had

> ... stirred the very life of the nation with his appeals to Kings and Congresses, and his vast experiments at New Harmony. Think of his family of nine hundred members on a farm of thirty thousand acres! A magnificent beginning, that thrilled the world!

But he had left William high and dry for the first few months in Utopia, without having first hammered out any details concerning housing, property rights and selection of members. Robert Owen called New Harmony 'the best half-way house I could procure for those who are going to travel this extraordinary journey with me.' William Owen wrote less optimistically in his journal:

> The enjoyment of a reformer, I should say, is much more in contemplation than in reality. . . . I doubt whether those who have been comfortable and contented in their old mode of life, will find an increase of enjoyment when they come here.

One enthusiastic New Harmonian commented wryly:

> Pone Bread & Musquetoes! How wonderfully efficient these will be in defeating the most feasible plan for improving the condition of mankind that was ever devised.

The fact was that Robert Owen was more interested in chasing 'the phantom which was public opinion' than in sorting out the minutiae of Utopia. Thus, while the father, back in Washington, DC, was proudly displaying an impressive model, specially made in England, of the parallelogram to be erected in Indiana, the son was writing from New Harmony:

> As for building houses, that is at present out of the question. We have

no lime, no rocks (ready blasted), *no brick, no timber, no boards, no shingles,* nothing requisite for buildings, and as to getting them from others, they are not to be had in the whole country. We must ourselves produce the whole of them, before we can build . . . to do all these things, we have no hands to spare, or the branches of business in the Society must stop, and they cannot stop, or the whole Society would stop too.

One contemporary quipped that Robert Owen 'might live in parallelograms, but he argued in circles.'

Owen senior returned to New Harmony periodically, but his visits always seemed to cause more problems than they solved. During one of these brief appearances, in May 1825, when 800 inhabitants were already installed in New Harmony, a committee of four was appointed and a constitution devised, giving Robert Owen complete control for the first three years. On a return visit in January 1826, however, Owen proposed a new constitution based on absolute equality and self-government. This was the second of seven constitutions drafted within two years, each one as inadequate as the last. Owen began to institute a 'labour currency' at New Harmony, wherein the amount added to the credit in each member's 'passbook' equalled the value of his or her labour, and the price of goods was based on the average labour time required for their manufacture. Owen believed that on a national scale this system, as long as the 'currency' in circulation corresponded to the amount produced, would make the economy immune to overproduction, depression and inflation.

Despite the general confusion at New Harmony, the rhetoric continued. On 4 July 1826, Robert Owen described to a gathering of New Harmonians the awful Trinity of Man's oppressors: 'Private property, Irrational Religion and Marriage', calling instead for liberation from both privilege and individual ownership. He went on to produce the successor to the Declaration of Independence of 1776, the Declaration of Mental Independence of 1826. All this was accompanied by a firework display, 'with all the crucibles and chemicals around him that money could buy', but which at the appointed time 'only sputtered and smoked', ending the meeting in 'confusion and disappointment'. Outsiders were deeply suspicious of Owen's unconventional views on religion and marriage, and some saw the horrible spectre of the French Revolution looming behind Owen's doctrines.

The one issue which contributed most to the eventual collapse of New

Harmony was membership. The crucial question of who were to be the first pioneers in Utopia was never addressed. One rumour had it that Owen was planning to bring over the entire population of New Lanark to begin his venture. Once in New Harmony, William Owen urged his father not to admit the locals but to consider applications from Europeans only. But, as another son, Robert Dale Owen, later explained:

A believer in the force of circumstances and of the instinct of self interest to reform all men, however ignorant or vicious, he admitted into his village all comers, without recommendatory introduction or any examination whatever. This error was the more fatal, because it is in the nature of any novel experiment, or any putting forth of new views which may tend to revolutionize the opinions or habits of society, to attract to itself . . . waifs and strays from the surrounding society; men and women of crude, ill-considered, extravagant notions; nay, worse, vagrants who regard the latest heresy but as a stalking-horse for pecuniary gain, or a convenient cloak for immoral demeanor.

Noyes remarked of Owen's recruitment policy that 'it was like advertising for a wife; and we never heard of any body's getting a good wife by advertising.' Participants and observers alike described the inhabitants of New Harmony as drunkards, 'black sheep', 'vagabonds and lazy worthless persons'.

A great many well-educated, respectable people also joined Owen's movement; however, their good intentions turned to despair when confronted with their fellow men. Sarah Pears wrote from New Harmony: 'Oh, if you could see some of the rough uncouth creatures here, I think you would find it rather hard to look upon them exactly in the light of brothers and sisters.' However much they were committed in theory to equality, it was not easy for recruits to leave the class distinctions of the outside world behind them. One visitor, the Duke of Saxe-Weimer, described how, during an evening's entertainment, 'young ladies turned up their noses apart at the democratic dancers'. One refined young woman, who had apparently joined New Harmony because of an unhappy love affair, nearly burst into tears when, in the middle of a recital on the pianoforte, 'she was told that the milking of the cows was her duty. . . . She betook herself to this servile employment, deprecating the new social system, and its so much prized equality.' A Russian woman confided to the Duke 'that the highly vaunted equality was not altogether to her taste; that some of the society were too low, and the table was below all criticism.' She added that 'she would enter a Shaker establishment near Vincennes.'

Even the arrival in early 1826 of an impressive array of scientists and educationalists in the 'boatload of knowledge' – 'more *learning* than ever was before contained in a boat' – could not save New Harmony. These East-coast intellectuals were, by Robert Owen's orders, treated like royalty, with special accommodation and fare provided for them. Enthusiastic to begin with, they too soon became discouraged. The educationalist William Maclure even despaired of his newly established school: 'I have so far lost the little confidence I had in adults or parents that I believe no system of education can have a fair trial but with orphans.'

The community of New Harmony soon divided into factions and the Owenite experiment came to an end in June 1827, after only a few years' trial. The downfall of New Harmony was due in large part to the democratic disease of individualism, as Tocqueville called it. Owen himself stated that no principle had ever 'produced so much evil as the principle of *individualism*'. William Maclure attributed the collapse of New Harmony to Owen's failure to recognize that 'the materials in this country are not the same as the cotton spinners at New Lanark, nor does the advice of a patron go so far.' The Owen sons stayed behind in America and one of them, Robert Dale Owen, entered government as a US Representative and pioneered the Indiana free-school system which was eventually adopted throughout the Midwest. Their father, financially worse off after his backwoods venture, returned to England with perhaps his most important work, in the British Trade Union movement, before him.

The New Harmony fiasco did nothing to extinguish the communitarian tradition in America. During the economic recession of the 1840s, a new generation came to believe, like their predecessors, that 'America itself having in some sense gone astray, utopianism would remake it in the small.' The American philosopher Ralph Waldo Emerson wrote to Thomas Carlyle in 1840:

We are all a little wild here with numberless projects of social reform. Not a reading man but has a draft of a new Community in his waistcoat pocket. . . . One man renounces the use of animal food; & another of coin; & another of domestic hired service; & another of the state.

In 1841 one of the best known experiments in America got under way at

Brook Farm, in Roxbury, Massachusetts. Described by one observer as 'a social poem fashioned out of Yankee homespun', it was destined to be immortalized by Nathaniel Hawthorne, one of America's greatest writers and an original Brook Farmer, in his novel *The Blithedale Romance*.

The recession in America which began with the Panic of 1837 grew more severe in the following decade. Ralph Waldo Emerson had noted in his diary on 22 April 1837:

> Cold April: hard times; men breaking who ought not to break; banks bullied into the bolstering of desperate speculators; all the newspapers a chorus of owls. . . . Sixty thousand laborers, says rumor, to be presently thrown out of work and these make a comfortable mob to break the banks, and rob the rich, and brave the domestic government.

Nathaniel Hawthorne, thinking back on this period, wrote in *The House of the Seven Gables* (1851) that 'amid the fluctuating waves of our social life, somebody is always at the drowning-point.' Something had to be done, but the intellectuals and artists of the day, most of whom subscribed to the Transcendentalist Movement, were divided on the remedy.

Transcendentalism was a uniquely American philosophy. It basically emphasized intuition as a means to knowledge, but perhaps the best definition is that offered by a Boston lady of the day who remarked 'with a wave of the hand that transcendentalism meant "a little beyond"'. Although the Transcendentalists were 'nonconformists who preached self-reliance and were hostile to any compromise of individual freedom', some among them argued that true freedom was impossible in a society which was unequal and impoverished, both financially and spiritually.

The founder of Brook Farm, a Unitarian minister named George Ripley, admitted that he preferred to be 'independent of the world, and of every man in it', but was prepared to sacrifice his personal heaven 'in the hope of a great social good'. As one scholar remarks, 'by establishing a new social order that would serve as alternative and model for reform, the transcendentalists proposed a rebirth of the spirit to precede a gradual regeneration of society from within.' However, in laying down the foundations of his new community, Ripley was determined to preserve the principle of individualism among its members. He insisted on a joint-stock scheme rather than fully fledged communism. To abolish private ownership, wrote Ripley, would 'so far destroy the independence of the individual as to interfere with the great object of all social reforms: namely, the development . . . of a race of free, noble, holy men and women instead of the dwarfish and mutilated specimens which now cover the earth.'

Brook Farm was a strange blend of millenarianism, communitarianism, Unitarianism and Transcendentalism. Its original constitution, published in January 1842, describes a pastoral idyll:

> Everything can be said of it, in a degree, which Christ said of his kingdom, and therefore it is believed that in some measure it does embody his idea. For its gate of entrance is strait and narrow. It is literally a pearl hidden in a field. Those only who are willing to lose their life for its sake shall find it. Its voice is that which sent the young man sorrowing away: 'Go sell all thy goods and give to the poor, and then come and follow me'.

Conservative circles remained sceptical of the venture: 'Are they fools, knaves, madmen, or mere sentimentalists? Is this Coleridge and Southey again, with their Pantisocracy and Susquehanna Paradise?'

Even some Transcendentalists remained unconvinced that this was the way to a better society, let alone true happiness. Emerson confided in his *Journal*:

> I wish to be convinced, to be thawed, to be made nobly mad before the kindlings before my eye of a new dawn of human piety. But this scheme was arithmetic and comfort. . . . It was not the cave of persecution which is the place of spiritual power, but only a room in the Astor House [Hotel] hired for the Transcendentalists.

Emerson declined Ripley's repeated invitations to join the Brook Farm experiment, claiming that

> . . . to join this body would be to traverse all my trumpeted theory, and the instinct which spoke from it, that one man is counterpoise to a city, that a man is stronger than a city, that his solitude is more prevalent and beneficient than the concert of crowds.

A change in attitude towards work was the key to Ripley's plan for social regeneration. He wrote to Emerson:

> Our objects, as you know, are to insure a more natural union between

intellectual and manual labor than now exists; to combine the thinker and the worker as far as possible in the same individual; to guarantee the highest mental freedom by providing all with labor adapted to their tastes and talents, and securing to them the fruits of their industry; to do away with the necessity of menial services by opening the benefits of education and the profits of labor to all; and thus to prepare a society of liberal, intelligent, and cultivated persons, whose relations with each other would permit a more simple and wholesome life than can be led amidst the pressure of our more competitive institutions.

He sought 'industry without drudgery, and true equality without its vulgarity'. A favourite subject for Sunday night debates at Brook Farm was the question: 'Is Labor in itself an ideal, or being unattractive in character, do we in effect clothe it with the spirit we bring to it?'

Hawthorne's opinion on the 'natural union between intellectual and manual labor' changed dramatically during his stay at Brook Farm. The struggling author had joined the Brook Farm community, investing $1000, in the hope that he could support himself and his bride-to-be, Sophia Peabody, by dividing his time equally between manual labour and his writing. His letters to Sophia show that Hawthorne was a zealous initiate in the mysterious ways of the dung piles and 'transcendental heifer[s]' at Brook Farm. In mid-April, soon after his arrival, he began to chop hay before breakfast with 'such "righteous vehemence" (as Mr Ripley says)' that he broke the machine within ten minutes.

After breakfast, Mr Ripley put a four-pronged instrument into my hands, which he gave me to understand was called a pitch-fork; and he and Mr Farley being armed with similar weapons, we all three commenced a gallant attack upon a heap of manure. . . . Dearest, I will never consent that thou come within half a mile of me, after such an encounter as that of this morning. Pray Heaven that this letter retain none of the fragrance with which the writer was imbued.

On 4 May 1841 he was still enthusiastic about his labours:

. . . there is nothing so unseemly and disagreeable in this sort of toil, as thou wouldst think. It defiles the hands, indeed, but not the soul. This gold ore is a pure and wholesome substance.

The 'gold mine' was Ripley's euphemism for the manure pile. However,

Hawthorne had changed his tune completely within a month, during which time he was working eight to ten hours a day, six days a week, in the fields and barns. He writes on 1 June, 'nearly 6 a.m.':

That abominable gold mine! Thank God, we anticipate getting rid of its treasurers, in the course of two or three days. Of all hateful places, that is the worst; and I shall never comfort myself for having spent so many days of blessed sunshine there. It is my opinion, dearest, that a man's soul may be buried and perish under a dung-heap or in a furrow of the field, just as well as under a pile of money.

By August, when he had made up his mind to withdraw his formal membership from Brook Farm and return only as a paying boarder, he exclaimed to Sophia:

Oh; belovedest, labor is the curse of this world, and nobody can meddle with it, without becoming proportionably brutified. Dost thou think it a praiseworthy matter, that I have spent five golden months in providing food for cows and horses? Dearest, it is not so. Thank God, my soul is not utterly buried under a dung heap.

Hawthorne was not alone in his feelings. Another participant told Emerson that 'the experience of Brook Farm was unanimous, "We have no thoughts."' (One woman member did, however, manage, at least for a time, to iron 'Community-collars, and, with book stuck open with two forks, [commit] German poems to memory'.)

In his *History of American Socialisms* Noyes's judgment of Hawthorne's sojourn at Brook Farm is unjustly harsh: 'Hawthorne, who joined it only to jilt it, has given the world a poetico-sneering romance about it.' In fact, Hawthorne's *Blithedale Romance* (1852) is one of the classics of American literature. Although a romance rather than a utopia, it offers an insight into the inevitable difficulties of communal living. Hawthorne states in his preface that he 'has ventured to make free with his old, and affectionately remembered home, at BROOK FARM, as being, certainly, the most romantic episode of his own life – essentially a daydream, and yet a fact – and thus offering an available foothold between fiction and reality.' A pretty good description of Utopia.

The narrator of the tale, a poet named Miles Coverdale, arrives at Blithedale, like his creator Hawthorne, in an April snow storm, fancying himself one of the Pilgrim Fathers. On that first night, Coverdale compares the window-panes glowing with warmth to 'the beacon-fire which we have kindled for humanity':

> If ever men might lawfully dream awake, and give utterance to their wildest visions, without dread of laughter or scorn on the part of the audience – yes, and speak of earthly happiness, for themselves and mankind, as an object to be hopefully striven for, and probably attained – we, who made that little semicircle round the blazing fire, were those very men.

As the Blithedale band sit warming themselves in front of the cheering fire, they encounter their first obstacle, one which had risen its ugly head at New Harmony and one which Coleridge and Southey had worried about – how to act the equal of those below you on the social ladder. Coverdale describes their first meal:

> We all sat down – grisly Silas Foster, his rotund helpmate, and the two bouncing handmaidens, included – and looked at one another in a friendly, but rather awkward way. It was the first practical trial of our theories of equal brotherhood and sisterhood; and we people of superior cultivation and refinement (for as such, I presume, we unhesitatingly reckoned ourselves) felt as if something were already accomplished towards the millennium of love. The truth is, however, that the laboring oar was with our unpolished companions; it being far easier to condescend, than to accept of condescension . . . if ever I did deserve to be soundly cuffed by a fellow-mortal, for secretly putting weight upon some imaginary social advantage, it must have been while I was striving to prove myself ostentatiously his equal, and no more.

After a few weeks shovelling manure and digging in the fields, Coverdale mirrors Hawthorne's own disenchantment with the community's principle of labour: 'The peril of our new way of life was not lest we should fail in becoming practical agriculturalists, but that we should probably cease to be anything else.' In his novel Hawthorne also identifies a more fundamental problem with the theory of labour and economics practised at Brook Farm. The 'Arcadians' found themselves, not in harmony with their country neighbours, but in stiff competition in the market for cash crops. Coverdale notes the irony of the situation and comments:

'. . . as regarded society at large, we stood in a position of new hostility, rather than new brotherhood.' At one point in the story, Coverdale, like Hawthorne before him, feels the need to get away:

> It was now time for me, therefore, to go and hold a little talk with conservatives, the writers of the North American Review, the merchants, the politicians, the Cambridge men, and all those respectable old blockheads, who still, in this intangibility and mistiness of affairs, kept a death-grip on one or two ideas which had not come into vogue since yesterday morning.

Hawthorne was not the only member to desert the real Brook Farm. Many utopian enthusiasts floated among the numerous communities, both religious and secular, which dotted the hillsides from Massachusetts to Indiana in the 1840s. By 1844 a number of Brook Farmers had either transferred to another community or, like Hawthorne, returned to civilization. Those who remained behind took up a number of different fads and fashions. Some members formed a Grahamite table at mealtimes. The former preacher Sylvester Graham advocated vegetarianism as a cure for social ills and invented the wholesome graham cracker, today a staple in the American diet (his spiritual successor, John Harvey Kellogg, created cornflakes to improve America's moral fibre as part of this utopian health-food craze). A Brook Farmer recounted that, in addition, 'rough wooden crosses, and pictures of the Madonna, began to appear, and I suspected rosaries rattling under the aprons.' However, 'Fourier and finance' became a more engrossing topic than Catholicism or even vegetarianism at Brook Farm through the efforts of Fourier's devoted American disciple Albert Brisbane.

Brisbane, the son of a wealthy land speculator, was born in the Burnt Over Region of New York State in 1809. He was educated in New York City, after which he set off on a Grand Tour of Europe, where he 'whirled through several of the major trends in contemporary social philosophy' and met many of the great celebrities of the day. One contemporary called him a metaphysical 'windmill'. Walt Whitman said of him: 'Somehow or other he always looks as if he is attempting to think out some problem a little too hard for him.'

Brisbane was looking for a system. In the first two decades of the nineteenth century, Charles Fourier, Robert Owen and Henri de Saint-Simon were bitter utopian rivals. The impressionable Brisbane was initially attracted to Saint-Simon's heirs, the Saint-Simonians and their 'religion of love'. He had heard the sect's leader, the charismatic Barthélemy Prosper Enfantin, speak in Paris. But, after the scandalous dissolution of the Ménilmontant experiment in 1831, Brisbane lost enthusiasm. Owen continued to be a greatly respected figure in Europe; however, the failure of New Harmony had tainted his reputation among America's intellectuals and communitarians.

Fourier took full advantage of his rivals' misfortunes and published the pamphlet *Pièges et Charlatanisme des Deux Sectes: Saint-Simon et Owen, Qui Promettent l'Association et le Progrès* ('Snares and Charlatanism of the Two Sects: Saint-Simon and Owen, Who Promise Association and Progress') in 1831. Although Fourier had spent most of his life looking for a patron to implement his great phalanx, he refused to acknowledge any of the experimental schemes which were founded in his name, such as the 'Societary Colony' at Condé in France (1832). By thus distancing himself from these utopian communities, which inevitably ended in failure, Fourier kept the principles of Association (his term for the system) pure and unsullied.

In the 1820s Fourier had toyed with the notion of setting up his utopia in America – in fact, his idea was that Robert Owen give financial backing to the building of a phalanstery in New Harmony. Fourier had courted the American embassy in Paris, claiming that his system would pacify the Indians and prevent division between the North and South over slavery. The American consul commented that Fourier was 'either a genuine curiosity or the emanation of a disturbed brain'. When Brisbane met the old and embittered prophet in Paris in 1832, he was immediately converted to Fourier's brand of utopian socialism.

Brisbane returned to the United States in 1834 with a mission. His 'sole thought' was to 'transmit the thought of Charles Fourier to my countrymen'. Brisbane admired Fourier's critique of contemporary society and his ideas of social harmony, the co-operative society, the phalanstery and 'passionate attraction'. The principle of Fourier which most appealed to Brisbane was that work, the curse of civilization, should be organized to provide variety and job satisfaction. This was to be achieved through the mechanism of the 'passionate series': groups joined together by a common liking for a particular task. Brisbane hoped to apply Fourierism to harness the new forces of industrialization.

He proclaimed Fourierism in the millenarian rhetoric of the day: 'The Paradise itself will be the Moral Harmony of the Passions in Associative Unity, the Kingdom of Heaven which comes to this terrestrial world.' Brisbane prophesied that Fourier's theory of Association would do for society 'what the mariner's compass did for navigation, the telescope for astronomy, and steam for machinery.' And Fourier's ideas, as interpreted and preached by Brisbane, found ready followers among the floating population of utopians in America. One historian summarizes Fourierism's appeal to Americans: Fourierists

> ... argued that far from repudiating American values, utopian socialism was merely a more effective way to realize the goals of republicanism, democracy, Christianity, and missionary nationalism. They promised that the new order would bring an abundant, satisfying, and equal society without renouncing conventional ways or liberal beliefs. And their phalanxes incorporated familiar capitalist features such as private property, interest, and a modified wage system inside the communitarian frame. In this sense the Fourierists were proposing not just a cooperative substitute for competitive capitalism but an alternative, more community-minded version of the American Dream.

Many believed that Fourierism, sympathetic as it was to many of capitalism's principles, would solve once and for all the scourges of capitalism, unemployment, decreasing wages, and social instability. Perhaps most importantly, Fourier's egalitarianism was in tune with American thinking: equality of opportunity, but not equality of goods. The New York journalist Parke Godwin likened Fourier's system to the United States' motto *E Pluribus Unum*, 'that beautiful arrangement for combining the most perfect independence of the separate members with complete harmony and strength in the federal heart'.

Brisbane proved to be a brilliant publicist. Through his writings, lectures and translations, he could boast at the end of 1843, six years after Fourier's death: 'The name of FOURIER is now heard from the Atlantic to the Mississippi.' By the next year Brisbane, who had close links with the Transcendentalists, had succeeded in claiming Brook Farm as his most distinguished convert.

Fourier's ideas had at first met with a mixed reaction. One Brook Farmer said of Fourier: 'A rare and original mind; ... but our nobler part protests at much which a genuine descendant of the Puritans must always find it hard to swallow.' George Ripley's wife Sophia also found certain aspects of Fourierism too French for New Englanders:

> His general principles should be cautiously separated from the details which accompany their exposition, many of which are so exclusively

adapted to the French character as to prejudice their reception with persons of opposite habits and associations.

But Brisbane persevered and 'to the regret of some, the readings of Dante or rendering of Beethoven were often renounced because Mr Brisbane insisted on propounding the doctrine that was destined to bring peace and plenty to mankind.' Noyes called Brisbane's success at Brook Farm

> . . . a great move. A more brilliant attorney could not have been found. The concentrated genius of Unitarianism and Transcendentalism was at Brook Farm. It was the school that trained most of the writers who have created the newspaper and magazine literature of the present time.

A modern historian has called it 'one of the most interesting ideological experiments of the nineteenth century: the joining of American Transcendentalism and European utopian socialism in a communal venture'.

The transition to Fourierism gave Brook Farm a new lease of life. By 1844 its membership had dwindled to only a dozen. But Fourier's prestige was such that, within a few months of the community's rebirth as the Brook Farm Association for Industry and Education, sixty-seven new recruits had joined. The new Association introduced a number of Fourierist measures in order to prop up its ailing economy. These included wage differentials to encourage labour, diversified production and mixed industry. The members also set about building a large communal dwelling – though nothing as ambitious as Fourier's original design for a phalanstery. The system of joint stock was retained and refined.

On a more mundane level, the community adopted Fourier's concept of the juvenile Hordes, rechristened the Sacred Legion, to perform the more distasteful chores. Their services were especially appreciated in the dining room, where the method of serving griddle cakes at breakfast had completely broken down. Both the Transcendentalists and the Fourierists agreed that education should be a high priority, and the Brook Farm school was duly famous. George Ripley ran a preparatory school for young men destined for Harvard University; his daughter, Miss Marianne Ripley, dubbed 'Her Perpendicular Majesty', oversaw the primary school.

By the close of 1844, Brook Farm was showing a profit for the first time. But then three disasters struck the community: an epidemic of smallpox, a fire which destroyed the newly built (and uninsured) 'phalanstery' and a suit lodged by Nathaniel Hawthorne claiming the money still due him from his original investment in Brook Farm. The community was understandably demoralized by these misfortunes, and the last two proved to be its financial undoing. Brook Farm was disbanded in the autumn of 1847.

Yet it was more than bad luck that had led to the dissolution of Brook Farm. All of the nearly thirty American phalanxes established in the 1840s, from Massachusetts to Iowa, were short-lived, and critics were soon referring to Fourierists as 'four-year-ites' (they were also called 'fury-ites' because of their fanatic zeal). Emerson called Brook Farm 'a perpetual picnic, a French Revolution in small; an Age of Reason in a patty-pan' – in short, 'a buzz in the ear'. His criticism of Fourier could well extend to all utopian projects:

> Fourier had skipped no fact but one, namely life, [for human nature] spawns and scorns systems and system-makers . . . eludes all conditions . . . [and] makes or supplants a thousand phalanxes and New Harmonys with each pulsation.

It is easy to share Emerson's dismissive tone about the communitarian movement. Its pretensions can seem ridiculous, its failures predictable. Yet communitarianism has remained a vital and seemingly irrepressible expression of America's utopian nature. By the end of the nineteenth century a new and vigorous wave of communities was establishing itself on the West Coast, from Point Loma in San Diego to Puget Sound in Washington State, and the communes of the 1960s and '70s were just the latest manifestation of this movement.

Communitarianism reflects the exceptionally fluid and dynamic nature of American society; it redeems the promise of the Declaration of Independence that Americans will be free to pursue happiness in their own way. If the communitarian movement were ever to die away completely, America would have lost something of its soul. Today, the movement is experiencing one of its periodic phases of quiescence. Yet we should expect it to flower again, perhaps fuelled by frustration at the way late twentieth-century living fractures all sense of community, so that once more the experimental utopia can fulfil its role as, in the words of one nineteenth-century Owenite, 'a light-house, pointing to the rocks on which so many have been wrecked, or to the haven in which the few have found rest'.

11. The Great Trust

To many reform-minded Americans in the second half of the nineteenth century it seemed as if the rapid industrialization of the continent was leading to ever greater exploitation and injustice, and that capitalism as an economic system was straining to breaking point. In *Looking Backward*, Edward Bellamy compares the society of his day

> . . . to a prodigious coach which the masses of humanity were harnessed to and dragged toilsomely . . . Despite the difficulty of drawing the coach at all along so hard a road, the top was covered with passengers who never got down, even at the steepest ascents. . . . Well up out of the dust, their occupants could enjoy the scenery at their leisure, or critically discuss the merits of the straining team. . . . Oh, yes, commiseration was frequently expressed by those who rode for those who had to pull the coach, especially when the vehicle came to a bad place in the road, as it was constantly doing . . . At such times the passengers would call down encouragingly to the toilers of the rope, exhorting them to patience, and holding out hopes of possible compensation in another world for the hardness of their lot.

Growing economic and social inequity was placing the American vision of Utopia under strain. To many people, Tocqueville's 'equality of condition' seemed increasingly inadequate: the Industrial Revolution was making a mockery of the guarantees in the name of which the American Revolution had been fought. It was in response to this unease that the last direct descendant of Fourierism emerged in the late 1880s in the guise of Bellamy's Nationalist movement. It was nothing less than an attempt to fire the American imagination with a nationwide utopia hitherto foreign to the United States: Marxist socialism.

Bellamy had known Albert Brisbane as an older man, and he was a keen student of the antebellum communitarian movement in America, which he deemed 'one of the most significant as well as most picturesque chapters of American history'. Bellamy stated that 'the Brook Farm Colony and a score of phalansteries' were the 'precursors' of his own utopian vision. Many of the innovations in Bellamy's Boston of the year 2000 owe their existence to the imagination of Fourier and his disciples, including, as we have seen in previous chapters, the 'industrial army', covered walkways and pneumatic tubes. (The last were Brisbane's invention; the US Congress spent $15,000 constructing an underground tube between the Capitol and the Government Printing Office, but it collapsed and the project was abandoned.) However, Bellamy was convinced that the small-scale communitarian approach to reform was outdated: the social problems in America had to be tackled on a national level. He declared at his Nationalist meetings: 'We nationalists are not trying to work out our individual salvation, but the weal of all. . . . A slight amendment in the condition of the mass of men is preferable to elysium attained by the few.' As one historian remarks: 'It was Bellamy's call for action on a national scale rather than the Fourierists' decentralized communitarianism which set the agenda for the next generations of American radicals.'

Edward Bellamy was born in Chicopee Falls, Massachusetts, into a family of ministers. He grew up in a religious household rigorously presided over by his Calvinist mother, and became a rebel as a young man, showing a decided preference for beer and fast horses over conventional piety. Edward may have taken after his boyhood hero, the black sheep of the family, Captain Samuel Bellamy, whose profession in the eighteenth century was piracy. The captain's views, according to Philip Gosse's *The Pirates' Who's Who* (1924) 'were distinctly socialistic'.

Edward's attraction to socialism was strengthened not only by an aversion to his Calvinist upbringing but also by the economic and social change which was turning his cherished Chicopee Falls from a thriving village into an ugly factory town. One historian states that the 'Bellamys' unpretentious frame house with its picket fence – a symbol of the besieged old Yankee – was located near the grimy mills, rows of brick tenements, and mansions of factory owners.' After his studies at Union College in Schenectady, New York, a year's sojourn in Germany and a miserable year as a journalist in New York City, Bellamy returned to his home town, married Emma Sanderson, his parents' ward, and remained in Chicopee Falls for the rest of his life, writing articles, short stories and eventually *Looking Backward*. His newspaper pieces, with titles such as 'Overworked Children in Our Mills', 'Riches and Rottenness', 'Wastes and Burdens of Society', reveal his distress at what he saw around him, and his reformist leanings.

However, Bellamy was not entirely forward looking. This was a man who admitted having 'a deep-seated aversion to change' and dreaded any journey, 'however brief', away from home. A key to Bellamy's philosophy and to his utopian romance, *Looking Backward*, is his attitude to the past: a 'nostalgia for the future'. What has been said of Jules Verne's science fiction also applies to Bellamy's utopian fiction of the same period: his 'progress-oriented society may well have experienced, in depth, a nostalgia for reassuring patterns of recurrence, and therefore often preferred, even in its political moods, to think forward by looking backward.' Even Dr Leete, the time-traveller Julian West's host in the year 2000, succumbs to nostalgia as he reminds his guest of a time when 'the individual workman was relatively important and independent in his relations to the employer . . . when a little capital or a new idea was enough to start a man in business for himself . . . and there was no hard and fast line between the two classes.' Leete adds, 'Labor unions were needless then, and general strikes were out of the question.' Ultimately, Bellamy adhered to Saint-Simon's dictum: '*Looking Backward* was written in the belief that the Golden Age lies before us and not behind us.'

But Bellamy's backward looking was extremely selective. He only wanted to remember the good things; indeed a major theme of his fiction is how to eradicate those unpleasant memories which haunt us and, according to both Bellamy and modern psychiatry, hold us back. In his novel *Dr Heidenhoff's Process* (1880), the doctor solves the mystery of 'galvano-therapeutics' (or 'thought extirpation') so that he can remove a patient's bad memories or 'inconvenient recollections . . . as readily as a dentist pulls a tooth': 'Memory is the principle of moral degeneracy. Remembered sin is the most utterly diabolical influence in the universe.' The cure for original sin is to eradicate the memory of it. In *Looking Backward*, Julian West, having acknowledged the advances of the future, looks back from the year 2000 and declares: 'The past was dead, crushed beneath a century's weight.'

Bellamy's own memory proved faulty immediately following the publication of *Looking Backward*, when he declared, 'I have never been in any sense a student of socialistic literature, or have known more of the various socialistic schemes than any newspaper reader might.' This statement is false on two counts. First, Bellamy was, on the contrary, well read in socialist literature; his brother testified that Edward's year in Germany (1869–70) was spent studying the country's language and socialism. Secondly, Bellamy was not just 'any newspaper reader'; he was a journalist covering the stories of the day, and socialism was a well known (though certainly not well understood) phenomenon of the time. Why, then, did Bellamy deny any socialist influence?

The communitarians, Owen and the Fourierists, had first introduced socialism to America in the 1820s and 1840s. Americans were receptive to this early socialism which represented itself as the true expression of the egalitarianism of the Declaration of Independence. The Transcendentalist Octavius Brooks Frothingham remarked that socialism seemed 'to be fast assuming in the United States a national character'. In 1886, while on a tour of the United States, Karl Marx's daughter Eleanor Marx Averling commented on the 'unconscious socialism' of the people she met: the 'American people . . . were waiting to hear in their own language what socialism was.' Although few of Marx's works had been translated into English, his ideas were propagated in America via pamphlets and newspapers. Marx had written for the Fourierist newspaper the *New York Tribune* until the outbreak of the Civil War in 1861, and America was home to the First International, the international workers' association which had become unpopular in Europe, from 1872.

However, by the time Bellamy was writing, the word 'socialism' had become somewhat disreputable. It was partly the failures of the communitarian experiments which had given socialism a bad name (one former Owenite, revisiting New Harmony fifteen years after the community had disbanded, recounts how he was 'cautioned not to speak of Socialism, as the subject was unpopular'). But, more importantly, a rash of industrial disputes in the 1880s caused socialists to become associated in the public mind with violent unrest. This 'red scare' reached its climax in 1886, the year before *Looking Backward* was written, when four socialist campaigners for shorter working hours were executed for their alleged part in the Haymarket riot, in which a bomb was thrown, killing a policeman. Bellamy's disclaimer *vis à vis* socialism, therefore, was more than a literary pretence; he did not want *Looking Backward* to be branded, and thus discounted, as subversive literature. Bellamy described his mixed feelings regarding socialism in a letter to his friend, William Dean Howells:

Every sensible man will admit there is a big deal in a name, especially in making first impressions. In the radicalness of the opinions I have expressed, I may seem to out-socialize the socialists, yet the word socialist is one I could never well stomach. In the first place it is a foreign word in itself, and equally foreign in all its suggestions. It smells to the average American of petroleum, suggests the red flag, with all manner of sexual novelties, and an abusive tone about God and religion, which in this country we at least treat with decent respect. . . . whatever German and French reformers may choose to call themselves, socialist is not a good name for a party to succeed in America. No such party can or ought to succeed that is not wholly and enthusiastically American and patriotic in spirit and suggestions.

Bellamy believed most Americans of his generation, 'considered socialism a license for bomb throwing and inflammatory speechmaking by bearded radicals', as one scholar comments. In *Looking Backward*, Dr Leete criticizes the 'followers of the red flag' of the nineteeth century, claiming that 'they had nothing to do with it [the transformation of society] except to hinder it.'

But, Bellamy 'doth protest too much'. Julian West falls asleep in Boston in 1887 and wakes up in the year 2000 to discover the city and the whole United States transformed into what the modern reader immediately recognizes as a socialist state, with nationalized industry and full economic as well as social equality. West is understandably puzzled as to how the strike-torn capitalist America of the late nineteeth century has been transformed into this communist paradise. In fact, *Looking Backward* is unusual among utopian romances in that it not only describes the ideal state, but also lays considerable emphasis on how it came about.

Bellamy was writing at a time of great change in the structure of American capitalism. Small independent manufacturers were being consolidated into large corporations or trusts ruled by a handful of 'Robber Barons'. Men like Rockefeller, Morgan, Vanderbilt and Carnegie were rapidly acquiring monopolistic control of industrial production in the United States. At one point two of them, Rockefeller (oil) and Morgan (railroads), controlled twenty per cent of the nation's wealth. The creation of these monopolies was the cause of much concern and eventually prompted anti-trust legislation. But Bellamy saw the trusts as the logical precursors of the ultimate monopoly of industry by the state itself. Thus, according to Dr Leete,

> ... the movement toward the conduct of business by larger and larger aggregations of capital, the tendency toward monopolies, which had been so desperately and vainly resisted, was recognized at last, in its true significance, as a process which only needed to complete its logical evolution to open a golden future to humanity.

> Early in the last century the evolution was completed by the final consolidation of the entire capital of the nation. The industry and commerce of the country, ceasing to be conducted by a set of

irresponsible corporations and syndicates of private persons at their caprice and for their profit, were entrusted to a single syndicate representing the people, to be conducted in the common interest for the common profit. The nation, that is to say, organized as the one great business corporation in which all other corporations were absorbed; it became the one capitalist in the place of all other capitalists, the sole employer, the final monopoly in which all previous and lesser monopolies were swallowed up, a monopoly in the profits and economies of which all citizens shared.

Bellamy saw the capitalists of his day operating on an ever greater scale, and simply projected this trend into the future. As Dr Leete says, 'the epoch of trusts had ended in The Great Trust.' The idea that the socialist state is an inevitable product of the evolution of capitalism echoes Marx, as we shall see in the next chapter. And, indeed, Dr Leete's use of the term 'evolution' lends to his account the same scientific aura that Marx and his followers claimed for their ideas. In a response to a review of his book, Bellamy was even more explicit:

> *Looking Backward*, although in form a fanciful romance, is intended, in all seriousness, as a forecast, in accordance with the principles of evolution, of the next stage in the industrial and social development of humanity.

But, whereas Marx believed that the proletariat would be the agents of change, for Bellamy it is the corporations who head the transition. Dr Leete describes the public's attitude to the corporations on the eve of the nationalization of industry:

> The most violent foes of the great private monopolies were now forced to recognize how invaluable and indispensable had been their office in educating the people up to the point of assuming control of their own business. . . . Thus it came about that, thanks to the corporations themselves, when it was proposed that the nation should assume their functions, the suggestion implied nothing which seemed impracticable even to the timid.

As if to reassure readers who shared Bellamy's distaste for bomb-throwing radicals, Dr Leete explains that 'there was absolutely no violence. The change had been long foreseen. Public opinion had become fully ripe for it, and the whole mass of the people was behind it.'

In *Looking Backward* Bellamy was attempting to Americanize Marxism, to create a socialist utopia that, free from foreign influences and the 'smell of petroleum', would appeal to his patriotic fellow-countrymen. Bellamy calls the single party which rules the United States in the year 2000 the Nationalist Party. The Nationalists' themes, objectives and rhetoric are drawn from the example of the Founding Fathers. In the sequel to *Looking Backward*, aptly termed *Equality* (1897), Dr Leete, still a fixture of the year 2000, remarks:

> As we look at it, the immortal preamble of the American Declaration of Independence, away back in 1776, logically contained the entire statement of the doctrine of universal economic equality guaranteed by the nation collectively to its members individually.

For Bellamy, the political equality promised in the Declaration of Independence could not be achieved unless there was an equal distribution of material resources. The Founding Fathers had not implemented this economic equality straightaway, according to Dr Leete, because in the largely agricultural America of the eighteenth century there were no great disparities of wealth. Only with industrialization did intolerable inequalities begin to appear. By the year 2000, however, the system had been properly adjusted; the promise of the American Revolution of 1776 had at long last been fulfilled. Dr Leete declares:

> The corner stone of our state is economic equality, and is not that the obvious, necessary, and only adequate pledge of these three birthrights – life, liberty, and happiness? What is life without its material basis, and what is an equal right to life but a right to an equal material basis for it? What is liberty? How can men be free who must ask the right to labor and to live from their fellow-men and seek their bread from the hands of others? How else can any government guarantee liberty to men save by providing them a means of labor and of life coupled with independence; and how could that be done unless the government conducted the economic system upon which employment and maintenance depend? Finally, what is implied in the equal right of all to the pursuit of happiness? What form of happiness, so far as it depends at all on material facts, is not bound up with economic conditions; and how shall an equal opportunity for the pursuit of

happiness be guaranteed to all save by the guarantee of economic equality?

The mechanism by which economic equality is achieved and maintained in *Looking Backward* is the industrial army, a sort of national service for industry, which every citizen joins at the age of twenty-one and leaves at forty-five. All workers receive the same 'wages', in the form of credits which can be exchanged for goods; honour and a sense of duty, not higher salaries, have become the incentives to work and to rise in the organization's hierarchy. For the details of this army, Bellamy looked not only to Fourier's *Nouveau Monde Industriel*, as we have seen in Chapter 6 but also, like Saint-Simon before him, to 'the idealized image of the Napoleonic army, in which ordinary soldiers had risen to be marshals, in which rank was at least in theory the reward of talent and merit.' Napoleon had been another boyhood hero of Bellamy. However, the spirit and morale of Bellamy's workforce were undoubtedly inspired by a wholly American theme: nostalgia for the Civil War (1861–65), fought during his childhood.

Many of Bellamy's contemporaries looked backed wistfully to the patriotism, courage and self-sacrifice displayed throughout the Civil War. Ralph Waldo Emerson voiced a commonly held opinion concerning America's recent experience:

War civilizes, for it forces individuals and tribes to combine, and act with larger views, and under the best heads, and keeps the population together, producing the effect of cities; for camps are wandering cities.

When in a nightmare Julian West returns to the misguided and corrupt Boston of 1887, he finds hope and consolation in the sight of a military parade:

A regiment was passing. It was the first sight in that dreary day which had inspired me with any other emotions than wondering pity and amazement. Here at last were order and reason, an exhibition of what intelligent co-operation can accomplish. The people who stood looking on with kindling faces – could it be that the sight had for them no more than but a spectacular interest? Could they fail to see that it was their perfect concert of action, their organization under one control, which made these men the tremendous engine they were, able to vanquish a mob ten times as numerous? Seeing this so plainly, could they fail to compare the scientific manner in which the nation went to war with the unscientific manner in which it went to work?

Bellamy's military machine is motivated by the same spirit of patriotism which inspired the soldiers of the Civil War, as Dr Leete explains to West:

> Not higher wages, but honor and the hope of men's gratitude, patriotism and the inspiration of duty, were the motives which were set before their soldiers when it was a question of dying for the nation. . . . The coarser motives, which no longer move us, have been replaced by higher motives wholly unknown to the mere wage earners of your age. Now that industry, of whatever sort, is no longer self-service, but service of the nation, patriotism, passion for humanity, impel the worker as in your day they did the soldier. The army of industry is an army, not alone by virtue of its perfect organization, but by reason also of the ardor of self-devotion which animates its members.

This ethos of patriotism and selflessness is cemented by the new religion that has arisen in Bellamy's utopia. The 'Religion of Solidarity' exalts the triumph of public spirit over 'excessive individualism', and acts as a sort of spiritual bludgeon to 'prevent any slackers from taking advantage' of the system.

Bellamy had first conceived of this religion when he was in his early twenties, no doubt to fill the void left by his rejection of his parents' brand of religious piety. The Religion of Solidarity is a ragbag of Transcendentalism and socialism. Bellamy admired the Transcendentalists – in his youth he even contemplated living as a hermit in the woods, Thoreau-style, though he never got any further than estimating the cost of his food and clothing. Like the Transcendentalists, Bellamy sought to 'recover a communion with "eternity."' He viewed the individual as 'of so little importance, of such trifling scope, that it should matter little to us what renunciations of its things we make.' 'The greatest of all loves,' Bellamy wrote in an early essay, 'is that of an individual for his remnant, the universe.'

However, Bellamy recognized an inherent weakness in Transcendentalism which had also troubled George Ripley. The Transcendentalist was an egocentric romantic at heart who took 'refuge in the bundle of mental and physical experiences which he calls himself as the only thing of which he is absolutely sure.' To overcome this inadequacy, Bellamy wedded Transcendentalism to the tenets of socialism to create the Religion of Solidarity. Dr Leete again:

> The equal wealth and equal opportunities of culture which all persons now enjoy have simply made us all members of one class, which corresponds to the most fortunate class with you. Until this equality of condition had come to pass, the idea of the solidarity of humanity, the brotherhood of all men, could never have become the real conviction and practical principle of action it is nowadays.

Within everyone, writes Bellamy, there is a 'passion for losing ourselves in others or for absorbing them into ourselves, [which] is the greatest law of solidarity.' The Religion of Solidarity is the antidote to the individualism which was so characteristic of America in Bellamy's time, as it is today, but which Bellamy believed constituted a major obstacle to the achievement of a just society. As Dr Leete explains:

> Individualism, which in your day was the animating idea of society, not only was fatal to any vital sentiment of brotherhood and common interest among living men, but equally to any realization of the responsibility of the living for the generation to follow.

Although he claimed to be fulfilling America's utopian destiny, Bellamy had, in fact, rejected the two basic principles which animate the American project: individualism and the limited egalitarianism of status that goes with it. Bellamy was, in effect, arguing that when the Founding Fathers declared that 'all men are created equal' they had in mind the radical economic equality advocated by European socialists. It is perhaps an indication of just how deeply the European view of equality had taken root in America since the communitarian experiments of the early nineteenth century that *Looking Backward* was successful beyond all expectation. Bellamy had succeeded in making socialism seem patriotic, and his utopian work captured the public imagination, not least because, like Marx, he portrayed it as the inevitable resolution of the upheavals of his day. A journalist wrote in 1890, 'Men read the Republic or the Utopia with a sigh of regret. They read Bellamy with a thrill of hope.'

Looking Backward sold half a million copies within the first few years of its publication. Bellamy graduated from utopian prophet to political leader almost overnight; his party, the Nationalists, took its name from his utopia. The first Nationalist Club, of which there were 162 in twenty-seven states by 1890, was formed in Boston by a group of retired army officers, many of whom had fought in the Civil War. The military regimentation in *Looking Backward* appealed to them, and 'they had pensions to spend and time to kill, and a light airy reading room on Boylston Street opposite the [Boston] Common.' Membership was exclusive, although, inevitably, it became a 'repository for malcontents of every description – prohibitionists, woman's righters, antimonopoly men, die-hard communitarians, socialists, and disgruntled small businessmen'.

The Nationalist Party joined ranks with the Populist (or People's) Party to 'conduct a new kind of campaign' in the bid for the White House in 1892, declaring that 'to nationalists, principles are more important than men, and the platform than the candidates.' Bellamy churned out dozens of newspaper editorials in support of Populism and the Nationalist cause. He continued the war-cry of *Looking Backward* and *Equality*: 'The Nationalist party is the legitimate heir to the principles and spirit of the patriots of 1776.' 'We are the true conservative party,' Bellamy told followers in 1890, 'because we are devoted to the maintenance of republican institutions.' It was the capitalists who were the real revolutionaries, trying to overthrow the republic. Bellamy appealed to the People's Party on the eve of the presidential election:

> We are today confronted by portentous indications in the conditions of American industry, society and politics, that this great experiment [America], on which the last hopes of the race depend, is to prove, like all former experiments, a disastrous failure. Let us bear in mind that, if it be a failure, it will be a final failure. There can be no more new worlds to be discovered, no fresh continents to offer virgin fields for new ventures.

The Populist candidate, General Weaver, carried six states with twenty-two electoral votes (a million popular votes) in 1892: not a disgraceful result, but not enough to win the election. Following the economic Panic of 1893, the membership of the Nationalists and Populists dwindled. Bellamy, whose health was failing, retired from politics, and the Populists merged with the more powerful Democratic party in 1896.

When Edward Bellamy died in 1898, the *American Fabian* wrote:

> It is doubtful if any man, in his own lifetime, ever exerted so great an

influence upon the social beliefs of his fellow-beings as did Edward Bellamy. Marx, at the time of his death, had won but slight recognition from the mass; and though his influence in the progressive struggle has become paramount, it is through his interpreters, and not in his own voice, that he speaks to the multitude. But Bellamy spoke simply and directly; his imagination conceived, and his art pictured, the social framework of the future in such clear and bold outlines that the commonest mind could understand and appreciate. Wherever, in all lands, men are striving for a fairer social order based upon an economic democracy, Bellamy is a recognized prophet of the ideal state.

The Fabians were wholly justified in mentioning Bellamy and Marx in the same breath since, as we have seen, Bellamy's vision of a socialist America was shaped by Marxist ideas. Certainly, the leaders of the Russian Revolution recognized, and approved of, Bellamy's Marxism. They even claimed to have drawn inspiration from *Looking Backward*, which was first translated into Russian by Leo Tolstoy, who called it 'an exceedingly remarkable book'. In 1906 Maxim Gorky remarked to an American audience: 'Edward Bellamy and his theories in *Looking Backward* are known to all the Russian students' – despite the fact that the Tsarist authorities had banned the book from public libraries in 1889. Another Russian, K. A. Koskin, a member of the Petersburg Soviet in 1905, remarked that *Looking Backward* was read during the first Russian Revolution by the workers and that it had won their hearts.

It seems paradoxical, then, that the advent of the Russian Revolution in 1917, the ideals of which were so close to Bellamy's, spelled the end of socialism as a real force in American politics. The White House, still adhering to its policy of supporting revolutions abroad, which dated from 1776, was the first power to extend diplomatic relations to the new Russian government in March 1917, seven days after the abdication of Tsar Nicholas II. But, with the Bolshevik *coup d'état* the following October (November in the Western calendar), the Revolution was seen to sin in American eyes on two counts. First, its violent excesses, like those of the French Revolution before it, shocked and frightened the contented classes of America.

Secondly, and more significantly, it proclaimed a revolutionary ideology which was in direct competition with America's own and 'threatened nothing less than the displacement of the United States from the vanguard of history.' Any subsequent attempts to advocate the equal distribution of wealth between rich and poor were associated in the American mind with this rival utopia of communism and, therefore, considered 'unpatriotic' and 'un-American'. The claim which had been so important to both the communitarians and socialistic-minded reformers like Bellamy, that they were patriots carrying to fruition the ideals of the Founding Fathers, would no longer wash. The United States, which had once so boldly welcomed revolutions as a reflection of its own glory, now saw them as a threat, a potential seedbed for communism. Instead, since 1917 successive American administrations have bolstered authoritarian regimes, from the Shah's in Iran to Duvalier's in Haiti.

Nevertheless, *Looking Backward* has had a lasting influence in America. When Bellamy's Nationalist supporters were absorbed into the Democratic Party, they took with them many of the planks of their reformist platform. These ideas resurfaced a generation later, during another time of crisis in America's history, the Great Depression of the 1930s. President Franklin D. Roosevelt's response, the New Deal, was planned by a staff of intellectuals, the 'Brains Trust', many of whom were influenced by Bellamy, including the Assistant Secretary of State, Adolph A. Berle, Jr, whose father had been a member of the Nationalist Club of Boston, and Bellamy's biographer, A. E. Morgan. Between 1933 and 1941, the Civilian Conservation Corps and the Civil Works Administration directed an army of six million workers in various projects to improve America's infrastructure. Industrial competition, which Bellamy had deprecated as wasteful and inefficient, was regulated under government supervision by the National Industrial Recovery Act. Many other reforms which Bellamy's Nationalists fought for were eventually adopted in piecemeal fashion: municipal gas and electricity systems, income tax, women's suffrage, state liquor licences, postal savings banks, parcel post, direct election of Senators (originally they were appointed), the referendum, free school books and lunches for the needy, raising the age of child labour from ten or thirteen to sixteen, the right to trade unions, a minimum wage and maximum hours.

Although *Looking Backward* has never been out of print, it has been largely forgotten. Americans reading it today would probably reject Bellamy's Marxism: it is all too easy to see why it would fail – any doubt on that score would have been removed by the collapse of the Soviet Empire. Nevertheless, faint echoes of Bellamy's ideas can still be heard in American politics. The problems of economic recession and growing social inequality which the Clinton administration now faces are those which so distressed Bellamy one hundred years ago. In the Clinton-Gore election manifesto, *Putting People First*, there are several passages which are reminiscent of Bellamy's programme. The 1992 manifesto requires that, after two years' unemployment benefit, *'those who can work . . . go to work'*. If they cannot find a job in the private sector, the government will employ them in community service jobs. The stipulation, put forward in the Democrats' 'New Social Contract', 'that if the society gives you a benefit, you must, if you are able, pay it back in some appropriate form', is a hesitant attempt to reawaken ties of mutual service and obligation similar to those which bind the members of Bellamy's industrial army to the nation.

America's self-defined role as a beacon for mankind has dimmed of late. The nation is now experiencing social problems on a scale far worse than many other Western democracies. Nonetheless, America's utopian role is something which most Americans still feel deeply. It would be interesting if the application of ideas first embraced, in America at least, by the communitarians and later by Bellamy, succeeded in reviving America's faith in itself as Utopia.

12. The Sacrificial Altar

From the perspective of our own times, perhaps the most interesting and unsettling thing about *Looking Backward* is the way Bellamy blends socialism and nationalism to create a state ideology that is clearly proto-Fascist. A perceptive reader in 1888 could have seen in Bellamy's utopia the nation-worship, authoritarianism and gerontocratic oligarchy which would prove endemic in twentieth-century totalitarian regimes. The 'goose-step' of the Fascist armies haunts the pages of *Looking Backward*, as does the rhetoric of Hitler's 'National Socialism', whose very name evokes Bellamy's Nationalist Party. Dr Leete explains to West that the purpose of the party

> ... was to realize the idea of the nation with a grandeur and complete-
> ness never before conceived ... as a family, a vital union, a common
> life, a mighty heaven-touching tree whose leaves are its people, fed from
> its veins, and feeding it in turn. The most patriotic of all possible parties,
> it sought to justify patriotism and raise it from an instinct to a rational
> devotion, by making the native land truly a father-land.

In picturing the nation as a living entity and the individual as simply its manifestation, Bellamy anticipates the language of Fascism and the exaltation of the state which characterize both Fascist and socialist regimes. Trees, of course, periodically shed their leaves, and lurking beneath Bellamy's metaphor is a premonition of the purges which disfigure the history of communism.

According to Bellamy, full economic equality was to be (and, in fact, can only be) achieved by ceding to the state total control over economic activity. But there is an heavy price to pay for this economic equality: Boston in the year 2000 is a deeply undemocratic society. The three top ranks of the industrial army, the generals of the individual guilds or trades, the major-generals of the larger divisions, and the general-in-chief, that is, the President of the United States, are the only elected officials. What is more, only officers from the rank immediately below can be candidates for these positions. The general population is only enfranchised on retirement from the industrial army, and then may only vote for the

231

President and for the generals of their own guilds. Dr Leete agrees with Julian West that 'if the workers had any suffrage to exercise, or anything to say about the choice' there would be intrigue and disorder: 'But they have nothing.' To allow the working members of the industrial army to vote for President 'would be perilous to its discipline, which it is the business of the President to maintain as the representative of the nation at large.'

Bellamy does not appear to realize that by effectively allowing the generals of the industrial army to select who may be candidates for their own positions he has created a self-perpetuating élite. One cannot but be struck by the parallels to the pre-*perestroika* Soviet Union where, whatever the election, all candidates had to be approved by the Communist Party. Truly, Boston in the year 2000 has become, in the phrase sometimes used to describe Harvard University, 'Moscow on the Charles'.

Reading *Looking Backward* with the wisdom of hindsight raises disturbing questions about Utopia. It is unnecessary to recount the crimes perpetrated in the Soviet Union and other socialist countries, but suffice it to say that they constitute a human disaster on an almost unparalleled scale. Yet communism also constitutes the great utopian experiment of the twentieth century: André Gide called the USSR 'a land where I imagined Utopia was in the process of becoming reality'. Should we, therefore, conclude that utopianism is inherently dangerous? Was Stalinist Russia so dreadful precisely because it was animated by the utopian impulse? According to Isaiah Berlin, the radical philosopher Alexander Herzen said of 1848, the year of revolutions, that 'a new form of human sacrifice had arisen in his time – of living human beings on the altars of abstractions – nation, church, party, class, progress, the forces of history – these have all been invoked in his day and ours.' Utopia must answer the charge of being the altar upon which the victims of Stalin's purges were sacrificed.

The origin of state socialism is to be found in a key text of the Enlightenment, Jean-Jacques Rousseau's work of utopian political philosophy, *Du Contrat Social* (1762). In the same way that Jefferson's 'pursuit of Happiness' embodied the New World Utopia, so Rousseau's 'general will' became the guiding principle of the Old World Utopia. Chapter 1 of *Du Contrat Social* opens with the famous declaration: 'Man is born free, and everywhere he is in chains.' As we saw in Chapter 7, Rousseau asserted in the *Discours sur l'Origine et les Fondements de l'Inégalité Parmi les Hommes* (1755) that man in a state of nature is solitary and free. But this blissful existence is destroyed as soon as people gather together in societies. It is the inevitable inequalities produced by social relations which forge the chains that bind mankind and rob him of his freedom. In *Du Contrat Social* Rousseau sets out to liberate humanity by describing an ideal state in which the obligations of society bear down on all citizens equally, and in which, therefore, everyone is perfectly equal and also perfectly free. As Rousseau himself puts it, his aim is:

To find a form of association that defends and protects the person and possessions of each associate with all the common strength, and by means of which each person, joining forces with all, nevertheless obeys only himself and remains as free as before.

It appears that Rousseau has set himself an impossible task. How can any society function which is dedicated to letting its members behave exactly as they please? But, in true utopian fashion, Rousseau claims to have found the answer. The ideal society will be one in which all citizens naturally and voluntarily submit to the collective general will, the sole source of legitimate sovereignty, which cannot but be directed towards the common good. However, for this social contract to work properly, the submission of the individual must be total: 'Each of us puts his person and all his power in common under the supreme control of the general will, and, as a body, we receive each member as an indivisible part of the whole.'

Although the general will is determined by vote at an assembly of the people (which Rousseau terms the 'sovereign'), it is more than simply the will of the majority. Rousseau makes the claim that the general will is, in fact, what is in the interests of *all* citizens, even if a minority of them are unaware of it. Thus to enforce the general will is not to benefit the majority at the expense of the minority: it is to advance the interests of all, even if not everyone sees it that way at the time.

The unchanging will of all the members of the state is the general will; through it, they are citizens and free. When a law is proposed in the assembly of the people, what they are being asked is not precisely whether they approve or reject the proposal, but whether or not it is consistent with the general will that is their own; each expresses his opinion on this point by casting his vote, and the declaration of the general will is derived from the counting of the votes. When, therefore, the opinion contrary to my own prevails, this merely proves that I was mistaken, and that what I considered to be the general will was not so. If my private opinion had prevailed, I would have done something other than what I had willed; it is then that I would not have been free.

It may seem that in stipulating that society must be governed in accordance with the general will, Rousseau is doing little more than advocating a democratic constitution in which the will of the majority prevails. Indeed, some modern critics have read *Du Contrat Social* in just this way, seeing Rousseau as a prophet of liberal democracy on the Western model. However, such liberal democracies are based on the realization that the citizens of a state may have diverging interests. What is good for some may not be good for others. It follows from this that enforcing what the majority desires may sometimes result in the persecution of the minority. To prevent their legitimate interests from being trampled upon in this way, liberal democracies endow their citizens with individual rights which are enforceable against the will of the majority.

But Rousseau's general will is, by definition, in everyone's interests, and so there is no need to place any restrictions on its scope; indeed, any such restrictions are positively harmful. To grant the minority of citizens, those who are 'mistaken' about the common good, individual rights in opposition to the general will would be to permit them to continue in the error of their ways, with results that could only be self-destructive. As Rousseau so chillingly puts it: 'Anyone who refuses to obey the general will shall be compelled to do so by the entire body; this means nothing else than that he will be forced to be free.'

Rousseau's neglect of the rights of the private citizen is a by-product of his utopianism. To maintain his claim to have squared the circle of perfect individual freedom within society, he is obliged to deny what the liberal democrat willingly admits, that even the most democratic government must discriminate between the competing interests of its populace. Rousseau asserts that a state governed by the general will can never act against the interests of any of its citizens. Therefore, they have no need of any rights.

The result is that in Rousseau's utopia the state has unlimited power over the individual. In an image which pre-figures Bellamy's 'mighty heaven-touching tree', Rousseau likens the state to the human body:

> Just as nature gives each man absolute power over all his members, the social pact gives the body politic absolute power over all its own. . . . It is agreed that each person alienates through the social pact only the part of his power, possessions, and liberty that will be important to the

community, but it must also be agreed that the sovereign alone is the judge of what is important.

This alienation of private 'power, possessions and liberty' is, in fact, the foundation of the new sort of liberty which mankind will enjoy under the social contract. In a key passage of *Du Contrat Social* Rousseau states:

> If we inquire into exactly what constitutes the greatest good of all, which should be the end of every system of legislation, we shall find that it comes down to these two principal objectives, *liberty* and *equality*. Liberty, because all private dependence is only so much force taken away from the body of the state; equality, because liberty cannot continue to exist without it.

Again, this sounds reassuring. Liberty and equality are the aims of any late twentieth-century social democrat. But a closer reading reveals that the freedom Rousseau has in mind is far closer to that offered till lately by the state socialist regimes of Eastern Europe. Rousseau sees liberty as freedom from 'all private dependence', that is, any obligations or restrictions placed upon one citizen by another. Such 'private dependence' is harmful because it limits the citizen's ability to serve 'the body of the state'. However, restrictions placed on an individual by the state do not, in Rousseau's view, limit liberty, because his ideal state always acts according to the general will. As Rousseau writes elsewhere, the liberty which man gains by entering into the social contract is 'civil liberty, which is limited by the general will'. That is why the basis of civil liberty is equality: it is only when all citizens have pooled their interests in the state and have an equal stake in it that every person will want the common good, and his particular desires will accord with the general will. In effect, Rousseau offers his citizens the freedom to go along with what the state requires, trusting that the reformation of human nature produced by the social contract will ensure that this is what they want to do anyway.

This improvement of the human character is central to *Du Contrat Social*, and one of its most characteristically utopian features.

> Anyone who dares to undertake the founding of a people should feel himself capable of *changing human nature*, so to speak, of transforming each individual, who by himself is a perfect and solitary whole, into part of a greater whole from which this individual receives, in a way, his life and his being; of altering the human constitution in order to strengthen

it; and of substituting a partial and artificial existence for the physical and independent existence we have all received from nature. He must, in a word, take away man's own forces in order to give him new ones which are alien to him.

This transformation will come about partly as a natural result of the egalitarianism of the ideal society, partly through a deliberate policy of state propaganda and education. In the *Discours sur l'Économie Politique* ('Discourse on Political Economy') he writes that if citizens are trained

> . . . early enough never to consider their own persons except in terms of their relations with the body of the state, and not to perceive of their own existence, so to speak, except as a part of that of the state, they may finally succeed in identifying themselves in some way with this greater whole, in feeling themselves members of the homeland, in loving it with that exquisite sentiment which every isolated man feels only for himself, in perpetually lifting up their souls toward this great objective, and thus in transforming into a sublime virtue that dangerous disposition from which all our vices arise.

This nation-worship is pernicious enough, but the problems with Rousseau's utopia do not end here. As we have seen, the general will has the strange property that it may be revealed to some but not to others. Although in *Du Contrat Social* Rousseau insists that the majority of citizens will always be so enlightened, it is obviously difficult to rule out the possibility that on occasions the general will might be apparent only to a chosen few, perhaps only to the government. Rousseau himself could not entirely resist this conclusion. In the *Discours sur l'Économie Politique* he writes:

> How, someone will ask me, can the general will be known in cases in which it has not expressed itself? Must the whole nation be assembled at every unforeseen event? It will be all the less necessary to do so, because it is by no means certain that its decision would be the expression of the general will, because this means is impracticable for a large people, and because it is rarely necessary when the government is well intentioned, for the leaders know very well that the general will is always on the side most favorable to the public interest, that is to say, the most equitable, so that it is necessary merely to be just to be assured of following the general will.

In *Du Contrat Social* Rousseau goes further. At times of great danger to the state it may be necessary to resort to dictatorship:

> If the peril is such that the legal apparatus is an obstacle to protecting the laws, then a supreme leader is named who silences all the laws and momentarily suspends the sovereign authority; in such cases, the general will is not in doubt, and it is evident that the people's primary intention is that the state should not perish.

Thus, the utopian notion of the general will leads Rousseau inexorably away from a democratic reliance on the good sense of the citizenry, towards what can be, and was, read as a justification of untrammelled state power wielded by one party or even just one man. Truly a case where, as Voltaire remarked in another context, 'the best is the enemy of the good.' Rousseau's avowed aim was to break the chains that bind, yet his ideas were taken up by his followers during the French Revolution in a way that only strengthened men's shackles.

The link between *Du Contrat Social* and the French Revolution was forged by the Abbé Emanuel Joseph Sieyès, a priest whose conscience would not allow him to preach a sermon or hear confession. He was the driving force behind the creation of the revolutionary National Assembly in June 1789, whose aim was to devise a new constitution for the French state. Sieyès was not satisfied with the first version of the Declaration of the Rights of Man and of the Citizen (August 1789), which, as we have seen, was drafted by Lafayette with the advice of Thomas Jefferson. The Abbé, an avowed disciple of Rousseau, subscribed wholeheartedly to the Swiss philosopher's sanctification of the state over and above the individual: 'The nation exists before all, it is the origin of everything. Its will is always legal, it is the law itself.' He duly injected Rousseau's concept of the general will into the Declaration, which act rendered its Jeffersonian guarantees of personal liberty worthless. Thus:

> Article Three: The source of all sovereignty resides essentially in the nation: no group, no individual may exercise authority not emanating expressly therefrom.
> Article Six: Law is the expression of the general will; . . . it must be the same for all, whether it protects or punishes.

The Declaration was no longer to be a contract recognizing two bodies,

237

the government and the people, as in the American model, which maintained that 'whenever any Form of Government becomes destructive of these ends, it is the Right of the People to alter or to abolish it.' The general will acknowledged only one authority, potentially a dictatorship, and the Declaration thus became a 'mandate for Terror': as the President of the Committee on Public Instruction was to declare at its height, 'The Revolution explains *The Social Contract.*'

Sure enough, by 1793 the general will was being invoked as a justification for dictatorship by Rousseau's most famous disciple, the Jacobin revolutionary Maximilien de Robespierre. Robespierre pictured himself as the lawgiver of Rousseau's ideal society described in *Du Contrat Social*, 'the engineer who invents the machine', whose greatest difficulty 'is not so much what must be established as what must be destroyed'. But Robespierre did not surrender control of the machine to the sovereign assembly of the people, as stipulated in *Du Contrat Social*. He saw the nine-member Committee of Public Safety and his party, the Jacobins, both of which obeyed his orders, as representing the general will: 'Notre volonté, c'est la volonté générale.' The historian Conor Cruise O'Brien remarks, 'This was a humble statement which claimed an awesome authority, and carried within it a lethal menace.' The turmoil of revolutionary France was Robespierre's pretext for carrying out the emergency measures prescribed by Rousseau: he became a *de facto* dictator. In 1793–94, during the Reign of Terror, Robespierre duly set out to destroy all those who were enemies of the general will, that is to say, of Robespierre and his Committee.

Perhaps the strangest application of Rousseau's ideas by Robespierre was the 'Cult of Reason'. Robespierre abolished Christianity, adopted a new calendar (each month to have three weeks of ten days), and in June 1794 held a Festival of the Supreme Being. This was, in effect, the civil religion which Rousseau had set forth in the last few pages of *Du Contrat Social*:

There is . . . a purely civil profession of faith, the articles of which are for the sovereign to determine, not precisely as religious dogmas, but as sentiments of sociability, without which it is impossible to be a good citizen or a faithful subject. Without being able to obligate anyone to them, the sovereign can banish from the state anyone who does not believe them; it can banish him not for being impious but for being unsociable, for being incapable of sincerely loving the laws and justice, and of sacrificing his life, if need be, for his duty. If, after having publicly acknowledged these same dogmas, someone behaves as though he does not believe them, let his punishment be death; he has committed the greatest of crimes, he has lied before the laws.

One historian remarks, concerning Robespierre's adoption of the cult of the Supreme Being:

> The barely disguised aim of the festival was to purge the individual of everything that distinguished him from the civic body, to impose a State dogma defining both public and private conscience, and thereby to make citizens turn themselves into parts of the whole.

Two days later, with patriotism now compulsory, Robespierre drafted the Prairial Law which deprived those brought before the revolutionary tribunal of the right to cross-examine witnesses 'if material or moral proofs exist independently of witnesses' evidence' and declared that 'the rule of judgment is the conscience of jurors enlightened by love of fatherland.' This last measure finally proved too much for the delegates to the National Convention, who justifiably feared for their own lives. Robespierre and twenty-one of his adherents were arrested and executed at the end of July.

The French Revolution set off a chain reaction of utopianism in Europe which has only just – perhaps – come to an end. Whereas the American War of Independence had been a short period of upheaval which brought stability in its wake, the French Revolution became an on-going event, a revolution *en permanence*. According to the philosopher Hegel, it ushered in 'a new age of rapid change and increasing instability, an age that would stand under the category of "becoming"'. In the 1870s Jakob Burckhardt opened a course of lectures on the Revolution with the statement, 'We know that the same storm which hit mankind in 1789 is still driving us into the future.' That storm would drive humanity on to the rocks of socialist tyranny.

Although Rousseau does not use the word 'socialism' (it had not yet been coined), he can in some respects be seen as the father of twentieth-century state socialism. The subordination of liberty to equality in *Du Contrat Social* and the definition of freedom as complete identification with the state are the true hallmarks of socialism in the twentieth century. More and Campanella believed in equality and either explicitly or implicitly associated it with the common good, but the identification of the common good with the state was a phenomenon born of the French

Revolution and Rousseau's general will. This is the most dangerous of the new forms of human sacrifice which Herzen detected in the failed revolutions of 1848. Fittingly, it was in that same year that the most influential of all socialist texts, the *Communist Manifesto*, was published; by the end of the nineteenth century its author, Karl Marx, had become the leading prophet of the socialist movement.

Ironically, Marx led a somewhat conventional, even bourgeois existence. He came from a liberal, middle class German family, but was something of a disappointment to his parents. As a young student at the University of Bonn he was thrown in gaol for drunkenness and slightly wounded in a duel. He transferred to the more academic University of Berlin, but his father grumbled that 'degeneration in a learned dressing-gown with uncombed hair has replaced degeneration with a beer glass.'

After university, Marx worked as a newspaper editor in Cologne, but his radical views provoked the government to suppress the paper. Marx moved to Paris in 1843 to become co-editor of a German-French publication. While in Paris, he met his compatriot Friedrich Engels. Engels's father was a textile manufacturer in Germany, and Friedrich worked for the firm's cotton mill in Manchester, eventually securing a partnership in the business along with a large private income. Although he worked behind enemy lines, as it were, he took a great interest in the conditions of the working class, and was to devote himself to Marx and his ideas for the rest of his life.

Between 1844 and 1848 Marx and Engels were actively involved in politics. In 1847 Marx went to London to state his views at the Congress of the Communist League on how communism would come about. The upshot of the congress was the *Communist Manifesto*, in which Marx and Engels set out 'in the face of the whole world' the views, aims and tendencies of the communists. The *Manifesto* was to become the classic summary of Marx's theory, but its first publication in February 1848 was badly timed. The outbreak of revolution in France during that same month sparked off similar political turmoil throughout Europe. However, it all ended in failure and disappointment, dashing the hopes of socialist revolutionaries. (The historian A.J.P. Taylor called the Revolution of 1848 the historical turning-point at which 'history did not turn'.) Disillusioned, Marx returned to Cologne to found a new radical newspaper which also met with government disapproval. He was forced to leave the Rhineland, and in August 1849 he and his family took refuge in England, which was to be his home until his death.

On taking up residence in London, Marx withdrew from the political fray and became a fixture in the British Library, working on his *magnum opus, Das Kapital* ('Capital'). Initially, Marx and his family lived in great poverty, supported by Engels out of the meagre profits from the Manchester cotton mill. (Marx's mother thought it a shame her son 'merely wrote about capital and had never acquired any'.) Nevertheless, through a series of inheritances, Marx's life eventually became 'like that of any comfortably off bourgeois family: they moved to a larger house, spent a good deal on furnishing it, sent their children to a ladies' seminary, and travelled to fashionable Continental spas. Marx even claimed to have made money on the stock exchange.'

In 1864 Marx returned to active politics with the formation in London of the International Workingman's Association, later known as the First International; Marx was elected to the General Council. However, the First International found itself in an awkward position regarding the Paris Commune of 1871, the workers' uprising which ruled Paris for two months after France's military defeat by Prussia. Although the International had not been involved in this event, the public nevertheless associated it with the success – and eventual failure – of the Paris Commune. Engels explained that the International had been 'thrust into the forefront of European history at a moment when it had everywhere been deprived of all possibility of successful practical action.' Marx, therefore, made the 'heroic' decision to save the organization by withdrawing it 'from the stage for the time being by transferring the General Council to America'. The French delegates remarked that 'one might as well remove it to the moon.' It seems that Marx wanted the International to die a peaceful death (it was dissolved in 1876), out of reach of his European rivals for the soul of communism.

In exploring Marxist theory, the best starting point is the 'materialist' conception of history which Marx developed, largely from Saint-Simon's ideas, as the 'guiding thread for my studies'. It asserts that in any historical epoch, all forms of social life are determined by the economic relations which underpin society. As Marx put it: 'The anatomy of civil society is to be sought in political economy.' Accordingly, the actions of an individual reflect primarily his economic relationship to the other members of society. These differing relationships divide humanity into classes: the feudal nobility, the bourgeoisie and so forth. All of history is in reality the struggle for dominance between these classes. Engels deemed this to be his friend's most important revelation: 'Just as Darwin discovered the law of development of organic nature, so Marx discovered the law of development of human history.' The analogy is apt, because Marx held up his theory not as philosophical postulation but as scientific fact. Previously, Engels states, no one had asked the question 'what the driving causes of the political changes are':

> Now Marx has proved that the whole of history hitherto is a history of class struggles, that in all the manifold and complicated political struggles the only thing at issue has been the social and political rule of classes of society, the maintenance of domination by older classes and the conquest of domination by newly arising classes.

History for Marx, therefore, was more than simply 'one damned thing after another'. Adapting the ideas of Hegel, he asserted that events follow a discernible pattern and are moving in a definite direction – towards human freedom. History is made up of a number of distinct epochs, each inaugurated by a violent revolutionary upheaval which liberates a hitherto oppressed class. This class assumes for a while the leadership of society. Inevitable technological and social advances in the methods of production lead to conflict between the classes, a new revolution and the hegemony of a new class. This pattern, however, would not recur forever. In fact, the penultimate upheaval had already taken place with the French Revolution, which had ushered in bourgeois rule. The liberation of the bourgeoisie left only one stratum below the rest of society, one class which alone remained enslaved – the landless, propertyless proletariat. Because the proletariat had been stripped to its bare humanity, because there was no other class below it, by securing its own emancipation it would emancipate all mankind, and so end all social conflict, establishing in its place an unending era of peace and plenty. Marx believed that this final cataclysm was at hand. As Engels wrote in 1877, the scientific study of history leads inevitably to the conclusion that:

> . . . the ruling big bourgeoisie has fulfilled its historic mission, that it is no longer capable of the leadership of society and has even become a hindrance to the development of production, as the trade crises, and especially that last great crash [the Panic of 1873], and the depressed condition of industry in all countries have proved; that historical leadership has passed to the proletariat, a class which, owing to its whole position in society, can only free itself by abolishing altogether all class rule, all servitude and all exploitation; and that the productive

forces of society, which have outgrown the control of the bourgeoisie, are only waiting for the associated proletariat to take possession of them in order to bring about a state of things in which every member of society will be enabled to participate not only in production but also in the distribution and administration of social wealth, and which so increases the productive forces of society and their yield by planned operation of the whole of production that the satisfaction of all reasonable needs will be assured to everyone in an ever-increasing measure.

Once the final revolution had taken place, Marx imagined that society would take on a communist form. The description of this state is rather vague, but the division of labour will disappear, and with it the evils of poverty and exploitation; in fact, in some passages Marx envisioned what can only be described as a Marxist Cockaigne:

In communist society, where nobody has one exclusive sphere of activity but each can become accomplished in any branch he desires, society regulates the general production and thus makes it possible for me to do one thing today and another tomorrow, to hunt in the morning, fish in the afternoon, rear cattle in the evening, criticize after dinner, just as I have a mind, without ever becoming hunter, fisherman, shepherd or critic.

This certainly sounds like Utopia, and this impression is strengthened by the debt which Marx and Engels acknowledged they owed to their utopian socialist predecessors. As Engels wrote:

German theoretical Socialism will never forget that it stands on the shoulders of Saint-Simon, Fourier, and Owen, three men who despite their fantasies and utopianism are to be reckoned among the most significant minds of all times, for they anticipated with genius countless matters whose accuracy we now demonstrate scientifically.

Marx reserved special admiration for Robert Owen, praising him as one of those 'really doughty natures who, once having struck out on a revolutionary path, always draw fresh strength from their defeats and become more decisive the longer they swim in the flood tide of history.' The young Engels contributed to Owen's journal, *New Moral World*, and later said that he had found there 'not only the most clear-cut communism possible ... but also the most comprehensive project of the future communist community, with its groundplan, elevation, and bird's-eye view'.

Yet Marx professed to abhor utopianism: 'The man who draws up a programme for the future is a reactionary.' In Marx's eyes, utopians

> ... endeavour, and that consistently, to deaden the class struggle and to reconcile the class antagonisms. They still dream of experimental realisation of their social Utopias, of founding isolated *'phalanstères'*, of establishing 'Home Colonies' [Robert Owen], of setting up a 'Little Icaria' [Étienne Cabet] – duodecimo editions of the New Jerusalem.

In part, Marx's disavowal of these utopians was motivated by his desire to proclaim his own originality, part of his struggle for the intellectual leadership of the radical movement, in which cause Marx never tired of attacking his rivals in a sometimes abusive tone. (It was the fear of being associated with these utopians and 'social quacks' which led Marx and Engels to reject the title 'Socialist Manifesto' in favour of the *Communist Manifesto*.) But his anti-utopianism also reflects a fundamental aspect of Marx's theory: the belief that 'it is not the consciousness of men that determines their being, but, on the contrary, their social being that determines their consciousness.' In other words, the ideas, and ideals, that men hold are a product of their historical circumstances. Utopian schemes do little more than reflect the class bias of their authors; they certainly never have their claimed absolute and universal validity. In *Socialism: Utopian and Scientific*, Engels mocks the utopian socialists for their pretensions:

> To all these Socialism is the expression of absolute truth, reason, and justice, and has only to be discovered to conquer all the world by virtue of its own power. And as absolute truth is independent of time, space, and of the historical development of man, it is a mere accident when and where it is discovered. With all this, absolute truth, reason, and justice are different with the founder of each different school.

For Marx, his forerunners all shared the illusion that society could be reformed, that history could be changed, by the actions of a few determined individuals. But, according to Marx, social development was solely the result of the class struggle, from which utopian scheming was simply a dangerous distraction. The urgent task was to intensify the class war in the hope of bringing the inevitable day of decision closer. But the first step was to understand the laws that governed historical change; only then would one know where to stand to be 'on the side of history'. In this regard every utopian dreamer from Thomas More to Robert Owen was equally unhelpful, since they were all prisoners of their own time; only Marx, living in the mid-nineteenth century, enjoyed a vantage point which enabled him to perceive clearly the forces of history as they approached the final crisis.

Above all, Marx avowed that his was a scientific theory, based upon a mountain of facts culled from the Blue Books of government statistics in the British Library. Marxism described what *was*, not what ought to be. As Lenin remarked:

> In their scientific works, Marx and Engels were the first to explain that socialism is not the invention of dreamers, but the final aim and necessary result of the development of the productive forces in modern society.

However, of all Marx's assertions, his claim to scientific status is the least plausible. The predictions he made, that wages will always tend to fall to subsistence level, that the rate of profit will decline, that capitalism will force more and more people down into the working class, and so forth, were already proving wrong in Marx's lifetime. The philosophical centre of gravity of his thought is the very unscientific idea that history obeys natural laws and yet is moving towards a definite goal. Today, the epithet 'scientist', valued by Marx perhaps above all others, is denied to him even by otherwise sympathetic commentators.

Stripped of their scientific veneer, Marx's ideas reveal their utopian nature. As we have seen, history's final resting place, the communist society, has many of the classical attributes of Utopia: it is universal; it satisfies the material and spiritual desires of all men; it has obliterated the past; since the motor of social change, the class struggle, has been dismantled, communism will presumably be unchanging and eternal; and in it all men will be perfectly equal and therefore perfectly free. Even the aspect of Marxist theory that sets it apart from the tradition of utopian thought, the denial that the individual will can affect the course of history, is belied by Marx's own life of committed revolutionary struggle. Indeed, Marx reveals the utopian temper of his thinking most clearly in the way he assigns an important role in the drama of history to a dedicated revolutionary élite.

It is an important element of Marxist theory that until the proletariat becomes conscious of its true situation and thus the historical necessity of overthrowing bourgeois society, no successful revolution can take place. The masses must be educated, and Marx saw the communists as their instructors. According to the *Communist Manifesto*:

> The Communists ... are on the one hand, practically, the most advanced and resolute section of the working-class parties of every country, that section which pushes forward all others; on the other hand, theoretically, they have over the great mass of the proletariat the advantage of clearly understanding the line of march, the conditions, and the ultimate general results of the proletarian movement.

Thus Marx anoints the Communists with the 'leading role' in the class struggle. It was a part which they proved reluctant to relinquish. In entrusting knowledge of a universal truth (the laws of history) to an élite whose task is to guide humanity towards the Promised Land, Marx is following a utopian tradition that goes back to Plato's Guardians. Most striking is the parallel with Rousseau's conception of the general will: an entity which belongs to all and yet may sometimes be known only to a few. Conor Cruise O'Brien remarks that 'Rousseau's "general will" becomes Marx's "History". Communists were people who knew the will of History and executed it.' It is fitting that the *Communist Manifesto* ends where *Du Contrat Social* began:

> The proletarians have nothing to lose but their chains. They have a world to win.

WORKING MEN OF ALL COUNTRIES, UNITE!

Marx's writings received their warmest reception in Russia, a fact which surprised their author, who had a fairly low opinion of Russians (he referred to them as 'clodhoppers'). Isaiah Berlin states that 'the Russian radicals read the *Communist Manifesto* and declamatory passages of *Das Kapital* with the sense of exhilaration with which men had read Rousseau in the previous century.' Before the emergence of Lenin, however, Marxism remained a theory, and a much misinterpreted one, so that even Marx declared towards the end of his life, 'All I know is that I am not a Marxist.' Nevertheless, by 1895, when he was campaigning for the overthrow of the Tsar and formulating his views on socialism in

Russia, Lenin knew that *he* was a Marxist and that Marxism must be 'the party's world-outlook'.

Lenin's aim was to fashion his wing of the Russian Social Democrats, the Bolsheviks ('majority'), into the vanguard of the proletariat which Marx had prescribed. But Lenin went further than Marx in claiming that, without such a vanguard, true proletarian class-consciousness would not arise:

> There can be no question of an independent ideology formulated by the working masses themselves in the process of their movement . . . the spontaneous development of the working-class movement leads to its subordination to bourgeois ideology.

Once this proposition was accepted (and it was the subject of bitter debates within the party), Lenin's conclusion followed logically: while it is the party's task to lead the proletariat, it must nevertheless keep itself separate from the broader working-class movement, and should be composed not of workers but, in Lenin's words, 'first and foremost of people who make revolutionary activity their profession.'

Lenin professionalized the revolution, creating a small, centralized party of men and women who regarded themselves not as workers or intellectuals, but simply as revolutionaries, devoting all their time to party activities. Unlike the more open, broad-based workers' movement, the conspiratorial nature of such a party made democratic control impractical: party members had to have the discipline to carry out the orders of the leadership unquestioningly. What is more, Lenin's assertion that the working class was incapable of spontaneously achieving a true socialist consciousness meant that, paradoxically, the workers' movement was a bourgeois movement unless subordinated to the party. In other words, what defines a true proletarian movement is not that it consists of workers, but that it is guided by the 'correct' Marxist ideology (interpreted, of course, by the party). The Polish historian Leszek Kolakowski summarizes:

> Thus, according to Lenin, the party with its 'correct' theoretical consciousness embodies the proletarian consciousness irrespective of what the real, empirical proletariat may think of itself or about the party. The party knows what is in the 'historical' interest of the proletariat and what the latter's authentic consciousness ought to be at any particular moment, although its empirical consciousness will generally be found

lagging behind. The party represents that consciousness not because the proletariat agrees that it should, but because the party knows the laws of social development and understands the historical mission of the working class according to Marxist theory.

Lenin interpreted Marx in the same way that Robespierre interpreted Rousseau: the key to the ideal society of perfect freedom, whether the 'general will' or the 'laws of history', became the exclusive property of a tiny group of revolutionaries, and, eventually, of a single person. Lenin thus cast himself in the classic utopian role of 'lawgiver'; only the fig-leaf of 'science' disguised Bolshevism's thorough-going utopianism.

Despite, or rather because of, its utopianism, Lenin's strategy proved highly effective when it came to seizing and holding power, and in that respect at least it was entirely faithful to Marx's intentions as laid out in the *Communist Manifesto*: 'The immediate aim of the Communists is the same as that of all the other proletarian parties: formation of the proletariat into a class, overthrow of the bourgeois supremacy, conquest of political power by the proletariat.'

Once the Communist Party had achieved power in 1917, it quickly assumed the guise of a nationalist movement, as predicted in the *Communist Manifesto*: 'Since the proletariat must first of all acquire political supremacy, must rise to be the leading class of the nation, must constitute itself *the* nation, it is, so far, itself national, though not in the bourgeois sense of the word.' Nevertheless, Lenin believed that the working classes of Europe, under the guidance of the party, would follow Russia's example and fulfil Marx's dream of an international workers' revolution. When it became clear that the workers everywhere were not going to unite, Soviet Russia suddenly became 'the advance guard of the revolution'. As such it became 'the world proletariat's most precious possession', and so the interests of the international working class became identical with that of Soviet Russia: clearly whatever was good for the Soviet state was good for the world proletariat.

Indeed, as Kolakowski states, 'You were a Marxist . . . because you were prepared to accept whatever the supreme authority might proclaim today, tomorrow, or in a year's time':

When the party is identified with the state and the apparatus of power, and when it achieves perfect unity in the shape of a one-man tyranny, doctrine becomes a matter of state and the tyrant is proclaimed infallible. Indeed, he really *is* infallible as far as the content of

Marxism is concerned, for there is no Marxism but that which the party asserts in its capacity as the mouthpiece of the proletariat, and the party, having once achieved unity, expresses its will and its doctrine through the leadership embodied in the dictator's person.

In 1939 the philosopher Maurice Cornforth described the mental acrobatics which the Communist Party in Britain had to perform to stay in line with the rhetoric flowing out of the Soviet Union:

> If one loses any of that faith in the Soviet Union one is done for as a Communist and Socialist . . . a socialist state . . . can do no wrong, and is doing no wrong, and this is what we have to stick to, so these are the reasons why personally I commenced to turn political somersaults, because that is what it means.

The concentration of power in the hands of one man was made doubly pernicious by the central doctrine of Marxist theory: that ideas are essentially a reflection of material conditions. Liberal concepts of freedom and morality are, therefore, tainted by their bourgeois origins and must be completely done away with. As Marx and Engels wrote in the *Communist Manifesto*: 'The abolition of bourgeois individuality, bourgeois independence and bourgeois freedom is undoubtedly aimed at.' Lenin was never more faithful to Marx than when he wrote:

> They who serve the cause of freedom in general without serving the specific cause of proletarian utilization of this freedom, the cause of turning this freedom to account in the proletarian struggle for socialism, are, in the final analysis, plainly and simply fighters for the interests of the bourgeoisie.

For Marx, as for Rousseau, 'higher' freedom, as opposed to freedom as defined by the bourgeoisie, was to be found in the unity of mankind that would be achieved by the resolution of class antagonisms in communism. From this it follows that the more unity there is, the more freedom there is; since, by abolishing private property, the party had achieved the 'objective' conditions of unity, this act alone guaranteed freedom for all. Soviet citizens exercised their liberty when they followed the lead of the Communist Party; expressions of dissent were merely relics of bourgeois thinking to be ruthlessly expunged.

Marxist 'historical materialism' subordinates all aspects of civil society to the class struggle. Art, law, morality, all must serve the interests of the proletariat, interests which were defined by the party. As Lenin made explicit:

> We say that our morality is entirely subordinated to the interests of the proletariat's class struggle. . . . To a Communist all morality lies in this united discipline and conscious mass struggle against the exploiters.

In Kolakowski's words:

> Thus the abolition of law as a mediating institution between individuals and the state, and the principle of servility in every manifestation of culture, could be regarded as a perfect embodiment of Marxist theory.

Marxist theory made a tremendous impact not only on the political system in Russia but also on the very land itself. For Marx, the essential goal of humanity was to escape its fate as the plaything of forces beyond its control. These forces are both economic and natural. Man must wrest control not only from the reactionary classes, but also from Nature. This emphasis on the mastery of Nature, a product of Marx's nineteenth-century scientism and a constant theme of his philosophy, found full expression in the gargantuan development projects of Stalin and his successors. In the name of the communist millennium, Soviet technocrats ploughed up the steppes, diverted rivers and altered drainage patterns. The result was ecological catastrophe on a continental scale. Marxist ideology must bear some responsibility for the environmental degradation that is palpably a legacy of the communist regimes.

When, after Stalin's death, the Communist Party acknowledged his crimes, they sought to portray him simply as an evil tyrant who had, regrettably, wrested control of the party and dragged it away from the true Marxist-Leninist path. Today, the consensus of historians is that the foundations of Stalin's Great Terror were laid by Lenin. Yet the roots of state socialist tyranny went deeper. They drew their strength from the utopianism of Marx – and ultimately of Rousseau. Kolakowski concludes in his magisterial study *Main Currents of Marxism* that 'Marxism has been the greatest fantasy of our century.' It is not a scientific doctrine, as Marx, Lenin and Stalin claimed, but the very opposite: a doctrine 'of blind confidence that a paradise of universal satisfaction is awaiting us around the corner' – in other words, a utopia. However, in one important respect, Marxist theory is not utopian: there is no detailed description of what the future communist society will be like, no 'speaking picture' of the Promised Land. Marx's followers subscribed to the view expressed by Lenin that 'what Socialism will look like when it takes on its final forms we do not know and cannot say.' This lack of specificity makes Marx's goal of History less utopian and more treacherous.

Without a blueprint, there was no standard by which the proletariat could judge the progress and results of their self-appointed leaders – and this was just what Marx intended. In his *Critique of the Gotha Programme*, Marx shows his disdain for any attempts to predict the future by his rival communists:

> But to draw up programmes of principles (instead of waiting till a longish spell of common activity has prepared the ground for that sort of thing) is to set up bench marks for all the world to see, whereby it may gauge how far the party has progressed.

Thus, the only visions provided by the Communist Party in the Soviet Union were empty slogans: in the 1930s, it was 'socialism is largely built', in the '50s, 'socialism is completely won', in the '60s and '70s, 'in the process of socialism's perfection'. The vagueness of Marxism was a priceless political asset to the dictators of Russia. The tragedy is that Marx was both too utopian, and not utopian enough.

The communist revolutionaries of the twentieth century saw themselves as heirs of the French Revolution. Lenin and his followers, returning from exile in 1917, are said to have sung the battle-hymn of the Revolution, the 'Marseillaise', as they crossed the border into Russia. Mao Tse-Tung remarked, when asked to describe the implications of the French Revolution, 'It is a little too early to say.' However, with the fall of the Berlin Wall and the disintegration of the Soviet Union coinciding neatly with the bicentenary of the French Revolution, we are now in a position to venture an assessment. The great utopian experiment inaugurated by the reflections of Jean-Jacques Rousseau has failed, utterly and irrevocably. It failed because it was utopian: in striving to create at one and the same time perfect equality and perfect freedom, it was forced to bend the diversity of human desires to a single end, that of the state. In so doing it crippled both citizens and the state itself. The lesson, as Kolakowski observes, is that 'perfect equality can only be imagined under a system of extreme despotism.' The Roman emperor Marcus Aurelius put it another way: 'Never hope to realize Plato's Republic, for who can change the opinions of men? And without a change of sentiments what can you make but reluctant slaves and hypocrites?'

Where does this leave utopianism? If to strive for perfection is a dangerous thing, then should we close up More's little book, with a sigh of regret, or perhaps relief? The recent histories of Russia, China, Cambodia, as well as numerous exhausted and dispirited small and poor nations around the world, are indeed black passages in the chronicle of Utopia. But many of the most positive political developments of the past half-millennium have also drawn nourishment from the utopian tradition: the rise of science, of female emancipation, of democracy itself. The Founding Fathers sought not to fashion the wishes of men into a perfect unity, but to found a Utopia upon their diversity. America is not a perfect society, but it has endured and it is still seeking its own betterment. Utopianism has proved its worth as a stimulus to activity within existing political institutions, in focusing discontent, in prefiguring reform. If attempts to refashion a complete society as a fully fledged utopia have crashed to failure, it is because Utopia is spice for the meat of politics, and, as John Humphrey Noyes discovered, a diet of unadulterated cayenne pepper leads to madness.

Epilogue: On the Uses of Utopia

Progress, wrote Oscar Wilde in 'The Soul of Man under Socialism', is the realization of Utopias. But Wilde did not live to see the triumph and disaster of the socialist utopia in the twentieth century. Today, with our ears filled with the din of collapsing ideologies, not all of them in the East, we might more readily echo a disillusioned Tocqueville, who in the 1850s found himself asking 'where this voyage will end. I am tired of thinking, time and again, that we have reached the coast and finding it was only a misleading bank of fog. I often wonder whether that solid ground we have so long sought really exists, or whether our destiny is not rather to sail a storm-tossed sea for ever.' If Utopia is just so much sea-mist, it may seem safer to give up the idea of a landing altogether, and resign ourselves to a long cruise. After all, heading towards fog banks is a sure recipe for ending up on the rocks.

However, to extend the nautical metaphor, utopianism has been one of mankind's principal navigational instruments for at least five hundred years. Though the voyage through history has ended in shipwreck for some, others have made safe and profitable landfall. It would be folly to throw the sextant overboard simply because we have wandered off course. Instead, we must attempt to master it. The task is to re-learn the uses of Utopia, for humanity stands in urgent need of its help.

We have argued in this book that both former Cold War adversaries have a utopian history: Russia crushed beneath the vast monolith of Marxist utopianism; America the great geographical *tabula rasa*, waiting to be colonized and cultivated by a diversity of utopias. Nevertheless, for as long as Eastern state socialism was a force to be reckoned with, Western liberal democracy, basking in the flattering light of relative prosperity and stability, generally preferred to pose as the pragmatic antithesis of all grandiose utopian scheming. Now, however, with the Wall breached, we are able to pass through and look back at Western society from a new vantage point. When we do so, we find the Wall is also a looking-glass: from the utopian perspective, the two systems have some uncomfortable similarities.

The fundamental problem which More addressed in *Utopia* was the unjust distribution of material goods in contemporary European society.

The remedy he explores is to share out in equal measure the meagre resources of his imaginary community. This was not Marx's solution. Marx follows most utopians from Bacon onwards by insisting that the rational, planned economy of the future will produce goods in such abundance that all problems of scarcity will evaporate: 'The satisfaction of all reasonable needs will be assured to everyone in an ever-increasing measure.' Under these conditions of plenty all problems of the distribution of wealth would evaporate, since, as Robert Owen put it, 'individual accumulation of wealth will appear as irrational as to bottle up or store water in situations where there is more of this invaluable liquid than all can consume.'

But this, of course, has also been the strategy of Western liberal governments. They too have sought to ameliorate social problems through economic growth. The difference is that the West has made the strategy work. The lesson which the twentieth century teaches is that such a superfluity of material goods cannot be achieved by a planned economy, but that it is characteristically the product of the competitive capitalism which socialists before and after Marx condemned as wasteful and irrational.

Today we can, perhaps, discern a limit to this economic expansion. It may be that future historians will regard the very rapid rise in living standards of the post-war period as an anomaly brought about by an unprecedented and unsustainable plundering of the planet's natural capital, a piece of creative accounting on a global scale. Around the world many welfare states are showing signs of strain: while the Swedes begin to restrict their once-legendary social benefits, New Zealanders are wondering whether they can any longer afford a National Health Service. Of course, it is always possible that a technological advance of similar importance to the development of the internal combustion engine will release new productive forces and so re-invigorate Western economies. But it is at least as probable that this will not happen. Experience suggests that the settlement between haves and have-nots which underpins liberal democratic societies is predicated on economic growth. If so, it may turn out that we in the West have only postponed the problem of the just distribution of wealth, not abolished it, and that we face a social crisis of truly millennial proportions.

If the utopian looking-glass helps us to discern ominous storm clouds coming up behind, can it also illuminate the way forward? Unfortunately, the other great lesson of this century is that asking for a blueprint of the ideal society is asking for trouble. Nevertheless, clear thinking about our situation may be aided if we use Utopia as More intended, as a political thought experiment. It is an established and useful technique in the physical sciences to imagine what would transpire in a situation that cannot in fact be brought about; it was a favourite device of Einstein. The point of such a mental experiment is not to design a real one, but to stand instead of it. In effect, the imaginary procedure is used to test scientific ideas, not against the real world, but against each other, to reveal the connections between them and to seek out contradictions.

Utopia can serve us in the same way. Rather than merely advocating reform, the utopian is forced to depict the desired reformation in action. In doing so, the utopia may make clear consequences which would otherwise remain unforeseen. The literary utopia is by no means always attractive, as Morris's reaction to *Looking Backward* shows. But that fact makes it more, not less, useful as a tool of political thought. In a well-ordered world political parties would present their manifestos in the form of utopian romances. If we can read the utopia properly, staying alert to the sleight of hand, the conjuring tricks that attempt to disguise the weak links, we can uncover the hidden corollaries of political action. Perhaps then utopias could forestall disaster rather than precipitating it.

There is another reason to advance the use of Utopia. The familiar categories of political thought, the old opposition of capitalism and socialism, of state and individual, are no longer adequate to the tasks that face us. We need to add new ideas to our mental armamentarium. Where better to seek novel political concepts than Utopia? The very act of imagining a society that steers by different stars forces us to look at our unexamined assumptions, to explore those things which otherwise remain undisputed and undiscussed. Somewhere among them lie the ideas we need, and Utopia is the perfect vehicle for carrying these ideas out into the light of discourse and argument, the field of opinion where they can influence social change.

But, most of all, utopianism is useful to us because it is a uniquely effective form of politics. Utopias never, as their authors usually hope, remake society in their own image. Instead, elements of the utopia are gradually assimilated by the outside world, altering it in subtle but sometimes profound ways, as we have seen. Utopias are realized piecemeal, but realized they frequently are. For those who wish to change the world, Utopia will always remain a powerful weapon.

It is powerful because, in the end, we need it. Sailors on a storm-tossed sea, we are not psychologically provisioned for an indefinite voyage. We need to believe, whatever Tocqueville's scepticism, that there is indeed

255

a farther shore. Without that hope, we face mutiny or worse. Wilde was right: Utopia is the country at which we are always landing, and from which we are always setting sail. Utopia is our reason for going on.

A Gallery of Utopians

ALBERTI, Leon Battista (1404–1472). Greatly influenced by classical Roman architecture, Alberti sought to discover the laws of harmony and proportion to which he believed the ancients had adhered in their art. In his treatise *De Re Aedificatoria*, Alberti identified the centrally planned building with Christ, the essence of perfection and harmony, and gave architecture a moral vision, thus laying the intellectual foundations of the ideal city. See pp. 40–42.

ARISTOTLE (384–322 BC). A pupil of Plato, the Greek philosopher Aristotle was the first and most important critic of Plato's *Republic*. His main objection, that Plato's communism ignores human nature, is set down in the second book of the *Politics*. By the end of this work, Aristotle succumbs to the temptation to outline his own formula for the ideal constitution, but this soon turns into a discussion of education and music, and is left unfinished. See pp. 12–13.

ATWOOD, Margaret (1939–). Margaret Atwood is the author of the feminist dystopia, *The Handmaid's Tale* (1985), set in the near future in an America where the sexual liberation of the late twentieth century has been replaced by a repressive puritanism. See pp. 168–169.

BACON, Francis, first Baron Verulam and Viscount St Albans (1561–1626). Lord Chancellor from 1618 to 1621, Francis Bacon was the founder of modern scientific method. He believed that science and technology could be harnessed to benefit mankind. His utopian work, *New Atlantis*, describes a society centred on a specialist research institution called variously the College of the Six Days' Works and Salomon's House. This institution inspired the creation of the Royal Society in 1662. See Chapter 5.

BELLAMY, Edward (1850–1898). An American journalist influenced by Marxism and Fourierism, Edward Bellamy wrote the popular utopian novel *Looking Backward* (1888). Its hero falls asleep in 1887 and wakes up in the year 2000 to find that America has evolved into an urban 'engine' with the efficiency and spirit of a professional army. The book inspired an important political movement, the Nationalists. For the main discussion, see Chapter 11; also town planning, pp. 63–65; work, pp. 112–116; sex, pp. 158–159.

BRISBANE, Albert (1809–1890). Born in the state of New York, Brisbane set off as a young man on a Grand Tour of Europe looking for a philosophical system. Initially attracted to the Saint-Simonians, Brisbane eventually became a disciple of Charles Fourier. He returned home in 1834 and made Fourierism an influential movement in America. He converted George Ripley's utopian community Brook Farm to Fourierism, and nearly thirty phalanxes as well as numerous Fourierist clubs were founded in the 1840s. See pp. 212–215.

BRUNELLESCHI, Filippo (1377–1446). Originally a goldsmith, in 1420 Brunelleschi undertook the construction of the dome of Florence's cathedral. His innovations in both building techniques and organization enabled the dome to be completed in sixteen years. With Brunelleschi, the architect replaces the medieval master-mason, thus allowing architecture to become a utopian calling. See pp. 39–40.

CADBURY, George (1839–1922). George Cadbury, owner of the Birmingham chocolate factory, founded Bournville in 1879, although its development into a model housing estate for workers, following the example of Lever's Port Sunlight, did not begin until 1894. Cadbury was a prominent member of Ebenezer Howard's Garden City Association. See p. 69.

CAMPANELLA, Tommaso (1568–1639). Born in Calabria, southern Italy, the Dominican monk Campanella was persecuted, gaoled and tortured as a heretic by the Catholic Church for most of his life. His work *La Città del Sole* (1601) advocates communism, eugenics and an education programme in which the illustrated walls of the city form the classroom. Campanella's utopia was the inspiration behind Lenin's Monumental Propaganda Plan. For the main discussion, see pp. 49–55; also work, pp. 84–85; sex, pp. 135–137.

COLERIDGE, Samuel Taylor (1772–1834). In his youth, the English poet and author Coleridge, inspired by the French Revolution, planned with Robert Southey to set up a Pantisocratic community on the banks of the Susquehanna in Pennsylvania. The main tenets of the community were to be communism and absolute equality. Their plans came to nothing, although 'Pantisocracy' became a byword for radical and wildly idealist utopian ventures. See pp. 197–199.

A GALLERY OF UTOPIANS

DIDEROT, Denis (1713–1784). One of the French *philosophes* and editor of the *Encyclopédie*, Diderot condemned the Catholic Church's stance on both celibacy and marriage as unnatural and harmful. Inspired by Louis-Antoine de Bougainville's voyage to the South Seas, Diderot wrote the utopian dialogue *Supplément au Voyage de Bougainville*, in which a Catholic monk learns from his Tahitian host that a nation's sexual morality should depend upon the relation of population to resources. See pp. 141–148.

ENFANTIN, Barthélemy Prosper (1796–1864). Leader of the disciples of Henri de Saint-Simon, Enfantin designated himself 'Supreme Father' of the newly formed Church of the Saint-Simonians. This group established a utopian community at Ménilmontant outside Paris in the 1830s. Their espousal of free love outraged contemporary society, and the experiment was dissolved following a scandalous court case. Embracing Saint-Simon's faith in industry, Enfantin and other former Saint-Simonians went on to become the 'architects of French capitalism'. See pp. 107–108.

ENGELS, Friedrich (1820–1895). Engels was the son of a German textile manufacturer. He worked for the firm's cotton mill in Manchester, eventually securing a partnership in the business and a private income. He took a great interest in the conditions of the working class. In 1843 he met Karl Marx in Paris, and devoted the rest of his life to assisting the German philosopher, both financially and in his writings. See pp. 240–249.

FILARETE [Antonio Averlino] (*c.* 1400–*c.* 1470). The sculptor and architect Filarete (the name is Greek for 'lover of virtue') worked in Milan under the patronage of Duke Francesco Sforza. Influenced by Alberti, Filarete sought in his *Trattato di Architettura* to design a city, Sforzinda, whose principles of aesthetic harmony would be reflected in the behaviour of its citizens. His advocacy of the centrally planned building greatly influenced Leonardo da Vinci and Donato Bramante. See pp. 42–46.

FOURIER, Charles (1772–1837). Born in Besançon, Fourier worked most of his life as a travelling salesman in textiles. In a series of utopian treatises, he describes the 'phalanstery', a large communal building housing 1,600–1,800 people, who are organized according to the notion of 'passionate attraction'. Every comfort, talent, pleasure and sexual whim is accommodated, and both work and love are enjoyable and fulfilling. Fourier never found a patron for his schemes. For town planning, see pp. 61–63; work, pp. 109–112; sex, pp. 152–155.

GILMAN, Charlotte Perkins (1860–1935). The American feminist and writer Gilman advocated women in the workforce, collective house-keeping and centralized kitchens. She argued that the first step to real social change must be the liberation of women. She also venerated motherhood, and her utopian novel, *Herland* (1915), tells of three male explorers in Africa who discover a lost civilization without men. The women, who are strong and intelligent, bear children by parthenogenesis. See pp. 165–168.

GRAHAM, Sylvester (1794–1851). Sylvester Graham was a minister who also lectured in America on a regulated system of diet, exercise and general hygiene. He advocated hard mattresses, cold shower baths and a vegetarian regime of stale wholewheat bread, fruit and vegetables. Ralph Waldo Emerson called him the 'poet of bran bread and pumpkins', and Grahamite tables became a fixture of many utopian communities, including Ripley's Brook Farm. Today graham crackers are still a staple of the American diet. See p. 212.

HAWTHORNE, Nathaniel (1804–1864). The American writer Nathaniel Hawthorne was a descendant of one of the original Puritan settlers. He joined the utopian community of Brook Farm, set up by George Ripley near Boston, but soon became disillusioned with the experiment and left within the first year. His novel *The Blithedale Romance* (1852) is based on his experiences there. See pp. 207–212.

HOWARD, Sir Ebenezer (1850–1928). Originally a stenographer, Howard conceived of the Garden City as a remedy for the overcrowded and unhealthy cities of Britain. He envisioned a series of manageable towns, with well-built houses and gardens, each surrounded by a green belt of countryside. This idea became a reality with the establishment around London of satellite towns such as Letchworth and Welwyn Garden City. The Garden City Movement was extremely influential in Russia, Western Europe and America. See pp. 71–75.

HUXLEY, Aldous (1894–1963). The grandson and brother of eminent biologists, Aldous Huxley nevertheless scorned the faith men had put in reason, progress and science. In his dystopia *Brave New World*, rather than creating institutions to serve its citizens, society, through a combination of chemistry and brainwashing, moulds the citizens to serve its institutions. Huxley's later utopia, *Island*, which advocates ecology, drugs and Eastern philosophy, lacks the power of *Brave New World*. See pp. 119–123.

JEFFERSON, Thomas (1743–1826). Jefferson, one of the Founding Fathers, was the third President of the United States. His Declaration of Independence (1776) set out America's utopian agenda, 'Life, Liberty, and the pursuit of Happiness'. His egalitarianism was based not on a levelling of material circumstances, but on a levelling of status. Jefferson continued to support revolutions abroad and helped to draft the Declaration of the Rights of Man (1789), the manifesto of the French Revolution. See pp. 193–196.

KELLOGG, John Harvey (1852–1945). Kellogg, a follower of Ellen White, prophetess of the Seventh Day Adventists, was a surgeon in Battle Creek, Michigan. He advocated good dietary habits and, to this end, created and marketed cornflakes and, later, branflakes as 'part of a good breakfast'. The Kellogg Company is still based in Battle Creek. See p. 212.

LE CORBUSIER [Charles-Edouard Jeanneret] (1887–1965). Born in the Swiss watchmaking town of La Chaux-de-Fonds, Le Corbusier was the founder of the Modernist Movement in architecture. He glorified the big city run by a strong bureaucracy, and envisioned such projects as the 'Contemporary City for Three Million People' and the 'Radiant City'. Le Corbusier believed that the 'total architecture' and centralized administrations of these cities would bring order and harmony to their inhabitants. See pp. 75–79.

LEDOUX, Claude-Nicolas (1736–1806). *Architecte du Roi*, Ledoux designed and built the royal saltworks at Arc-et-Senans. Surrounding it, he planned the ideal city of Chaux, whose strikingly futuristic designs he published in *L'Architecture Considerée* (1804). Though never built, this 'industrial park', set in the countryside, anticipates many of the concerns of modern town planning. See pp. 57–61.

LEE, Ann (1736–1784). Born in Manchester, 'Mother' Ann Lee was the founder of the millenarian sect, the 'Believers in Christ's Second Appearing', better known as the 'Shakers'. In 1774 the Shakers emigrated to America, where Mother Ann Lee and her followers set up a community in New Lebanon, New York. The main tenets of Shakerism were celibacy and the equality of the sexes. Their numbers grew from 1,000 at the time of Mother Ann Lee's death to nearly 6,000 in the 1840s. Today they number nine. See pp. 175–182.

LENIN, Vladimir Ilyich (1870–1924). After arrest and exile to Siberia for three years, Lenin left Russia in 1900 and spent most of the next seventeen years abroad in France, England and Germany. He fashioned his faction of the Russian Social Democratic Party, the Bolsheviks, into the vanguard of the proletariat which Marx had described. He returned to Russia in 1917, eventually staging the *coup d'état* which inaugurated seventy-four years of Communist rule. See pp. 55, 246–251.

LEVER, William Hesketh, later Viscount Leverhulme (1851–1925). Soap magnate and philanthropist, Lever tore down a slum in Liverpool to make way for a model estate, Port Sunlight, to house his workers. The design of Port Sunlight was influenced by the Arts and Crafts Movement. Lever was a prominent member of Howard's Garden City Association. See pp. 69–73.

LYCURGUS (between 800 and 600 BC). Almost nothing is known about this legendary legislator of Sparta. The Greek historian Plutarch and others claim that he was the founder of the Spartan constitution, which redistributed the land equally among the citizens and turned Sparta into a military state. Its regimented and communal life inspired Plato's *Republic* and many subsequent utopian works. See pp. 7–9.

MARX, Karl (1818–1883). Marx left his German homeland in 1843 when his radical views met with government disapproval. He moved first to Paris, where he met Friedrich Engels, then to England, which became his permanent home. Here he wrote his most important work, *Das Kapital*, which argues that history is moving inexorably towards the communist state. Although Marx criticized utopian thinkers, he borrowed their ideas and conceived of his own version of a socialist utopia. See pp. 240–251.

MORE, Sir Thomas (1478–1535). The English humanist and Lord Chancellor, Thomas More, both coined the word and framed the concept of 'utopia' in his work *Utopia* (1516), which describes the travels of one Raphael Hythloday to the eponymous island. More refused to take the oath demanded by the first Act of Succession and was beheaded in 1535, becoming a martyr to the Catholic faith. For the main discussion, see Chapter 2; also architecture, pp. 37, 51; work, pp. 83–85, 91; sex, pp. 133–135.

A GALLERY OF UTOPIANS

MORRIS, William (1836–1896). Morris, poet, artist, printer and socialist, wrote his utopian romance *News from Nowhere* (1890) as a riposte to Bellamy's *Looking Backward*, which he called a 'cockney paradise'. Morris's ecologically sound twenty-first century resembles an idealized medieval England: there are no suburbs or cities (except London). The Houses of Parliament store manure and work as both art and pleasure has replaced the machine. For town planning, see pp. 66–68; work, pp. 115–119; love, pp. 156–158.

NOYES, John Humphrey (1811–1886). Noyes, son of a US Congressman, rejected conventional theology and morality, declaring that salvation was a pleasurable process and sexual shame irrational. Noyes founded the Oneida Community in the backwoods of New York State where marital ties between men and women were dissolved to be replaced by 'complex marriage', a form of free love. Oneida was one of the most long-lived utopian ventures, lasting thirty years. See pp. 159–164.

OLMSTED, Frederick Law (1822–1903). Olmsted, the great American landscape architect, was a Fourierist sympathizer. He designed many city parks across America in the late nineteenth century, including Central Park in New York and Jackson Park in Chicago (originally for the Columbian Exposition of 1893). Olmsted intended them as congenial meeting places where social classes could mingle and a communal spirit be cultivated. See pp. 63, 65.

OWEN, Robert (1771–1858). Owen first became prominent with the social reforms he carried out at his mill in New Lanark, Scotland. He believed that a person's character was shaped by the environment and proposed dividing the population into self-supporting communities, miniature welfare states, housed in 'parallelograms'. In 1824 he established the utopian community of New Harmony, Indiana, which espoused radical equality and socialism. It soon failed. He returned to England and became a leading figure in the fledgling trades union movement. See pp. 199–206.

PAINE, Thomas (1737–1809). Born in Norfolk, Paine emigrated to America and aided the cause of American Independence through his writings, such as *Common Sense* (1776). He declared that America had 'made a stand, not for herself only, but for the world'. In 1792 Paine travelled to France to support the French Revolution, believing it to be the 'first ripe fruits of American principles transplanted into Europe'. See pp. 183, 193–194.

PLATO (427–347 BC). The Greek philosopher Plato founded the Academy in Athens as a school for statesmen, where would-be politicians might learn to be philosopher rulers. Plato's dialogue the *Republic* discusses education, ethics and philosophy, as well as the ideal constitution for a state. It was an important model for Sir Thomas More's *Utopia*. Plato describes the lost island of Atlantis in his dialogues the *Critias* and *Timaeus*. For the *Republic*, see pp. 9–14; for Atlantis, pp. 91–92.

QUIROGA, Vasco de (d. 1565). Vasco de Quiroga went to New Spain (Mexico) as a judge in 1531. He tried to implement reforms based upon Thomas More's *Utopia* to relieve the Indians' sufferings. He failed to win over the Spanish government but established hospital-villages in Santa Fe organized along the lines of More's work. See pp. 32–33.

RIPLEY, George (1802–1880). Ripley, a Unitarian minister, founded the utopian community of Brook Farm, near Boston, Massachusetts, in 1841. He hoped that it would initiate a regeneration of society. The community, a joint-stock scheme, advocated absolute equality and 'industry without drudgery'. Its most famous member was Nathaniel Hawthorne. Brook Farm came under the influence of Fourierism in 1844 (see Albert Brisbane above). See pp. 207–212.

ROBESPIERRE, Maximilien de (1758–1794). Robespierre emerged as one of the leading radicals of the French Revolution, and he and his fellow Jacobins came to dominate the Committee of Public Safety. In the spring of 1794 Robespierre established a dictatorship and initiated the Terror in which many were summarily executed. He believed that his party was the embodiment of Rousseau's 'general will'. Robespierre and twenty-one of his followers were executed in July 1794. See pp. 238–239.

ROUSSEAU, Jean-Jacques (1712–1778). One of the French *philosophes*, Rousseau attributed evil, not to sin, but to society. In the *Discours sur l'Origine de l'Inégalité* (1754), he elaborated the myth of the 'noble savage', claiming that in the original state of nature man was both good and happy. He developed his ideas further in *Du Contrat Social* (1762), which maintains that the ideal society must be governed according to the 'general will'. This concept was exploited by Robespierre in the French Revolution. For the noble savage, see pp. 137–141; general will, pp. 232–240.

SADE, Donatien Alphonse, Marquis de (1740–1814). The Marquis de

Sade, who gave his name to 'sadism', refused to conform to society, especially its sexual morality, and consequently spent most of his life in gaols and insane asylums. One of his pornographic works, *Philosophie dans le Boudoir*, sets out a utopian constitution which stipulates that no one may deny a citizen the satisfaction of any of his or her erotic desires. He was the first utopian to divorce sex from procreation. See pp. 148–151.

SAINT-SIMON, Henri de (1760–1825). Seeking to apply the principles of Newtonian physics to society, Saint-Simon was one of the founders of the social sciences. He saw history as falling into progressive stages of development and believed that the main agents of change in the nineteenth century would be scientists and industrialists. Many Marxist slogans originate in Saint-Simon's ideas. For his disciples, see Barthélemy Prosper Enfantin above. See pp. 101–109.

SALT, Sir Titus (1803–1876). Influenced by the Great Exhibition of 1851 and the Report of Health of Towns of 1846, which warned of possible social unrest, the Bradford mill-owner Titus Salt built the first model estate of workers' dwellings, Saltaire, an area of terraced houses on a grid plan. Saltaire influenced Lever's Port Sunlight and Cadbury's Bournville. See p. 69.

SKINNER, B. F. (1904–1990). One of the foremost psychologists of the twentieth century, Skinner denied the existence of human freedom, believing that behaviour is always controlled by the environment. He developed the concept of 'behavioural engineering', achieved through 'positive reinforcement'. Skinner's utopian fiction, *Walden Two* (1948), describes an experimental community based on the science of human behaviour. See pp. 123–129.

SMITH, Joseph (1805–1844). Joseph Smith grew up in the Burnt Over Region of New York State, where revivalism was strong. In 1823 an angel revealed to him the existence of an ancient text engraved on golden tablets. The Book of Mormon duly appeared in 1830, and Smith's millenarian sect, the Mormons, quickly grew. The group moved first to Ohio, then Missouri, then Indiana, always meeting with local hostility. Smith was assassinated in 1844; his successor was Brigham Young. See p. 182–189.

SOLON (c. 640 561 BC). The Athenian statesman and poet Solon has a semi-mythical status. He wrote verses to publicize and justify his political policies, which were aimed at ending serfdom, revising the severity of the laws and making property rather than high birth the basis of political power. Solon's achievements are an early example of pragmatic piecemeal reform. See p. 7.

SOUTHEY, Robert (1774–1843). In his youth, the English poet and writer, Robert Southey, planned with Samuel Taylor Coleridge to set up a Pantisocratic community in Pennsylvania. The plans came to nothing, and Southey looked back on the venture with bitterness. See pp. 197–199.

VESPASIANO GONZAGA COLONNA (1531–1591). A member of a cadet branch of the Gonzaga family of Mantua, Vespasiano oversaw the expansion and rebuilding of Sabbioneta into an ideal city between 1556 and his death in 1591. He regulated everything from the architecture, which reflects his fascination with the classical world, to daily life. See pp. 47–49.

YOUNG, Brigham (1801–1877). Young succeeded Joseph Smith as head of the Mormons in 1844. Under his direction, 1,700 Mormons migrated west to Utah, beyond the United States' borders. Utah became a US territory in 1849, and Young was appointed its first governor. It did not achieve statehood until 1896, after polygamy had been outlawed among the Mormons by the US government. The Mormons have since splintered, but the largest group, numbering in the millions today, is based in Salt Lake City. See pp. 186–189.

NOTES

The words in *italic* at the beginning of each note are the last few words of the text referred to. The numbers in the left-hand column refer to pages in the text.

The epigraph by Max Beerbohm is quoted in Richard Marius, *Thomas More: A Biography* (London: J. M. Dent & Son, 1985) p. 187.

Prologue

xi *164 occasions* Based on a search of the NEXIS database.
    wall of words Quoted in A. L. Morton, *The English Utopia* (London: Lawrence and Wishart, 1952) p. 10.
xii *word 'Yewtopia'* Stanley Morison, *The Likeness of Thomas More: An Iconographical Survey of Three Centuries*, ed. Nicolas Barker (London: Burns and Oates, 1963) p. 39. Our thanks to Nicolas Barker for this reference.

Chapter 1

3   *the blessed gods* Quoted in A. O. Lovejoy and G. Boas, *Primitivism and Related Ideas in Antiquity* (Baltimore: Johns Hopkins University Press, 1935; repr. ed., New York: Octagon Books, 1973) p. 27. See also F. E. Manuel and F. P. Manuel, *Utopian Thought in the Western World* (Oxford: Basil Blackwell, 1979) Part One.
    of wasting away Lovejoy and Boas, *Primitivism*, p. 30.
    the verdant oak Ovid, *Metamorphoses*, Book I, lines 90–112.
4   *no lamentation* Quoted in N. K. Sandars, Introduction to *The Epic of Gilgamesh* (Harmondsworth: Penguin, 1960) p. 39.
    salt yourself, stupid Lovejoy and Boas, *Primitivism*, p. 40.
5   *were fat then* Ibid., pp. 40–41.
6   *pay the bill* Quoted in Morton, *The English Utopia*, pp. 217–222.
    of whiskey too Ibid., p. 29.
    in a truck Idem. See also Hal Rammel, *Nowhere in America: 'The Big Rock Candy Mountain' and Other Comic Utopias* (Urbana and Chicago: University of Illinois Press, 1990).
    that invented work Morton, *The English Utopia*, p. 29.
7   *describe political effectiveness* John Ferguson, *Utopias of the Classical World* (London: Thames & Hudson, 1975) pp. 23–24.
    oligarchy and monarchy Herodotus, *The Histories*, III, 80–82.
    as arbitrator Aristotle, *Athenaion politeia*; quoted in Ferguson, *Utopias of*

the Classical World, p. 44.

to prevail unjustly Quoted in Plutarch, *Solon*, XVIII, 4.

8 *doubted by some* Plutarch, *Lycurgus*; Ferguson, *Utopias of the Classical World*, Chapter 4. For Solon and Lycurgus, see also Oswyn Murray, *Early Greece* (London: Fontana, 1980) Chapters 10 and 11.

poverty and wealth Plutarch, *Lycurgus*, VIII, 1–2.

equality through conformity Murray, *Early Greece*, p. 168.

throttle a bull Quoted in Ferguson, *Utopias of the Classical World*, p. 37.

9 *unknown among them* Plutarch, *Lycurgus*, XV, 9.

miracle true philosophers Quoted in Desmond Lee, Introduction to Plato, *The Republic*, 2nd rev. ed., trans. D. Lee (London: Penguin, 1987) p. 16. Lee's translation of the *Republic* is used throughout. See also Ferguson, *Utopias of the Classical World*, Chapter 8.

10 *foundation of both* Lee, Introduction to Plato, *Republic*, pp. 17–19, 21, 31–32.

and the whole community Plato, *Republic*, 416e–417b.

of the whole community Ibid., 420b.

11 *in the Guardian class* Ibid., 464a.

common between friends Ibid., 423e.

child its parent Ibid., 457c–d.

half a state Plato, *The Laws*; quoted in Lee, Introduction, ibid., p. 47n.

as well as men Plato, *Republic*, 455d.

and a crime Ibid., 461a.

the weaker parties Ibid., 455d, 460e.

Managerial Meritocracy Lee, Introduction, ibid., p. 50.

12 *multiplicity and change* Plato, *Republic*, 484b.

of earthly paradise Ibid., 517c, 519c.

a clean canvas Ibid., 501a.

form of autocracy Lee, Introduction, ibid., p. 20.

difficult to implement A. E. Taylor, Introduction to Plato, *The Laws* (London: J. M. Dent & Sons, 1960) p. xxxv.

13 *themselves personally concerned* Quoted in Ferguson, *Utopias of the Classical World*, p. 83.

unity and uniformity Lee, Introduction to Plato, *Republic*, p. 48.

it into effect Sir Karl Popper, *The Open Society and Its Enemies*, 2 vols. (London: Routledge & Kegan Paul, 1945).

confer on the community Plato, *Republic*, 519e–520a.

the Third Reich G. R. Morrow, 'Plato and the Rule of Law', in Renford Bambrough, ed., *Plato, Popper and Politics* (Cambridge: Heffer, 1967) pp. 49–50.

herself gain control Plato, *Republic*, 458a–b, 499c–d.

Chapter 2

15 *Thomas More, Knight* From the second edition of Ralph Robinson's translation, published in 1556; the first edition is dated 1551.

NOTES

bird's-eye view Friedrich Engels on Robert Owen; quoted in Manuel and Manuel, *Utopian Thought*, p. 706.

born for it Erasmus to Ulrich von Hutten, 23 July 1519; *The Collected Words of Erasmus*, vols. I-VIII: *The Correspondence of Erasmus*, trans. R. A. B. Mynors and D. F. S. Thomson (Toronto: University of Toronto Press, 1974–1988) vol. VII, no. 999, p. 19. For Thomas More and *Utopia*, see also Marius, *Thomas More*; *The Complete Works of Sir Thomas More*, vol. IV: *Utopia*, eds. E. Surtz and Hexter (New Haven and London: Yale University Press, 1965); Dominic Baker-Smith, *More's 'Utopia'* (London: Harper Collins, 1991).

16 *her first youth* Correspondence of Erasmus, vol. VII, no. 999, p. 21.

family in Chelsea More to Erasmus, 17 February 1516; ibid., Vol. III, no. 388.

but God's first J. B. Trapp and H. S. Herbrüggen, *'The King's Good Servant': Sir Thomas More 1477/8–1535* (London: National Portrait Gallery, 1977) no. 253.

18 *Raphael told us* Thomas More, *Utopia*, translated with an Introduction by Paul Turner (Harmondsworth: Penguin, 1965) p. 29. This translation is used throughout.

to go there Ibid., pp. 30–31.

on his travels Ibid., pp. 33–34.

when at leisure Correspondence of Erasmus, vol. VII, no. 999, p. 24.

every social evil More, *Utopia*, p. 33.

19 *everyone's reading about* Ibid., p. 38.

easy to find: Ibid., p. 40.

and useful advice Ibid., p. 41.

20 *his great eminence* Ibid., p. 43.

down their throats Ibid., p. 46.

these pernicious practices Ibid., p. 48.

21 *my advice at Court* Ibid., p. 57.

experience with Dionysius Idem.

community of men Quoted in Quentin Skinner, 'Sir Thomas More's *Utopia* and the Language of Renaissance Humanism', in *The Languages of Political Theory in Early Modern Europe*, ed. Anthony Pagden (Cambridge: Cambridge University Press, 1987) p. 130.

wrong as possible More, *Utopia*, p. 64.

heat of the moment Correspondence of Erasmus, vol. VII, no. 999, p. 24.

trifles of princes More to Erasmus, 25 October 1517; ibid., vol. V, no. 688.

connexion between them More, *Utopia*, p. 64.

22 *system of private property* Ibid., pp. 65–66.

punished and safeguarded Hexter, Introduction, *Complete Works*, vol. IV: *Utopia*, p. cxiii.

distribution of goods Quoted in Skinner, 'Sir Thomas More's *Utopia*', p. 139.

23 *protection of private property* Our thanks to Dr David Starkey for this point.

shared in common Vespucci, *Quatuor Navigationes*; quoted in More, *Utopia*, p. 135n.

modern about Utopia Hexter, Introduction, *Complete Works*, vol. IV: *Utopia*, p. cxiv.

24 *so well organized* More, *Utopia*, p. 67.

now my name Ibid., p. 27.

nation in the world Ibid., pp. 69–70.

25 *calls them bourgeois* Manuel and Manuel, *Utopian Thought*, p. 133.

the domestic atmosphere More, *Utopia*, p. 126.

every ten years Ibid., p. 73.

the New World Ibid., p. 136n.

with his job Ibid., pp. 75–76.

for eight hours Ibid., p. 76.

26 *first thing every morning* Idem.

your spare time Ibid., p. 84.

is Watching You Paul Turner, Introduction, ibid., p. 13.

these precious commodities More, *Utopia*, p. 136n.

to the embassy Ibid., p. 88.

because he's rich Ibid., p. 89.

27 *view of nobility* Skinner, 'Sir Thomas More's *Utopia*', p. 144.

wholly in pleasure More, *Utopia*, p. 91.

community as well Ibid., pp. 92–93.

identify true happiness Ibid., p. 91.

own private ends Ibid., p. 120.

28 *idleness and greed* Marius, *Thomas More*, p. 167.

acting virtuously More, *Utopia*, p. 93.

anywhere on earth Ibid., p. 99.

29 *speaks for God* Ibid., p. 102.

the lower animals Ibid., p. 109.

piece of property Ibid., p. 80.

30 *by rational argument* Ibid., p. 119.

fights shy of Ibid., p. 122.

truly Christian communities Ibid., p. 118.

31 *shalt lead me* Ibid., p. 128.

the heathen Utopians Skinner, 'Sir Thomas More's *Utopia*', pp. 148–152.

the Englishman's name Correspondence of Erasmus, vol. VII, no. 999, p. 19; Manuel and Manuel, *Utopian Thought*, p. 131; More to Erasmus, 3 September 1516; *Correspondence of Erasmus*, vol. IV, no. 461.

the other, reason Our thanks to Dr David Starkey for this point.

troubles in the commonwealth Erasmus to Guillaume Cop, 24 Februry 1517; *Correspondence of Erasmus*, vol. IV, no. 537.

knew it best Ibid., vol. VII, no. 999, pp. 23–24.

32 *Common Run of Christians* These marginal notes are translated and

reprinted in *Complete Works*, vol. IV: *Utopia*, pp. 125, 157, 181; see also ibid., pp. 280–281n.

stands up to comparison Skinner, 'Sir Thomas More's *Utopia*', pp. 154–155.

adopted in Europe More, *Utopia*, p. 132.

a unanimous vote More to Peter Gilles, printed in the second edition of *Utopia* (Paris 1517); translated and reprinted in *Complete Works*, vol. IV: *Utopia*, pp. 249–251.

in the New World Silvio Zavala, 'The American Utopia of the Sixteenth Century', *Huntington Library Quarterly* IV (August 1947) p. 341.

Chapter 3

35 *are upon us* E. S. Morgan, ed., *The Founding Fathers of Massachusetts: Historians and Sources* (Indianapolis: Bobbs-Merrill, 1964) p. 203.

erects it in reality Quoted in D. D. Egbert, 'Socialism and American Art', in D. D. Egbert and S. Persons, eds., *Socialism and American Life*, 2 vols. (Princeton: Princeton University Press, 1952) vol. I, p. 642.

its gardens green Quoted in Peter Hall, *Cities of Tomorrow: An Intellectual History of Urban Planning and Design in the Twentieth Century* (Oxford: Basil Blackwell, 1988) p. 86.

37 *in other words, utopia* Lewis Mumford, 'Utopia, the City and the Machine', in F. E. Manuel, ed., *Utopias and Utopian Thought* (Boston: Houghton Mifflin, 1965; repr. ed., London: Souvenir Press, 1973) p. 13.

beasts and heroes Aristotle, *The Politics*, 1253.a.3.

rough it for too long More, *Utopia*, pp. 70–71.

38 *by bricks alone* Robert Fishman, 'Utopia in Three Dimensions: The Ideal City and the Origins of Modern Design', in Peter Alexander and Roger Gill, eds., *Utopias* (London: Duckworth, 1984) p. 95.

displayed in their architecture Giulio C. Argan, *The Renaissance City* (London: Studio Vista, 1969) pp. 13–15.

39 *equal to the task*: For Brunelleschi and Il Duomo, see Peter Murray, *The Architecture of the Italian Renaissance*, 3rd ed. (London: Thames & Hudson, 1986) pp. 31–37; Howard Saalman, *Filippo Brunelleschi: The Cupola of Santa Maria del Fiore* (London: A. Zwemmer, 1980). For Italian architecture, see also L. H. Heydenreich and W. Lotz, *Architecture in Italy 1400 to 1600*, trans. Mary Hottinger (Harmondsworth: Penguin, 1974); Leonardo Benevolo, *The Architecture of the Renaissance*, trans. Judith Landry, 2 vols. (London: Routledge & Kegan Paul, 1978).

40 *aimed to recover* For Alberti, see Murray, *Architecture*, pp. 51–62; Rudolf Wittkower, *Architectural Principles in the Age of Humanism*, Studies of the Warburg Institute, vol. XIX (London: Warburg Institute, 1949) *passim*.

41 *for the worse* Quoted in Murray, *Architecture*, p. 11. For a complete English translation, see Leon Battista Alberti, *On the Art of Building in Ten Books*, trans. J. Rykwert, N. Leach and R. Tavernor (Cambridge, Mass.: MIT Press, 1988).

the outstretched arms Quoted in Murray, *Architecture*, p. 11.
42 *Man of Sorrow* Wittkower, *Architectural Principles*, p. 27.
haunted their imagination Ibid., p. 13.
shared with Vitruvius Alberti, *De Re Aedificatoria*, Book IV.
Milan in the 1460s For Filarete, see Murray, *Architecture*, pp. 105–109;
Fishman, 'Utopia in Three Dimensions', pp. 98–101; Benvolo, *Architecture of the Renaissance*, vol. I, pp. 148–153; Filarete, *Treatise on Architecture*, translated with an Introduction by J. R. Spencer, 2 vols. (New Haven and London: Yale University Press, 1965).
43 *to the whole society* Fishman, 'Utopia in Three Dimensions', p. 98.
barbarous modern style Quoted in Murray, *Architecture*, p. 107.
for Francesco Sforza Filarete, *Treatise on Architecture*, vol. I, pp. xix, 3–4.
its own time Ibid., p. 12.
44 *bear the expense* Ibid., p. 21.
leader of Sforzinda Fishman, 'Utopia in Three Dimensions', p. 100.
not have relatives Filarete, *Treatise on Architecture*, vol. I, pp. 234–236.
45 *separate the planets* Ibid., pp. 247–249.
conceded to it Ibid., p. 45.
who had it done Idem.
as well as technically Benvolo, *Architecture of the Renaissance*, vol. I, p. 148;
see also Martin Kemp, *Leonardo da Vinci: The Marvellous Works of Nature and Man* (London: J. M. Dent & Sons, 1981) pp. 110, 161.
research in anatomy Murray, *Architecture*, pp. 109–112.
46 *these early structures* For Bramante, see ibid., pp. 112–142.
was ever written Quoted ibid., p. 109.
47 *hardly be over-estimated* Idem.
during his lifetime For Sabbioneta, see Umberto Maffezzoli, *Sabbioneta: A Tourist Guide to the City*, 2nd ed. (Modena: Il Bulino, 1992); K. W. Forster, 'From "Rocca" to "Civitas": Urban Planning at Sabbioneta', *L'Arte* V (1969) pp. 5–40.
state-of-the-art Maffezzoli, *Sabbioneta*, p. 9.
town's visual interest Alberti, *On the Art of Building*, IV, 5.
48 *a new Rome* Maffezzoli, *Sabbioneta*, p. 9.
49 *in un teatro* Forster, 'From "Rocca" to "Civitas"', p. 27.
50 *and the new science* For Campanella, see Manuel and Manuel, *Utopian Thought*, Chapter 10; D. J. Donno, Introduction to Tommaso Campanella, *La Città del Sole: Dialogo Poetico, The City of the Sun: A Poetical Dialogue*, trans. D. J. Donno (Berkeley: University of California Press, 1981). This translation is used throughout.
51 *desires of others* Quoted in P. F. Grendler, *Critics of the Italian World 1530–1560: Anton Francesco Doni, Niccolò Franco and Ortensio Lando* (Madison: University of Wisconsin Press, 1969) pp. 197–198.
52 *of astonishing design* Campanella, *La Città del Sole*, pp. 27, 29.
seen them all More, *Utopia*, p. 71.

representations of God Ibid., p. 125.
always kept burning Campanella, *La Città del Sole*, p. 31.
submit to them Ibid., p. 67.
war 'by craft' Ibid., p. 69.
53 *union of the world* Ibid., p. 121.
of the spheres Ibid., p. 123.
and nations operate Ibid., p. 45.
sed sensu Quoted in Donno, Introduction, ibid., p. 5.
of sacred history Manuel and Manuel, *Utopian Thought*, p. 272.
54 *used in medicine* Campanella, *La Città del Sole*, pp. 33, 35.
are ten years old Ibid., p. 37.
55 *the new generation* Quoted in Egbert, 'Socialism and American Art', p. 681.
See also V. Tolstoy, I. Bibikova and C. Cooke, *Street Art of the Revolution: Festivals and Celebrations in Russia* (London: Thames & Hudson, 1990).
the first Communists Francesco Grillo, *Tommaso Campanella in America: A Critical Bibliography* (New York: S. F. Vanni, 1954) p. 75; citing an anonymous article 'A Dominican Communist' (1934).
schools in the Soviet Union Ibid., p. 85; citing John Somerville, *Soviet Philosophy* (1946).
heroes of the Russian Revolution Manuel and Manuel, *Utopian Thought*, p. 268.

Chapter 4

57 *society as a whole* Fishman, 'Utopia in Three Dimensions', p. 102.
as a museum For Ledoux and Arc-et-Senans, see ibid., pp. 102–104; Valérie-Noëlle Jouffre, *The Royal Saltworks of Arc-et-Senans* (Arcs-et-Senans: Fondation Claude-Nicolas Ledoux, 1990); Anthony Vidler, *The Writing of the Walls: Architectural Theory in the Late Enlightenment* (Princeton: Princeton Architectural Press, 1987) *passim*; Anthony Vidler, *Claude-Nicolas Ledoux: Architecture and Social Reform at the End of the Ancien Régime* (Cambridge, Mass.: MIT Press, 1990). There is no complete English translation of Ledoux's works.
58 *in its course* Quoted in Jouffre, *Royal Saltworks*, p. 23.
'production' of salt Vidler, *Ledoux*, pp. 98–99.
59 *happy fireside evenings* Quoted in Jouffre, *Royal Saltworks*, p. 34.
hôtels in miniature Vidler, *Ledoux*, p. 107.
that undertake them Quoted in M. Higonnet and P. Higonnet, 'Ledoux's New Order of Building', Review of *Ledoux*, by Vidler, in *Times Literary Supplement*, 22 February 1991, p. 15.
temple de surveillance Quoted in Vidler, *Ledoux*, p. 113.
60 *and time keeping* Ibid., p. 107.
mustering of his needs Quoted in Vidler, *Writing of the Walls*, p. 41.
in perpetual circles Quoted in Vidler, *Ledoux*, p. 266.
access to natural beauty Fishman, 'Utopia in Three Dimensions', p. 103.
a sturdy podium Idem; quoting Emil Kaufman.

61 *their 'libertine pleasures'* Quoted in Vidler, *Ledoux*, p. 356.
    is it not sublime Quoted ibid., p. 276.
    of architectural order Quoted ibid., p. 302.
    shape of a bottle Quoted in Vidler, *Writing of the Walls*, p. 48.
    should be honored Quoted in Vidler, *Ledoux*, p. 298.
62 *imitation in Harmony* Jonathan Beecher, *Charles Fourier: The Visionary and His World* (Berkeley: University of California Press, 1986) p. 246. For Fourier's architecture, see also Vidler, *Writing of the Walls*, pp. 109–114.
    of architectural harmony Ibid., p. 110.
    I immediately determined Fourier, *Traité de l'Association Domestique-Agricole*; quoted in Vidler, *Writing of the Walls*, p. 110.
    pleasure and whim Ibid., p. 112.
    sumptuous resort hotel Beecher, *Fourier*, p. 243.
    curiosity-seekers: Fourier, *Traité de l'Association*; in Jonathan Beecher and Richard Bienvenue, eds., *The Utopian Vision of Charles Fourier: Selected Texts on Work, Love and Passionate Attraction* (London: Jonathan Cape, 1972) pp. 240–241.
63 *quantity of attraction* Ibid., p. 238.
    selfish individualism C. J. Guarneri, *The Utopian Alternative: Fourierism in Nineteenth-Century America* (Ithaca and London: Cornell University Press, 1991) pp. 380, 400.
    happiness of each Olmsted, 'Public Parks and the Enlargement of Towns' (1870); quoted in Guarneri, *Utopian Alternative*, p. 400.
    on every side Edward Bellamy, *Looking Backward 2000–1887*, edited with an Introduction by Cecilia Tichi (Harmondsworth: Penguin, 1982) p. 55.
64 *reign of comfort* Ibid., p. 216.
    recreation seemed lacking Ibid., p. 126.
    enormously valuable Fourier, *Traité de l'Association*; in Beecher and Bienvenue, *Utopian Vision*, p. 245.
    with its spray Bellamy, *Looking Backward*, p. 92.
    adornment of the city Ibid., p. 57.
    between-decks Ibid., p. 225.
    are always pagan Quoted in A. E. Morgan, *Edward Bellamy* (New York: Columbia University Press, 1944) p. 94.
    rest in vacations Bellamy, *Looking Backward*, p. 126.
65 *runs all by itself* Ibid., pp. 139–140.
    a 'tremendous engine' Ibid., p. 225.
    harmonious social order Hall, *Cities of Tomorrow*, p. 179; quoting P. S. Boyer. See also W. H. Wilson, *The City Beautiful Movement* (Baltimore and London: Johns Hopkins University Press, 1989).
66 *the National Guard* For the armouries, see R. M. Fogelson, *America's Armories: Architecture, Society, and Public Order* (Cambridge, Mass.: Harvard University Press, 1989).
    as he imagines Morris to John Glasier, 13 May 1889; quoted in Krishan Kumar, *Utopia & Anti-Utopia in Modern Times* (Oxford: Basil Blackwell,

1987) p. 132. For architecture in *News from Nowhere*, see Mark Pearson, 'The Hammersmith Guest House Again: William Morris and the Architecture of Nowhere', in Stephen Coleman and Paddy O'Sullivan, eds., *William Morris & 'News from Nowhere': A Vision for Our Time* (Bideford: Green Books, 1990) pp. 137–149.

67 *neat and pretty* Morris, *News from Nowhere, or an Epoch of Rest: Being Some Chapters from a Utopian Romance* (London: Longmans, Green & Co., 1910) pp. 79–80.

  the general country Ibid., p. 76.

  the eddying stream Ibid., p. 8.

  using his eyes Ibid., pp. 13–14.

68 *doing in one* Ibid., p. 97.

  rule amongst us Ibid., p. 71.

  workmanship and individuality Pearson, 'Hammersmith Guest House', p. 141.

  drive them to Chartism Quoted in Leonardo Benevolo, *The Origins of Modern Town Planning*, trans. Judith Landry (London: Routledge & Kegan Paul, 1967) p. 118.

  the Working Classes For the Great Exhibition and modern town planning in general, see Benevolo, *Origins of Modern Town Planning*; Hall, *Cities of Tomorrow*; Robert Fishman, *Urban Utopias in the Twentieth Century: Ebenezer Howard, Frank Lloyd Wright and Le Corbusier* (New York: Basic Books, 1977); Paul Greenhalph, *Ephermeral Vistas: The Expositions Universelles, Great Exhibitions and World's Fairs, 1851–1939* (Manchester: Manchester University Press, 1988).

  their mouths open Fishman, *Urban Utopias*, p. 60.

  patron and philanthropist Edward Hubbard and Michael Shippobottom, *A Guide to Port Sunlight Village* (Liverpool: Liverpool University Press, 1988) p. 4. For Port Sunlight, see also Charles Dellheim, 'Utopia Ltd: Bournville and Port Sunlight', in Derek Fraser, ed., *Cities, Class and Communication: Essays in Honour of Asa Briggs* (New York and London: Harvester Wheatsheaf, 1990) pp. 44–57.

69 *of wealth-producers* Quoted in Hubbard and Shippobottom, *Guide to Port Sunlight*, p. 6.

70 *health and loveliness* Dellheim, 'Utopia Ltd', p. 52; quoting from the journal *Progress* (1900).

  influence for the good Quoted in Hubbard and Shippobottom, *Guide to Port Sunlight*, p. 6.

  housing estate in England Ibid., p. 49; quoting Theo Crosby.

  and convenient centres: Quoted ibid., p. 20.

71 *prosperity-sharing* Ibid., p. 4.

  most admirably executed Quoted ibid., p. 6.

  you think best Quoted ibid., p. 40.

  state of Nebraska For Howard and the Garden City Movement, see Fishman, *Urban Utopias*, pp. 23–88; Hall, *Cities of Tomorrow*, *passim*;

Stanley Buder, *Visionaries and Planners: The Garden City Movement and the Modern Community* (New York and Oxford: Oxford University Press, 1990).

72 *The Master Key* Title of an illustration in Ebenezer Howard, *To-morrow: A Peaceful Path to Reform* (London: Swan Sonnenschein & Co., 1898).
community-building in the air Hall, *Cities of Tomorrow*, p. 91.
Social City Ibid., p. 93.

73 *gas and water socialism* Fishman, *Urban Utopias*, p. 49.
while politically neutral Buder, *Visionaries and Planners*, p. 65.
with Lantern Slides Fishman, *Urban Utopias*, p. 25.
an imaginary Phalanstery Quoted in Buder, *Visionaries and Planners*, p. 51.
Mr Wells' Martians Ibid., p. 77; quoting Edward Pease, *Fabian News*.
small matter to Utopians Quoted in Fishman, *Urban Utopias*, p. 54.
land like England Howard, *Daily Mail*; quoted in Buder, *Visionaries and Planners*, p. 54.
their money back Hall, Cities of Tomorrow, pp. 94, 96.
Howard in To-morrow Quoted in Buder, *Visionaries and Planners*, p. 78.
a practical turn Quoted ibid., p. 79.

74 *at five percent* Fishman, *Urban Utopias*, p. 46.
a soap magnate Ibid., p. 66.
toga and sandals Quoted ibid., p. 72.
tone of dustmen Buder, *Visionaries and Planners*, p. 91.
women in other towns Hall, *Cities of Tomorrow*, p. 97; quoting D. Macfadyen.
city on a hill Buder, *Visionaries and Planners*, p. 109.
suburban nightmare For the Green Belt, see Roger Gill, 'In England's Green and Pleasant Land', in Alexander and Gill, eds., *Utopias*, pp. 109–117.

75 *communities in Britain* Buder, *Visionaries and Planners*, p. 139.
garden cities and woodlands S. O. Khan-Magomedov, *Pioneers of Soviet Architecture: The Search for New Solutions in the 1920s and 1930s*, trans. A. Lieven, ed. C. Cooke (London: Thames & Hudson, 1987) pp. 271–273. For Russian town planning and architecture, see also W. C. Brumfield, ed., *Reshaping Russian Architecture: Western Technology, Utopian Dreams* (Cambridge: Cambridge University Press, 1990).
petit-bourgeois intellectual Quoted in Buder, *Visionaries and Planners*, p. 140.
fantasy and utopia Quoted in Milka Bliznakov, 'The Realization of Utopia: Western Technology and Soviet Avant-Garde Architecture', in Brumfield, ed., *Reshaping Russian Architecture*, p. 145.
to conduct business Khan-Magomedov, *Pioneers of Soviet Architecture*, pp. 280–283.
considered state treason B. A. Ruble, 'Moscow's Revolutionary Architecture and Its Aftermath: A Critical Guide', in Brumfield, ed., *Reshaping Russian Architecture*, pp. 111–115.

was their god Hall, *Cities of Tomorrow*, p. 201. For Le Corbusier, see ibid., pp. 204–240; Fishman, *Urban Utopias*, pp. 163–63; Fishman, 'Utopia in Three Dimensions', pp. 104–106; *Le Corbusier: Architect of the Century* (London: Arts Council of Great Britain, 1987).

76 *can be avoided* Le Corbusier, *Vers une Architecture*; quoted in Fishman, *Urban Utopias*, p. 187.

one huge manufactory Ibid., p. 166; quoting Marx, *Das Kapital*.

dared to aspire Quoted ibid., p. 177.

out of gear Quoted ibid., p. 187.

constructed geometrically Quoted in Hall, *Cities of Tomorrow*, pp. 208–209.

77 *Le Corbusier sought* Fishman, *Urban Utopias*, pp. 163–164.

construction and enthusiasm Quoted ibid., p. 189.

by man or nature Ibid., p. 190.

in a practical sense Quoted in *Le Corbusier: Architect of the Century*, p. 210.

and open space Fishman, *Urban Utopias*, pp. 190, 192.

78 *houses or land* Ibid., pp. 197, 233. See also Fishman, 'Utopia in Three Dimensions', pp. 104–106

doesn't matter who Quoted in Hall, *Cities of Tomorrow*, p. 210.

Messieurs les Non Fishman, *Urban Utopias*, p. 255.

proletarian dictatorship Quoted in *Le Corbusier: Architect of the Century*, p. 174.

feeling 'insulted' Jean-Louis Cohen, *Le Corbusier and the Mystique of the USSR: Theories and Projects for Moscow 1928–1936* (Princeton: Princeton University Press, 1992) Chapter 7.

subtopia Hall, *Cities of Tomorrow*, pp. 222–223; quoting I. Nairn.

79 *and dynamited* David Harvey, *The Condition of Postmodernity* (Oxford: Blackwell, 1989) p. 39.

of past forms Ibid., p. 66.

their utopian dreams Fishman, 'Utopia in Three Dimensions', pp. 95–98.

Chapter 5

81 *the upper hand* Francis Bacon, *Works*, eds. J. Spedding, R. L. Ellis and D. D. Heath, 2nd ed., 14 vols. (London: Longmans & Co., *et al.*, 1862–1875) vol. XII, p. 52.

the social order Henri de Saint-Simon, *Selected Writings on Science, Industry and Social Organisation*, translated with an Introduction by Keith Taylor (London: Croom Helm, 1975) p. 136.

comfort for civilization Quoted in P. E. Firchow, *The End of Utopia: A Study of Aldous Huxley's 'Brave New World'* (Lewisburg: Bucknell University Press, 1984) p. 57.

83 *is man's curse* Barbara Goodwin, 'Economic and Social Innovation in Utopia', in Alexander and Gill, eds., *Utopias*, p. 75.

else in the world More, *Utopia*, p. 76.

of a happy life Ibid. p. 79.
a 'comfortable life' Ibid., pp. 76–77.
84 *forms of pleasure* Ibid., p. 77.
around doing nothing Ibid., p. 75.
with your job Ibid., p. 84.
that preserve it Campanella, *La Città del Sole*, p. 81.
85 *the greatest nobility* Ibid., p. 43.
themselves and more Ibid., p. 63.
of man's estate Bacon, *Advancement of Learning*; quoted in H. B. White, *Peace among the Willows* (The Hague: Martinus Nijhoff, 1968) p. 4. For Bacon and *New Atlantis*, see ibid; J. C. Davis, *Utopia and the Ideal Society: A Study of English Utopian Writing 1516–1700* (Cambridge: Cambridge University Press, 1981) Chapter 5; C. D. Bowen, *Francis Bacon: The Temper of a Man* (Boston: Little, Brown & Co., 1963); Benjamin Farrington, *The Philosophy of Francis Bacon: An Essay on its Development from 1603 to 1609* (Liverpool: Liverpool University Press, 1964); Nell Eurich, *Science in Utopia: A Mighty Design* (Cambridge, Mass.: Harvard University Press, 1967) *passim*.
it more perfect Quoted in *DNB*, vol. I, p. 803.
86 *London and Highgate* Quoted in Bowen, *Francis Bacon*, pp. 225–226.
87 *nature in action* Francis Bacon, *'New Atlantis' and 'The Great Instauration'*, edited with an Introduction by Jerry Weinberger, 2nd ed. (Arlington Heights, Ill.: Harlan Davidson, 1989) pp. 16, 21. This translation of *New Atlantis* is used throughout.
manner of More's Utopia Bowen, *Francis Bacon*, p. 167.
power to effect Bacon, *New Atlantis*, p. 36.
and in Spanish Ibid., p. 38.
88 *presage of good* Ibid., p. 39.
much less expected Ibid., 46.
twice paid Ibid., p. 41.
in tall ships Ibid., p. 52.
and savage people Ibid., pp. 54–55.
89 *so happily established* Ibid., p. 56.
but for a dream Ibid., p. 57.
is that country Ibid., p. 60.
touch of it Ibid., pp. 66–67.
90 *had been placed* Ibid., p. 70.
all things possible Ibid., p. 71.
learn many things Ibid., p. 72.
all the world Ibid., p. 59.
91 *Adam and Eve's pools* Ibid., p. 68.
and endless abundance Plato, *Critias*, 115a–b.
measure of mortality Ibid., 121a.
from proceeding further Ibid., 108e–109a.
92 *small the world is* J. H. Elliott, 'The World After Columbus', *New York*

NOTES

Review of Books, 10 October 1991, p. 10; quoting a letter to St Francis Borja from his son.

sober man hope Bacon, *Novum Organum*; quoted in White, *Peace among the Willows,* p. 20.

man [Plato] saith Bacon, *New Atlantis,* p. 54.

motto Plus Ultra Sir Peter Medawar, 'On "The Effecting of All Things Possible"', *The Advancement of Science* XXVI (1969) p. 2.

93 *age and century* Bacon, *Redargutio Philosophiarum*; quoted in Farrington, *Philosophy of Francis Bacon,* pp. 131–132.

degrees before it Bacon, *New Atlantis,* p. 36.

[the] Instauratio Magna Eurich, *Science in Utopia,* p. 141.

preceding Natural History Bacon, *New Atlantis,* p. 36.

fit to utter Bacon, *Advancement of Learning,* in *Works,* vol. III, pp. 473–474.

through their science For example, Weinberger, Introduction to Bacon, *New Atlantis,* pp. XII, XXX–XXXI.

94 *state of creation* Davis, *Utopia and the Ideal Society,* pp. 124–125.

of the new men Quoted in Eurich, *Science in Utopia,* p. 109.

preceding four thousand Campanella, *La Città del Sole,* p. 121.

these mechanical discoveries Bacon, *Novum Organum*; quoted in Kumar, *Utopia & Anti-Utopia,* p. 31.

Magic, and Alchemy Bacon, *Advancement of Learning*; quoted in Eurich, *Science in Utopia,* p. 138.

95 *out of Plato's cave* Bacon, *Historia Naturalis et Experimentalis*; quoted in Eurich, *Science in Utopia,* p. 135.

descending to works Bacon, *Novum Organum*; quoted in Margery Purver, *The Royal Society: Concept and Creation,* with an Introduction by Hugh Trevor-Roper (London: Routledge & Kegan Paul, 1967) p. 39.

model of the world Hugh Trevor-Roper, Introduction, ibid., p. xvi.

axioms out of them Bacon, *New Atlantis,* p. 81.

than the former Ibid., p. 82.

96 *and lasts forever* Bacon, 'On the Interpretation of Nature'; quoted in Eurich, *Science in Utopia,* pp. 261–262.

wits and pens Ibid., p. 142.

97 *passeth all understanding* Bowen, *Francis Bacon,* pp. 171–172.

since they sat The Diary of Samuel Pepys, eds. R. Latham and W. Matthews, vol. V (London: G. Bell & Sons, 1971) p. 33 (1 February 1663/4).

renowned French Academy H. Fisch and H. W. Jones, 'Bacon's Influence on Sprat's *History of the Royal Society*', *MLQ* XII (1951) p. 400. For Bacon and the Royal Society, see also Purver, *Royal Society*; Eurich, *Science in Utopia, passim*; Thomas Sprat, *History of the Royal Society* (London 1667).

Works of Nature Ibid., p. 64.

of humane life Ibid., p. 2.

had despair'd of Ibid., p. 318.

Professions of Life Ibid., pp. 62–63.
Scheam of the Royal Society Joseph Glanvill, *Scepsis Scientifica* (London 1665) p. (c)1v.
now set on foot Sprat, *History, p. 35.*
98 *to graft on* Quoted in Purver, *Royal Society*, p. 79.
search it out Bacon, *Novum Organum*; quoted in Eurich, *Science in Utopia*, p. 265.
a wise administration Sprat, *History*, pp. 79–80.
contemptible progress Bacon, *Novum Organum*; quoted in Purver, *Royal Society*, pp. 33–34.
99 *not yet exist* Quoted in H. B. White, 'The Influence of Bacon on the Philosophes', *Studies on Voltaire and the Eighteenth Century* XXVII (1963) p. 1850.
greatest of philosophers Quoted ibid., p. 1863.
eagle spirit soared Quoted ibid., p. 1869.
was ever written H. G. Wells, 'Utopias'; quoted in Kumar, *Utopia & Anti-Utopia*, p. 30.
and some not Bacon, *New Atlantis*, p. 82.
100 *with atomic power* Quoted in W.H.G. Armytage, 'Utopias: The Technical and Educational Dimension', in Alexander and Gill, eds., *Utopias*, p. 87.
adorned or swelling Bacon, *New Atlantis*, p. 80.
mysteries of God Bacon, *Advancement of Learning*; quoted in Manuel and Manuel, *Utopian Thought*, p. 259.
but in proceeding Medawar, 'On "The Effecting of All Things Possible"', p. 9.

Chapter 6

101 *all was light* Alexander Pope, *Epitaphs*, 'Intended for Sir Isaac Newton'.
descent from Charlemagne For Saint-Simon, see Keith Taylor, Introduction to Saint-Simon, *Selected Writings*; Manuel and Manuel, *Utopian Thought*, Chapters 24 and 25; F. E. Manuel, *The New World of Henri Saint-Simon* (Cambridge, Mass.: Harvard University Press, 1956).
'revolutionaries' of them Quoted in Taylor, Introduction to Saint-Simon, *Selected Writings*, p. 14.
102 *I set myself Lettres à un Américain*; ibid., p. 162.
of Europe lived Ibid., p. 163.
school of improvement Quoted in Taylor, Introduction, ibid., p. 16.
counter-revolutionary Ibid., p. 17.
social physiology Ibid., p. 19.
103 *must be organisational* Quoted ibid., p. 34.
crushed by it Quoted in Manuel, *New World of Henri Saint-Simon*, p. 67.
Royal Society of London Lettres d'un Habitant de Genève; in Saint-Simon, *Selected Writings*, pp. 66–82.

NOTES

104 *rival the Church* Taylor, Introduction, ibid., pp. 20–21.

confirmed by experience Introduction aux Travaux Scientifiques du XIXe Siècle; ibid., pp. 88, 90.

is not hindered Lettres à un Américain; ibid., p. 165.

with power politics Taylor, Introduction, ibid., p. 36.

105 *favourable to production Esquisse du Nouveau Système Politique*; ibid., p. 206.

attached to a workshop Lettres d'un Habitant de Genève; ibid., p. 80.

develop their intelligence De l'Organisation Sociale; ibid., p. 266.

106 *carrying out useful work Esquisse du Nouveau Système Politique*; ibid., pp. 203–204.

hasten towards it Ibid., pp. 135–136.

European Community Keith Taylor, 'Henri de Saint-Simon: Pioneer of European Integration', *European Community* VI (June 1972) pp. 22–23.

107 *the public good Adresse aux Philanthropes, Du Système Industriel*; ibid., p. 224.

Supreme Fathers For the Saint-Simonians, see Taylor, Introduction, ibid., pp. 49–55; Manuel and Manuel, *Utopian Thought*, Chapter 26; F. E. Manuel, *The Prophets of Paris* (Cambridge, Mass.: Harvard University Press, 1962) Chapter 4.

emancipator of her sex Manuel and Manuel, *Utopian Thought*, p. 616.

108 *into a scandal* Quoted ibid., p. 637.

planners and entrepreneurs J. L. Talmon, *Romanticism and Revolt: 1815–1845* (London: Thames & Hudson, 1967) p. 68.

109 *missed by Newton* Quoted in Beecher and Bienvenue, Introduction, *Utopian Vision*, p. 1. For Fourier, see also Beecher, *Fourier*; Manuel and Manuel, *Utopian Thought*, Chapter 27.

Hannibalic Oath Beecher and Bienvenue, Introduction, *Utopian Vision*, p. 3.

110 *low the mighty* Quoted ibid., p. 11.

as it is Quoted in Manuel and Manuel, *Utopian Thought*, p. 647.

an unhealthy workshop Quoted in Beecher and Bienvenue, Introduction, *Utopian Vision*, p. 29.

RIGHT TO WORK Quoted in Beecher, *Fourier*, p. 213.

they now aspire Quoted in Beecher and Bienvenue, Introduction, *Utopian Vision*, pp. 30–31.

of his integrity Ibid., p. 43.

111 *the imitative mania* Quoted in Beecher, *Fourier*, p. 263.

cultivation of a fruit Quoted in Beecher and Bienvenue, Introduction, *Utopian Vision*, p. 46.

reason, duty and constraint Quoted ibid., p. 47.

pleasure to pleasure Quoted ibid., p. 48.

sleep very little Le Nouveau Monde Industriel; ibid., p. 277.

a hundred years Quoted in Beecher and Bienvenue, Introduction, ibid., p. 53.

112 *with dirty things* Le Nouveau Monde Industriel; ibid., p. 317.
service in return Bellamy, *Looking Backward*, p. 38.
in house-building Ibid., p. 42.

113 *horde of barbarians* Ibid., p. 177.
of efficient production Ibid., p. 178.
The Great Trust Ibid., pp. 65–66.
had become unmistakable Ibid., p. 61.
for political purposes Ibid., p. 66.

114 *industries of the country* Ibid., p. 155.
all but runs itself Ibid., p. 140.
before undreamed of Ibid., p. 65.
the former system Ibid., pp. 176–177.
any good thing Ibid., p. 85.
gold used to be Ibid., p. 118.
of Von Moltke Ibid., p. 177.

115 *satisfactorily to himself* Ibid., p. 71.
all sorts of industry Ibid., p. 102.
permit no lagging Ibid., p. 105.
under rational conditions Ibid., pp. 100–101.
instincts of men Ibid., p. 196.
is his humanity Ibid., p. 87.
of human action Ibid., p. 68.

116 *Bellamy's consumer paradise* For Morris's utopia, see Coleman and O'Sullivan, eds., *William Morris & 'News from Nowhere'*.
Morrow of the Revolution Morris, *News from Nowhere*, p. 1.
the underground railway Ibid., p. 2.
up amongst them Morris, 'Looking Backward'; quoted in Kumar, *Utopia & Anti-Utopia*, p. 162.
a regimented obligation Quoted in Paddy O'Sullivan, Introduction to Coleman and O'Sullivan, eds., *William Morris & 'News from Nowhere'*, p. 30. See also Ray Watkinson, 'The Obstinate Refusers: Work in *News from Nowhere*', ibid., pp. 91–106.

117 *everything was sacrificed* Morris, *News from Nowhere*, p. 103.
developments of machinery Morris, 'Looking Backward'; quoted in Kumar, *Utopia & Anti-Utopia*, p. 166.
the Combined Workers Morris, *News from Nowhere*, p. 122.
without a tragedy Ibid., p. 147.

118 *soon began to grow* Ibid., p. 148–150.
works of art Ibid., pp. 201–202.

119 *immensely improved machinery* Ibid., p. 108
we don't want Ibid., p. 190.
Banded-workshops Ibid., p. 50.
it once was Ibid., p. 108.
Small is Beautiful Kumar, *Utopia & Anti-Utopia*, p. 406. For Morris and ecology, see Paddy O'Sullivan, 'The Ending of the Journey: William Morris,

NOTES

News from Nowhere and Ecology', in Coleman and Sullivan, eds., *William Morris & 'News from Nowhere'*, pp. 169–181.

damage to the environment Kumar, *Utopia & Anti-Utopia*, p. 406; quoting D. Dickson.

straightforward utopia Ibid., pp. 264–265. For Huxley and *Brave New World*, see ibid., Chapter 7; Firchow, *End of Utopia*.

120 *grew before. Progress* Aldous Huxley, *Brave New World* (London: Chatto & Windus, 1932; repr. ed., London: Granada, 1977) p. 17.

applied to biology Ibid., p. 18.

the written word Henry Ford, *My Philosophy of Industry* (1925); quoted in Firchow, *End of Utopia*, p. 105.

natural step forward Ford, *Moving Forward* (1930); quoted ibid., p. 106.

in uniform batches Huxley, *Brave New World*, p. 18.

Directors of Hatcheries Ibid., p. 22.

121 *embryo below par* Ibid, p. 23.

unescapable social destiny Ibid., p. 24.

botany all their lives Ibid., p. 29.

physico-chemically equal Ibid., p. 67.

force of all time Ibid., p. 33.

stupid to be able Idem.

122 *Bill of Rights* Aldous Huxley, *Brave New World Revisited* (London: Chatto & Windus, 1959; repr. ed., London: Triad/Panther, 1983) p. 114.

holiday from them Huxley, *Brave New World*, p. 180.

wheels stop turning Ibid., p. 190.

owes to industrial society Firchow, *End of Utopia*, p. 103; quoting Garet Garrett.

123 *purely technological progress* Kumar, *Utopia & Anti-Utopia*, p. 254; quoting Sir Isaiah Berlin.

to be unhappy Huxley, *Brave New World*, p. 192.

life for everyone B. F. Skinner, *Walden Two* (New York: Macmillan, 1948; repr. ed., 1976) p. 180. For Skinner and *Walden Two*, see Kumar, *Utopia & Anti-Utopia*, Chapter 9; Sohan Modgil and Celia Modgil, eds., *B. F. Skinner: Consensus and Controversy* (New York: Falmer, 1987); R. Puligandla, *Fact and Fiction in B. F. Skinner's Science & Utopia* (St Louis, Mo.: Warren H. Green, 1974).

foot and note disease Armytage, 'Utopias: The Technical and Educational Dimension', p. 89.

when positively presented Glenn Negley and J. Max Patrick, eds., *The Quest for Utopia: An Anthology of Imaginary Societies* (New York: Henry Schuman, 1952; repr. ed., College Park, Md.: McGrath, 1971) p. 590.

Maharishi and whatnot Quoted in Larry Rohter, 'Isolated Desert Community Lives by Skinner's Precepts', *New York Times*, 17 November 1989, pp. C1, 8. For another community in Virginia, see Kathleen Kinkade, *A Walden Two Experiment: The First Five Years of Twin Oaks Community* (New York: William Morrow, 1973).

124 *shocked by the fence* Skinner, *Walden Two*, p. 16.
except when sick Ibid., p. 88.
irritation and frustration M. H. Hall, 'An Interview with "Mr Behaviorist"
B. F. Skinner', *Psychology Today* I (September 1967) pp. 21–23, 68–71.
to build strength Skinner, *Walden Two*, p. 105.
a satisfactory level Ibid., p. 114.
125 *hands of society* Ibid., p. 96.
non-social environments Skinner, *Beyond Freedom and Dignity*; quoted in
Kumar, *Utopia & Anti-Utopia*, p. 369.
would be absurd Skinner, *Walden Two*, pp. 241–242.
of behavior in the ocean Ibid., p. 240.
of behavioral engineering Idem. See also Kumar, *Utopia & Anti-Utopia*,
pp. 353–359.
science of human behavior Skinner, *Walden Two*, p. 182.
126 *they think best* Ibid., p. 251.
follow almost miraculously Ibid., p. 25.
tells us nothing Ibid., p. 181.
well-endowed arts centre Douglas Bethlehem, 'Scolding the Carpenter',
in Modgil and Modgil, eds., *B. F. Skinner: Consensus and Controversy*, p. 94.
born of weariness Skinner, *Walden Two*, p. 32.
weakness of the family Ibid., p. 128.
to raise children Ibid., p. 132.
do a good job Hall, 'An Interview with "Mr Behaviorist"'.
127 *see to that* Skinner, *Walden Two*, p. 54.
sport or play Ibid., p. 110.
working for himself Ibid., p. 53.
by anyone else Ibid., p. 50.
and the loom: Kumar, *Utopia & Anti-Utopia*, p. 351; quoting Kathleen
Kinkade.
conquest of man Skinner, *Walden Two*, p. 69.
the 'Superorganism' Ibid., p. 276.
intelligent co-operation Ibid., pp. 176–177.
see a difference Ibid., p. 273.
128 *cleaning up the county* Ibid., p. 183.
to the new order Ibid., pp. 215–216.
study of behaviour Skinner, *Science and Human Behaviour*; quoted in
Kumar, *Utopia & Anti-Utopia*, p. 368.
its past too Roger Hahn, *Laplace as a Newtonian Scientist* (Los Angeles:
Clark Memorial Library, 1967).
129 *the way they do* Skinner, *Walden Two*, pp. 246–247.

Chapter 7

133 *Beatles' first LP* Philip Larkin, 'Annus Mirabilis', in Larkin, *High Windows*
(London: Faber & Faber, 1974).

134 *a beautiful soul* More, *Utopia*, p. 103.

relations with her Marius, *Thomas More*, p. 220; quoting More's early biographer, Nicholas Harpsfield.

choose between them Turner, Introduction to More, *Utopia*, p. 11; citing John Aubrey, *Brief Lives*.

unpleasant after-effects More, *Utopia*, p. 93.

functioning of the body Ibid., p. 96.

as they're necessary Ibid., p. 98.

135 *sexual intercourse otherwise* Ibid., p. 103.

make them happier Ibid., p. 104.

to be forgiven Ibid., p. 126.

136 *in their offspring* Campanella, *La Città del Sole*, p. 55.

the cell doors Idem.

no means be permitted Ibid., p. 63.

troubled by Venus Ibid., p. 53.

become a wanton Ibid., p. 59.

137 *the weaker parties* Plato, *Republic*, 454d-e, 455e.

depraved or evil Original French quoted in Franco Venturi, *Utopia and Reform in the Enlightenment* (Cambridge: Cambridge University Press, 1971) p. 97.

138 *real and imagined* For Rousseau, see Maurice Cranston, *The Noble Savage: Jean-Jacques Rousseau 1754–1762* (London: Penguin, 1991); Alan Ritter and Julia Conaway Bondanella, eds., *Rousseau's Political Writings*, trans. J. C. Bondanella (New York and London: W. W. Norton, 1988). This translation is used throughout.

authorized by natural law Ibid., p. 3.

his needs satisfied Ibid., p. 11.

opportunity, and desire Ibid., p. 22.

to be good Ibid., pp. 26–27.

is naturally good Ibid., p. 16n.

a city-dweller Aristotle, *Politics*, 1253.a.3.

their true origin Ritter and Bondanella, eds., *Rousseau's Political Writings*, pp. 9–10.

139 *founder of civil society* Ibid., p. 34.

the human species Rousseau, *Émile*; quoted in Manuel and Manuel, *Utopian Thought*, p. 439.

decrepitude of the species Ritter and Bondanella, eds., *Rousseau's Political Writings*, p. 39.

conflict and injustice Douglas Johnson, 'A Waistcoat Soaked in Tears', Review of *The Noble Savage*, by Maurice Cranston, in *London Review of Books*, 27 June 1991, pp. 15–16.

his primitive state Ritter and Bondanella, eds., *Rousseau's Political Writings*, p. 39.

140 *disputes among themselves* Ibid., p. 30.

fatal to men Ibid., p. 31.

going back to it Voltaire to Rousseau, 30 August 1755; quoted ibid., pp. 191–192.

141 *most enduring epoch* Ibid., pp. 39–40.

142 *protect her limbs* Otis Fellows, *Diderot*, 2nd ed. (Boston: Twayne, 1989) p. 138. For Diderot, see also J. H. Mason, *The Irresistible Diderot* (London: Quartet, 1982); A. M. Wilson, *Diderot* (Oxford: Oxford University Press, 1972); P. N. Furbank, *Diderot: A Critical Biography* (London: Secker & Warburg, 1992); Wilda Anderson, *Diderot's Dream* (Baltimore: Johns Hopkins University Press, 1990).

can be imagined Quoted in Mason, *Irresistible Diderot*, p. 307.

in a small cell Original French quoted in W. F. Edmiston, *Diderot and the Family: A Conflict of Nature and Law* (Saratoga, Calif.: ANMA Libri, 1985) p. 92.

to remain constant Stephen Werner, 'Diderot's *Supplément* and the Late Enlightenment Thought', *Studies on Voltaire and the Eighteenth Century* LXXXVI (1971) pp. 254–257.

Sur les Femmes The text of *Sur les Femmes* referred to throughout is reprinted in A. L. Thomas, Denis Diderot, and Madame d'Epinay, *Ou'Est-ce Qu'une Femme?*, with an Introduction by Elisabeth Badinter (Paris: P.O.L., 1989).

143 *biologically and socially* Wilson, *Diderot*, p. 615.

more or less machiavellian Diderot, *Sur les Femmes*, pp. 179–180.

children you are Ibid., p. 172.

be most obliged Ibid., p. 180.

extreme of desire Ibid., pp. 166–167.

against a woman Ibid., p. 174; translated in Wilson, *Diderot*, p. 616.

144 *without strife* Original French quoted in Peter Jimack, *Diderot, 'Supplément au Voyage de Bougainville'*, Critical Guides to French Texts, no. 75 (London: Grant & Cutler, 1988) p. 10.

courtesy of Tahiti Supplément au Voyage de Bougainville, in Diderot, *Dialogues*, trans. F. Birrell (London: George Routledge & Sons, 1927) p. 116. This translation is used throughout.

145 *our future slavery* Ibid., pp. 119–120.

146 *beside this girl* Ibid., pp. 126–128.

wife of his host Ibid., p. 146.

natural economics Anderson, *Diderot's Dream*, p. 134.

more in Tahiti Diderot, *Supplément*, p. 134.

object of nature Werner, 'Diderot's *Supplément*', pp. 259–261.

147 *better than thine* Diderot, *Supplément*, p. 127.

how to calculate Ibid., pp. 144–145.

science of community planning M. L. Perkins, 'Community Planning in Diderot's *Supplément au Voyage de Bougainville*', *Kentucky Romance Quarterly* XXI (1974) p. 411.

mechanisms are distorted Anderson, *Diderot's Dream*, p. 165.

148 *savage in Tahiti* Diderot, *Supplément*, pp. 157–158.

women on appearances Original French quoted in Jimack, *Diderot, 'Supplément'*, pp. 71–72.

potent as creation Werner, 'Diderot's *Supplément*', pp. 279, 283–286. For Sade, see also Donald Thomas, *The Marquis de Sade* (London: Allison & Busby, 1992).

sex without cruelty David Coward, 'Pornocrat or Libertarian?', Review of Sade, *Oeuvres*, edited by M. Delon, in *Times Literary Supplement*, 15 February 1991, p. 5.

149 *maps of hell* Idem.

sharing your tastes Philosophie dans le Boudoir, in Sade, '*The Complete Justine*', '*Philosophy in the Bedroom*' *and Other Writings*, trans. R. Weaver and A. Wainhouse (New York: Grove Press, 1965) p. 325. This translation is used throughout.

de la patrie Ibid., p. 322.

followers of Saint-Simon Angela Carter, *The Sadeian Woman* (London: Virago Press, 1979) p. 119.

150 *to satisfy them*: Sade, *Philosophie dans le Boudoir*, p. 321.

misfortune to occur Ibid., p. 276.

in our womb Ibid., p. 249.

Nature wills it Ibid., pp. 322–323.

tortures and murders Sade, '*The 120 Days of Sodom*' *and Other Writings*, trans. R. Weaver and A. Wainhouse (New York: Grove Press, 1966). This translation is used throughout.

151 *service of women* Carter, *Sadeian Woman*, p. 37.

between man and man Simone de Beauvoir, 'Must We Burn Sade?', in Sade, *120 Days of Sodom*, p. 64.

trouble the government Sade, *Philosophie dans le Boudoir*, p. 317.

Chapter 8

152 *all social progress* Fourier, *Théorie des Quatre Mouvements*; in Beecher and Bienvenue, eds., *Utopian Vision*, pp. 195–196.

individual erotic needs Beecher, *Fourier*, p. 301.

reinforcement of social harmony Idem.

153 *closed too soon* Quoted in Beecher and Bienvenue, Introduction, *Utopian Vision*, p. 40.

through the window Quoted in Manuel and Manuel, *Utopian Thought*, p. 662.

happiness of all Quoted in Beecher and Bienvenue, Introduction, *Utopian Vision*, pp. 42–43.

his or her desire Quoted ibid., p. 60.

to please them Fourier, *Le Nouveau Monde Amoureux*; ibid., p. 350.

154 *a general distraction* Ibid., pp. 389–390.

grubby provincial hotels Manuel, *Prophets of Paris*, p. 225.

disappointing in-laws Fourier, *Traité de l'Association*; in Beecher and Bienvenue, eds., *Utopian Vision*, p. 179.

155 *and of religion* Quoted in Beecher and Bienvenue, Introduction, ibid., p. 57.

civilization now is Fourier, *Le Nouveau Monde Amoureux*; ibid., p. 395.

Jill, tumbling after Frances Bartkowski, *Feminist Utopias* (Lincoln, Nebr. and London: University of Nebraska Press, 1989) pp. 25–26; quoting Corre Moylan Walsh. For women and Utopia, see also L. F. Jones and S. W. Goodwin, eds., *Feminism, Utopia, and Narrative* (Knoxville: University of Tennessee Press, 1990); C. F. Kessler, ed., *Daring to Dream: Utopian Stories by United States Women 1836–1919* (Boston: Pandora, 1984).

156 *economic unit of society* Quoted in Jan Marsh, 'Concerning Love: *News from Nowhere* and Gender', in Coleman and O'Sullivan, eds., *William Morris & 'News from Nowhere'*, pp. 107–108.

likely to be serious William Morris to George Bernard Shaw, 18 March 1885; quoted ibid., p. 110.

157 *our time are* Morris, *News from Nowhere*, p. 14.

forms of flirtation Ibid., pp. 65–66.

which then obtained Ibid., p. 67.

158 *prudery and prurience* Ibid., p. 68.

under house arrest Tichi, Introduction to Bellamy, *Looking Backward*, p. 25.

indefatigable shopper Bellamy, *Looking Backward*, p. 90.

maximum physical vigor Ibid., p. 185.

159 *very happy in it* Ibid., p. 186.

the nation's children Ibid., p. 188.

of woman was possible Ibid., p. 189.

to the pedestal Tichi, Introduction, ibid., p. 25.

such as cayenne pepper Quoted in M. L. Carden, *Oneida: Utopian Community to Modern Corporation* (Baltimore: Johns Hopkins University Press, 1969) p. 29. For Noyes and the Oneida Community, see also Lawrence Foster, *Religion and Sexuality: Three American Communal Experiments of the Nineteenth Century* (New York and Oxford: Oxford University Press, 1981) Chapter 3; R. D. Thomas, *The Man Who Would Be Perfect: John Humphrey Noyes and the Utopian Impulse* (Philadelphia: University of Pennsylvania Press, 1977).

regeneration of the heart Quoted in Foster, *Religion and Sexuality*, p. 87.

160 *yea, radically changed* Quoted in Carden, *Oneida*, p. 47.

does the most good Quoted ibid., p. 14.

war with nature Quoted ibid., p. 54.

abolished on earth Quoted ibid., p. 8.

marriage 'worketh wrath' Noyes, *Bible Communism* (1848); in Albert Fried, ed., *Socialism in America: From the Shakers to the Third International* (Garden City, NY: Doubleday, 1970) p. 57.

God's universal family Quoted in Foster, *Religion and Sexuality*, p. 83.

NOTES

161 *of man to God* Noyes, *Bible Communism*; in Fried, ed., *Socialism in America*, p. 58.

first to be solved Quoted in Foster, *Religion and Sexuality*, p. 86.

makes labor attractive Noyes, *Bible Communism*; in Fried, ed., *Socialism in America*, p. 61.

but en masse Quoted in Foster, *Religion and Sexuality*, p. 92.

public spirit Carden, *Oneida*, p. 58.

Special love Foster, *Religion and Sexuality*, p. 74.

162 *and social restraints* Idem; quoting Charles Nordhoff.

any private family Ibid., p. 72; quoting Noyes, Oneida Community *Handbooks* of 1867 and 1871.

companion and 'helpmeet' Noyes, *Bible Communism*; in Fried, ed., *Socialism in America*, p. 59.

of unloading it Quoted in Foster, *Religion and Sexuality*, p. 94. See also M. P. Ryan, *Cradle of the Middle Class: The Family in Oneida County, New York, 1790–1865* (Cambridge: Cambridge University Press, 1981).

produces disease Noyes, *Bible Communism*; in Fried, ed., *Socialism in America*, p. 59.

over the falls Quoted in Carden, *Oneida*, p. 50.

163 *never been before* Quoted in Foster, *Religion and Sexuality*, p. 97.

skirts over trousers Ibid., p. 98.

for the passive Quoted in Thomas, *The Man Who Would Be Perfect*, p. 103.

glory of man Quoted in Carden, *Oneida*, p. 67.

is to . . . animals Quoted ibid., p. 61.

164 *and true Communism* Quoted ibid., pp. 61–62.

women and children Quoted ibid., p. 113.

value to mankind Quoted in Foster, *Religion and Sexuality*, p. 120.

165 *the domestic sphere* Bartkowski, *Feminist Utopias*, p. 9.

foundation stone of a society Nan Bowman Albinski, ' "The Laws of Justice, Nature, and of Right": Victorian Feminist Utopias', in Jones and Goodwin, eds., *Feminism, Utopia, and Narrative*, p. 51. For Gilman, see Ann J. Lane, Introduction to Gilman, *Herland* (London: Women's Press, 1979; repr. ed., 1992); Lane, Introduction to *The Charlotte Perkins Gilman Reader: 'The Yellow Wallpaper' and Other Fiction* (London: Women's Press, 1981; repr. ed., 1987).

166 *rarely carefree pleasure* Ibid., pp. xxxv–xxxvi.

Desirable and Undesirable Gilman, *Herland*, p. 21.

Girls and Girls Ibid., p. 7.

a back seat Ibid., p. 8.

cordon of London police Ibid., p. 23.

and the girls Ibid., p. 31.

167 *With Her in Ourland* First published in *The Forerunner* VII (1916); repr. ed., Westport, Conn.: Greenwood Press, 1968.

help them grow Lane, Introduction to Gilman, *Herland*, p. xxi.

all the bundles Gilman, *Herland,* p. 69.
collectively to one another Ibid., p. 95.
frills and furbelows Ibid., p. 81.
daringly for the future Ibid., p. 111.
and spoils you Ibid., p. 142.
calls it 'Ma-land' Ibid., p. 146.
it's all done Ibid., p. 99.
mutually devoted Ibid., p. 127.
enjoy being mastered Ibid., p. 131.

Chapter 9

174 *the here and now* J.F.C. Harrison, *The Second Coming: Popular Millenarianism 1780–1850* (London: Routledge & Kegan Paul, 1979) Chapter
1. For religion and Utopia, see also Mark Holloway, *Heavens on Earth*
(London: Turnstile, 1951); D. E. Pitzer, 'Collectivism, Community and
Commitment: America's Religious Communal Utopias from the Shakers
to Jonestown', in Alexander and Gill, eds., *Utopias,* pp. 119–135.
dreamed of an Utopia Keith Thomas, 'The Utopian Impulse in Seventeenth-
Century England', *Dutch Quarterly Review of Anglo-American Letters* III
(1985) p. 173; quoting Gerrard Winstanley.
George-Hill in Surrey Quoted in A.E. Bestor, *Backwoods Utopias: The
Sectarian and Owenite Phases of Communitarian Socialism in America,
1663–1829* (Philadelphia: University of Pennsylvania Press, 1950) p. 21.
where to find it Quoted in Mircea Eliade, 'Paradise and Utopia: Mythical
Geography and Eschatology', in Manuel, ed., *Utopias and Utopian
Thought,* p. 262.
175 *fought in America* Garry Wills, *Under God: Religion and American Politics*
(New York: Simon & Schuster, 1990) pp. 138–139.
of brotherly love Thomas, 'Utopian Impulse', p. 172.
accepted her leadership For the Shakers, see E. D. Andrews, *The People
Called Shakers: A Search for the Perfect Society* (New York: Oxford
University Press, 1953); Harrison, *Second Coming,* pp. 163–175; Foster,
Religion and Sexuality, Chapter 2; June Sprigg and David Larkin, *Shaker:
Life, Work, and Art* (New York: Stewart, Tabori & Chang, 1987; repr.
ed., London: Cassell, 1988); Henri Desroche, *The American Shakers:
From Neo-Christianity to Pre-Socialism,* trans. J. K. Savacool (Amherst:
University of Massachusetts Press, 1971); R. E. Whitson, ed., *The Shakers:
Two Centuries of Spiritual Reflection,* with a preface by Gertrude M. Soule
(New York: Paulist Press, 1983); Mick Gidley and Kate Bowles, eds.,
*Locating the Shakers: Cultural Origins and Legacies of an American
Religious Movement* (Exeter: University of Exeter Press, 1990); S. J.
Stein, *The Shaker Experience in America: A History of the United Society
of Believers* (New Haven and London: Yale University Press, 1992).
176 *flesh with him* Testimonies of Mother Ann Lee; quoted in Foster, *Sexuality*

and Religion, p. 27.

really a woman Ibid., pp. 32–33.

lay monasticism Harrison, *Second Coming*, p. 165.

subject of controversy Stein, *Shaker Experience*, passim.

in-through-with us all Whitson, Introduction, *Shakers*, p. 12.

Christ for Glory' Ibid., p. 1.

177 *agreement with Hell* Quoted in Harrison, *Second Coming*, p. 168.

truth of this remark. Calvin Green and Seth Y. Wells, *A Summary View of the Millennial Church* (1823); quoted in Foster, *Religion and Sexuality*, p. 46.

sisters in the World: Alison M. Newby, 'Shakers as Feminists? Shakerism as a Vanguard in the Antebellum American Search for Female Autonomy and Independence', in Gidley and Bowles, eds., *Locating the Shakers*, pp. 97.

178 *humanity, male and female* Whitson, Introduction, *Shakers*, pp. 13–14.

doing what men do Newby, 'Shakers as Feminists?', p. 101; quoting D'Ann Campbell.

bolts and bars Quoted in Sprigg and Larkin, *Shaker*, p. 68.

chaste parking meters Madeline Drexler, 'New Eden in New England', *New York Times*, 14 July 1991, sect. XX, pp. 8, 20.

or earthly ties Quoted in Foster, *Religion and Sexuality*, p. 31.

179 *if so, 'How much'* Membership form, displayed in the Shaker House at Fruitlands Museum, Harvard, Massachusetts.

when they copulate The 'Millennial Laws' are listed in Andrews, *People Called Shakers*.

subordination of self Harrison, *Second Coming*, p. 175.

penguin kind of motion Quoted in Sprigg and Larkin, *Shaker*, p. 246.

180 *cutting up capers* Anonymous, 'Four Months among the Shakers, 1842–1843'; in Fried, ed., *Socialism in America*, pp. 50–53.

to look at it Quoted in Sprigg and Larkin, *Shaker*, p. 176.

have suspected it Charles Dickens, *American Notes for General Circulation*, eds. J. S. Whitley and A. Goldman (London: Penguin, 1972) pp. 257–261.

181 *the poor workers* Quoted in Desroche, *American Shakers*, pp. 294–296.

will attend you Quoted in Sprigg and Larkin, *Shaker*, p. 68.

singing glory hallelujah Quoted ibid., p. 246.

with Victorian tastes Our thanks to the Shaker community at Sabbathday Lake, Maine, for pointing out this and several other common misconceptions concerning the Shakers.

Architects of modern times Noyes, *History of American Socialisms* (Philadelphia: J. B. Lippincott & Co., 1870) p. 192.

the true work Green and Wells, *Summary View*; quoted in Bestor, *Backwoods Utopias*, p. 52.

182 *a thousand by 1910* Harrison, *Second Coming*, p. 165.

several thousand a week L. J. Arrington and D. Bitton, *The Mormon Experience: A History of the Latter-Day Saints*, 2nd ed. (Urbana and

Chicago: University of Illinois Press, 1992) pp. 342–343. See also Harrison, *Second Coming*, pp. 176–192; Foster, *Religion and Sexuality*, Chapters 4 and 5; K. H. Winn, *Exiles in a Land of Liberty: Mormons in America, 1830–1846* (Chapel Hill and London: University of North Carolina Press, 1989).
the millennial reign Quoted in Harrison, *Second Coming*, p. 177.

183 *upon the land* Winn, *Exiles*, p. 1; quoting the *Book of Mormon*.
upon this continent Quoted in Harrison, *Second Coming*, p. 182.
friendship nor safety L. S. Kramer, ed., *Paine and Jefferson on Liberty* (New York: Continuum, 1988) p. 49.

184 *chloroform in print* Quoted in N. O. Hatch, *The Democratization of American Christianity* (New Haven and London: Yale University Press, 1989) p. 115.
rights of man Quoted in Harrison, *Second Coming*, p. 184.
grew up in Winn, *Exiles*, p. 17.
owed to their God Quoted ibid., pp. 26–27.
was a republican Ibid., p. 35.

185 *strength of a nation* Sir Richard Burton, *The City of the Saints and across the Rocky Mountains to California*, with a Foreword by B. H. Morrow (Niwot, Colo.: University of Colorado Press, 1990) p. 383.
age of sixteen Ibid., pp. 427, 430.
to seduce women Foster, *Religion and Sexuality*, p. 171.

186 *'quixotic' campaign* Ibid., p. 142.
our republican institutions Quoted in Winn, *Exiles*, p. 219.
Revolution of '76 Quoted ibid., p. 220.
nation of Israel Quoted ibid., p. 236.
to the settlement Burton, *City of the Saints*, p. 198.
as the breadth Dolores Hayden, *Seven American Utopias: The Architecture of Communitarian Socialism, 1790–1975* (Cambridge, Mass.: MIT Press, 1976) pp. 110–111.
disembarking in New York Burton, *City of the Saints*, pp. 193, 225–227.

187 *Home Sweet Home* Ibid., pp. 349–350.
was in office Ibid., pp. 310–311.
word of fear Ibid., p. 2.
the US Army Ibid., pp. 354–355; see also pp. 168–169, 245, 338–342.
abiding resentment Ibid., p. 250.
the next president Ibid., p. 251.
being an American Ibid., p. 306.
if not in deed Ibid., p. 351.

188 *strife and wickedness* Ibid., p. 314.
strengthen not efface Ibid., p. 250.
331,000 new converts Arrington and Bitton, *Mormon Experience*, p. 342.
them look bad Quoted in Diane Johnson, 'The Lost World of the Mormons', Review of *The Chincilla Farm*, by Judith Freeman, *et al.*, in *New York Review of Books*, 15 March 1990, p. 30.
Utah and the West Harrison, *Second Coming*, p. 189.

advanced social planning Pitzer, 'Collectivism', pp. 125–126; quoting V. F. Calverton.

an older America Winn, *Exiles*, p. 39.

189 *from the Apocalypse* Wills, *Under God*, p. 150.

never been dissolved Alexis de Tocqueville, *Democracy in America*, trans. Henry Reeve, with an Introduction by D. J. Boorstin, 2 vols. (New York: Vintage Books, 1990) vol. I, p. 300.

than in America Ibid., p. 303.

pre-millenarian sect 'Saving the World: Fighting Back', *Everyman*, BBC1 (3 May 1992).

find a priest Tocqueville, *Democracy*, vol. I, pp. 306–307.

stumbling over each other Wills, *Under God*, p. 29. See also, Frances Fitzgerald, *Cities on a Hill: A Journey through Contemporary American Culture* (New York: Simon & Schuster, 1986; repr. ed., London: Picador, 1987) pp. 121–201.

they proved prophets Wills, *Under God*, p. 25.

Chapter 10

191 *realized in full* Epigraph to Huxley, *Brave New World*.

193 *but for the world* Paine, *Rights of Man*; in Kramer, ed., *Paine and Jefferson*, p. 106.

194 *transplanted into Europe* Quoted in D. Brion Davis, *Revolutions: Reflections on American Equality and Foreign Liberations* (Cambridge, Mass.: Harvard University Press, 1990) p. 3. See also G. S. Wood, 'Americans and Revolutionaries', Review of *Revolutions*, by D. Brion Davis, in *New York Review of Books*, 27 September 1990, pp. 31–36.

ambassador in Paris Conor Cruise O'Brien, 'The Decline and Fall of the French Revolution', Review of *The Critical Dictionary of the French Revolution*, edited by F. Furet and M. Ozouf, in *New York Review of Books*, 15 February 1990, p. 48.

of international revolution Wood, 'Americans and Revolutionaries'.

the term popular Geoffrey Best, Introduction to *The Permanent Revolution: The French Revolution and Its Legacy 1789–1989* (London: Fontana, 1988) p. 4.

until the Civil War Wood, 'Americans and Revolutionaries', p. 33.

success in it Quoted ibid., p. 34.

195 *cause of human liberty* Quoted idem.

pursuit of Happiness Kramer, ed., *Paine and Jefferson*, p. 63.

constantly terminated Tocqueville, *Democracy*, vol. I, p. 3.

196 *made their place* E. S. Morgan, 'The Second American Revolution', Review of *The Radicalism of the American Revolution*, by G. S. Wood, in *New York Review of Books*, 25 June 1992, p. 23.

197 *his social relations* Quoted in Richard Holmes, *Coleridge: Early Visions* (London: Hodder & Stoughton, 1989) p. 66.

Trinity Colleges, Cambridge John Morrow, *Coleridge's Political Thought: Property, Morality and the Limits of Traditional Discourse* (London: Macmillan, 1990) p. 4.

by a tiger Holmes, *Coleridge*, p. 62.

198 *of perpetual improvement* Quoted in David Spadafora, *The Idea of Progress in Eighteenth-Century Britain* (New Haven and London: Yale University Press, 1990) pp. 388–389; also Harold Silver, Introduction to *Robert Owen on Education* (Cambridge: Cambridge University Press, 1969) p. 12.

modern Unitarianism Morrow, *Coleridge's Political Thought*, p. 6.

Characters make money Coleridge to Southey, 1 September 1794; in *The Letters of Samuel Taylor Coleridge*, ed. E. L. Griggs, 6 vols. (Oxford: Oxford University Press, 1956–1971) vol. I, no. 55, p. 99.

following the plough Quoted in Holmes, *Coleridge*, p. 75.

199 *disturbs the earth* Robert Southey, *Sir Thomas More: Colloquies on the Progress and Prospects of Society*, 2 vols. (London: John Murray, 1829) vol. I, pp. 18–19.

new moral world Between 1836 and 1844 Owen published *The Book of the New Moral World*.

theft was very general *The Life of Robert Owen by Himself* (1957); in A. L. Morton, ed., *The Life and Ideas of Robert Owen* (London: Lawrence & Wishart, 1962) p. 74.

unenlightened rivals Leszek Kolakowski, *Main Currents of Marxism: Its Origins, Growth and Dissolution*, trans. P. S. Falla, 3 vols. (Oxford and New York: Oxford University Press, 1978; repr. ed., 1981) vol. I, p. 193.

lot of the poor Quoted in J.F.C. Harrison, *Robert Owen and the Owenites in Britain and America* (London: Routledge & Kegan Paul, 1969) p. 11. See also Manuel and Manuel, *Utopian Thought*, Chapter 27; Bestor, *Backwoods Utopias, passim*.

200 *interference with industry* Morton, Introduction, *Life and Ideas of Robert Owen*, pp. 26–27.

from his birth Quoted in Silver, Introduction, *Owen on Education*, p. 16.

person's work place *Life of Robert Owen by Himself*; in Morton, ed., *Life and Ideas of Robert Owen*, pp. 77–78.

not BY himself Quoted in Manuel and Manuel, *Utopian Thought*, p. 683.

tone of voice Quoted in Silver, Introduction, *Owen on Education*, p. 28.

wishes and desires Quoted in Kolakowski, *Main Currents*, vol. I, p. 195.

cradle to the grave Bestor, *Backwoods Utopias*, p. 141.

201 *government of nations* Quoted in Morton, Introduction, *Life and Ideas of Robert Owen*, p. 20.

most extravagant customer Quoted in Harrison, *Owen and the Owenites*, p. 12.

but one interest Quoted in Bestor, *Backwoods Utopias*, p. 10.

all can consume Quoted ibid., p. 81.

will rapidly multiply Quoted ibid., p. 12.

community on each Quoted in Benvolo, *Origins of Modern Town Planning*, pp. 49–50.

202 *Who are you* Life of Robert Owen by Himself; in Morton, ed., *Life and Ideas of Robert Owen*, p. 112.

disagreeable truths Gregory Claeys, Introduction to *Robert Owen: 'A New View of Society' and Other Writings* (London: Penguin, 1991) p. xii.

which I propose Bestor, *Backwoods Utopias*, p. 114.

sons of men Quoted in Silver, Introduction, *Owen on Education*, pp. 29–30.

203 *at Harmony, Indiana* W. H. G. Armytage, 'Owen and America', in S. Pollard and J. Salt, eds., *Robert Owen: Prophet of the Poor* (London: Macmillan, 1971) p. 225.

thrilled the world Noyes, *American Socialisms*, p. 22.

journey with me Quoted in Armytage, 'Owen and America', p. 214.

when they come here Quoted in Bestor, *Backwoods Utopias*, pp. 115–116.

was ever devised William Pelham, in *New Harmony as Seen by Participants and Travellers*, The American Utopian Adventure, 2nd ser. (Philadelphia: Porcupine Press, 1975) f. 25 (originally published 1916).

was public opinion Bestor, *Backwoods Utopias*, p. 122.

204 *Society would stop too* Ibid., p. 130.

argued in circles Ibid., p. 61; quoting Harriet Martineau.

inadequate as the last Morton, Introduction, *Life and Ideas of Robert Owen*, p. 34.

depression and inflation Kolakowski, *Main Currents*, vol. I, pp. 194, 196.

confusion and disappointment Noyes, *American Socialisms*, pp. 45–46.

behind Owen's doctrines Bestor, *Backwoods Utopias*, p. 126.

205 *from Europeans only* Ibid., p. 121.

for immoral demeanor Quoted in Morton, Introduction, *Life and Ideas of Robert Owen*, pp. 34–35.

wife by advertising Noyes, *American Socialisms*, p. 56.

black sheep Ibid., p. 35.

lazy worthless persons Duke of Saxe-Weimer, in *New Harmony as Seen by Participants*, f. 34v.

brothers and sisters Harrison, *Owen and the Owenites*, p. 185.

democratic dancers New Harmony as Seen by Participants, f. 41.

prized equality Ibid., f. 40.

206 *establishment near Vincennes* Ibid., f. 37–37v.

contained in a boat Quoted in Bestor, *Backwoods Utopias*, p. 133.

provided for them Armytage, 'Owen and America', p. 217.

but with orphans Quoted ibid., p. 236n.

Tocqueville called it Tocqueville, *Democracy*, vol. II, pp. 98–99.

principle of individualism Quoted in Bestor, *Backwoods Utopias*, p. 8.

go so far Quoted ibid., p. 63.

throughout the Midwest. Kumar, *Utopia & Anti-Utopia*, p. 92.

in the small Irving Howe, *Politics and the Novel* (New York: Horizon Press, 1957) p. 170.

another of the state Emerson to Carlyle, 30 October 1840; in *The Correspondence of Emerson and Carlyle*, ed. J. Slater (New York and London: Columbia University Press, 1964) pp. 283–284.

Yankee homespun Howe, *Politics*, p. 167; quoting V. L. Parrington.

207 *the domestic government* Quoted in E. R. Curtis, *A Season in Utopia: The Story of Brook Farm* (New York: Thomas Nelson & Sons, 1961) p. 31.

at the drowning-point Quoted in A. N. Kaul, 'The Blithedale Romance and the Puritan Tradition', in Harold Bloom, ed., *Nathaniel Hawthorne* (New York: Chelsea House, 1986) p. 65.

a little beyond W. H. Harrison, Introduction to Louisa May Alcott, *'Transcendental Wild Oats' and Excerpts from the Fruitlands Diary* (Harvard, Mass.: Harvard Common Press, 1981) p. 6.

financially and spiritually Guarneri, *Utopian Alternative*, pp. 44–45.

great social good Curtis, *Season in Utopia*, pp. 49–50.

society from within Taylor Stoehr, 'Art vs. Utopia: The Case of Nathaniel Hawthorne and Brook Farm', *Antioch Review* XXXVI:1 (1978) p. 91.

208 *cover the earth* Quoted in Guarneri, *Utopian Alternative*, p. 49.

come and follow me Noyes, *American Socialisms*, p. 116.

Susquehanna Paradise G. W. Curtis, in Joel Myerson, ed., *The Brook Farm Book: A Collection of First-Hand Accounts of the Community* (New York and London: Garland, 1987) p. 96.

for the Transcendentalists Quoted in Curtis, *Season in Utopia*, p. 46.

concert of crowds Quoted ibid., p. 49.

209 *equality without its vulgarity* Quoted ibid., pp. 53–54.

we bring to it Quoted ibid., p. 76.

transcendental heifer[s] Hawthorne to Sophia Peabody, 13 April 1841; in *The Centenary Edition of the Works of Nathaniel Hawthorne*, vol. XV: *The Letters, 1813–1843*, eds. T. Woodson, L. Smith and N. H. Pearson (Columbus: Ohio State University Press, 1984) p. 527.

writer was imbued Ibid., p. 528.

and wholesome substance Hawthorne to Sophia Peabody, 4 May 1841; ibid., p. 542.

210 *pile of money* Hawthorne to Sophia Peabody, 1 June 1841; ibid., p. 545.

a dung heap Hawthorne to Sophia Peabody, 12 August 1841; ibid., p. 558.

have no thoughts Quoted in Stoehr, 'Art vs. Utopia', p. 92.

poems to memory Georgina Bruce Kirby, in Myerson, ed., *Brook Farm Book*, p. 108.

romance about it Noyes, *American Socialisms*, p. 107.

fiction and reality Hawthorne, *The Blithedale Romance*, with an Introduction by Tony Tanner (Oxford and New York: Oxford University Press, 1991) p. 2.

211 *kindled for humanity* Ibid., p. 25.

those very men Ibid., p. 19.

equal, and no more Ibid., pp. 24–25.

to be anything else Ibid., p. 65.
212 *than new brotherhood* Ibid., p. 20.
since yesterday morning Ibid., p. 141.
in the 1840s Bestor, *Backwoods Utopias*, pp. 55–59.
health food craze Wills, *Under God*, p. 145.
under the aprons Georgina Bruce Kirby, in Myerson, ed., *Brook Farm Book*, p. 149.
Fourier and finance Ibid., p. 152.
metaphysical 'windmill' Guarneri, *Utopian Alternative*, p. 26; quoting Horatio Greenough.
too hard for him Quoted ibid., p. 25.
looking for a system For Brisbane and Fourierism, see ibid., Chapter 1.
Condé, in France Ibid., pp. 23–24.
213 *phalanstery in New Harmony* Beecher, *Fourier*, pp. 367–368.
a disturbed brain Quoted in Guarneri, *Utopian Alternative*, p. 24.
to my countrymen Quoted ibid., p. 30.
this terrestrial world Quoted in Curtis, *Season in Utopia*, p. 133.
214 *steam for machinery* Quoted in Hayden, *Seven American Utopias*, p. 20.
the American Dream Guarneri, *Utopian Alternative*, p. 9.
the federal heart Noyes, *American Socialisms*, p. 220.
to the Mississippi Quoted in Guarneri, *Utopian Alternative*, p. 60.
hard to swallow Georgina Bruce Kirby, in Myerson, ed., *Brook Farm Book*, p. 166.
215 *habits and associations* Quoted in Curtis, *Season in Utopia*, pp. 95–96.
plenty to mankind Ibid., p. 145.
of the present time Noyes, *American Socialisms*, p. 209.
a communal venture Guarneri, *Utopian Alternative*, p. 35.
retained and refined Ibid., pp. 57–59.
completely broken down Georgina Bruce Kirby, in Myerson, ed., *Brook Farm Book*, pp. 166–167; Curtis, *Season in Utopia*, p. 68.
Her Perpendicular Majesty Ibid., pp. 62, 70.
216 *four-year-ites* Guarneri, *Utopian Alternative*, p. 3.
fury-ites Curtis, *Season in Utopia*, p. 98.
in a patty-pan Quoted ibid., p. 92.
buzz in the ear Quoted ibid., p. 105.
with each pulsation Guarneri, *Utopian Alternative*, p. 53.
have found rest Noyes, *American Socialisms*, p. 4; quoting A. J. MacDonald.

Chapter 11

217 *of their lot* Bellamy, *Looking Backward*, pp. 39–40.
own utopian vision Guarneri, *Utopian Alternative*, p. 401; quoting Bellamy, 'Progress of Nationalism in the United States' (1892).
218 *project was abandoned* Ibid., pp. 503–504n.

attained by the few Ibid., p. 404; quoting Bellamy, 'Concerning the Founding of Nationalist Colonies' (1893).

of American radicals Ibid., pp. 404–405.

distinctly socialistic Morgan, *Bellamy*, p. 9. For Bellamy, see also J. L. Thomas, Introduction to Bellamy, *Looking Backward 2000–2887* (Cambridge, Mass. Harvard University Press, 1967); S. E. Bowman, *The Year 2000: A Critical Biography of Edward Bellamy* (New York: Bookman Associates, 1958); Daphne Patai, ed., *Looking Backward, 1988–1888: Essays on Edward Bellamy* (Amherst: University of Massachusetts Press, 1989); Kumar, *Utopia & Anti-Utopia*. Chapter 5; Tichi, Introduction to Bellamy, *Looking Backward*.

mansions of factory owners Milton Cantor, 'The Backward Look of Bellamy's Socialism', in Patai, ed., *Looking Backward, 1988–1888*, p. 23.

Burdens of Society Tichi, Introduction to Bellamy, *Looking Backward*, p. 11.

however brief Quoted in Morgan, *Bellamy*, p. 150.

219 *by looking backward* Victor Brombert, 'Looking Back to the Future', Review of *The Mask of the Prophet*, by A. Martin, in *Times Literary Supplement*, 16–22 November 1990, p. 1231.

out of the question Bellamy, *Looking Backward*, p. 63.

not behind us Ibid., p. 234.

dentist pulls a tooth Bellamy, *Dr Heidenhoff's Process* (New York: D. Appleton & Co., 1880) pp. 100–101.

in the universe Ibid., p. 120. See also Sylvia Strauss, 'Gender, Class, and Race in Utopia', in Patai, ed., *Looking Back-ward, 1988–1888*, pp. 83–84; W. W. Wagar, 'Dreams of Reason: Bellamy, Wells, and the Positive Utopia', ibid., pp. 111–112.

a century's weight Bellamy, *Looking Backward*, p. 208.

newspaper reader might Quoted in Morgan, *Bellamy*, p. 372.

220 *a national character* Quoted in Kumar, *Utopia & Anti-Utopia*, p. 83.

what socialism was Bowman, *Year 2000*, p. 95.

subject was unpopular Noyes, *American Socialisms*, p. 42; referring to A. J. MacDonald.

221 *spirit and suggestions* Bellamy to Howells, 17 June 1888; quoted in Bowman, *Year 2000*, p. 114.

by bearded radicals Thomas, Introduction to Bellamy, *Looking Backward* (1967), p. 77.

to hinder it Bellamy, *Looking Backward*, p. 182.

the nation's wealth H. Kinder and W. Hilgemann, *The Penguin Atlas of World History*, trans. E. A. Menze, 2 vols. (London: Penguin, 1978) vol. II, p. 117.

222 *The Great Trust* Bellamy, *Looking Backward*, pp. 65–66.

development of humanity Bellamy, 'The Rate of the World's Progress' (1888); quoted in Bellamy, *Looking Backward*, p. 232.

223 *was behind it* Ibid., pp. 66–67.

its members individually Bellamy, *Equality* (New York: D. Appleton &

Co., 1897) p. 16. See also Kumar, *Utopia & Anti-Utopia*, pp. 144–146.

224 *guarantee of economic equality* Bellamy, *Equality*, p. 17.

talent and merit Manuel and Manuel, *Utopian Thought*, p. 603.

boyhood hero of Bellamy Morgan, *Bellamy*, p. 145.

wandering cities Quoted in Kumar, *Utopia & Anti-Utopia*, p. 158.

225 *went to work* Bellamy, *Looking Backward*, pp. 224–225.

animates its members Ibid., p. 89.

excessive individualism Ibid., p. 57.

from taking advantage Strauss, 'Gender, Class, and Race', p. 76.

food and clothing Morgan, *Bellamy*, p. 89.

communion with 'eternity' Cantor, 'Backward Look', p. 26.

remnant, the universe Wagar, 'Dreams of Reason', p. 111; quoting Bellamy, 'The Religion of Solidarity' (1874).

226 *is absolutely sure* Thomas, Introduction to Bellamy, *Looking Backward* (1967), pp. 15–16.

it is nowadays Bellamy, *Looking Backward*, p. 125.

law of solidarity Quoted in Tichi, Introduction to Bellamy, *Looking Backward*, p. 13.

generation to follow Bellamy, *Looking Backward*, 192.

thrill of hope Morgan, *Bellamy*, p. ix; quoting H. P. Peebles.

227 *the [Boston] Common* Ibid., pp. 248–249. For the Nationalist Movement, see ibid., Chapter 11; Kumar, *Utopia & Anti-Utopia*, pp. 136–140; Thomas, Introduction to Bellamy, *Looking Backward* (1967), pp. 69–88.

disgruntled small businessmen Ibid., p. 73.

than the candidates Ibid., p. 80.

patriots of 1776 Quoted in Morgan, *Bellamy*, p. 277.

of republican institutions Quoted in Thomas, Introduction to Bellamy, *Looking Backward* (1967), p. 77.

for new ventures Bellamy, 'Letter to the People's Party' (1892); quoted in Kumar, *Utopia & Anti-Utopia*, p. 139.

228 *prophet of the ideal state* Quoted ibid., p. 133.

libraries in 1889 Ibid., p. 135.

won their hearts Franklin Rosemont, 'Bellamy's Radicalism Reclaimed', in Patai, ed., *Looking Backward, 1988–1888*, p. 201n.

vanguard of history Wood, 'Americans and Revolutionaries', p. 35.

229 *Duvalier's in Haiti* Ibid., p. 32.

and maximum hours For Bellamy's policies and the New Deal, see Morgan, *Bellamy*, pp. xii, 279–296, 304; Wagar, 'Dreams of Reason', pp. 120–121; J. L. Thomas, *Alternative America: Henry George, Edward Bellamy, Henry Demarest Lloyd and the Adversary Tradition* (Cambridge, Mass.: Belknap Press, 1983) pp. 361–364.

230 *some appropriate form* Quoted in Joan Didion, 'Eye on the Prize', *New York Review of Books*, 24 September 1992, p. 65.

Chapter 12

231 *Nationalist Party* Kumar, *Utopia & Anti-Utopia*, pp. 158–160.
a father-land Bellamy, *Looking Backward*, p. 183.
232 *they have nothing* Ibid., p. 144
nation at large Ibid., p. 146.
of becoming reality Quoted in Kumar, *Utopia & Anti-Utopia*, p. 382.
his day and ours Sir Isaiah Berlin, *The Crooked Timber of Humanity: Chapters in the History of Ideas*, ed. Henry Hardy (London: John Murray, 1990; repr. ed., London: Fontana, 1991) p. 16.
is in chains Ritter and Bondanella, eds., *Rousseau's Political Writings*, p. 85.
233 *as free as before* Ibid., p. 92.
234 *not have been free* Ibid., p. 151.
forced to be free Ibid., p. 95.
235 *what is important* Ibid., p. 101–102.
exist without it Ibid., pp. 115–116.
limited by the general will Ibid., p. 96.
236 *alien to him* Ibid., p. 108.
our vices arise Ibid., p. 73. See also Robert Nisbet, 'Rousseau & Equality', ibid., pp. 244–260.
following the general will Ibid., p. 66.
237 *should not perish* Ibid., p. 163.
the law itself Quoted in O'Brien, 'Decline and Fall', p. 48. See also Jean Starobinski, 'Rousseau in the Revolution', *New York Review of Books*, 12 April 1990, pp. 47–50.
protects or punishes Quoted in O'Brien, 'Decline and Fail,' p. 49.
238 *to abolish it* Kramer, ed., *Paine and Jefferson*, p. 63.
mandate for Terror O'Brien, 'Decline and Fall', p. 49.
explains the Social Contract Starobinski, 'Rousseau in the Revolution', p. 47.
invents the machine Ritter and Bondanella, eds., *Rousseau's Political Writings*, p. 108.
must be destroyed Ibid., p. 115.
a lethal menace O'Brien, 'Decline and Fall', p. 50.
239 *lied before the laws* Ritter and Bondanella, eds., *Rousseau's Political Writings*, p. 172.
parts of the whole Starobinski, 'Rousseau in the Revolution', pp. 49–50; quoting Patrice Gueniffey.
love of fatherland Ibid., p. 50.
category of 'becoming' Eugene Kamenka, 'Revolutionary Ideology and "The Great French Revolution of 1789–?"', in Best, ed., *The Permanent Revolution*, p. 78.
into the future Neal Ascherson, 'Where Will this Voyage End?', Review of *Echoes of the Marseillaise*, by E. J. Hobsbawm, in *London Review of Books*, 14 June 1990, p. 3.

NOTES

240 *with a beer glass* Quoted in Peter Singer, *Marx*, Past Masters (Oxford and New York: Oxford University Press, 1980) p. 2. For Marx and Marxism, see also Kolakowski, *Main Currents*; Sir Isaiah Berlin, *Karl Marx*, 4th ed. (Oxford: Oxford University Press, 1978); Terrell Carver, ed., *The Cambridge Companion to Marx* (Cambridge: Cambridge University Press, 1991); Karl Marx and Friedrich Engels, *Selected Works in One Volume*, rev. ed. (London: Lawrence & Wishart, 1991).

of the whole world Ibid., p. 35.

did not turn Quoted in J. J. Sheehan, 'The Revolution Marx Didn't Make', Review of *Rhineland Radicals*, by J. Sperber, in *Times Literary Supplement*, 31 January 1992, p. 11.

241 *never acquired any* Carver, Introduction, *Cambridge Companion to Marx*, p. 10.

the stock exchange Singer, *Marx*, p. 9.

General Council to America Engels, 'Karl Marx'; in Marx and Engels, *Selected Works*, pp. 354–355.

soul of communism Berlin, *Marx*, p. 192.

thread for my studies Quoted in Singer, *Marx*, p. 28.

in political economy Quoted in Berlin, *Marx*, p. 92.

242 *development of human history* Engels, 'Karl Marx's Funeral'; in Marx and Engels, *Selected Works*, p. 411.

newly arising classes Engels, 'Karl Marx'; ibid., p. 355.

243 *ever-increasing measure* Ibid., p. 357.

shepherd or critic Quoted in Kumar, *Utopia & Anti-Utopia*, p. 57.

demonstrate scientifically Quoted in Manuel and Manuel, *Utopian Thought*, p. 702. See also Steven Lukes, 'Marxism and Utopianism', in Alexander and Gill, eds., *Utopias*, pp. 153–167.

flood tide of history Manuel and Manuel, *Utopian Thought*, p. 706.

244 *bird's-eye view* Idem.

is a reactionary Ibid., p. 698.

the New Jerusalem Communist Manifesto; in Marx and Engels, *Selected Works*, p. 60.

of the Communist Manifesto Engels, Preface to the *Communist Manifesto* (1890); ibid., pp. 32–34.

determines their consciousness Berlin, *Marx*, pp. 96–97.

each different school Marx and Engels, *Selected Works*, p. 387.

245 *forces in modern society* Lenin, 'Frederick Engels'; ibid., p. 15.

246 *the proletarian movement* Ibid., p. 45.

and executed it O'Brien, 'Decline and Fall', p. 50.

ALL COUNTRIES, UNITE Marx and Engels, *Selected Works*, p. 62.

as 'clodhoppers' Berlin, *Marx*, p. 199.

the previous century Ibid., p. 200.

not a Marxist Quoted in Singer, *Marx*, p. 38.

247 *party's world-outlook* Quoted in Kolakowski, *Main Currents*, vol. III, p. 3.

bourgeois ideology Quoted ibid., vol. II, p. 387.

activity their profession Quoted idem.

248 *according to Marxist theory* Ibid., pp. 390–391.

power by the proletariat Marx and Engels, *Selected Works*, p. 46.

sense of the word Ibid., p. 50.

the world proletariat Kolakowski, *Main Currents*, vol. II, p. 478.

249 *the dictator's person* Ibid., vol. III, p. 4.

what it means Quoted in Francis King and George Matthews, eds., *About Turn: The Communist Party and the Outbreak of the Second World War: The Verbatim Record of the Central Committee Meetings 1939* (London: Lawrence & Wishart, 1990) p. 131.

undoubtedly aimed at Marx and Engels, *Selected Works*, p. 47.

interests of the bourgeoisie Quoted in Kolakowski, *Main Currents*, vol. II, pp. 395–396.

250 *against the exploiters* Quoted ibid., pp. 515–516.

embodiment of Marxist theory Ibid., vol. I, p. 419.

fantasy of our century Ibid., vol. III, p. 523.

around the corner Ibid., p. 526.

251 *and cannot say* Quoted in Kumar, *Utopia & Anti-Utopia*, p. 51.

party has progressed Marx to Wilhelm Bracke, 5 May 1875; in Marx and Engels, *Selected Works*, p. 299.

of socialism's perfection John Lloyd, 'The Party's Over', *London Review of Books*, 25 July 1991, p. 9.

border into Russia Conor Cruise O'Brien, 'Paradise Lost', Review of *Crooked Timber*, by Isaiah Berlin, in *New York Review of Books*, 25 April 1991, p. 57.

too early to say Christopher Huhne, 'The Open Society and Its Enemies', Review of *Reflections on the Revolution in Europe*, by R. Dahrendorf, in *London Review of Books*, 25 October 1990, p. 8.

extreme despotism Kolakowski, *Main Currents*, vol. III, p. 528.

252 *slaves and hypocrites* Quoted in Kumar, *Utopia & Anti-Utopia*, p. 100.

Epilogue

253 *sea for ever* Quoted in Ascherson, 'Where Will this Voyage End?', p. 3.

255 *undisputed and undiscussed* Helen King, 'In Praise of Geoffrey Lloyd', Review of *Methods and Problems in Greek Science*, by G. E. R. Lloyd, in *London Review of Books*, 8 October 1992, p. 15; citing Pierre Bourdieu.

Select Bibliography

Alberti, Leon Battista. *On the Art of Building in Ten Books*. Translated by J. Rykwert, N. Leach and R. Tavernor. Cambridge, Mass.: MIT Press, 1988.

Albinski, Nan Bowman. ' "The Laws of Justice, Nature, and of Right": Victorian Feminist Utopias'. In Jones and Goodwin, eds. *Feminism, Utopia, and Narrative*, pp. 50–67.

Alcott, Louisa May. *'Transcendental Wild Oats' and Excerpts from the Fruitland Diary*. Introduction by W. H. Harrison. Harvard, Mass.; Harvard Common Press, 1981.

Alexander, Peter, and Gill, Roger, eds. *Utopias*. London: Duckworth, 1984.

Anderson, Wilda. *Diderot's Dream*. Baltimore: Johns Hopkins University Press, 1990.

Andrews, E. D. *The People Called Shakers: A Search for the Perfect Society*. New York: Oxford University Press, 1953.

Argan, Giulio C. *The Renaissance City*. London: Studio Vista, 1969.

Armytage, W. H. G. 'Owen and America'. In S. Pollard and J. Salt, eds. *Robert Owen: Prophet of the Poor*, pp. 214–238. London: Macmillan, 1971.

——. 'Utopias: The Technical and Educational Dimension'. In Alexander and Gill, eds. *Utopias*, pp. 85–94.

Arrington, L. J., and Bitton, D. *The Mormon Experience: A History of the Latter-Day Saints*. 2nd ed. Urbana and Chicago: University of Illinois Press, 1992.

Ascherson, Neal. 'Where Will this Voyage End?'. Review of *Echoes of the Marseillaise*, by E. J. Hobsbawm. *London Review of Books*, 14 June 1990, p. 3.

Atwood, Margaret. *The Handmaid's Tale*. London: Jonathan Cape, 1986; repr. ed., London: Virago Press, 1987.

Bacon, Francis. *'New Atlantis' and 'The Great Instauration'*. Edited with an Introduction by Jerry Weinberger. 2nd ed. Arlington Heights, Ill.: Harlan Davidson, 1989.

——. *Works*. Edited by J. Spedding, R. S. Ellis, and D. D. Heath. 2nd ed. 14 vols. London: Longmans & Co., *et al.*, 1862–1875.

Baker-Smith, Dominic. *More's 'Utopia'*. London: Harper Collins, 1991.

Bartkowski, Frances. *Feminist Utopias*. Lincoln, Nebr. and London: University of Nebraska Press, 1989.

Beauvoir, Simone de. 'Must We Burn Sade?'. In the Marquis de Sade. *'120 Days of Sodom' and Other Writings*, pp. 1–64.

Beecher, Jonathan. *Charles Fourier: The Visionary and His World*. Berkeley: University of California Press, 1986.

——, and Bienvenue, Richard, eds. *The Utopian Vision of Charles Fourier: Selected Texts on Work, Love and Passionate Attraction*. London: Jonathan Cape, 1972.

Bellamy, Edward. *Dr Heidenhoff's Process*. New York: D Appleton & Co., 1880.

——. *Equality*. New York: D Appleton & Co., 1897.

——. *Looking Backward 2000–1887*. Edited with an Introduction by Cecilia Tichi. Harmondsworth: Penguin, 1982.

Benevolo, Leonardo. *The Architecture of the Renaissance*. Translated by Judith Landry. 2 vols. London: Routledge & Kegan Paul, 1978.

——. *The Origins of Modern Town Planning*. Translated by Judith Landry. London: Routledge & Kegan Paul, 1967.

Berlin, Sir Isaiah. *The Crooked Timber of Humanity: Chapters in the History of Ideas*. Edited by Henry Hardy. London: John Murray, 1990; repr. ed., London: Fontana, 1991.

——. *Karl Marx*. 4th ed. Oxford: Oxford University Press, 1978.

Best, Geoffrey, ed. *The Permanent Revolution: The French Revolution and Its Legacy 1789–1989*. London: Fontana, 1988.

Bestor, A. E. *Backwoods Utopias: The Sectarian and Owenite Phases of Communitarian Socialism in America, 1663–1829*. Philadelphia: University of Pennsylvania Press, 1950.

Bethlehem, Douglas. 'Scolding the Carpenter'. In Modgil and Modgil, eds. *B. F. Skinner: Consensus and Controversy*, pp. 89–97.

Bliznakov, Milka. 'The Realization of Utopia: Western Technology and Soviet Avant-Garde Architecture'. In Brumfield, ed. *Reshaping Russian Architecture*, pp. 145–175.

Bowen, C. D. *Francis Bacon: The Temper of a Man*. Boston: Little, Brown & Co., 1963.

Bowman, S. E. *The Year 2000: A Critical Biography of Edward Bellamy*. New York: Bookman Associates, 1958.

Brumfield, W. C., ed. *Reshaping Russian Architecture: Western Technology, Utopian Dreams*. Cambridge: Cambridge University Press, 1990.

Buder, Stanley. *Visionaries and Planners: The Garden City Movement and the Modern Community*. New York and Oxford: Oxford University Press, 1990.

Burton, Sir Richard. *The City of the Saints and across the Rocky Mountains to California*. Foreword by B. H. Morrow. Niwot, Colo.: University of Colorado Press, 1990.

Campanella, Tommaso. *La Città del Sole: Dialogo Poetico, The City of the Sun: A Poetical Dialogue*. Translated with an Introduction by D. J. Donno. Berkeley: University of California Press, 1981.

Cantor, Milton. 'The Backward Look of Bellamy's Socialism'. In Patai, ed. *Looking Backward, 1988–1888*, pp. 21–36.

Carden, M. L. *Oneida: Utopian Community to Modern Corporation*. Baltimore: Johns Hopkins University Press, 1969.

Carter, Angela. *The Sadeian Woman*. London: Virago Press, 1979.

Carver, Terrell, ed. *The Cambridge Companion to Marx*. Cambridge: Cambridge University Press, 1991.

Claeys, Gregory, ed. *Robert Owen: 'A New View of Society' and Other Writings*. London: Penguin, 1991.

Cohen, Jean-Louis. *Le Corbusier and the Mystique of the USSR: Theories and Projects for Moscow 1928–1936*. Princeton: Princeton University Press, 1992.

Coleman, Stephen, and O'Sullivan, Paddy, eds. *William Morris & 'News from Nowhere': A Vision for Our Time*. Bideford: Green Books, 1990.

Coleridge, Samuel Taylor. *The Letters of Samuel Taylor Coleridge*. Edited by E. L. Griggs. 6 vols. Oxford: Oxford University Press, 1956–1971.

Curtis, E. R. *A Season in Utopia: The Story of Brook Farm*. New York: Thomas Nelson & Sons, 1961.

Davis, D. Brion. *Revolutions: Reflections on American Equality and Foreign Liberations*. Cambridge, Mass.: Harvard University Press, 1990.

Davis, J. C. *Utopia and the Ideal Society: A Study of English Utopian Writing 1516–1700*. Cambridge: Cambridge University Press, 1981.

Dellheim, Charles. 'Utopia Ltd: Bournville and Port Sunlight'. In Derek Fraser, ed. *Cities, Class and Communication: Essays in Honour of Asa Briggs*, pp. 44–57. New York and London: Harvester Wheatsheaf, 1990.

Diderot, Denis. *Dialogues*. Translated by F. Birrell. London: George Routledge & Sons, 1927.

Desroche, Henri. *The American Shakers: From Neo-Christianity to Pre-Socialism*. Translated by J. K. Savacool. Amherst: University of Massachusetts Press, 1971.

Edmiston, W. F. *Diderot and the Family: A Conflict of Nature and Law*. Saratoga, Calif.: ANMA Libri, 1985.

Egbert, D. D. 'Socialism and American Art'. In D. D. Egbert and S. Persons, eds. *Socialism and American Life*, vol. I, pp. 623–751. 2 vols. Princeton: Princeton University Press, 1952.

Eliade, Mircea. 'Paradise and Utopia: Mythical Geography and Eschatology'. In Manuel, ed. *Utopias and Utopian Thought*, pp. 260–280.

Emerson, Ralph Waldo. *The Correspondence of Emerson and Carlyle*. Edited by J. Slater. New York and London: Columbia University Press, 1964.

Erasmus, Desiderius. *The Collected Works of Erasmus*. Vols. I–VIII: *The Correspondence of Erasmus*. Translated by R.A.B. Mynors and D.F.S. Thomson. Toronto: University of Toronto Press, 1974–1988.

Eurich, Nell. *Science in Utopia: A Mighty Design*. Cambridge, Mass.: Harvard University Press, 1967.

SELECT BIBLIOGRAPHY

Farrington, Benjamin. *The Philosophy of Francis Bacon: An Essay on its Development from 1603 to 1609*. Liverpool: Liverpool University Press, 1964.

Fellow, Otis. *Diderot*. 2nd ed. Boston: Twayne, 1989.

Ferguson, John. *Utopias of the Classical World*. London: Thames & Hudson, 1975.

Filarete [Antonio Averlino]. *Treatise on Architecture*. Translated with an Introduction by J. R. Spencer. 2 vols. New Haven and London: Yale University Press, 1965.

Firchow, P. E. *The End of Utopia: A Study of Aldous Huxley's 'Brave New World'*. Lewisburg: Bucknell University Press, 1984.

Fisch, H., and Jones, H. W. 'Bacon's Influence on Sprat's *History of the Royal Society*', *MLQ* XII (1951) pp. 399–406.

Fishman, Robert. *Urban Utopias in the Twentieth Century: Ebenezer Howard, Frank Lloyd Wright, and Le Corbusier*. New York: Basic Books, 1977.

——. 'Utopia in Three Dimensions: The Ideal City and the Origins of Modern Design'. In Peter Alexander and Roger Gill, eds. *Utopias*, pp. 95–107.

Fitzgerald, Frances. *Cities on a Hill*: *A Journey through Contemporary American Culture*. New York: Simon & Schuster, 1986; repr. ed., London: Picador, 1987.

Fogelson, R. M. *America's Armories*: *Architecture, Society, and Public Order*. Cambridge, Mass.: Harvard University Press, 1989.

Forster, K. W. 'From "Rocca" to "Civitas": Urban Planning at Sabbioneta', *L'Arte* V (1969) pp. 5–40.

Foster, Lawrence. *Religion and Sexuality*: *Three American Communal Experiments of the Nineteenth Century*. New York and Oxford: Oxford University Press, 1981.

Fried, Albert, ed. *Socialism in America*: *From the Shakers to the Third International*. Garden City, NY: Doubleday, 1970.

Furbank, P. N. *Diderot*: *A Critical Biography*. London: Secker & Warburg, 1992.

Gidley, Mick, and Bowles, Kate, eds. *Locating the Shakers: Cultural Origins and Legacies of an American Religious Movement*. Exeter: University of Exeter Press, 1990.

Gill, Roger. 'In England's Green and Pleasant Land'. In Alexander and Gill, eds. *Utopias*, pp. 109–117.

Gilman, Charlotte Perkins. *The Charlotte Perkins Gilman Reader: 'The Yellow Wallpaper' and Other Fiction*. London: The Women's Press, 1981; repr. ed., 1987.

——. *Herland*. Introduction by Ann J. Lane. London: The Women's Press, 1979; repr. ed., 1992.

——. *With Her in Ourland*. In *The Forerunner* VII (1916); repr. ed., Westport, Conn.: Greenwood Press, 1968.

Goodwin, Barbara. 'Economic and Social Innovation in Utopia'. In Alexander and Gill, eds. *Utopias*, pp. 69–83.

Greenhalph, Paul. *Ephemeral Vistas: The Expositions Universelles, Great Exhibitions and World's Fairs, 1851–1939*. Manchester: Manchester University Press, 1988.

Grendler, P. F. *Critics of the Italian World 1530–1560: Anton Francesco Doni, Niccolo Francò and Ortensio Lando*. Madison: University of Wisconsin Press, 1969.

Grillo, Francesco. *Tommaso Campanella in America: A Critical Bibliography*. New York: S. F. Vanni, 1954.

Guarneri, C. J. *The Utopian Alternative: Fourierism in Nineteenth-Century America*. Ithaca and London: Cornell University Press, 1991.

Hahn, Roger. *Laplace as a Newtonian Scientist*. Los Angeles: Clark Memorial Library, 1967.

Hall, M. H. 'An Interview with "Mr Behaviorist" B. F. Skinner', *Psychology Today* I (September 1967) pp. 21–23, 68–71.

Hall, Peter. *Cities of Tomorrow: An Intellectual History of Urban Planning and Design in the Twentieth Centiury*. Oxford: Basil Blackwell, 1988.

Harrison, J. F. C. *Robert Owen and the Owenites in Britain and America*. London: Routledge & Kegan Paul, 1969.

——. *The Second Coming: Popular Millenarianism 1780–1850*. London: Routledge & Kegan Paul, 1979.

Harvey, David. *The Condition of Postmodernity*. Oxford: Blackwell, 1989.

Hatch, N. O. *The Democratization of American Christianity*. New Haven and London: Yale University Press, 1989.

Hawthorne, Nathaniel. *The Blithedale Romance*. Introduction by Tony Tanner. Oxford and New York: Oxford University Press, 1991.

——. *The Centenary Edition of the Works of Nathaniel Hawthorne*, vol. XV: *The Letters, 1813–1843*. Edited by T. Woodson, L. Smith and N. H. Pearson. Columbus: Ohio State University Press, 1984.

Hayden, Dolores. *Seven American Utopias: The Architecture of Communitarian Socialism, 1790–1975*. Cambridge, Mass.: MIT Press, 1976.

Heydenreich, L. H., and Lotz, W. *Architecture in Italy 1400 to 1600*. Translated by Mary Hottinger. Harmondsworth: Penguin, 1974.

Holloway, Mark. *Heavens on Earth*. London: Turnstile, 1951.

Holmes, Richard. *Coleridge: Early Visions*. London: Hodder & Stoughton, 1989.

Howard, Ebenezer. *To-morrow: A Peaceful Path to Reform*. London: Swan Sonnenschein & Co, 1898.

Howe, Irving. *Politics and the Novel*. New York: Horizon Press, 1957.

Hubbard, Edward, and Shippobottom, Michael. *A Guide to Port Sunlight Village*. Liverpool: Liverpool University Press, 1988.

Huxley, Aldous. *Brave New World*. London: Chatto & Windus, 1932; repr. ed., London: Granada, 1977.

——. *Brave New World Revisited*. London: Chatto & Windus, 1959; repr. ed., London: Triad/Panther, 1983.

Jimack, Peter. *Diderot, 'Supplément au Voyage de Bougainville'*. Critical Guides to French Texts, no. 75. London: Grant & Cutler, 1988.

Jones, L. F., and Goodwin, S. W., eds. *Feminism, Utopia and Narrative*. Knoxville: University of Tennessee Press, 1990.

Jouffre, Valérie-Noëlle. *The Royal Saltworks of Arc-et-Senans*. Arcs-et-Senans: Fondation Claude-Nicolas Ledoux, 1990.

Kamenka, Eugene. 'Revolutionary Ideology and "The Great French Revolution of 1789–?"'. In Geoffrey Best, ed. *The Permanent Revolution*, pp. 78–99.

Kaul, A. N. '*The Blithedale Romance* and the Puritan Tradition'. In Harold Bloom, ed. *Nathaniel Hawthorne*, pp. 59–70. New York: Chelsea, 1986.

Kessler, C. F., ed. *Daring to Dream: Utopian Stories by United States Women 1836–1919*. Boston: Pandora, 1984.

Khan-Magomedov, S. O. *Pioneers of Soviet Architecture: The Search for New Solutions in the 1920s and 1930s*. Translated by A. Lieven. Edited by C. Cooke. London: Thames & Hudson, 1987.

King, Francis, and Matthews, George. *About Turn: The Communist Party and the Outbreak of the Second World War: The Verbatim Record of the Central Committee Meetings 1939*. London: Lawrence & Wishart, 1990.

Kinkade, Kathleen. *A Walden Two Experiment: The First Five Years of Twin Oaks Community*. New York: William Morrow, 1973.

Kolakowski, Leszek. *Main Currents of Marxism: Its Origins, Growth and Dissolution*. Translated by P. S. Falla. 3 vols. Oxford and New York: Oxford University Press, 1978.

Kramer, L. S., ed. *Paine and Jefferson on Liberty*. New York: Continuum, 1988.

Kumar, Krishan. *Utopia & Anti-Utopia in Modern Times*. Oxford: Basil Blackwell, 1987.

Le Corbusier [Charles-Edouard Jeanneret]. *Le Corbusier: Architect of the Century*. London: Arts Council of Great Britain, 1987.

Ledoux, Claude-Nicolas. *L'Architecture Considerée Sous le Rapport de l'Art, des Moeurs et de la Législation*. 2 vols. Paris: H.-L. Perroneau, 1804.

Lovejoy, A. O., and Boas, G. *Primitivism and Related Ideas in Antiquity*. Baltimore: Johns Hopkins University Press, 1935; repr. ed., New York: Octagon Books, 1973.

Lukes, Steven. 'Marxism and Utopianism'. In Alexander and Gill, eds. *Utopias*, pp. 153–167.

Maffezzoli, Umberto. *Sabbioneta: A Tourist Guide to the City*. 2nd ed. Modena: Il Bulino, 1992.

Manuel, F. E. *The New World of Henri Saint-Simon*. Cambridge, Mass.: Harvard University Press, 1956.

——. *The Prophets of Paris*. Cambridge, Mass.: Harvard University Press, 1962.

——, ed. *Utopias and Utopian Thought*. Boston: Houghton Mifflin, 1965; repr. ed., London: Souvenir Press, 1973.

——, and Manuel, F. P. *Utopian Thought in the Western World*. Oxford: Basil Blackwell, 1979.

Marius, Richard. *Thomas More: A Biography*. London: J. M. Dent & Son, 1985.

Marsh, Jan. 'Concerning Love: *News from Nowhere* and Gender'. In Coleman and O'Sullivan, eds. *William Morris & 'News from Nowhere'*, pp. 107–125.

Marx, Karl, and Engels, Friedrich. *Selected Works in One Volume*. Rev. ed. London: Lawrence & Wishart, 1991.

Mason, J. H. *The Irresistible Diderot*. London: Quartet, 1982.

Medawar, Sir Peter. 'On "The Effecting of All Things Possible"', *The Advancement of Science* XXVI (1969) pp. 1–9.

Modgil, Sohan, and Modgil, Celia, eds. *B. F. Skinner: Consensus and Controversy*. New York: Falmer, 1987.

More, Thomas. *The Complete Works of Sir Thomas More*. Vol. IV: *Utopia*. Edited by E. Surtz and J. H. Hexter. New Haven and London: Yale University Press, 1965.

——. *Utopia*. Translated with an Introduction by Paul Turner. Harmondsworth: Penguin, 1965.

Morgan, A. E. *Edward Bellamy*. New York: Columbia University Press, 1944.

Morris, William. *News from Nowhere, or an Epoch of Rest: Being Some*

Chapters from a Utopian Romance. London: Longmans, Green & Co., 1910.

Morrow, G. R. 'Plato and the Rule of Law'. In Renford Bambrough, ed. *Plato, Popper and Politics*, pp. 49–70. Cambridge: Heffer, 1967.

Morrow, John. *Coleridge's Political Thought: Property, Morality and the Limits of Traditional Discourse.* London: Macmillan, 1990.

Morton, A. L. *The English Utopia.* London: Lawrence & Wishart, 1952.

——. ed. *The Life and Ideas of Robert Owen.* London: Lawrence & Wishart, 1962.

Mumford, Lewis. 'Utopia, the City and the Machine'. In F. E. Manuel, ed. *Utopias and Utopian Thought*, pp. 3–24.

Murray, Oswyn. *Early Greece.* London: Fontana, 1980.

Murray, Peter. *The Architecture of the Italian Renaissance.* 3rd ed. London: Thames & Hudson, 1986.

Myerson, Joel, ed. *The Brook Farm Book: A Collection of First-Hand Accounts of the Community.* New York and London: Garland, 1987.

Negley, Glenn, and Patrick, J. Max, eds. *The Quest for Utopia: An Anthology of Imaginary Societies.* New York: Henry Schuman, 1952; repr. ed., College Park, Md.: McGrath, 1971.

Newby, Alison M. 'Shakers as Feminists? Shakerism as a Vanguard in the Antebellum American Search for Female Autonomy and Independence'. In Gidley and Bowles, *Locating the Shakers*, pp. 96–105.

New Harmony. *New Harmony as Seen by Participants and Travellers.* The American Utopian Adventure, 2nd ser. Philadelphia: Porcupine Press, 1975.

Nisbet, Robert. 'Rousseau & Equality'. In Ritter and Bondanella, eds. *Rousseau's Political Writings*, pp. 244–260.

Noyes, John Humphrey. *History of American Socialisms.* Philadelphia: J. B. Lippincott & Co., 1870.

O'Brien, Conor Cruise. 'The Decline and Fall of the French Revolution'. Review of *The Critical Dictionary of the French Revolution*, edited by F. Furet and M. Ozouf. *New York Review of Books*, 15 February 1990, pp. 45–50.

SELECT BIBLIOGRAPHY

O'Sullivan, Paddy. 'The Ending of the Journey: William Morris, *News from Nowhere* and Ecology'. In Coleman and Sullivan, eds. *William Morris & 'News from Nowhere'*, pp. 169–181.

Patai, Daphne, ed. *Looking Backward, 1988–1888: Essays on Edward Bellamy*. Amherst: University of Massachusetts Press, 1989.

Pearson, Mark. 'The Hammersmith Guest House Again: William Morris and the Architecture of Nowhere'. In Coleman and O'Sullivan, eds. *William Morris & 'News from Nowhere'*, pp. 137–149.

Perkins, M. L. 'Community Planning in Diderot's *Supplément au Voyage de Bougainville*', *Kentucky Romance Quarterly* XXI (1974) pp. 399–417.

Pitzer, D. E. 'Collectivism, Community and Commitment: America's Religious Communal Utopias from the Shakers to Jonestown'. In Alexander and Gill, eds. *Utopias*, pp. 119–135.

Plato. *The Republic*. Translated with an Introduction by Desmond Lee. 2nd rev. ed. London: Penguin, 1987.

Popper, Sir Karl. *The Open Society and Its Enemies*. 2 vols. London: Routledge & Kegan Paul, 1945.

Puligandla, R. *Fact and Fiction in B. F. Skinner's Science & Utopia*. St Louis, Mo.: Warren H. Green, 1974.

Purver, Margery. *The Royal Society: Concept and Creation*. Introduction by Hugh Trevor-Roper. London: Routledge & Kegan Paul, 1967.

Rammel, Hal. *Nowhere in America: 'The Big Rock Candy Mountain' and Other Comic Utopias*. Urbana and Chicago: University of Illinois Press, 1990.

Ritter, Alan, and Bondanella, Julia Conaway, eds. *Rousseau's Political Writings*. Translated by J. C. Bondanella. New York and London: W. W. Norton, 1988.

Rosemont, Franklin. 'Bellamy's Radicalism Reclaimed'. In Patai, ed. *Looking Backward, 1988–1888*, pp. 147–209.

Ruble, B. A. 'Moscow's Revolutionary Architecture and Its Aftermath: A Critical Guide'. In Brumfield, ed. *Reshaping Russian Architecture*, pp. 111–144.

Ryan, M. P. *Cradle of the Middle Class: The Family in Oneida*

County, New York, 1790–1865. Cambridge: Cambridge University Press, 1981.

Saalman, Howard. *Filippo Brunelleschi: The Cupola of Santa Maria de Fiore*. London: A. Zwemmer, 1980.

Sade, Donatien Alphonse, Marquis de. *'The Complete Justine', 'Philosophy in the Bedroom' and Other Writings*. Translated by R. Weaver and A. Wainhouse. New York: Grove Press, 1965.

——. *'The 120 Days of Sodom' and Other Writings*. Translated by R. Weaver and A. Wainhouse. New York: Grove Press, 1966.

Saint-Simon, Henri de. *Selected Writings on Science, Industry and Social Organisation*. Translated with an Introduction by Keith Taylor. London: Croom Helm, 1975.

Silver, Harold, ed. *Robert Owen on Education*. Cambridge: Cambridge University Press, 1969.

Singer, Peter. *Marx*. Past Masters. Oxford and New York: Oxford University Press, 1980.

Skinner, B. F. *Walden Two*. New York: Macmillan, 1948; repr. ed., 1976.

Skinner, Quentin. 'Sir Thomas More's *Utopia* and the Language of Renaissance Humanism'. In *The Languages of Political Theory in Early Modern Europe*, pp. 125–135. Edited by Anthony Pagden. Cambridge: Cambridge University Press, 1987.

Southey, Robert. *Sir Thomas More: Colloquies on the Progress and Prospects of Society*. 2 vols. London: John Murray, 1829.

Spadafora, David. *The Idea of Progress in Eighteenth-Century Britain*. New Haven and London: Yale University Press, 1990.

Sprigg, June, and Larkin, David. *Shaker: Life, Work and Art*. New York: Stewart, Tabori & Chang, 1987; repr. ed., London: Cassell, 1988.

Starobinski, Jean. 'Rousseau in the Revolution', *New York Review of Books*, 12 April 1990, pp. 47–50.

Stein, S. J. *The Shaker Experience in America: A History of the United Society of Believers*. New Haven and London: Yale University Press, 1992.

SELECT BIBLIOGRAPHY

Stoehr, Taylor. 'Art vs. Utopia: The Case of Nathaniel Hawthorne and Brook Farm', *Antioch Review* XXXVI:1 (1978) pp. 89–102.

Strauss, Sylvia. 'Gender, Class, and Race in Utopia'. In Patai, ed. *Looking Backward, 1988-1888*, pp. 68-90.

Talmon, J. L. *Romanticism and Revolt: 1815–1845*. London: Thames & Hudson, 1967.

Taylor, Keith. 'Henri de Saint-Simon: Pioneer of European Integration', *European Community* VI (June 1972) pp. 22–23.

Thomas, A. L., Diderot, Denis, and Madame d'Epinay. *Qu'Est-ce Qu'une Femme?*. Introduction by Elisabeth Badinter. Paris: P.O.L., 1989.

Thomas, Donald. *The Marquis de Sade*. London: Allison & Busby, 1992.

Thomas, J. L. *Alternative America: Henry George, Edward Bellamy, Henry Demarest Lloyd and the Adversary Tradition*. Cambridge, Mass.: Belknap Press, 1983.

——. Introduction to Edward Bellamy, *Looking Backward 2000–1887*. Cambridge, Mass.: Harvard University Press, 1967.

Thomas, Keith. 'The Utopian Impulse in Seventeenth-Century England', *Dutch Quarterly Review of Anglo-American Letters* III (1985) pp. 162–188.

Thomas, R. D. *The Man Who Would Be Perfect: John Humphrey Noyes and the Utopian Impulse*. Philadelphia: University of Pennsylvania Press, 1977.

Tocqueville, Alexis de. *Democracy in America*. Translated by Henry Reeve. Introduction by D. J. Boorstin. 2 vols. New York: Vintage Books, 1990.

Tolstoy, V., Bibikova, I., and Cooke, C. *Street Art of the Revolution: Festivals and Celebrations in Russia*. London: Thames & Hudson, 1990.

Trapp, J. B., and Herbrüggen, H. S., *'The King's Good Servant': Sir Thomas More 1477/8–1535*. London: National Portrait Gallery, 1977.

Venturi, Franco. *Utopia and Reform in the Enlightenment*. Cambridge: Cambridge University Press, 1971.

Vidler, Anthony. *The Writing of the Walls: Architectural Theory in the Late Enlightenment*. Princeton: Princeton Architectural Press, 1987.

——. *Claude-Nicolas Ledoux: Architecture and Social Reform at the End of the Ancien Régime*. Cambridge, Mass.: MIT Press, 1990.

Wagar, W. W. 'Dreams of Reason: Bellamy, Wells, and the Positive Utopia'. In Patai, ed. *Looking Backward, 1988–1888*, pp. 106–125.

Watkinson, Ray. 'The Obstinate Refusers: Work in *News from Nowhere*'. In Coleman and O'Sullivan, eds. *William Morris & 'News from Nowhere'*, pp. 91–106.

Werner, Stephen. 'Diderot's *Supplément* and the Late Enlightenment Thought', *Studies on Voltaire and the Eighteenth Century* LXXXVI (1971) pp. 229–292.

White, H. B. *Peace among the Willows*. The Hague: Martinus Nijhoff, 1968.

——. 'The Influence of Bacon on the *Philosophes*', *Studies on Voltaire and the Eighteenth Century* XXVII (1963) pp. 1849–1869.

Whitson, R. E., ed. *The Shakers: Two Centuries of Spiritual Reflection*. Preface by Gertrude M. Soule. New York: Paulist Press, 1983.

Wills, Garry. *Under God: Religion and American Politics*. New York: Simon & Schuster, 1990.

Wilson, A. M. *Diderot*. Oxford: Oxford University Press, 1972.

Wilson, W. H. *The City Beautiful Movement*. Baltimore and London: Johns Hopkins University Press, 1989.

Winn, K. H. *Exiles in a Land of Liberty: Mormons in America, 1830–1846*. Chapel Hill and London: University of North Carolina Press, 1989.

Wittkower, Rudolf. *Architectural Principles in the Age of Humanism*. Studies of the Warburg Institute, vol. XIX. London: Warburg Institute, 1949.

Wood, G. S. 'Americans and Revolutionaries'. Review of *Revolutions*, by D. Brion Davis. *New York Review of Books*, 27 September 1990, pp. 31–36.

Zavala, Silvio. 'The American Utopia of the Sixteenth Century', *The Huntington Library Quarterly* IV (August 1947), pp. 337–347.

Index

INDEX

319

INDEX

History of American Socialisms
181, 210

O'Brien, Conor Cruise 238, 246
Olmsted, Frederick Law 63, 65, 72, 263
Oneida Community 159, 161–4,
181, 263
Oppenheimer, Robert 99
Organisateur, L' 105
original sin 22–3, 27, 93, 137, 173–4,
177, 198, 219
Orwell, George: *Nineteen Eighty-Four*
26, 123
Ovid: *Metamorphoses* 3
Owen, Robert 199–206, 212–13, 219,
243–4, 254, 263
A New View of Society 201
Owen, Robert Dale 72, 205–6
Owen, William 203, 205

Paine, Thomas 193–4, 263
Common Sense 183, 263
Palladio, Andrea 48
Panama Canal 102, 108
Pantisocracy 197–8, 258, 266
Paris 62, 66, 78
passionate series 111, 213, 259
paternalism 68–70, 199
Penn, William 175
phalanstery 62, 64, 68, 77, 213, 217, 259
phalanxes 110, 153–5, 216, 258
philosopher ruler 9, 11–13, 21, 24,
91, 263
philosophes 99, 101, 137, 141–2,
148, 152
philosophy 10–14, 21, 27
Plato 13, 15, 21–2, 41, 95, 246, 263–4
Critias 91, 94, 264
The Laws 12
Republic 9–14, 17, 21, 23–4, 28, 37,
91, 136–7, 257, 262–3
Timaeus 264
pleasure 27–8, 134, 148, 153
Plutarch 8
political institutions 105
politics 7, 13, 86
polygamy 185, 188
'Poor Man's heaven' 6
Pope, Alexander 101
Popper, Sir Karl: *Spell of Plato* 13

Populist Party 227
pornography 151, 169, 264
Port Sunlight 69–71, 74, 262
Post-modernism 79
Priestley, Joseph 197–8
propaganda 55, 236, 258
property 7, 10, 12, 22–4, 105, 107, 139,
145, 204
puritanism 155–6, 165, 257
Pythagoras 41

Quayle, Dan 168
Quiroga, Vasco de 32–3, 264

Ranters 174
rationality 27–9, 33
Rawley, William 87, 90, 93
Reagan, Ronald 188, 191
religion 27–8, 30–1, 173–89, 204
civil 238–9
religious tolerance 30–1
Renaissance 17, 38, 42–9
Revelation, Book of 173–5, 186, 189
revolution 174, 193–4, 228, 261
Richmond, Cora 72
Ripley, George 207–9, 215, 225,
258, 264
Ripley, Sophia 214–15
Robespierre, Maximilien de 238–9, 264
Romans 3, 21, 39–41, 47–8
Rome 46
Roosevelt, Franklin D. 229
Roper, William 134
Rousseau, Jean-Jacques 99, 101, 145,
240, 246, 250–1, 264
Discours sur l'Économie Politique 236
Discours sur l'Origine de l'Inéqalité
137–41, 232–3, 264
Du Contrat Social 138, 232–9, 264
Royal Society 97–8, 103, 257
Russia *see* Soviet Union
Russian Revolution 55, 228

Sabbioneta 47–9, 266
Sade, Marquis de 148–52, 155, 168, 264
Les 120 Journées de Sodome 150–1
Philosophie dans le Boudoir 149, 264
Saint-Simon, Henri de 81, 101–8, 110,
112, 120, 125, 212, 224, 241, 243, 265

321